Scrap Craft

LUMBER

Scrap Craft

105 PROJECTS

Written
and Illustrated by

Michael Carlton Dank

Dover Publications, Inc., New York

Published in Canada by General Publishing Company, Ltd., 30 Lesmill Road, Don Mills, Toronto, Ontario.
Published in the United Kingdom by Constable and Company, Ltd., 10 Orange Street, London WC 2.

This Dover edition, first published in 1969, is an unabridged republication of the text of the work originally published by Greenberg Publisher in 1946 under the title *Adventures in Scrap Craft.*
A new selection of photographs replaces those shown in the original edition.

Standard Book Number: *0-486-21999-2*
Library of Congress Catalog Card Number: 69-17471
Manufactured in the United States of America
Dover Publications, Inc.
180 Varick Street
New York, N.Y. 10014

Affectionately Dedicated

to the

Memory of my Father

ABRAHAM H. DANK

PREFACE

Creating something out of nothing is what some of the students in my shop classes often call it. Actually, they are referring to the many exciting projects which we develop from a great variety and plentiful supply of materials, costing practically nothing.

A discarded oatmeal container may be transformed miraculously into an attractive knitting bag; a wooden cheese box into a decorative wall shelf; and a used, cast-off corrugated carton into a beautiful wastepaper basket. These are only a few of the many craft adventures which are made possible through the use of scrap materials.

The realization that arts and crafts programs in all sections of the country are frequently handicapped because of the lack of materials due to limited budgets or market shortages, and that the use of waste and discarded materials is an excellent solution to this problem, has inspired me to write SCRAP CRAFT—105 PROJECTS.

Although the idea of this book is primarily concerned with the utilization of scrap materials, there is no reason why the techniques and projects presented here cannot be advantageously applied in connection with the use of new or regular craft supplies.

To insure successful results in building the wide range of projects in this book, I have carefully supervised the construction of each model in my own shop classes.

Youngsters everywhere will derive benefit from the excellent training in thrift and ingenuity which is provided through the creation of handwork with scrap materials.

It is hoped, too, that SCRAP CRAFT—105 PROJECTS will

inspire our many home craftsmen to make playthings for their children and gifts for their friends from the odds and ends usually found in abundance in the kitchen, attic, basement, or local grocery store.

Also that teachers of arts and crafts, club leaders, camp counselors, and all other handicraft enthusiasts will find in this book the answers to such important problems as "What can we make?" and "What can we use for materials?"

This book is written not only to instruct those interested in all forms of handwork procedures, but also to encourage them to make toys, gifts, and other useful and attractive articles. Creating things either wholly or partially is always accompanied by a high degree of satisfaction and a sense of accomplishment.

For instance, there are unlimited design possibilities in the formation of the different parts of a wall shelf, a picture frame, or a stationery rack. Likewise, there are many different models and styles for fashioning such popular children's playthings as auto trucks, doll furniture, airplane models, trains, and so forth.

In the presentation of each scrap craft adventure in this book, the author's plan is to select a certain model as the key project, describe it in detail, and follow it with a brief discussion of related projects.

In conclusion, I wish to thank the many students of my arts and crafts classes, both children and adults, who have so graciously aided in the preparation of this work. Collecting quantities of scrap materials of almost every kind, assisting in the construction of the many models here presented, and offering many valuable and practical suggestions, are only a few of their contributions.

Appreciation is also extended to the publishers of this book for their cooperation during the period of its development.

My expression of gratitude would not be complete without acknowledging the continued faith and encouragement of my wife, Helen B. Dank, who helped to make this book an actuality.

MICHAEL CARLTON DANK
Brooklyn, N. Y.

CONTENTS
and LIST of PROJECTS

CHAPTER ONE

THE PLACE OF SCRAP MATERIALS IN CRAFT WORK

SOME people call them odd and discarded materials. Others refer to them as secondhand, odds and ends, or substitute materials. Still others have been known to describe them as waste or junk or trash. The term "scrap materials," however, is used by the author as representative of all such handicraft materials, irrespective of kind or source. The title of this book, SCRAP CRAFTS, is meant to designate all sorts of handicraft construction wherein every type of scrap materials is utilized.

It is interesting to observe that our children are pioneers in the technique of using scrap materials. For boys, it has always been a simple matter to build a scooter by cleverly joining a pair of old roller skates to a sturdy crate board equipped with a discarded soap box. For girls, it has always been just as easy to make a doll from mother's material remnants and bits of wool and thread always found about the house.

The use of scrap materials in educational handwork for preschool and kindergarten children is today recognized as an important element in this early training. This is due to the availability of many types of suitable scrap materials and to the cheapness with which they may be employed.

Building and furnishing a playhouse with discarded corrugated cartons and wooden crates; transforming a cheese or cigar box into different types of toy cars, trucks, trains, boats; building sandtable panoramas from lolly pop sticks, sea shells, differently proportioned cardboard boxes, odds and ends of crepe paper; and making cardboard toys and games out of discarded laundry cards and shoe boxes, are only a few examples of simple handwork suitable for young children.

Scrap materials are also used extensively in the arts and crafts classes of the higher elementary school grades. This is in accordance with the principles of progressive education which stress the value of "activities" and recognize handwork as an integral part of the regular school curriculum. Children are now acquiring a more vital and vivid understanding of history, geography, and the sciences through the construction of all types of models, dioramas and mechanical devices. Scrap materials play an important part in these activities because they make excellent substitutes for first grade materials which are often difficult to obtain. When there is a shortage of such materials as wood, tin, cardboard, leather, plastics, linoleum, crepe paper, rope, and string, what a blessing it is to have on hand an ample and well organized stock of scrap materials, ready for use. Progressive elementary school teachers engaged in this type of work will find that a scrap pile well stocked with all of these items is of great advantage in teaching handicrafts.

In children's clubs and recreational centers, as well as in all institutions where regular craft supplies may not be plentiful, odd and discarded materials can take their place. Cardboard boxes, crates, cigar and cheese boxes, cardboard tubes, wall paper, oatmeal and coffee containers, tin cans and felt are eminently suitable for use in these arts and crafts centers. Scout leaders and camp counselors will also find scrap materials of considerable value in many kinds of popular handwork.

In addition to the materials already mentioned, such plentiful products of nature as twigs, branches, birch bark, leaves, pine cones, plant dyes, sea shells, pebbles, seeds, stones, and sand are all excellent craft materials which afford endless creative possibilities.

Scrap materials, then, furnish an abundant, cheap, and entirely adequate source of supply for any successful arts and crafts program. It is a wise plan for all teachers of handwork, therefore, to start right in saving, salvaging, and accumulating all sorts of scrap materials. If they do so their students will at all times have plenty of wood, leather, plastics, and many other materials, to keep them happily at work.

Craftsmen and hobbyists who love to make things in their home workshops will also find it both expedient and advantageous to build up a good scrap pile of various odd and discarded materials. For example, an old shelf board can easily be converted into a beautiful bookcase, a shoe-shine box, and many other useful articles for the home. Similarly, old felt hats can be transformed into such gifts as change purses, bookmarks, table mats, and so forth, and many other excellent project ideas in the utilization of scrap materials will be found later in this book.

From the above we can readily understand why scrap materials of all kinds play an important part in all branches of educational and recreational handicrafts.

CHAPTER
TWO

TYPES AND SOURCES OF SCRAP MATERIALS

THERE are three distinct kinds of scrap materials:

1. Waste or leavings of manufactured products.

2. Worn out, broken, and discarded articles.

3. Natural materials.

The following lists offer a wide variety of scrap materials in each of these three groups. Familiarity with these items will prove of considerable benefit to workers in almost every branch of arts and crafts.

The extensive assortment of handicraft materials, found everywhere about us in the form of waste or discarded materials, can be transformed into many different kinds of useful and attractive articles through the application of various simple handwork techniques. The reader will find a large variety of such projects and craft procedures, utilizing many scrap materials, in each of the lists in the Project Section of this book.

Factories, grocery stores, confectionery and hardware stores, as well as the garages, attics, and basements of our homes, and nature, itself, are ready providers of scrap materials.

These should be stored in suitable containers, properly marked, so as always to be ready for use.

The following lists give the respective sources and specific types of each item represented.

SCRAP LIST NO. 1

WASTE OR LEAVINGS OF MANUFACTURED PRODUCTS

This list furnishes general types of scrap materials, commonly found in the form of waste or leftovers at factories producing wearing apparel, household goods, toys and gifts. Such scrap is ordinarily disposed of as refuse, and, in most cases, is gladly furnished free of cost to those who ask for it. Under the heading "Source," the reader will find several types of manufacturers who regularly have ample quantities of such scrap on hand.

It is of interest to note that these waste products are almost always obtainable in excellent condition and in fairly good sized pieces. Thus they are especially valuable for use in arts and crafts.

NAME OF ARTICLE	SOURCES
Cotton, Wool, and Silk Scraps	*Manufacturers of children's and adults' wearing apparel, burlap bags, furniture covers, draperies, and so forth.*
Cork Sheet Scraps	*Manufacturers of luncheon sets, knitting tubes, scrap books and photo albums, wastepaper baskets, and so forth.*
Felt Scraps	*Manufacturers of stuffed toys, children's purses, pin cushions, pennants and banners, lapel ornaments, and so forth.*
Leather and Suede Scraps	*Manufacturers of gloves, ladies' bags, sport jackets, shoes and slippers, picture frames, and so forth.*
Leatherette Scraps	*Manufacturers of inexpensive ladies' bags, comb cases, key holders, picture frames, belts, leatherette seat pads, and so forth.*
Linoleum Scraps	*Linoleum dealers' remnants or discontinued samples.*
Metal Scraps	*Manufacturers of metal stampings, castings, and wire goods. Among these products are fly swatters, serving trays,*

TYPE OF MATERIAL	SOURCES
	dust pans, children's sand sets, and other playthings.
Paper and Cardboard Scraps	*Manufacturers of paper and cardboard containers, cardboard toys and games. Printers of paper and cardboard advertising matter.*
Plastic Scraps	*Manufacturers of costume jewelry, picture frames, children's tea sets, ladies' bag frames, and so forth.*
Rubber Scraps	*Manufacturers of balloons and other rubber playthings, rubber bands, ice bags, rain coats, shower curtains, and so forth.*
Wood Scraps	*Manufacturers of wooden toys, household utensils, furniture, house trim, store fixtures. Also lumber yards, carpenters and small local cabinet makers. These same sources can also furnish, free of cost, sawdust or wood shavings, which are useful in certain hand work procedures.*

SCRAP LIST NO. 2

WORN, BROKEN, AND DISCARDED MATERIALS

This list covers a wide variety of articles which are generally discarded as waste. Many of these items may also be found in the average home, garage, attic, or basement, taking up space and serving no useful purpose at all.

The articles included in this scrap list should be cleaned and then stored in labeled containers of suitable size. For by utilizing these scraps, the alert and ingenious craftsman has a wealth of fine handwork material at his command.

Later in this book, the reader will find instructions for making a wide variety of toys, novelties and useful gifts for the home, which can easily be made from worn, broken, or discarded materials such as those listed here.

Name of Article	Types
Bags and Sacks	*Paper, cloth and burlap varieties, including flour, potato, and fruit sacks as well as paper bags used for carrying all forms of merchandise.*
Cardboard Boxes (Square Shaped)	*Suit and dress boxes, shoe boxes, candy boxes, shirt boxes, toy and game boxes, small match boxes, cracker and cereal boxes, and so forth.*
Cardboard Boxes (Round Shaped)	*Oatmeal boxes, salt boxes, pint and quart size ice cream and coffee containers, ladies' and men's hat boxes and cosmetic boxes.*
Cardboard (Sheets)	*Laundry shirt supports, used advertising posters, discarded window display signs, and so forth.*
Cardboard Tubes	*Box makers' paper roll tubes, mailing tubes, paper towel tubes, and toilet tissue tubes.*
Corrugated Cardboard Containers	*Various sizes, used for packing and shipping canned goods, household articles, wearing apparel, cigarettes, candies.*
Cellophane	*Straws, cigarette package wrappings, men's shirt coverings, window type cake and candy boxes, toy and game box wrappings.*
Celluloid	*Toy dishes and other children's playthings, tooth brush handles, gift boxes and merchandise display cases.*
Cheese Boxes	*Large and small sizes, used to pack cream cheese and other cheeses.*
Cigar Boxes	*Large and small sizes and assorted shapes. Both the wood and composition board varieties are good.*
Cotton Printed Goods	*Dresses, curtains, men's shirts, table covers, pajamas, aprons, and so forth.*

Name of Article	Types
Felt, Wool, and Silk Goods	*Sport jackets, men's hats, women's and girls' hats and bags, umbrellas, stockings, sweaters, sport belts, and ties.*
Floor Coverings	*Carpets, rugs, and linoleum.*
Glass Bottles	*Jelly, peanut butter, mayonnaise, and many other types of food bottles in a variety of shapes and sizes.*
Glass Mirrors	*Different types of home mirrors, women's bag mirrors, shelf mirrors, table mat mirrors, and so forth.*
Glass (Sheet)	*Window panes, tray and picture frame glass.*
Jewelry (Costume)	*Brooches, necklaces, pendants, earrings, and bracelets.*
Leather Goods	*Women's bags and purses, sport jackets, boots and shoes, belts, book jackets, picture frames, and wallets.*
Lolly Pop and Ice Cream Sticks	*Both the round and flat types are useful.*
Metal Kitchen Utensils	*Aluminum pots and pans, copper cooking utensils, and all types of kitchen gadgets.*
Metal Hardware Fittings and Accessories.	*Screws, nails, screw eyes, cup hooks, cotter pins, brass fasteners, paper clips, hair pins, hat pins, and so forth.*
Metal Miscellaneous Articles	*Razor blades, roller skates, electric irons, wash boards, watering cans, funnels, bottle caps, pen points, umbrella staves, lead and brass pipes.*
Metal Strapping	*Such as used to strap bales of paper, shipping cartons, and crates.*
Oil Cloth	*Table covers and shelvings of many types, oil cloth playthings, and so forth.*

Name of Article	Types
Paper Goods	*Crepe paper, tracing paper, tissue paper, shelf papers, wrapping paper, newspapers, cigar bands, wall paper rolls and sample books, paper plates, used postage stamps and magazines.*
Picture Frames	*Metal, leather, leatherette, plastic, and wood varieties.*
Plastic Goods	*Playing chips, radio cabinets, lapel ornaments, tooth and clothes brushes, picture frames, combs, letter openers, statuettes, children's tea sets, and other playthings.*
Pottery and Earthenware	*Vases, flower pots, ornamental fignres, bowls, and jars.*
Rope, String, Thread and Yarn	*Clothes line, packaging string and cord, knitting yarn, heavy rope, cotton and silk threads in assorted colors, and braided cord.*
Round Sticks	*Broom and mop handles, curtain rods, rug poles, lolly pop sticks, and chair rails.*
Rubber Goods	*Rubber sheets, gloves, shower curtains, auto tires and tubes, rubber balls, washers, hot and ice water bags, jelly jar rings, kneeling pads, children's playthings, rubber bands, elastic braids and cords.*
Spools	*Wooden thread spools of assorted sizes, and cardboard spools used for winding braidings and lacings.*
Tin Cans (Round Shaped)	*Stewed fruit cans, coffee cans, candy boxes, paint and varnish cans, auto oil cans, cigar and tobacco cans.* *sets.*
Tin Cans (Square Shaped)	*Turpentine cans, candy boxes, chalk containers, and tea containers.*

NAME OF ARTICLE	TYPES
Tin Foil	*Cigarette and smoking tobacco packages, tea wrappings, liquor bottles, and so forth.*
Tools	*Boring drill points, auger bits, screw drivers, nail files, nut picks, ice picks, brad awls, and other small tools.*
Wire Goods	*Bottle top wire, coat hangers, springs, wire mesh doors, dish drying trays, bird cages, electric wire, pipe cleaners, and so forth.*
Wooden Baskets	*Such as used to pack grapes, peaches, cherries, and various types of berries.*
Wooden Furniture and Fixtures	*Chairs, tables, tabourettes, cabinets, book cases, desks, ping pong tables, ladders, partitions, show cases, and shelvings.*
Wooden Miscellaneous Items	*Golf tees, clothes pins, checkers, buttons, buckles, curtain rings, umbrella handles, doily hoops, tongue depressors, pen holders, small ice cream spoons, and so forth.*
Wooden Packing Crates and Boxes	*Round vegetable and fruit crates, square shaped soap and canned goods boxes, egg crates, thick wood crates for packing heavy goods such as hardware, furniture and plumbing supplies, veneer packing cases, and so forth.*
Wooden Toys and Games	*Pull toys, toy guns, bow and arrow sets, building blocks, toy wagons, toy carts, scooters, hockey and golf sticks, and garden sets.*
Wooden Tubs and Barrels	*Butter and lard tubs, sugar, potato and flour barrels.*

SCRAP LIST NO. 3

NATURAL MATERIALS

The natural products listed below can all be used effectively in the construction of a wide variety of arts and crafts projects.

They are offered here as a distinct classification of scrap materials, because they are not ordinarily considered in List No. 1 or in the broken and worn out materials of List No. 2.

These natural products are presented here because, like the other types of scrap materials, they are, with few exceptions, obtainable free of cost.

The reader will find several models in the "Scrap Craft Project Section" of this book, which utilize different kinds of natural materials in their construction. For instance, pebbles are used for the maraccas (Project No. 77); acorns are used for the costume jewelry (Projects No. 69 and 70); birch bark and birch branches for the tie rack (Project No. 74) and so forth.

More and more uses for these natural products will be discovered by every craft enthusiast as he progresses in his work, for the possibilities are almost unlimited.

As an aid to the reader, a few craft uses or project suggestions are given after each item here listed.

NAME OF NATURAL PRODUCT	CRAFT USES
Acorns	*Necklaces, lapel ornaments, bracelets, buttons, box cover knobs.*
Animal Skins and Furs	*Coverings for boxes and tin cans, wallets, mittens, book jackets, drums, purses and bags, lapel and hat ornaments.*
Bamboo Sticks	*Flutes and whistles, walking canes, whips, woven table mats, bow and arrow*
Bark of Trees	*Tie racks, Indian tents, toy canoes, coverings for tin cans and gift boxes.*
Lima Beans and Other Dried Hard Beans	*Necklaces, bracelets, lapel pins, bean bags, and games.*
Bees Wax	*Backing for thin copper modeling work, mould making.*
Bones	*Buttons, puppets, castanets, pipes, whistles, rings, necklaces, tie slides, and so forth.*
Branches and Twigs	*Bow and arrow sets, letter openers, decorative wall plaques, thermometers, mallets, window boxes, candle holder, coasters, buttons, rustic furniture, table mats, bird houses, and doll furniture.*

Name of Natural Product	Craft Uses
Butterflies	*Decorative wall plaques, dioramas, serving trays, and table mats.*
Clay	*Papier-mâché work, general clay modeling, casting and moulding of tiles, pottery, brooches, lapel ornaments.*
Cocoanut Shells	*Puppet heads, wall plaques, lanterns, bird houses and bird baths, toy boats, flower pots, and so forth.*
Corn Kernels	*Jewelry such as necklaces, bracelets, lapel ornaments and earrings, rattle and bean bag fillers, and so forth.*
Cranberries	*Dolls, Christmas tree ornaments, flower vase decorations, necklaces, bracelets, boutonnieres, holiday gift package decorations, rolling games, foundations for string balls.*
Egg Shells	*Foundations for papier-mâché doll and puppet heads, toy animals and figures.*
Feathers	*Darts, quill pens, Indian headdresses, costumes, stuffing for dolls and other playthings, fans, hat ornaments, and so forth.*
Fish Scales	*Jewelry, costume trimmings, vase decorations.*
Flowers	*Decorative wall plaques, block prints, serving trays, spatter painting.*
Fungus	*Decorative pictures and dioramas.*
Gourds	*Rattles, bird houses and bird baths, grotesque animals, toy banks, ash trays, brush and pen and pencil holders, gift boxes, fruit and candy trays, Christmas tree decorations, decorative Mexican wall bunches.*

NAME OF NATURAL PRODUCT	CRAFT USES
Horns (Deer, Goat, and Bull)	*Tie and hat racks, napkin rings, wall plaques, ash trays, horns, tie slides, rings, and so forth.*
Leaves	*Leaf painting, spraying and blue printing, nature scrap books, plaster mould ana cast work, lapel ornaments, favors, greeting cards, and so forth.*
Peach Stones	*Tie slides, necklaces, novelty rings, and so forth.*
Pebbles and Stones	*Miniature rock gardens, diorama construction, fillers for rattles and maraccas, bean bag fillers, mosaic inlay decorations for tiles and bottles, and so forth.*
Pine Cones	*Christmas tree ornaments, necklaces, humorous bird and animal figures, shade pulls, box handles, dolls, boutonnieres, and so forth.*
Seeds (Pumpkin, Melon, Squash, and Sunflower)	*Necklaces, earrings, bracelets, boutonnieres, hat ornaments, decorative bottle or tin can coverings, and belt ornaments.*
Reed	*Table mats, coasters, baskets, serving trays, seat weaving.*
Sand	*Cement work, sandpainting, bottle book ends, diorama construction.*
Sea Shells	*Bracelets, necklaces, earrings, lapel ornaments, ash trays, painted wall plaques, buttons.*
Tusks (Elephant, Boar, and Walrus)	*Tie and hat racks, horns, rings, ash trays, napkin rings.*
Walnut Shells	*Bath tub boats, novelty lapel and hat ornaments, tie slides, toy figures, turtles, castanets, buckles, and checkers.*
Weeds	*Decorative vase bouquets, diorama construction, spray work, metallic hand painting, wall decorations, lapel and hat ornaments, picture frame, and calendar decorations.*

CHAPTER THREE

PLANNING AND EQUIPPING YOUR HANDICRAFT SHOP

IN THIS chapter, as well as in chapters four and five, the reader will find many practical suggestions concerning the tools, materials, equipment, and handwork procedures which are essential to the successful application of the scrap craft projects presented in this book.

The author is fully cognizant of the fact that in a great many school work shops, club and church recreation centers, and home work shops, arts and crafts budgets are often inadequate. Thus, the use of new, expensive, or regular tools and equipment in such craft shops is, of course, quite impossible. Because of this situation, every effort is made by the author to provide information concerning the preparation, installation, and use of various working tools and equipment which can easily be made from different kinds of odd and discarded materials at little or no cost.

The information presented here is based on the author's personal experience, over a period of many years, as an instructor and supervisor of educational and recreational handicrafts in public and private schools, craft schools for adults, and summer camps. A study has also been made of handwork activities in occupational therapy centers, schools for handicapped children, girl and boy scout organizations, children's clubs and Sunday school groups.

It is accordingly hoped that the suggestions given below concerning working tools, materials, and equipment for craft shops will help craft teachers and home craftsmen to solve their own problems in these matters, and that it will help them to get off to a good start in this fascinating creative work.

I. Planning the Size and Location of the Shop

Whether you are a teacher of handicrafts in a school or camp, or whether you are an amateur craftsman who likes to make beautiful things at home, the following facts and considerations should prove helpful to you in planning the location and building of your workshop.

First, the shop must be dry, well ventilated, and equipped for good lighting. It must be located where it can be readily heated when necessary. A damp shop is not only uncomfortable and unwholesome to work in, but also causes the tools to rust and the equipment to warp out of shape and become hardly workable. A poorly ventilated shop is a health hazard because of the paint, stain, turpentine, and other chemical odors, as well as various forms of dust resulting from craftwork. A shop with inadequate lighting is detrimental to the eyes and hardly conducive to accurate, satisfactory workmanship.

A workshop with a wooden floor is far more comfortable and healthful to work in than one with a cement floor. This is especially true on damp, stormy days, and in places where ample heat is not always available. Do not work in a room which is without heating facilities. Home craftsmen will find that an attic room or a corner section of a finished basement, which is dry, well lighted for day or evening work, sufficiently ventilated, and which can be heated when necessary, is a most appropriate place to set up a workshop. Of course, even though the shop is located in the basement or attic, it should be kept in order at all times by all who use it.

Still another important consideration in the selection of the work shop is whether it provides adequate working space. Sufficient room must be allowed for a good size work table, tool cabinet, stock or material bin and lumber rack. A mistake is too often made by home craftsmen in setting up a workshop which is entirely too small and cramped for comfort or for successful work. Although a shop may seem adequate at the beginning, the situation changes when new tools or equipment are added or when the scope and variety of work are expanded. It is, therefore, wise when planning and setting up your home workshop, to allow sufficient room for future development and advancement, as well as for comfort and orderliness as the shop progresses.

These suggestions in regard to good lighting and ventilation, proper heating facilities and ample working space, apply equally to the building or installation of handicraft shops in schools, summer camps, recreation centers, churches, clubs, and so forth.

When planning workshops for children's handicraft activities, it is essential to build them large enough to accommodate the approximate number of children that will work in the shop at a single time. For instance, it may be planned as a ten unit shop, to accommodate an average number of ten children at a time. Or, it may be necessary to construct a twenty unit shop for the use of an average number of twenty children at a time.

In each size workshop unit, provision must be made for a proportionate number of children's work sections. Thus a shop built on a ten unit basis, must provide ample working space at the work tables or benches where an average of ten children may comfortably participate in craft activities. In a shop of this size, a sufficient amount of room must also be provided for the orderly storing of tools, supplies, unfinished work—a wardrobe or clothes rack, a painting table and paint cabinet, and any other essential items. Twenty or thirty unit shops should be planned in the same fashion.

II. Suggested Equipment for Home Workshops

The average home workshop, suitable for the production of various types of scrap craft projects, should include the following equipment:

A. A practical work bench or work table sturdily built and large enough for comfort and convenience. The bench should be equipped with either a regular woodworking vise or a good size metalworking vise.

B. A solidly constructed chair of proper height for working conveniently at the particular work bench or table used in the shop.

C. A tool rack or tool chest, specially constructed and arranged to accommodate the particular assortment of tools used in the shop. A good place to locate the tool rack is on that section of the shop wall which is immediately above the work bench. The rack must not be built too high, so that each tool can easily be reached and replaced as needed. The tool rack, in fact, may be built as part of the work bench or work table itself.

In planning the tool rack, a definite and appropriate place should be allocated to each separate tool. It is a good idea to employ some fool-proof plan for indicating the exact place of each tool, such as painting a black silhouette of each tool on the tool board or numbering the tool and its respective place on the tool board. Thus, a silhouettte of a boring brace may be painted on the tool chest board at the exact place where the brace is to hang or be supported. Or the brace may bear the number Five, for instance, and the same number appear on the tool board at the spot where this particular tool is to be located. Still another idea, is to have the words "boring brace" printed or lettered on the board immediately below or just above the boring brace holder or supporting device employed.

For proper tool holding devices you may use either the metal-type clasps or tool grips which are simply screwed to the tool chest board, or, better still, especially prepared tool supports or racks, each to fit the special tool it is planned for, which you can easily make from scrap pieces of wood or narrow strips of band-iron. The use of either nails or screws for holding the tools in place on the tool board, is impracticable and unsatisfactory; for the tool rack made up in this manner presents a slovenly and uncraftsmanlike appearance and does not function properly. Thus, a holder for a backsaw, crosscut saw or ripsaw, may be made by forming a block of wood to the same shape as the open section of the saw handle, permitting the saw to hang neatly from this block in its special place on the tool rack. A holder for chisels or files may be made by cutting proper size notches in a strip of wood. Such tool racks are best made of 3/4 inch thick hardwood. Wooden tool holders may easily be screwed to the tool board with proper size, roundhead screws.

If possible, the tool rack should be equipped with two hinged doors which can be padlocked when the shop is not in use. These doors will also help considerably to prevent the tools from rusting or from being removed from the rack by intruders. All you need do is first to build a wooden frame of 3/4 inch lumber all around the edges of the tool board. The frame may vary from 4 inches to 6 inches in width, depending on the particular types of tools used. Then make two doors, each half the width and just as high as the tool rack board, and fasten the doors to the frame by means of proper size brass hinges. The doors may be made simply of 3/8 inch to 5/8 inch plywood or in panel-door form. In this latter type of construction, use 3/4 inch stock for the door frames and 1/4 inch plywood for the door panels.

When planning the arrangement for the different tools on the tool rack board, it is a good idea to keep all edge tools such as planes, saws, chisels, gouges, and so forth, toward the lower section of the board. Blunt tools such as hammers, pliers, boring braces, mallets, and so forth, may be placed in the upper section of the rack. Such an arrangement will result in greater safety when using the tools and may prevent serious accidents.

A good finish for the tool cabinet and its inside tool board is an appropriate color of oil or varnish stain such as oak or walnut.

D. Stock-bins and shelves for storing various scrap materials and working supplies such as leather, metal, plastic, steel wool, sandpaper, and emery cloth. A series of bins or cabinets for storing these items can easily be placed under the workbench. Or, they can be built along another wall of the shop room. If the latter arrangement is used, it is advisable to construct a shelf or two just above the bins for the storing of smaller size items of materials or supplies, such as nails, screws, cotter-pins, pin-backs, earring clasps, glue, paste, cement, stamping tools, and plastic wood. It is a practical plan to make plywood doors for the bins to keep dust from spoiling the supplies. These doors should be hinged and hasps can be added for padlocking the doors if desired.

E. Lumber rack for storing and stocking various shapes and sizes of scrap wood such as flat boards, wooden rods or dowels, vegetable crate bases, discarded cigar and cheese boxes, scrap pieces of plywood, sheets of corrugated and composition boards, and so forth. The best place for locating the lumber rack is at any corner of the shop. A few lengths of 2 inch by 4 inch wood joists, properly arranged, are all you will need for making a sturdy, practical lumber rack to accommodate all the scrap wood material you will require for your craft work. Besides allowing a tall stall for long boards placed vertically in the rack, it is also wise to add a plywood board shelf or two for storing smaller items of scrap wood such as odds and ends of wood, discarded cheese and cigar boxes, crate bases and end boards.

F. A metal paint cabinet for storing paints, stains, shellac, varnish, acids, brushes, and so forth. Such a paint supply cabinet can easily be made of an odd or old sheet of galvanized iron and fastened to the wall at some convenient place on one of the workshop walls. It is a good idea, too, to have this paint cabinet fitted with a hinged door. Also to have a few holes drilled at the sides of the cabinet or at the top part of the door as air vents. The size of the cabinet can vary according to individual requirements.

G. Carpenters' "horses," used as supports for ripping or cross-cutting large wood boards, plywood and composition board sheets and so forth. Also useful as foundations for nailing or gluing together larger projects and for laying out work. These "horses" can be made of scrap pieces of 3/4 inch stock for the legs, and 2 by 4 inch joists for the top, cross beams. The legs, which should be 4 inches in width, are fastened at the top to the 2 by 4 inch beams and extend outward at the bottom. The overall height of the horses is about 24 inches. Each horse is built of four legs, two at each end. For best construction of the "horses" use sturdy wood screws, rather than nails. For most practical purposes, the horses are used in pairs, placing one "horse" under one end of the board to be sawed or work to be assembled, and one under the other end. Of course, the "horses" are placed at such distance apart as may be required by the particular job in work. These "horses" are extremely handy and should be part of every home craftsman's shop equipment.

III. Suggested Equipment for Craft Shops in Summer Camps, Recreation Centers, Clubs, Hospitals, Churches, and so forth.

Of course, if you can have the use of regular two-unit woodworking benches, each bench equipped with two vises and two tool cabinets, and enough of such work benches to accommodate the average number of craft students for whom the shop is planned, you will have an ideal work bench set-up. However, since bench equipment of this regular type is far too expensive for most children's camps, clubs and recreation centers, here is another work bench arrangement which is also very practical and satisfactory and which will cost comparatively little to install.

A. Work bench.

Using 2 inch by 4 inch wooden joists of about 30 inch length for the legs and the same stock, in required lengths, for the rails, and several lengths of 3/4 inch thick boards of about 10 inch width for the top, build a sturdy work table or work bench long and wide enough to provide working sections for twelve children, six on each side. If a larger number of children are to be accommodated and there is ample room in the shop, then it is suggested that two such tables be constructed and put to use.

For the construction of these craft shop work tables, you can use second hand lumber, if you find new stock too costly. To be most practical, it is important that work tables be built very sturdily, using upper and lower cross-rails, also built of 2 inch by 4 inch joist stock, to reinforce the leg supports, as well as several cross-rails along the length of the table, located immediately below the table top. These interior section cross-rails will prevent the top from sagging, especially at the center. In addition to using large, sturdy screws in the assembling of the leg and rail table parts, it is also good to employ several proper size angle-irons to provide reinforcement and a more solid construction. Angle irons may be used to fasten the work tables to the floor, in their proper locations, to prevent the tables from being shifted when in use.

Should you be fortunate enough to procure two or three large size, sturdy library tables, you can use them in place of the homemade work tables previously described. Work tables or benches of either the homemade or manufactured kind are excellent for use in children's craft shops in summer camps and recreation centers, since they can be utilized for the successful conduct and presentation of most handicrafts. The author has found it most practical to locate such work tables in the center of the workshop so that either chairs or benches, preferably the latter, can be placed along both sides of the tables. It is also advisable not to use these tables for any extra heavy handwork procedures, such as planing wood, ripping or crosscutting wood or heavy assembling work, but to use these tables only for lighter forms of handwork, such as sawing out wood parts with the coping saw, stippling wood, tapping metal, tooling leather and coloring. For heavy work, it is best to use a separate, extra strong, special work table described below.

B. Sitting benches.

As indicated above, it is better to have the children sit on benches when working at their handicrafts than on chairs, since benches allow greater freedom and comfort for the children at work. Such sitting benches can easily be built of second hand boards, 3/4 inch thick and about 10 inches wide. The length of the benches should be the same as the length of the tables with which they are to be used.

When the shop is swept, it is a simple matter to lift up the sitting benches and place them on the work tables. Or, when it is necessary for the children to work in a standing position, it is simple enough to move the benches as far from the tables as desired.

Both the work tables and sitting benches may be finished in some appropriate color of varnish stain such as walnut or oak, or they may be painted in a suitable color of enamel. The selection of any particular color of varnish stain or enamel paint, however, should always be determined by its harmonious relationship with the coloring of the other fixtures and equipment in the shop.

C. The heavy-duty or special work table.

This special work table, which should be built in a well lighted corner or against a well lighted wall of the work shop, should be employed for such working operations such as planing wood, ripping and crosscutting wood, grinding and whetting edge tools, mitre-box saw cutting, and so forth. This table may also be employed as a support for any form of power tools which may be in use in the shop, such as a drill press, a polishing machine, a jig saw, an annealing furnace and so forth. One or two large size, metalworking vises should also be fastened to this table for the general use of the children whenever required for their work.

This heavy duty work table should be built in an especially strong form of construction and should be securely fastened to the wall as well as to the floor. It is also suggested that the top of this table be made of extra heavy wood, at least 1-1/2 inches in thickness.

D. Supply bins, racks and shelves.

The installation and use of supply bins, racks and shelves in any arts and crafts shop depends upon the construction, arrangement and size of each shop, and the special conditions under which the work has to be conducted. It is thus left to the individual instructor or director to employ his own ingenuity in making the most advantageous use of his shop space and facilities in the construction of this equipment. Generally speaking, however, a rack for the convenient and orderly stocking of regular lumber, plywoods, composition boards and so forth is always best located in some appropriate corner of the workshop. In addition to a tall stall for long boards, the rack should also be fitted with two or three shelf compartments for storing smaller sizes of scrap wood, discarded cigar and cheese boxes, round wooden rods, and so forth.

Supply bins for storing such working materials as scrap felt, leather, plastic, cork, sheet metal and so forth may be placed beneath the special worktable which, as previously advised, is best located at one of the lighter corners of the shop, or which may be built along some other available wall space which is also well lighted. The use of plywood doors with small size hasps attached for padlocking is also a practical idea for these supply bins. Adding a few shelves immediately above the table top of such a series of supply bins, to stock small hardware fittings, such as pin and earring clasps, drawing and tracing papers, nails, brads and screws, is still another idea which may be applied in connection with the installation of equipment.

These supply bins, shelves and lumber rack should be painted in the same fashion as the work tables, sitting benches and other shop equipment.

E. Metal paint cabinet.

Some form of metal paint cabinet should be employed for the storing of all painting materials, shellac, acids, brushes, varnish, lacquer, glues, and so forth. Such a cabinet is not only practical, but also serves as a precaution against fire. The cabinet should be fitted with air vents and firmly fastened to the wall. If it happens to be a tall cabinet, its base may rest on the floor; if it is short, it may be affixed to the wall with its base resting on top of the supply bins or on the top of the heavy duty work table. This paint cabinet should also be painted in harmony with the rest of the shop equipment.

F. Wall display boards for children's work and instructor's models.

The author has found from his own handicraft teaching experience that a children's craft shop which has a plentiful, carefully selected and neatly arranged display of finished models on the wall, representative of the various craft techniques presented in the shop, is always inspiring and helpful to the children at work. Such a display also helps to produce a high standard of workmanship. The models can be made especially attractive and imposing when mounted in an orderly fashion on a suitable size plywood or composition board, neatly trimmed with some kind of narrow moulding. The display board can be labeled, "Suggested Handicraft Projects." If possible, it is even a better idea to display each craft technique separately. Such display boards may then be labeled, "Suggested Leathercraft Projects," "Working with Plastics," and so forth.

Besides displaying the instructor's own samples of leathercraft, metalwork, woodwork, and so forth, it is a good idea to exhibit the work completed by the children themselves. This board may also be neatly trimmed with moulding and labeled.

Additional wall space may be used for charts, design suggestions, step-by-step diagrams, and other forms of visual representation directly related to the craft techniques employed in the shop.

G. The instructor's desk and demonstration table.

Any type of flat-top desk will serve satisfactorily for these two important shop functions. Children requiring individual instruction will find it convenient and profitable to come up to the instructor's desk. The instructor, on the other hand, can conveniently offer his assistance without always having to bend low over each child's section at the work table. The instructor's desk can also be used for demonstrating certain craft procedures to the children as a group, and for preparing all necessary shop records and lesson plans. Furthermore, the desk drawers can be used for storing small but essential items such as thumbtacks, paper clips, rubber bands and drawing instruments.

H. First aid cabinet.

All children's craft shops should always be furnished with some kind of well equipped first aid cabinet. Any small wood or metal cabinet can be used satisfactorily for this purpose. A red cross may be painted on the outside of the cabinet door, in order to identify the cabinet easily.

I. Sink, broom, and dustpan.

These items of equipment may seem trivial, but the author has found them to be essential to the proper conduct of every craft shop. A sink in the shop is not only convenient, but actually necessary for leatherwork, papier-mâché work, plaster-of-Paris molding and casting, corrugated cardboard construction, water color or tempera painting, and various types of handwork. It is also useful for refreshing the children when they become tired or thirsty, and for washing up after they have indulged in some "messy" form of craft activity.

Having the children make good use of the broom and dust pan at the close of each craft session is not only a healthful and sanitary practice, but trains them in the habits of neatness and cleanliness.

IV. Equipment for Scrap Craft Work in Regular School Classrooms.

In this phase of our discussion we are not going to consider the type of equipment which should be installed in regular school workshops. The reason for this is very obvious, since regular workshops or arts and crafts shops installed in our progressive schools are generally complete with all standard equipment. This is especially true in the large cities where the manual training or arts and crafts shops are generally equipped with two-vise work benches, a long handwork table, a special table for supporting a mitre-box, oil stones, a grindstone and so forth, a metal-topped painting, staining and finishing table, supply closets, a lumber rack, and frequently an electric polishing machine and a pottery kiln.

The author wishes rather to offer a few helpful suggestions about working equipment to grade teachers who are interested in introducing simple handwork, such as the scrap craft projects presented later in this book in their regular school classrooms.

Since the average school classroom is usually furnished with a large number of regular writing or study desks, equipped with stationary chairs, the first consideration is to use these desks and chairs to best advantage. Then when we have planned our handwork instruction accordingly, we should add whatever other working aids and equipment are necessary to facilitate the teaching of handwork.

Thus the children can easily work with a coping saw at their regular desks by fastening a notched end sawing board to the desk top with a small metal clamp. (You will find this sawing board and clamp device in Fig. 3, Illustration 10.)

A 1/4 inch thick plywood or composition wallboard, cut to the same size as the desk top, can be employed under the saw board and over the desk top to protect the desk top from injury. This plywood or composition board desk top cover can be used as a working foundation for such other interesting and fascinating craft procedures as cutting and tooling leather, simple woodcarving, soap carving, papier-mâché work, linoleum work, felt craft, simple plastic work, and various other handicrafts described later in this book.

For storing supplies, the craft teacher can utilize any form of wall cabinet, usually part of the equipment of the average classroom. Since craft work, as presented in the modern elementary school, is only part of the regular integrated curriculum, its scope is necessarily limited. For this reason the closet space required for craft supplies need not be as large as that needed in the regular workshop exclusively devoted to the teaching of arts and crafts.

For necessary heavy-type or general kind of handwork procedures, such as backsawing, crosscutsawing, planing, drilling holes, nailing and gluing together rather large size projects, sharpening edge tools, cutting large size sheets of metal, leather, felt, plastic, cardboard and other materials to smaller sizes for the use of the children, it is an excellent idea to have one or two regular work benches installed at the rear of the classroom. Should these regular work benches which come equipped with two screw-type woodworking vises be unobtainable, you can satisfactorily substitute any old sturdy library table or solidly constructed work table. Adding one or two removable metalworking vises to each table will make it practically as serviceable as the regular expensive type of work bench.

If regular work benches are part of the classroom equipment, the handwork tools used should be neatly arranged in the bench cabinets, usually provided with standard benches. If library tables or similar heavy tables are used, any resourceful teacher will find it a simple matter to build some convenient form of tool rack or cabinet underneath each table. Of course, if the tables are furnished with one or more drawers, tool compartments may be unnecessary.

Other practical hints for classroom teachers of handwork are as follows:

A display board of medium size, showing the teacher's finished models, should be hung prominently on the classroom wall. Another display board should be used to exhibit the best work produced by the children during the course of the term.

All painting and staining should be done on an old kitchen table, the entire top of which can be covered with a sheet of galvanized iron. This table can be made even more useful by being fastened solidly against the wall in some convenient section of the classroom, and by having a small metal cabinet, preferably with a door, attached to the wall section of its top. This cabinet can be used for storing paints, stains, shellac, turpentine, brushes and other such items. A suitable type of metal paint cabinet is provided by an old kitchen cabinet, bread box, or medicine chest, or, if necessary, a paint cabinet can be made from a scrap sheet of metal or from wood lined with scrap pieces of metal.

And, above all, remember the first aid cabinet, which should always be conveniently located and properly supplied.

CHAPTER FOUR

ESSENTIAL TOOLS AND OTHER USEFUL DEVICES FOR SCRAP CRAFT WORK

ALTHOUGH the tools, jigs, stamping and modeling implements, and other working devices described in this chapter, are needed for the various forms of scrap craft treated in this book, it is not absolutely necessary for every shop to be equipped with a complete assortment of these tools.

The reason for this is quite obvious since no two handicraft shops are exactly alike in their physical set-up or the extent of their working equipment; nor are all home craftsmen or children's craft groups interested in or capable of working with the same types of construction materials and techniques. While some home craftsmen or children's craft groups may wish to work with leather, felt, or paper and cardboard scraps, others may prefer such materials as wood, metal and plastics.

At any rate, the complete and extensive list of suggested tools and other working devices given below should afford the reader a perspective of all essential tools which are available. Even if certain of these tools are not immediately required, he should, nevertheless, know something about them. Very often good makes of shopworn or second hand tools may be procured at a considerable saving in cost. Such used tools can easily be put into good working order by the use of emery cloth, steel wool, and machine oil.

Furthermore, a good many of the tools described below can be improvised from various kinds of odd or discarded materials. For instance, a practical mallet can easily be built by inserting a proper length of a broom stick handle or curtain rod, into a 4 inch long end section of a discarded baseball bat. In fact, several differently formed and useful types of wooden mallets can be made from the same old baseball bat. The author himself has found it necessary to make various kinds of wooden mallets which proved most useful in such popular forms of simple craft techniques as wood and metal tapping, simple woodcarving, metal ash-tray construction, and so forth.

The same situation exists in regard to the preparation of various forms of stippling, tapping, modeling and stamping implements, from broken drill bits, odd pieces of tool steel strips, wire nails, old nut-picks and so forth. Suggestions for making these tools are given below.

Although these tools, jigs, and other working implements are planned for use in connection with the scrap craft projects presented later in this book, they can, of course, be satisfactorily employed in handwork activities utilizing new materials or for crafts not represented in this book.

The quantity of each kind of tool which should be provided for every craft shop is up to the individual home craftsman or instructor. Generally, however, one of each type is adequate for the home craftsman. In children's craft shops, one or two of such tools as rip or crosscutting saws, hacksaws, and boring braces is ample; while coping saws, mallets, try-squares, hammers, chisels, gouges, and so forth are needed in somewhat greater quantities, depending upon the number of children in each handicraft class.

I. Suggested Scrap Craft Tools

A. Saws

1. Back Saw—Has a thin, steel blade, about 3 inches in width, which is reinforced at the top edge with a heavy strip of metal. Has specially small teeth for cutting small pieces of flat wood, dowel rods, and so forth. Can be used only for straight line sawing. The smaller sizes, 10 inch to 12 inch long, are most suitable for general scrap crafts. Usually used over a hardwood benchhook in the manner shown in Fig. 7, Illustration 11.

2. Rip Saw—Used for cutting flat boards lengthwise, or in the direction of the grain. The 20 inch long, six points to the inch, type of rip saw is best for simple handwork. Teeth are larger than those of the crosscut saw described below, and look like little chisels at their tips. May be used while wood is clamped in a vise, clamped to the work bench top, or supported over two "horses."

3. Crosscut Saw—For sawing flat wood boards across the grain. A 20 inch long crosscut saw is most practical for scrap crafts. Its teeth are shaped like little knife points at the tips. A crosscut saw may also be used for ripping wood, but is not as efficient as the rip saw.

4. Coping Saw—An important type of saw for scrap crafts. Mostly used for cutting irregular shapes in thin woods, plastics, composition wall board, plywoods and similar materials. Comes with wire or wooden handles and stationary or swivel-type notches for holding the saw blades. Better grades are made with bright steel frames, while cheaper grades are made with heavy spring wire frames. Usually used with some kind of notched sawing board, in the manner shown in Fig. 3, Illustration 10. Finer grade coping saw blades may be used with the frames for smaller, more complicated forms of coping saw work, while heavier grade blades may be used for larger, less involved forms of coping saw cutting.

5. Hack Saw—A metal-framed saw equipped with a fine-toothed, hard steel blade, about 1/2 inch wide. Used for straight line sawing of all types of thick metals. The size with a 10 inch long blade is most practical for this work. Unlike most other types of saws, the hack saw is worked by both hands, with forward strokes, just as when using a wood or metal file.

6. Jeweler's Saw—A metal-framed saw, furnished with a very fine-toothed cutting blade. Used especially in jewelry or art metal work for sawing out irregularly shaped parts when working with thin gauge sheet metals, especially copper, brass, aluminum, bronze and silver. Jeweler's saws may also be employed for better, more complicated forms of plastic work. Though these saws are fairly expensive, a satisfactory type of saw for scrap craft work may be purchased for about 75 cents.

B. Hammers

1. Claw-type Nailing Hammer—This hammer is suggested for assembling all kinds of wooden articles. A medium size claw-type craft work. The flat end of the head of this hammer is used for driving nails, while the claw end, at the top of the head, is employed hammer, of 10 ounce to 12 ounce weight, is best for use in scrap

for extracting nails from wood whenever required. For an example of a claw-type hammer in use, see Fig. 3, Illustration 1.

2. Ball-Peen Hammer—This type of hammer is used mainly in art metal work, for such important art procedures as peening or tect-uring metal surfaces, fastening rivets in place when joining metals together, tapping and "chasing" designs on metal and so forth. Ball peen hammers have a rounded striking surface at one end of the head and a flat surface at the other end. Small size ball peen hammers, of a suitable grade, may be purchased for as little as 25 cents. For an example of a ball peen hammer in use, see Fig. 2, Illustration 14.

C. Mallets

The most useful form of mallet for scrap craft work is the type which is flat at one end of its head section and round at the other. To be practical and durable, mallets must be made of some hard wood such as maple, hickory, or birch. The flat end of the mallet can be used for tapping designs on wood, simple carving techniques, flattening and bending metals. The round end of the head of the mallet can be employed for concave-forming of the parts of metal projects, such as ashtrays and bowls.

As previously indicated in this book, suitable grade mallets of the type just described can easily be made in any desired quantity from short lengths of discarded baseball bats and proper lengths of broomsticks, curtain rods, mop handles, the handles of old garden rakes, and so forth. A 4 inch to 5 inch section of the top or bottom ends of a discarded baseball bat will provide a readymade round end for these homemade mallets. Of course, if you so desire, you can make separate mallets for woodwork with both ends of the flat head.

For the use of large groups of young children you can produce a good mallet in whatever quantity may be required by gluing 10 inch lengths of 1/4 inch dowels into 4 inch strips of 2 inch by 4 inch wooden joist stock. These "baby" mallets are especially useful in such elementary forms of craft work as tapping designs on metal or wood, simple woodcarving techniques, and so forth.

D. Planes

The most useful kind of plane for scrap craft work is the one commonly known as the smoothing plane. The type which measures from 8 inches to 9 inches in length at its base is suggested as best for this work. A suitable smoothing plane may be purchased at a cost of from $1.00 to $1.25 each. For very small planing work it is a good idea to use what is known as the "block plane", which is from 4 inches to 5 inches long at its base. Another useful plane is the "jack-plane", about 14 inches in length, which is used to smooth and true edges of larger size woodwork. If your craft budget makes it possible for you to include these extra two planes in your equipment of tools, be sure to have them on hand at all times, since they can do certain planing jobs better than the smoothing plane. Of course, should they be unobtainable, you will be able to manage well enough with the smoothing plane alone.

E. Files

There are many different kinds of files, each designed for a special type of filing. To meet the requirements of our scrap craft work we shall need the following useful kinds of files:

1. An 8 inch half-round, single-cut bastard, and an 8 inch, half-round, double-cut bastard for ordinary smoothing of the edges of wood boards;

2. An 8 inch, half-round rasp bastard for extra rough filing of wood board edges;

3. One each of the 8 inch half-round, double-cut, second-cut and the double-cut smooth grades of files for filing metal and plastic edges and surfaces;

4. A few small 6 inch size taper files, 6 inch round files, and a few 6 inch square files, for filing extra fine and small areas, edges, and so forth, of metal and plastic projects.

Of course, later on in your work, you may find it necessary to add other kinds of files, but the assortment recommended above will get you off to a good start.

For best results in the use of all types of files, it is wise to have wooden handles attached to the top of each file. Have a regular file brush on hand and ready for use at all times to keep the files clean and in good working order. All files of the same kind should be kept in the same section or rack of the tool chest or cabinet.

F. Boring tools

For drilling medium and large holes in wood, it is best to use a regular boring brace of the type seen in use in Fig. 4, Illustration 5. With these boring braces you can use either auger bits, with threaded tips, or twist drill bits with non-threaded tips, in a variety of sizes. For drilling small holes in wood or metal it is best to use the hand-drill type of boring tool shown in use in Fig. 6, Illustration 12. These hand-drills are equipped with a special form of drill points with short, thin shanks. These drill points are designed to bore small holes, from 1/32 inch to 1/4 inch in diameter. Some hand-drills have a compartment at the top of the handle for holding a full assortment of different size drill points.

Another tool which can be used advantageously for boring small size holes when working in wood, leather, cardboard or other soft materials is the small and very inexpensive tool known as the "brad-awl". You will see one of these brad-awls in use in Fig. 3, Illustration 27. This little tool is especially useful in simple coping saw work.

G. Metal cutting snips

The shears used to cut various kinds of metals by hand are commonly known as "snips." Snips come in two types, namely, the straight-lip snips, which are used for general metal cutting purposes, and the curved-lip snips, which are used primarily for making concave cuts. It is a good idea to have both types of snips, of a medium size, included in the shop equipment. It is important not to attempt to cut with snips any metal which is too thick or too hard for ordinary hand cutting. Thicker metals must either be cut with a hack-saw or by means of a footpower machine cutter.

H. Chisels and gouges

Chisels, which have flat steel blades, are used only in woodworking, and generally in combination with a wooden mallet. Chisels are most often used in the preparation of various joints, such as the half-lap joint, dado-joint, and mortise-and-tenon joint. The chisel sizes most useful in scrap craft work are the 1/4 inch, 1/2 inch, 3/4 inch and 1 inch sizes. These chisels are also employed in scrap craft work for simple low-relief woodcarving techniques.

Another chisel suggested for use in scrap craft work is the cold chisel, used mostly in various art metal working techniques. An application of this type of chisel is shown in Figure 2, Illustration 14. Cold chisels which are made entirely of steel, come in various sizes, each suited to a particular form of work. Best sizes are the 1/4 inch and the 1/2 inch kind.

Gouges, which are really chisels with curved instead of straight cutting blades, are used in scrap crafts for making concave grooves and other simple woodcarving processes. Best gouge sizes for this work are the 1/2 inch, 3/4 inch and the 1 inch sizes.

When using either chisels or gouges employ only a wooden mallet to obtain the necessary working force. But, when using any type of cold chisel in metal work, it is necessary to employ a ball-peen hammer or any other metal working hammer.

I. Oil Stone and Grinder

For keeping all edge tools such as plane bits, chisels, and knives in good working order, use a double-action or "two-faced" carborundum stone. One face of this type of oil stone has a rough surface for removing nicks and other irregularities from cutting edges, while the other face has a very smooth surface for the final whetting or sharpening of the tool. To keep carborundum stones in good working condition, always have a can of oil on hand to lubricate the stone when in use.

Craft shops which can afford it should have as part of their equipment a hand-grinder or a motor-driven grinding machine. Either of these machines is useful in quickly removing all edge-tool nicks, and either can be employed in the preparation of various types of wood and metal tapping, stamping, chasing and modeling implements.

J. Marking Gauge

This tool is commonly used in woodworking although it can be employed in metal working as well. It is used for marking or incising straight lines, parallel to an edge or surface of either a board of wood or a sheet of metal. It consists of a slender bar or beam which is about 8 inches long and has a sharply pointed metal pin inserted at its forward end, and a sliding head-piece which can be fastened securely to the beam by means of a set-screw, at any required distance from the marking pin. As the pin is moved along the wood or metal surface, with the head of the gauge held tightly against the guiding edge or flat surface of the material, the marking pin leaves a sharp, parallel scratched-in line at whatever distance the marking pin or gauge has been set. Most gauges have their beams marked with divisions of 1/16 inch to 1 inch measurements.

K. Try-squares

This tool is mainly used in the laying out and squaring up of wood. It is also employed to test the squareness and trueness of edges, ends, and flat surfaces of wood, subsequent to the planing or sawing operations. It consists of a thin steel blade, inscribed with measurements similar to those on a ruler, and has a thick wood or metal handle attached at right angles to one end of the try-square blade.

The most useful try-square for scrap craft work is that which has a 7 inch long blade. However, it is advisable to have a 10 inch blade try-square as part of your shop equipment as well.

II. More Scrap Craft Tools

A. Steel Rule and Steel Square

Both of these instruments are essential to various kinds of scrap crafts. The steel rule may be had in 12 inch or 24 inch lengths, and is used for measuring and laying out work in wood, metal, leather, felt, cardboard, and various other materials. The steel rule is also used in combination with a knife for cutting certain craft materials, especially leather, cardboard, cork, and linoleum. It is practical to have both sizes of rulers in the shop.

A 12 inch size steel square with two 12 inch arms running at right angles to each other is another useful laying out and cutting accessory tool. It is especially good for laying out such thin materials as leather, felt, metal, cork, and cardboard. The steel square, like the steel rule, can also be employed as a guide or straight edge for cutting the above mentioned materials to smaller sizes.

B. Screw Drivers

This important tool, which is used for driving screws into wood when fastening parts together, consists of a round steel blade, flat at its working tip, and a sturdily built handle. The most practical screw driver for scrap craft work is the kind which is fitted with a metal-reinforced plastic or wooden handle and which has a 6 inch long metal blade fitted with a 1/4 inch wide driving tip. For craft shops doing large work, a large screw driver, preferably the size with a 10 inch long steel blade, and a driving tip of 1/2 inch, is needed.

C. Knives

A good, all-purpose knife for scrap craft work, is the commonly known "sloyd" or whittling knife. Besides using it for whittling wood, it may also be employed with a steel rule or square to cut such materials as leather, cork, cardboard and linoleum to required sizes. The blade of this knife is somewhat curved along its entire length and sharply pointed at its tip. Like all other edge tools it must be kept sharp and well conditioned at all times.

For shops doing airplane model construction, another type of knife is also recommended. This is equipped with three interchangeable, small-size cutting blades, made of fine, highly tempered steel. Each blade is differently shaped for a special kind of small cutting. Any one of the blades can easily be slipped into the lower end of the handle and interchanged as required.

D. Pliers

The two most useful types of pliers for scrap crafts are the long-nosed, side-cutting pliers for light work, and the flat-nosed, side-cutting pliers for heavy work. The latter is particularly useful for gripping, twisting, pulling, bending and cutting various thicknesses of wire and metal strips. The round-nose pliers are especially practical for bending and twisting thin wires and for making various kinds of curves and scrolls.

E. Soldering Iron

For all kinds of soft soldering work use either the electric soldering iron or the non-electric type requiring heating by a gas stove or blowtorch. The electric form of soldering is preferable, however, since it is easier and safer to handle. An 8 ounce size iron is the most practical for scrap craft work, although the size of the soldering iron, either the electric or non-electric type, should be determined by the particular requirements of each workshop.

F. Clamps

These important tools are used to hold wood, metal and other materials in position while they are being sawed, filed, drilled or glued together. There are two distinct kinds of clamps which are most suited for general scrap craft work. These are the 4 inch and 8 inch "C" clamps, and the adjustable bar-clamps, also known as "cabinet makers' clamps", and are used primarily in gluing together different kinds of woodworking projects, such as book-racks, doll houses, wall shelves, magazine racks, small tables, etc.

G. **Vises**

Shops equipped with work benches with regular wood-working vises, can utilize such vises for practically all of their handicraft requirements. Those not so equipped can now purchase a new, less expensive type of woodworking vise for as little as two dollars each. These smaller bench vises can easily be attached to any sturdy work table and will function satisfactorily in all kinds of light craft work. In addition to some form of woodworking vises, each craft shop should also be equipped with one or two removable metal working vises. These sturdily built vises are especially suited to all types of metal filing, wire bending, and metal drilling. A medium size metal working vise is most practical for scrap crafts.

H. Glass Cutter

This little tool is used to cut glass sheets to special sizes and shapes. It is made entirely of metal, with a conveniently formed handle at its top and a small steel cutting wheel at its working end. When pressed over the surface of the glass, the steel wheel makes a sharp scratch or incision fairly deep into the glass, making it easy to break the glass along the scored line. Glass cutters are usually used with a yardstick to assure straight line scoring.

I. Scissors

Small and medium size scissors are always important tools in every workshop. It is important, however, to restrict their use to soft materials only, such as string, paper, thin cardboard, felt, and cloth. Using scissors to cut thin metals or for any other hard material must always be avoided if the scissors are to be kept in good working order. Dull scissors, however, can be easily sharpened by being used repeatedly to cut pieces of fine-emery cloth or sandpaper.

J. Leather and Metal Foil Toolers

These important little instruments are used for modeling or tooling designs, decorations, and surface textures on leather and thin gauges of metal. One end of the tooler is pointed and curved, while the other end is broader and spoon-shaped. Good toolers for use in both leather and thin metal work can easily be improvised from old nut-picks or fashioned form odd pieces of round tooling steel. All modelers should have some convenient handle at the center. Such handles can be made by winding glue-soaked paper strips or string around the middle sections of the modelers.

K. Nail Sets

These all metal implements are used to set heads of wire brads below the surface of wood, so that they can be completely covered and made invisible through the use of putty or plastic wood. The size with a 1/16 inch diameter cup at its working tip is most useful in scrap craft work.

L. Special Drills and Bits

In addition to the common type auger-bits, twist-drill bits and metal drill bits which have already been suggested as necessary shop tools, there are a few other types of drills and bits which will be serviceable in scrap craft activities. Among these is the countersink, which has a corrugated, conical working tip. With this tool you can drill a conically shaped depression in any piece of wood, making it possible for the head of a flat head screw to be driven even with or below the wood surface. Countersinks are fastened into the jaws of a regular boring brace, just as auger bits are fastened.

Another bit is known as an "expansion bit", which is really an adjustable form of auger bit. Expansion bits can be adjusted to cut holes as large as 2 inches in diameter.

Still another useful bit is the screw-driver bit which is shaped exactly like a screw-driver, but which can be inserted into a regular boring brace in order to drive the screw into place more rapidly and effortlessly.

M. Punches, Stamping Tools, Chasing Tools

These important tools can easily be made from various discarded metal instruments, odd strips of tooling steel, flat-head nails, broken bits and drills. Their preparation and use is really an individual or personal matter as each crafts enthusiast likes to make them in accordance with his own preferences.

One of these little tools is the sharply pointed hard steel center-punch which is used to make shallow dents in metal before drilling holes clear through the metal. These dents prevent the drills from slipping.

Stamping tools are used for stamping designs, surface textures, or patterns on leather, wood and metal. They come in a wide variety of motifs, such as straight lines, triangles, circles, griddle or cross-line patterns, arrows, arcs or flower and leaf designs. Number and letter stamping tools are also available. Stamping tools of this latter kind can hardly be made by hand, but may be purchased at small cost. Stamping or stippling tools for use in tapping designs and surface textures on wood can easily be prepared from 3 inch long flat-head nails or from off strips of tooling steel.

Chasing tools are used primarily for metal surface decoration and for metal embossing or "repousse" work. For best working results with chasing tools, only high tempered tooling steel can be employed in their preparation. Popular styles of chasing tools are those in the form of rounded tips, arcs, ovals, rectangles, straight lines, diamond shapes, triangular shapes, and so forth. Since these chasing tools are quite expensive, it is a good plan to buy only a single set in whatever designs you need and employ this set as a sample from which you can make any number of duplicates. Chasing tools may be used over the top or under surface of the metal to produce both incised or indented as well as embossed decorative effects. All chasing, stamping, and punching tools must, of course, be worked together with some form of metal working hammer such as a sturdy grade ball-peen hammer.

CHAPTER FIVE

WORKING WITH SCRAP WOOD

WE ARE discussing this handicraft first, because wood, in all its forms, is the most popular and widely used of all types of craft materials.

Another reason for giving the use of scrap wood our first consideration is the fact that all kinds of scrap wood, including cheese boxes, cigar boxes, crates, plywoods, broom and mop stick handles, old shelving boards and discarded furniture are easily obtained and, in most cases, free.

Most important, perhaps, scrap wood offers home craftsmen and teachers of arts and crafts groups everywhere, an unlimited field of fascinating projects, ranging from the simplest to the most difficult.

Of course, it would be quite impossible to attempt to cover in this book every possible form or phase of construction work in the use of scrap wood. Instead, the author has selected for detailed discussion a few of the more important types of handwork in wood.

As the reader progresses he will notice that considerable emphasis has been placed on the use of common forms and sources of scrap wood. This has been accomplished through the use of a series of key or representative projects, in which certain definite types of scrap woods are employed. The reader will thus find titles such as "Cheese Box Wall Shelf", "Cigar Box Photo Album", "Photograph Frame Made of Broom Stick Handles", "Crate Wood Ring Toss Game", and "Plywood Toys, Novelties and Games".

Each of these key projects is treated in considerable detail so that the reader will be able to construct many other projects of the same type after he builds the demonstration model. Thus, having completed the Cheese Box Wall Shelf, for example, he might try his hand at making a cheese box corner shelf, or a cheese box tie rack.

Once familiar with the basic procedures in woodwork construction, the reader will enjoy making different kinds of articles in which

Plate 1. A varied assortment of articles made from scrap wood, including ornamental lapel pins, useful containers, a stationery holder, wooden shoes and a belt.

Plate 2. Scrap wood can be used to make coasters and trivets, as well as decorative wall plaques.

scrap wood of various kinds is used in combination with other scrap materials, such as wood with leather, wood with metal, wood with pipe cleaners, wood with linoleum, and wood with felt. Several projects in which wood is used in combination with some other material will be found later in this book.

Home craftsmen and teachers of arts and crafts are advised to assemble a good stock of all shapes, sizes and types of wood scraps, including such useful items as spools, checkers, wooden candy boxes lollypop sticks, tongue depressors, old curtain rods, broken wooden articles, and chair rails. It is also a good idea to clean and condition the wood as it is collected, removing dirt, advertising matter and so forth, and to arrange the different types of wood according to kind. In this way your wood scrap will always be ready for immediate use.

Our first key project is the cheese box wall shelf in which the wood parts of a common variety of cheese box are converted into a charming little curio shelf. The reader understands, of course, that this same style shelf can be built of several other kinds of thin wood, such as cigar box wood or plywood. In like manner, Project No. 8, Cigar Box Photo Album, can also be constructed of scrap plywood or any other thin wood of sufficient size. This principle applies to many other projects presented in this book.

For the proper construction of these models a few simple and inexpensive woodworking tools are needed. These tools are listed and illustrated as each key project is described. It is a good idea to equip your workshop with these tools so as to facilitate construction. Of course, many of the tools needed for woodwork can also be used with other scrap craft materials treated in this book.

Above all, it is important to work slowly, carefully, and exactly as directed in the project discussions which follow. Each one of the models presented has been tried and tested by the author's own arts and crafts students and is sure to be successful if faithfully constructed.

Build the key projects exactly as shown, as to design and coloring treatments and the sizes and shapes of their parts. When this has been done, the reader may make one or more of the same type of project, but employing his own specifications as to design, coloring effect, sizes and contours. This experience, being more creative, will afford even greater satisfaction than can be obtained by working from already established patterns.

CHEESE BOX WOOD

The cheese box is a particularly valuable type of scrap wood because it has so many uses and is so easily obtainable. Furthermore, it is made of two different thicknesses of light-colored, soft basswood, from which a wide variety of useful and attractive objects can be built.

The value of two different thicknesses of wood in light woodworking is apparent in the construction of the Cheese Box Wall Shelf, Figure 1, Illustration 1. In this case, the thin wood of the cheese box is used for the sides of the shelf while the thick wood, which forms the ends of the cheese box, is employed for the two horizontal shelf parts.

In order to give the reader a good idea as to how the cheese box can be used to excellent advantage in the construction of simple, useful articles of woodwork, several typical projects are given below in which the cheese box provides the essential material of construction. It is hoped these representative project applications in the use of this popular form of scrap wood will inspire the reader to build many fine "cheese box creations" of his own original planning and designing.

Project No. 1, Cheese Box Wall Shelf

See Figure 1, Illustration 1

I. Description

As the title suggests, the material required for the construction of this wall shelf consists of ordinary cheese box wood. The bottom of the box provides the back of the shelf; its sides give us the sides of the shelf; and its ends, slightly thicker than either the bottom or sides, furnish the two horizontal shelf pieces.

This project is certain to be popular in club, church and school craft shops because it is easy to make, is practical and attractive.

After building the shelf according to the diagrams and patterns given in Illustration 1, the reader may construct several other shelves of his own conception.

First draw the patterns of the shelf parts on pieces of cardboard and cut them out with scissors. When the pattern parts have been prepared, use liquid glue to join them together, as shown in Figure

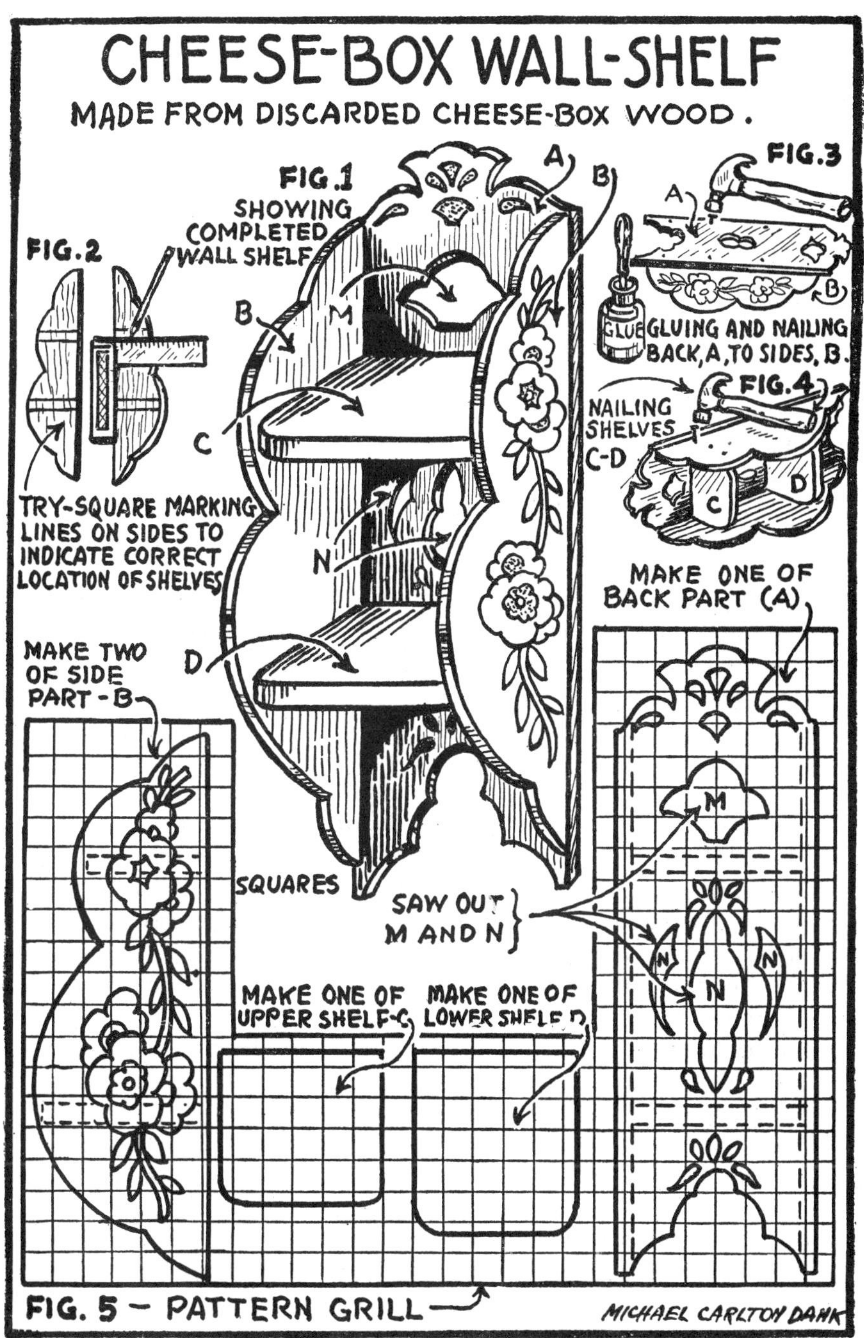
CHEESE-BOX WALL-SHELF
MADE FROM DISCARDED CHEESE-BOX WOOD.
FIG.1
SHOWING
COMPLETED
WALL SHELF
FIG.2
FIG.3
GLUE
GLUING AND NAILING
BACK, A, TO SIDES, B.
FIG.4
NAILING
SHELVES
C-D
TRY-SQUARE MARKING
LINES ON SIDES TO
INDICATE CORRECT
LOCATION OF SHELVES
MAKE ONE OF
BACK PART (A)
MAKE TWO
OF SIDE
PART - B
SQUARES
SAW OUT
M AND N
MAKE ONE OF
UPPER SHELF-C
MAKE ONE OF
LOWER SHELF D
FIG. 5 — PATTERN GRILL
MICHAEL CARLTON DANK

Illustration 1

1, Illustration 1. This will give an idea of the general appearance of the finished cheese box shelf. If it is satisfactory, take the cardboard pieces apart and use them as patterns or templates for tracing upon the cheese box wood. If slight corrections are necessary, make these with pencil and scissors before tracing.

By referring to Fig. 1, Illustration 1, you will note that the back of the shelf is perforated or sawed through, at sections M and N. Although this decorative treatment is very effective, these parts may be painted in, rather than sawed out. In this connection, it is suggested that the perforated design be used only by those who have had sufficient experience in the handling of the coping saw. Young or inexperienced craftsmen are advised to paint in the decorative sections. Below are given full directions for sawing out inside sections of wood parts.

The ornamentation of the top and bottom of the back piece and of the sides of the shelf is simply painted on according to instructions furnished later in the discussion of this project.

The construction diagrams and pattern grills furnished in Illustration 1, may also be employed for producing shelves of larger proportions than the cheese-box model. Suitable wood for building such models may be obtained from vegetable crates, food packing boxes, plywood partition panels, and several other sources found in the lists of discarded materials already furnished. To construct these larger shelves, simply use a larger size grill of squares than that of 1/2 inch squares suggested for reproducing the parts of the cheese-box shelf. Thus, to build a shelf twice as large as the cheese-box shelf, use a grill of 1 inch squares to reproduce each of the shelf parts. To produce a shelf three times as large as the cheese-box model, use 1-1/2 inch squares, and so on.

To make a neat, well-finished shelf, careful consideration must be given to accurate sawing of the wood parts, careful squaring up of all ends and edges, thorough sandpapering of all wood surfaces, well-planned and neatly applied coloring, and finally, accurate assembling of the shelf parts.

When properly completed, this trim little shelf looks quite like a manufactured product. Not only is it useful in the home but it can also be produced in quantity and sold at a profit in gift shops or at church and Red Cross bazaars.

In the directions which follow, it is assumed that the reader is already familiar with such general information as fastening devices used in woodwork, facts about using tempera colors, enamel paints and stains, use of shellac and varnish, care of brushes, and so forth. These matters have already been discussed in detail in Chapter 3 above and are accordingly treated only in brief form in the directions which follow.

II. Materials

A. The wood of one cheese box.

B. Sandpaper—Nos. 0 and 1.

C. Wire brads—size 1/2 inch by 20 inches.

D. Liquid glue.

E. Tempera colors.

F. Clear white shellac.

III. Tools

A. Coping Saw.

B. Sawing board and clamp.

C. Medium-coarse, half-round wood-file.

D. Sandpaper block.

E. Small, claw-style, nailing hammer.

F. Try-square.

G. Pointed brad-awl.

IV. Directions

A. Preparation Of Shelf Patterns.

1. The first step in the construction of this wall shelf is to prepare full-size patterns of each different wood part seen in the sketch of this project, in Fig. 1, Illustration 1.

2. As you will note by referring to this sketch, one pattern is required for the back part, one for the two sides, and one for each of the two different size shelf parts. These four patterns may easily be prepared by drawing an arrangement of squares in the manner shown in Fig. 5, Illustration 1. Use a sheet of drawing or wrapping paper, size 11 inches by 14 inches, and employ 1/2 inch squares instead of the reduced size squares seen in Fig. 5.

3. After the grill of 1/2 inch squares is all ruled and ready, copy shelf parts A, (back), B, (sides), and C and D, (shelf pieces), exactly as represented in the reduced size grill in Fig. 5. Be sure to include all exterior contours, the decorations which are to be painted on, and the perforated areas which are to be sawed out. When completed, each of the four required shelf patterns will be reproduced in its actual, full size.

4. The final step in preparing the patterns for our cheese-box shelf, is to cut the enlarged patterns apart so that each individual pattern may be separately traced to the wood. To do this, simply use a medium size pair of scissors to cut around the outside contours of each separate pattern. After they are cut out in this manner, they are ready to be transferred to the wood.

B. Taking cheese box apart

Since cheese box wood is rather thin and fragile, special care must be exercised in taking these boxes apart in their separate pieces. The author has found the following procedure both easy and practical.

1. With a medium size screw-driver, gradually pry up the bottom of the box at several points around the sides and ends. As a result of this step, the small, flat head nails, used to fasten the bottom in place, will be partially raised.

2. With a small size claw-hammer, pull out the nails, causing the bottom board to be completely free of the box.

3. With the flat head of the hammer, lightly tap the inside surfaces of the ends of the box, working gradually, until they are completely separated from the sides. Since the sides and

ends of a cheese box are only dove-tailed together, without the use of either glue or nails, simply tapping the inside surfaces of the end parts with the hammer, will cause the corner joints to loosen up, permitting the end and side boards to come apart easily, with practically no damage to their surfaces. Working in this manner, too, will prevent cracking the boards and wasting this fine lumber material.

C. Cleaning and smoothing board surfaces

1. Before the shelf patterns can be traced to the cheese-box boards, all printed matter must be completely removed and the board surfaces must be thoroughly cleaned and smoothed.

2. A good procedure for properly conditioning the boards, in preparation for the pattern transferring step, is as follows:

a. Clamp a strip of wood, of 1/8 inch thickness, to the top of the work-bench, at any convenient corner.

b. Place one of the cheese box boards on the bench, with printed side of the board facing upward, and with its forward end solidly propped up against the clamped strip of wood. The latter provides a form of bench stop to hold the board in place for the planing step which follows.

c. Using a medium size smoothing plane, set for fine shaving, plane the surface of the board carefully, and only enough to remove the printed matter. Too much planing will make the board too thin and unfit for use. Plane only in the direction of the grain.

d. Wrap a piece of No. 1 sandpaper, cut to about 4 inches square, around a block of wood, and then use this combination sandpaper and block to smooth the planed surface. In this step, as in planing, work only in the direction of the grain. Following this initial sanding step, wrap a piece of No. 0 sandpaper around the block and sand this same surface again, until a very smooth surface is produced.

e. Turn board so its unprinted side faces upward, and then proceed to sandpaper this side in the same way that you did for the printed side of the board. To condition this surface of the wood, just sandpapering without any planing will be sufficient.

f. Plane and sandpaper the flat surfaces of the other wood boards of the cheese-box in the same way, as directed for the first board.

D. Transferring shelf patterns to wood boards

1. The important point to remember in this pattern tracing step, is to be sure that each separate pattern is traced carefully and that each outline and all inside decorations are reproduced clearly, and exactly as indicated.

2. To transfer Pattern A, for back of shelf.

a. Place pattern A on board which formerly served as the bottom of the cheese box, so that the left, straight edge of the pattern coincides with the left edge of the board. Also, locate the pattern in about the center of the length of the board.

b. Holding pattern securely in place with left hand, place a sheet of carbon paper, with carboned face down, between the pattern and the wood.

c. Fasten pattern and carbon sheets to wood with two small strips of scotch-tape, placing one strip at the upper section and one at the lower section of the pattern.

d. With a sharpened pencil, now trace over all the inside decorations of this pattern as well as around its outside contours, working slowly and carefully.

e. After tracing this pattern, remove pattern and carbon sheets. If done correctly, the wood board will now have an exact copy of pattern A clearly reproduced on its surface.

3. To transfer Pattern B, for sides of shelf.

a. Place pattern B over one of the side boards of the cheese box, so that the straight edge of the pattern coincides with one of the straight edges of the wood board. In this case also, locate pattern in about the center of the board's length.

b. Place carbon paper between pattern and board, fasten the sheets in place with two or three small strips of scotch-tape, then trace as directed above, when tracing the pattern of the back part. When tracing the side piece patterns, it is important to remember that the flower decoration used on these parts, is to appear on the outside surface of each part. Therefore, it will be necessary to trace these side parts in reverse fashion.

Note: If no carbon paper is available, blacken under surface of pattern wih a soft pencil. This will serve satisfactorily as a means of transferring the complete contents of the pattern, in place of the carbon paper.

4. To transfer Patterns C and D, for shelf pieces.

In view of the fact that these shelf parts require no detail tracing but only a tracing of their outside contours, no carbon paper is necessary.

a. Place these shelf patterns over the end boards of the cheese box, so that the back, straight sides of the patterns coincide with the notchless edges of the boards.

b. Locate each pattern at the center of the board's length, and entirely free from the dove-tail notches at the ends of the boards.

c. Hold the shelf patterns firmly in this position.

d. Trace around the outside edges of the pattern with a pointed pencil.

E. Sawing out the wood parts

1. The tool used for cutting out the wood parts is commonly known as a coping-saw. In addition to this saw, a "V" notched sawing board, made of any sturdy wood, about 6 inches wide, 12 inches long, by 3/4 inches thick, and a small size, metal "C" clamp, are also essential equipment for this sawing procedure. See Fig. 3, Illustration 10.

2. A good method for cutting out shelf parts is as follows:

a. Clamp the "V" notched sawing board to a corner section of your work table or bench, allowing the forward end of the board to extend about 6 inches from the edge of the table.

b. Place the board, containing the tracing of the first part of the shelf, on the top of the saw board. Then, holding the work with the left hand, proceed to cut around its outside contours. Saw slowly and carefully and be sure to follow the traced pattern outlines exactly as indicated. Throughout this sawing step, hold the saw firmly in a perfectly upright position, with the handle of the saw located below the frame, and with the teeth of the saw blade pointing downward, toward the handle, just as shown in Fig. 3, Illustration 10.

c. In this same manner, saw out the other shelf parts, cutting only around their outside contours, as in the case of the first part.

d. After all parts have been cut out, in this manner, proceed to saw out the interior sections of Part A, the back part of the shelf. You will find these sections clearly indicated as M and N, in Fig. 1, Illustration 1.

3. To cut out the inside parts, first bore a small hole within the section which is to be sawed out. Then, unhook one end of the saw blade from the frame, insert it through the drilled hole, and hook it in its frame notch again. The interior section may now be cut out, working in the same manner as when sawing outside contours or edges. When finished, detach saw blade end, remove saw from wood, then fasten lose end of saw blade to its notch in the frame again.

4. For a more detailed explanation concerning the use of the coping-saw, see Chapter Four, Section I, A, 4. It should also be noted at this point, that those craftsmen who are fortunate enough to own an electrically driven band-saw or jig-saw, may, of course, use such motorized equipment to excellent advantage, in place of the hand-worked coping-saw, for cutting out the wood parts of this cheese box shelf.

F. Filing and sandpapering edges of cutout shelf parts

Following the sawing procedure just described, the next step in the construction of our cheese box shelf is that of filing and sandpapering all sawed edges, until they are smooth and neatly finished. These filing and sanding operations may be performed by using a bench-vise or by holding the boards in a flat position at the edge of the work table top.

Straight edges or smoothly sawed curved edges will not require any filing, as just sandpapering such edges will be sufficient. When sandpapering straight edges, simply wrap a piece of No. 0 sandpaper around a block of wood, measuring about 2 inches wide, by 4 inches long, by 3/4 inches thick, and then rub the edge of the wood firmly, until it is straight and smooth. Use a ruler to test the straightness of the edge after it is sandpapered. Straight edges as well as curved edges, should also be tested for squareness with the face or flat surface of the board. This important requirement for squareness of the edges of the board, may be satisfactorily complied with, by employing the tool known as a try-square. You will find this tool fully described in Chapter Four, Section I, K. It may also be seen in use in connection with another important operation, in Fig. 2, Illustration 1.

Any edges which have been sawed out in an uneven, jagged fashion must first be filed and later finished with sandpaper. A medium coarse, half-round file is most useful for this purpose. Best filing results are obtained by fastening the work in the bench-vise and by using the file with both hands. Use the flat side of the file for flat edge filing or for filing upward curves and the curved side of the file for downward curves. A good idea for sandpapering curved or irregular edges or edges resulting from interior sawing, is to wrap a piece of sandpaper about the half-round file, employing the file, in this case, as a convenient working handle for using the sandpaper easily and effectively. Use either the flat or round side of the sandpaper-wrapped file, according to the particular shape of the edge to be smoothed.

The front edges of the sides and horizontal shelf parts of our shelf project should be neatly rounded off to produce a pleasing, decorative effect. This may also be done through the use of the file and sandpaper.

After all the sawed edges of the shelf parts have been properly smoothed and finished by these filing and sandpapering methods, the parts are ready for assembling.

G. Assembling parts of cheese box shelf

The tools and materials required for properly assembling the parts of the shelf are a small size claw-hammer, a try-square, a pointed brad-awl, wire brads size 1/2 inch to 2 inches, liquid glue and any small brush suitable for applying the glue.

The correct procedure for assembling the shelf is as follows:

1. Using a sharpened pencil and a try-square, as in Fig. 2, Illustration 1, clearly mark off the lines on the back and inside surfaces of the side parts of the shelf, to indicate exactly where the horizontal shelf parts are to be located. You will find the locations for these assembling guide lines clearly indicated with dotted lines in the pattern grill on parts A and B. in Illustration 1.

2. Place one of the side pieces of the shelf in the bench-vise with the straight edge of the side piece facing upward.

3. Brush a little liquid glue along this edge and then nail one side of back part A in place, using 3 or 4 half-inch wire brads for this first nailing step, in the manner shown in Fig. 3, Illustration 1. Before driving the nails in place, make tiny holes with a pointed brad-awl, to get the nails off to a good start. Be sure the corner joint thus made is done evenly, without either of the parts overlapping.

4. Nail the other edge of the back part to the straight edge of the second side piece, in the same manner as in the case of the first side part. The correct placement of the back and side parts may easily be determined by referring to the dotted lines shown in part A. of the grill in Illustration 1.

5. After the sides are fastened to the back, glue and nail horizontal shelf parts C and D in their proper places, in the manner shown in Fig. 4, Illustration 1. Use three 1/2 inch wire brads at each side of the shelf in a neat, even arrangement. Be certain to nail the shelf parts perfectly straight and in their exact location, following the try-square guide lines previously marked off on the back and side pieces.

6. If any of the glue has oozed out from any of the joints just made, it can easily be removed by wiping with a damp cloth. A little additional sandpapering around the jointed sections may also be necessary.

H. Coloring and finishing the cheese box wall shelf

Although enamel paints or oil stains may be used satisfactorily for painting this shelf, the author has found that tempera colors are easiest to apply, least expensive, and generally most effective. This is especially true when children's craft groups are engaged in the construction of this project.

In addition to the tempera colors, you will also need small and medium size water color brushes, an inch wide, flat-style, shellacking brush, a few small mixing pans, a dish of plain water, and an old piece of cloth.

For best results in the coloring and finishing of our project, proceed as follows:

1. The first consideration is that of deciding upon a suitable color scheme which will harmonize with the coloring of the room in which the shelf is to be hung. The color scheme employed by the author for his model of this shelf consisted of an overall color of orange, a trimming treatment of medium blue and light green, and for coloring the floral decorations, a combination of yellow, red and dark green.

2. Prepare a sufficient quantity of the selected overall color in one of the mixing pans, then, using a No. 5, 6, or 7 water coloring brush, apply this color over all the surfaces of the shelf except the sections occupied by the floral decorations. Apply the paint in long, even strokes of the brush, using only as much paint as needed for a neat, uniform, complete coverage of all the wood parts.

3. After the overall coat is thoroughly dry, apply a trim of one or two colors around the edges on the outside surfaces of the side parts. Apply decorative trimming lines around the perforated areas, on the inside surface of the back part of the shelf, as well as along the top and bottom ends of this back part. Another good idea is to apply one of the colors employed in the color scheme, over the front edges of the two horizontal shelf pieces.

4. Color the floral decorations on the outside surfaces of the side parts of the shelf.

5. When all coloring work is completed and dry, use a flat-type brush to apply a coat of clear, white shellac over the entire shelf. When dry, rub this first coat lightly with fine, steel wool, and then apply a second coat of shellac.

Note: Many different effective coloring and finishing treatments can be worked out for this shelf project, depending upon the artistic skill and ingenuity of each craftsman. Teachers presenting this cheese-box shelf as a construction project to a group of children, should encourage each child to plan and work out his own coloring treatment and decorative scheme.

Footnote: For a more complete and more technical treatment of simple woodwork construction the reader is referred to another book by this Author, entitled "Creative Crafts In Wood" published by The Manual Arts Press, Peoria, Illinois.

RELATED CHEESE BOX PROJECTS

Based upon the working procedures given in connection with our key Project No. 1, Cheese Box Wall Shelf, shown in Fig. 1, Illustration 1.

Project No. 2, Combination Shelf and Towel Rack

See Figure 1, Illustration 2

I. Description

This unusually constructed cheese box project can be used to advantage either in the kitchen or bathroom. In the kitchen, it can serve as a holder for a small clock, salt and pepper shakers, and so forth, with its revolving arms providing a convenient rack for dish towels. In the bathroom, it can serve as a neat shelf for toilet articles while its arms hold a set of guest towels.

All the materials needed to build this practical combination shelf are a single cheese box, a small piece of 1/2 inch dowel, a narrow strip of scrap tin, a few 1/2 inch wire brads, a few 3/8 inch round head screws, a piece of medium grade sandpaper, a little liquid glue, and two or three colors of enamel paint. As for the

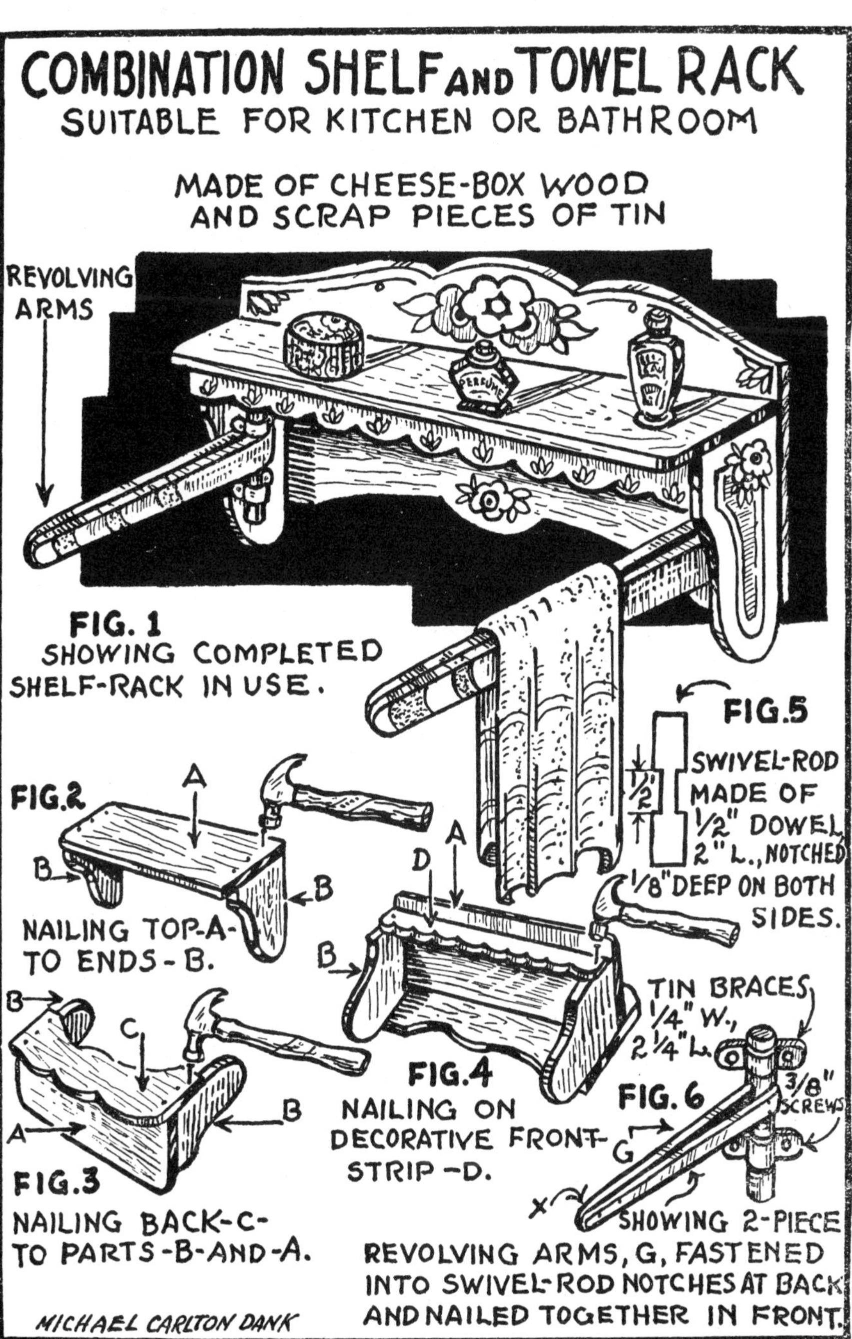
COMBINATION SHELF AND TOWEL RACK
SUITABLE FOR KITCHEN OR BATHROOM
MADE OF CHEESE-BOX WOOD
AND SCRAP PIECES OF TIN
REVOLVING ARMS
PERFUME
FIG. 1
SHOWING COMPLETED SHELF-RACK IN USE.
FIG.5
SWIVEL-ROD MADE OF 1/2" DOWEL, 2" L., NOTCHED 1/8" DEEP ON BOTH SIDES.
1/2
FIG.2
A
B
B
NAILING TOP-A-TO ENDS-B.
A
D
B
FIG.4
NAILING ON DECORATIVE FRONT-STRIP-D.
TIN BRACES 1/4" W., 2 1/4" L.
3/8" SCREWS
FIG. 6
G
X
SHOWING 2-PIECE REVOLVING ARMS, G, FASTENED INTO SWIVEL-ROD NOTCHES AT BACK AND NAILED TOGETHER IN FRONT.
B
C
A
B
FIG.3
NAILING BACK-C-TO PARTS-B-AND-A.
MICHAEL CARLTON DANK

Illustration 2

tools, all that is necessary is the inexpensive coping saw equipment shown in Fig. 3, Illustration 10, a small size nailing hammer, a brad-awl, a boring tool, and a smoothing plane.

The ends of this combination shelf and towel rack, are produced from the end boards of the cheese box. The back and top sections are made from the side boards of the cheese box. The scalloped strip at the front and the four narrow, tapered strips which form the two revolving arms of this article are fashioned from the bottom board of the cheese box.

II. Directions

Since most of the tooling procedures, required in the construction of this combination shelf and towel rack, are the same as those employed in the fashioning of our key project in this unit, the directions which follow are brief except when new or different tooling operations are involved.

Although this cheese-box project looks a little complicated in construction, it is really easy to build. Simply provide yourself with the few tools and materials indicated above, and proceed as follows:

A. Preparation of patterns

1. Draw a grill of 1/2 inch squares, using the same number and arrangement of squares as represented in the reduced form grill in Illustration 3. Use any medium weight, light colored paper. On this grill show Part A, top, Part B, ends, Part C, back, Part D, front, Part E, swivel rods, Part F, tin braces, and Part G, revolving arm strips. When completed, each part will be reproduced in the actual size of our project.

2. Be sure to include in the drawing of each pattern part all decorative and constructional details, exactly as represented in the reduced form pattern grill in Illustration 3.

3. Using a small pair of scissors, cut out each separate pattern part. Then place all completed patterns for this project in an envelope marked "Combination Shelf and Towel Rack."

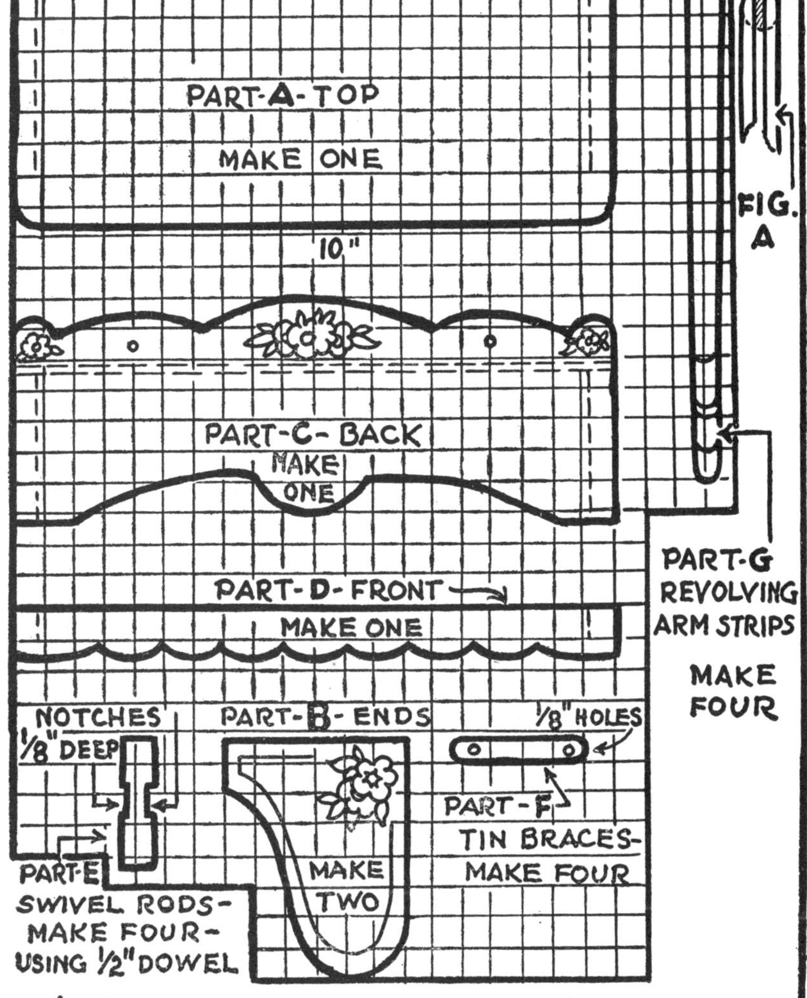

WORKING PATTERNS
FOR COMBINATION SHELF AND TOWEL RACK
SEE PREVIOUS ILLUSTRATION FOR SKETCH OF THIS PROJECT IN COMPLETED FORM.
ROUND BACK ENDS OF ARMS LIKE THIS
PART-A-TOP
MAKE ONE
FIG. A
10"
PART-C-BACK
MAKE ONE
PART-G
REVOLVING ARM STRIPS
MAKE FOUR
PART-D-FRONT
MAKE ONE
NOTCHES 1/8" DEEP
PART-B-ENDS
1/8" HOLES
PART-F
TIN BRACES-
MAKE FOUR
PART-E
SWIVEL RODS-
MAKE FOUR-
USING 1/2" DOWEL
MAKE TWO
USE 1/2 INCH SQUARES FOR ACTUAL SIZE DUPLICATION OF ABOVE PARTS
MICHAEL CARLTON DANK

Illustration 3

B. Taking cheese box apart

For directions see the instructions given for the Cheese Box Wall Shelf, Project No. 1, Section IV, B.

C. Cleaning and smoothing board surfaces

For filing and sandpapering, see text under Project No. 1, Cheese Box Wall Shelf, Section IV, C. Special attention is called to method of planing and smoothing printed wood surfaces of cheese boxes, also given under Section IV, C.

D. Transferring patterns to wood

Read instructions for similar procedure given for Cheese Box Wall Shelf, Project No. 1, Section IV, D. Then proceed as follows:

1. Make a tracing of Part A, top, to one of the side boards of the cheese box.

2. Make one tracing of Part C, back, to the other side board of the cheese box.

3. Make two tracings, in reverse fashion, of Part B, ends, using the end boards of the cheese box. These end boards of the cheese box are made of a thicker grade of wood than the sides or bottom section of the box, making possible a more solid form of construction.

4. Make one tracing of Part D, scalloped front strip, using a part of the bottom board of the cheese box.

5. Make four tracings of Part G, revolving arm strips, using the remainder of the bottom board of the cheese box.

6. Trace all decorations and dotted, constructional details exactly as indicated in each pattern part.

E. Sawing out the wood parts

Read directions for similar sawing procedure given under Project No. 1, Cheese Box Wall Shelf, Section IV, E, then proceed as follows:

1. Saw out traced wood parts A, B, C, D, and G, being careful to follow all traced outlines exactly as indicated. For this sawing step, use the equipment shown in Fig. 3, Illustration 10, being sure, at all times, to hold the coping saw in a perfectly upright position, just as illustrated in this same sketch.

2. Cut two 2 inch lengths of 1/2 inch diameter wooden dowel or any similar wooden material, to serve as Part E, swivel rods. In this cutting step, you may employ either the coping saw or the back-saw and bench-hook combination, the latter of which is shown in Figs. 2 and 3, Illustration 12.

3. Using the coping saw, cut out two 1/8 inch deep notches, 1/2 inch long, at the central section of each swivel-rod. See swivel-rod construction in use in the sketch of completed project, in Fig. 1, Illustration 2. Also see Figs. 5 and 6, Illustration 2.

F. Filing and sandpapering cutout wood parts

For these procedures, see text for corresponding steps in connection with the construction of the Cheese Box Wall Shelf, Project No. 1, as given under Section IV, F. Be sure, when sandpapering broad surfaces of wood parts, to work in the direction of the grain only. Also make certain that all edges and ends are smooth and neatly finished.

G. Assembling the parts

In this procedure, it is a good idea to refer again to the cheese box wall shelf, shown in Fig. 1, Illustration 1, since the basic principles for joining wood parts together in light woodwork construction, are there presented in detail. It is accordingly suggested that the reader first study the text given under Project No. 1, Section IV, G, and then proceed with the assembling of our present project as follows:

1. Nail top part A, to end parts, B, using liquid glue and 1/2 inch wire brads. Use three brads at each end and be sure the assembled parts are exactly flush at the back and ends, allowing the front edge of Part A, to extend forward about 3/4 inch. See Fig. 2, Illustration 2. In this step, as in the other assembling steps, it is a good

idea to be governed by the dotted construction lines as indicated in the pattern grill in Illustration 3.

2. Using glue and three 1/2 inch brads at each end, nail back piece, C, to assembled parts A and B, using as a guide the dotted construction lines as furnished in part C, in the grill, in Illustration 3. Also see Fig. 3, Illustration 2.

3. Nail scalloped front part, D, to front edge of end parts, B, locating this scalloped strip immediately under extended edge of top part, A. Use liquid glue on all contact surfaces and one 1/2 inch wire brad at each end of the strip. See Fig. 4, Illustration 2.

4. Nail a revolving arm strip, G, into each of the four cutout notches in the two previously prepared 1/2 inch dowel swivel rod parts. Use in this jointing step liquid glue and two 1/2 inch brads for the attachment of each arm.

5. Fasten together the tapered ends of each pair of revolving arm strips, using glue and two 1/2 inch brads for each pair of arms. See X, Fig. 6, Illustration 2.

6. Round off wide ends of revolving arm strips (ends which are attached to the revolving swivel rods), in the manner shown in Fig. A, Illustration 3, to permit the swivel rods to turn freely.

7. Attach completed swivel arm units to the inside sections of end parts B, locating the swivel rods approximately in the center of the width of parts B in the manner shown by the left section of our completed model, in Fig. 1, Illustration 2. In this procedure, it is important that one of the swivel rods be located about 1/2 inch either above or below the other swivel rod, in order that the two revolving arm units may properly interlock when they are folded beneath the shelf. To attach the swivel rods properly, cut four tin strips to the size of 1/4 inch by 2-1/4 inch. Then drill a 1/8 inch hole at both ends of each tin strip. See Part F, Illustration 3. Wrap a tin strip around the upper and lower sections of each swivel rod, E, placing them close to the revolving arm strips, as shown in Fig. 6, Illustration 2. Then, using a screw driver and 3/8 inch round head screws, fasten the swivel rods securely in place,

producing the convenient arm revolving arrangement sketched in Fig. 1, Illustration 2.

H. Coloring and finishing combination shelf and towel rack

Because of the particular use for which this project is intended, enamel paint is suggested as the most practical coloring medium. Good overall enamel colors for this purpose are light green, pink, light blue, light yellow, pale violet, or white. Of course, the color selected will in most cases be determined by the color scheme of the kitchen or bathroom in which the rack is to be used.

In addition to the selected overall enamel paint, it is a good plan to use some other color of enamel as a trim around the edges of the project as well as for the flower designs used for the decoration of parts B and C. You will find these trimming and floral unit decorations clearly indicated in the pattern grill, in Illustration 3. This additional color must be carefully selected so that it will harmonize with the overall enamel paint. Thus, with light green, for example, a good trimming color would be pink, or yellow. If you use yellow as the overall color, a suitable trimming color would be violet or brown.

To apply the enamel paints properly, proceed as follows:

1. Be sure all wood surfaces of the assembled project are sandpapered smooth and clean.

2. Apply a thin coat of white or orange shellac over the entire project and allow to dry thoroughly. For this shellacking step, use a 1 inch wide, flat-type brush. If shellac is too thick, thin with alcohol.

3. Select a suitable overall color of enamel paint and stir thoroughly until it is of an even consistency. If the enamel is too thick, add a little turpentine to thin it.

4. Using another flat style brush, also about 1 inch wide, apply the enamel paint evenly over all shellacked surfaces of the rack. Use long, uniform strokes of the brush, and be sure the painted surfaces are smooth, neat, and free from irregular brush strokes or paint puddles. Allow project to dry thoroughly.

5. Select a suitable color of enamel for use as a trim around the edges of the rack and for painting on the floral designs on parts B and C. See pattern grill for locations and drawings of these decorations.

6. Using a small size, pointed style brush, first paint on the floral designs and then trim the edges. Do not fill in the floral units. Use only an outlining form of treatment, and maintain a thin quality of line throughout. Before painting the decorations, it is a good idea to outline them just lightly with a sharply pointed pencil. These pencil outlines serve as a guide, when one is applying the second color of enamel for the trimming effects. It is suggested that the reader use Fig. 1, Illustration 2, as a model for pencilling the decorative outlines.

When the second or trimming color of enamel paint has dried, the combination shelf and towel rack is finished and ready to use in the kitchen or bathroom. The completed model will be as attractive as the one pictured in. Fig. 1, Illustration 2, if the directions above are followed.

Project No. 3, Cheese Box Corner Shelf

This corner shelf is built according to the general tooling procedures presented earlier in this unit in connection with the construction of the Cheese Box Wall Shelf, Project No. 1, shown in Fig. 1, Illustration 1.

The essential difference between the two models is the formation of their horizontal shelf parts. In the straight type cheese box wall shelf, the shelf parts are square shaped, while those of the corner shelf model are triangular in shape. The front edges of the horizontal shelf parts in the corner shelf project are neatly curved and rounded, just as those used for the straight shelf model, shown in Fig. 1, Illustration 1.

The sides of the cheese box corner shelf are fashioned exactly like those of the straight shelf. Since all sawing, nailing, and coloring directions are the same for both models, the reader is referred to the text given under Project No. 1, for complete building details.

Both the straight and corner type shelf models are equally attractive when completed. Both styles have proven popular with the boys and girls in the author's own shopwork classes.

Project No. 4, Cheese Box Tie Rack

This is another project which can be constructed easily and effectively through the use of discarded cheese box wood.

In the building of this model, the end boards of the cheese box, which are made of a thicker grade of wood than the rest of the box, are employed as the supports for the tie bars. The bottom board of the cheese box can be used for the back, or supporting board of the tie rack. The tie bars, of which there may be one, two, or three, as desired, can be made from one of the side boards of the cheese box. Two bars, one fastened to the top and one to the lower section of the tie bar supports, will be found very practical.

In making the patterns for the sides, supporting back board, and tie bars, any number of attractive designs can be used for the contours and ornamentation of the different wood parts. Either tempera or enamel paint is suitable.

To fasten the wood parts together, use liquid glue and 1/2 inch wire brads. See text under Project No. 1 for further instructions.

Project No. 5, Cheese Box Toy Furniture

Most little girls enjoy playing with toy furniture of all kinds, but a good purchased set is often quite expensive. Sturdy and attractive toy furniture including tables, chairs, beds, dressers, bookcases, and so forth, can easily be made from discarded cheese boxes at practically no cost at all. Simply apply the directions given above for Project No. 1, The Cheese Box Wall Shelf.

Just make paper patterns of each piece of toy furniture which you wish to build. Then trace the patterns to the cheese box boards, saw out the toy furniture parts, sandpaper, assemble, color, and finish them as desired. When making patterns for the toy furniture particular attention should be given to the relative size of each piece. For example, in a bedroom set, the bed, the dresser, night-table, chair, and so forth, must be built in proper proportions exactly as in the construction of real furniture. In the dining room set, the chairs must be built in correct proportion to the table, and so forth.

The thick wood ends of the cheese box can be used to advantage in making toy chair seats, table legs, and bed posts. The sides and the bottom boards of the cheese box, which are made of thinner wood, are suitable for table tops, chair sides, chair rails, bookcase shelves and uprights.

To assemble cheese box toy furniture liquid glue is sufficiently strong; a few 1/2 inch wire brads of a thin gauge, however, can be used for extra strength if desired.

For coloring cheese box toy furniture use either tempera colors or enamel paints. You will find these coloring techniques fully described in the text, under Projects Nos. 1 and 2, respectively. Another good way to color furniture is through the use of oil stains such as walnut, golden oak or mahogany. Simply apply the stain over the smoothly sandpapered wood surfaces of the toy furniture pieces, and then rub off the excess stain with a soft cloth. The next day apply a coat or two of clear shellac or clear varnish over all the stained surfaces. A polished coat of wax may be used over the stained surfaces in place of the shellac or varnish, with equally good effect.

Project No. 6, Cheese Box Plant Box

This cheese box plant box is especially suitable for use in a child's room, kitchen or breakfast room. This plant box can serve as an ornamental receptacle for two or three small flower pots, or it can be filled with earth and used as a regular plant box. If used in the latter fashion, however, it is necessary to line the cheese box with either galvanized sheet iron or a coating of waterproof cement to make it waterproof and to prevent the wood from warping.

To convert a discarded cheese box into this little plant box:—

1. Take the cheese box apart and cut off all the dovetail sections from the ends of the side and end boards.

2. Using a coping saw, cut the top edges of the side and end boards of the cheese box in a scalloped line, using scallops of from 1/2 inch to 3/4 inch wide, and about 3/8 inch deep.

3. Sandpaper all ends, edges, and flat surfaces of the boards neatly. Then nail the ends and side boards together, using 3/4 inch long round head screws as fasteners. Be sure in this assembling step to keep the printed surfaces of the cheese box on the inside where they will remain out of view when the plant box is in use.

4. Nail the bottom board to the four assembled sides of the plant box.

5. Apply a coat of white or orange shellac over all outside and inside surfaces of the box and allow to dry.

6. Apply an overall coat of enamel paint in the desired color, and again allow to dry thoroughly.

7. Using another color of enamel which will blend with the first color applied, trim the edges of the plant box and add a few floral designs at the center and corners of each of the four box sides for decorative effect.

For further instructions, see the text under Projects Nos. 1 and 2.

Project No. 7, Cheese Box Pull-Toy

See Figure 1, Illustration 4

To build this pull-toy is really a much simpler job than one might suppose after glancing at the sketch in Figure 1, Illustration 4. Of course, there are quite a few parts to this cheese box model, but they are small in size and easy to prepare.

An interesting feature of the pull-toy is that, in addition to cheese box wood, various types of scrap wood such as 1-1/4 inch square joist strips (for the radiator), 1/4 inch, 3/4 inch and 2 inch diameter round stick stock (for the headlights and steering wheel parts), and 3/4 inch stock (for the axles) are employed. This model also uses scrap tin (in the preparation of the bumper and mud-guards).

Since the working plan for this pull-toy is self-explanatory, and since the basic working procedures involved are practically the same as those described in connection with other cheese box projects presented above, the directions which follow are brief, though in correct constructional sequence.

Having obtained a discarded cheese box, a short length of 1-1/4 inch square joist stock, a few strips of round stock in diameters mentioned above, a scrap piece of tin, a few 1/2 inch wire brads, four 1 inch round head screws, some liquid glue, a few colors of tempera paints, and a little clear white shellac, proceed as follows:

A. Preparation of patterns

1. Make thin cardboard patterns of wood and metal parts A, B, C, D, E, F, G, J, M, N, and O, as represented in the pattern grill, Figure 2, Illustration 4. For the preparation of these patterns it will be necessary for you to draw a grill of 1/2 inch squares, using the

same number and arrangement of squares as in the reduced form grill in Figure 2. By using the grill of 1/2 inch squares each part will be reproduced in actual size.

2. After pattern grill is completed, cut out each pattern into a separate unit and place all the cut out cardboard patterns into a labeled envelope until ready for use.

B. Cutting out parts of truck

1. Trace patterns A, C, D, E, G, and J to the thinner or side boards of the cheese box. Then cut them out with a coping saw. Be sure to note from pattern grill in Figure 2 how many parts of each separate pattern are required. See coping saw equipment and method of using same as represented in Figure 3, Illustration 10.

2. Trace patterns B, F and M to the thicker or end boards of the cheese box, and then cut out these parts with the coping saw. In this step, note how many of each part are required.

3. Trace patterns N and O to a piece of scrap tin and then proceed to cut out these parts with a pair of metal cutting shears.

4. Using a back-saw and a bench hook in the manner shown in Figure 7, Illustration 11, cut a strip of 1-1/4 inch square joist stock to a length of 1-3/4 inch to form the radiator part H, shown in Figure 5, Illustration 4. Bevel the two top corners as shown in Figure 5.

5. Cut a strip of 1/4 inch dowel to a length of 2 inches to form the steering wheel shaft, indicated as K in Figure 2. For this cutting step use the back-saw.

6. Cut a 1/4 inch thick disc from a 3/4 inch diameter dowel to form the steering wheel P. (Use back saw.)

7. Cut two 3/8 inch thick discs from a 1/2 inch diameter dowel or round stick to form the headlights L.

8. Cut four 1/2 inch thick discs from a 2 inch diameter round pole, such as a curtain pole, to form the truck wheels S. (These

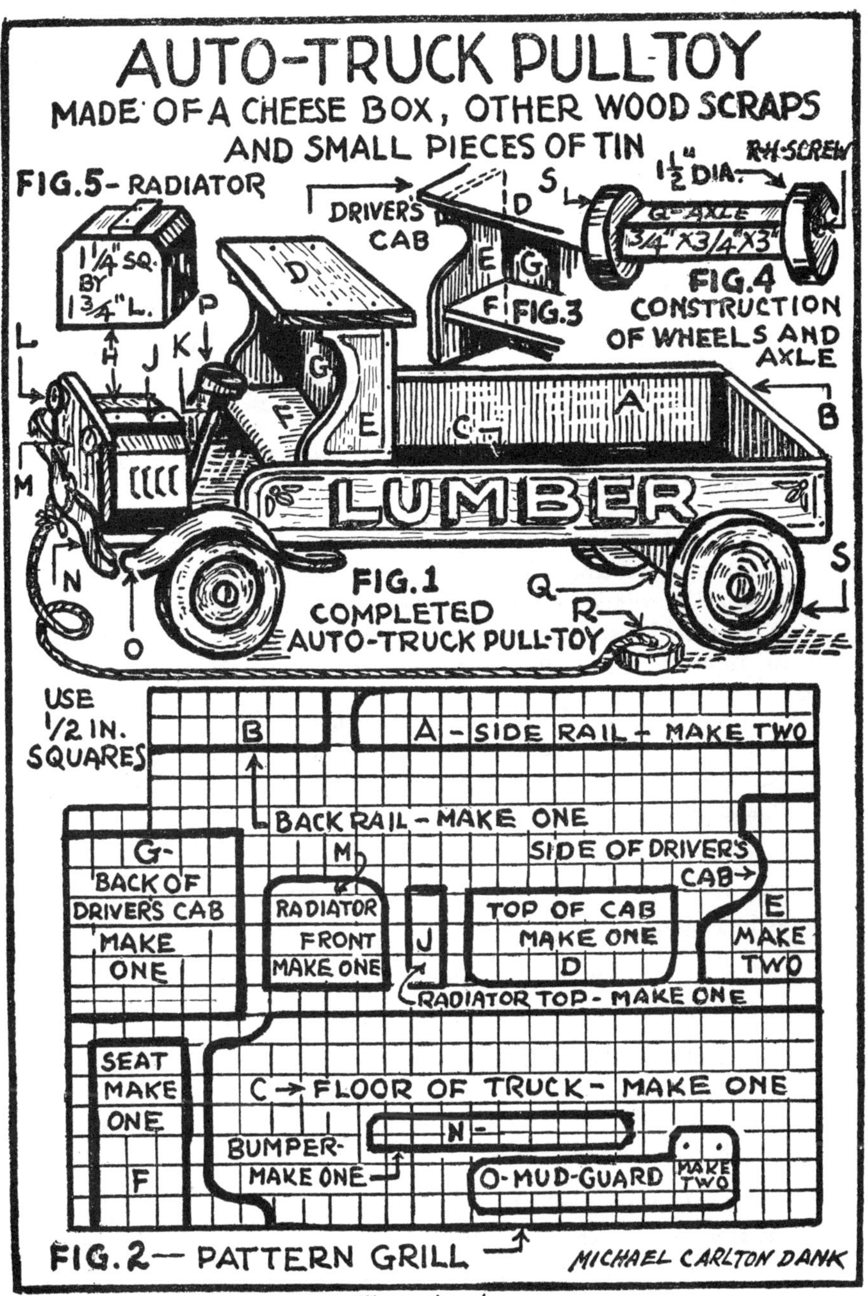
AUTO-TRUCK PULL-TOY
MADE OF A CHEESE BOX, OTHER WOOD SCRAPS
AND SMALL PIECES OF TIN
FIG.5- RADIATOR
1 1/4" SQ. BY 1 3/4" L.
DRIVER'S CAB
D
E
G
F
FIG.3
S
1 1/2" DIA.
R-H-SCREW
G-AXLE
3/4" X 3/4" X 3"
FIG.4
CONSTRUCTION OF WHEELS AND AXLE
L
H
J
K
P
M
A
B
C
LUMBER
N
O
FIG.1
COMPLETED AUTO-TRUCK PULL-TOY
Q
R
S
USE 1/2 IN. SQUARES
B
A - SIDE RAIL - MAKE TWO
BACK RAIL - MAKE ONE
G- BACK OF DRIVER'S CAB MAKE ONE
M
RADIATOR FRONT MAKE ONE
J
TOP OF CAB MAKE ONE D
SIDE OF DRIVER'S CAB
E MAKE TWO
RADIATOR TOP - MAKE ONE
SEAT MAKE ONE F
C → FLOOR OF TRUCK - MAKE ONE
N-
BUMPER- MAKE ONE
O-MUD-GUARD
MAKE TWO
FIG.2 — PATTERN GRILL
MICHAEL CARLTON DANK

Illustration 4

wheels may also be cut out of 1/2 inch scrap wood with a coping saw.)

9. Make two strips of wood size 3/4 inch by 3/'4 inch by 3 inch, to form the axle parts Q. The parts may easily be prepared by the use of a smoothing plane and a hack saw.

10. Be sure all cut out parts are neatly sandpapered.

C. Assembling the auto truck

1. Fasten side rails A to floor piece C, using liquid glue and 1/2 inch wire brads as fasteners. Locate the floor piece below the bottom edges of the rails.

2. In like fashion, nail back rail piece B into place in the manner shown in Figure 1.

3. Assemble the parts of the driver's cabin as a separate unit, following the method shown in Figure 3. First nail sides of cabin E to seat F. Next add top part D, and back of cabin G. After cabin unit is completed, glue and nail it into place about 1/2 inch back from the forward ends of the side rails A, as indicated in Figure 1.

4. Drill a 1/4 inch hole into back end of the radiator H, and into this hole glue the 2 inch long dowel steering wheel shaft K. Then drill a 1/4 inch hole in the center of the steering wheel P, and glue it to the top end of the shaft K.

5. Glue and nail radiator front piece M to radiator H. Also glue radiator top piece J to the central top section of radiator H, as in Figures 1 and 5.

6. Glue completed radiator, now equipped with its accessory parts, to the front end of floor piece C, as in Figure 1.

7. Drill 1/8 inch holes in the centers of the four wheel parts S and then fasten the wheels to their axles Q, as in Figure 4. Use 1" long round-head screws. Do not drive the screws in too tightly as the wheels must revolve freely.

8. Fasten the axles to the under surface of the floor C, locating the front one 2 inches in from the front end of the floor piece, and the back one 1 inch in from its back end.

9. Round the back ends of the 1/2 inch diameter headlights L, and then glue and nail them to the upper part of the radiator front part M, as shown in Figure 1.

10. Bend tin bumper N into proper shape, and nail it to the front end of floor part C, as in Figure 1.

11. Bend mudguards O into proper shape, and then nail their wide ends to the underneath sections of the floor piece C in the manner indicated in Figure 1.

12. Tie a string, about 3 feet long, to the middle section of the metal bumper. To the other end of the string attach an odd checker to serve as a convenient pull-handle. See R, Figure 1.

D. Coloring and finishing the pull-toy

To color the pull-toy, first apply an overall coat of white or orange shellac. When this is dry, paint the toy in some suitable bright shade of enamel. Red is a good color for this purpose. After the enamel is dry, use a harmonizing color to trim the edges of the truck parts, especially the side and back rail parts, the radiator, wheels and cabin parts, as indicated in Figure 1. After the trim color is dry, use a third color to letter the word "LUMBER" along the outside surfaces of the side rails, as shown in Figure 1. Of course, you may use any other lettering in place of the word "LUMBER," such as "ICE," "COAL" or "FRUITS AND VEGETABLES."

If the pull-toy is supposed to be a lumber truck, it is a good idea to fill the truck with a "pile" of unpainted wood strips or "boards." If it is intended to be an ice truck, a heap of small blocks painted white may be "loaded" into the truck. Or if it is to be a coal truck, it may be fitted with a load of pebbles, painted black to simulate coal.

The finished auto-truck pull-toy is sure to delight small children everywhere.

CIGAR BOX WOOD

Cigar box wood is another common type of thin scrap wood which offers amateur craftsmen and teachers of arts and crafts everywhere many possibilities in light woodwork construction.

Like cheese boxes, empty cigar boxes are always plentiful and easily obtainable at no cost. Cigar boxes may be used in craft work in box form, or they may be taken apart and used as separate sheets of thin wood.

For example, a cigar box in its original form may be employed to build a musical instrument simply by adding a few extra wood parts and necessary wire strings. It may also be used to make a child's toy cart by adding checkers as wheels and a pull-string. Another application of the cigar box is a miniature loom with which children can weave various simple articles such as small rugs, place mats or mittens. The cigar box can also be converted into a sewing kit, a jewelry or handkerchief box, and so forth, simply by covering the surfaces of the box with wallpaper, cork, or some attractive cotton print. As most of these original form cigar box projects are easy to make, the reader will experience little difficulty in working them out by himself.

In order to give the reader a comprehensive description of the uses of the cigar box as scrap wood, we are employing as our key project the snapshot album shown in Figure 1, Illustration 5. This particular project is specially designed for cigar box wood construction and involves all essential handwork procedures.

In the building of this snapshot album, the reader will learn how to take apart a cigar box into its separate boards, without cracking or breaking them. He will be informed how to clean and condition cigar box wood in preparation for use; how to cut it properly into various shapes and sizes; how to fasten the parts together securely; and how to color and finish this type of project.

In addition to our key project, the snapshot album, shown in Figure 1, Illustration 5, we are also presenting in this unit on cigar box wood, Project No. 9, Letter and Stationery Rack, shown in Figure 1, Illustration 6.

Both the snapshot album and the letter and stationery rack have proven popular in the author's own shop classes. When completed one could hardly surmise that they were built of discarded cigar box wood. Of course, they can also be built out of any other form of thin wood of suitable size with equally successful results.

Project No. 8, Cigar Box Snapshot Album

See Figure 1, Illustration 5

As you will note from the sketch of our completed cigar box snapshot album, in Figure 1, Illustration 5, the top and bottom covers of this project are each built in two parts, neatly joined to-

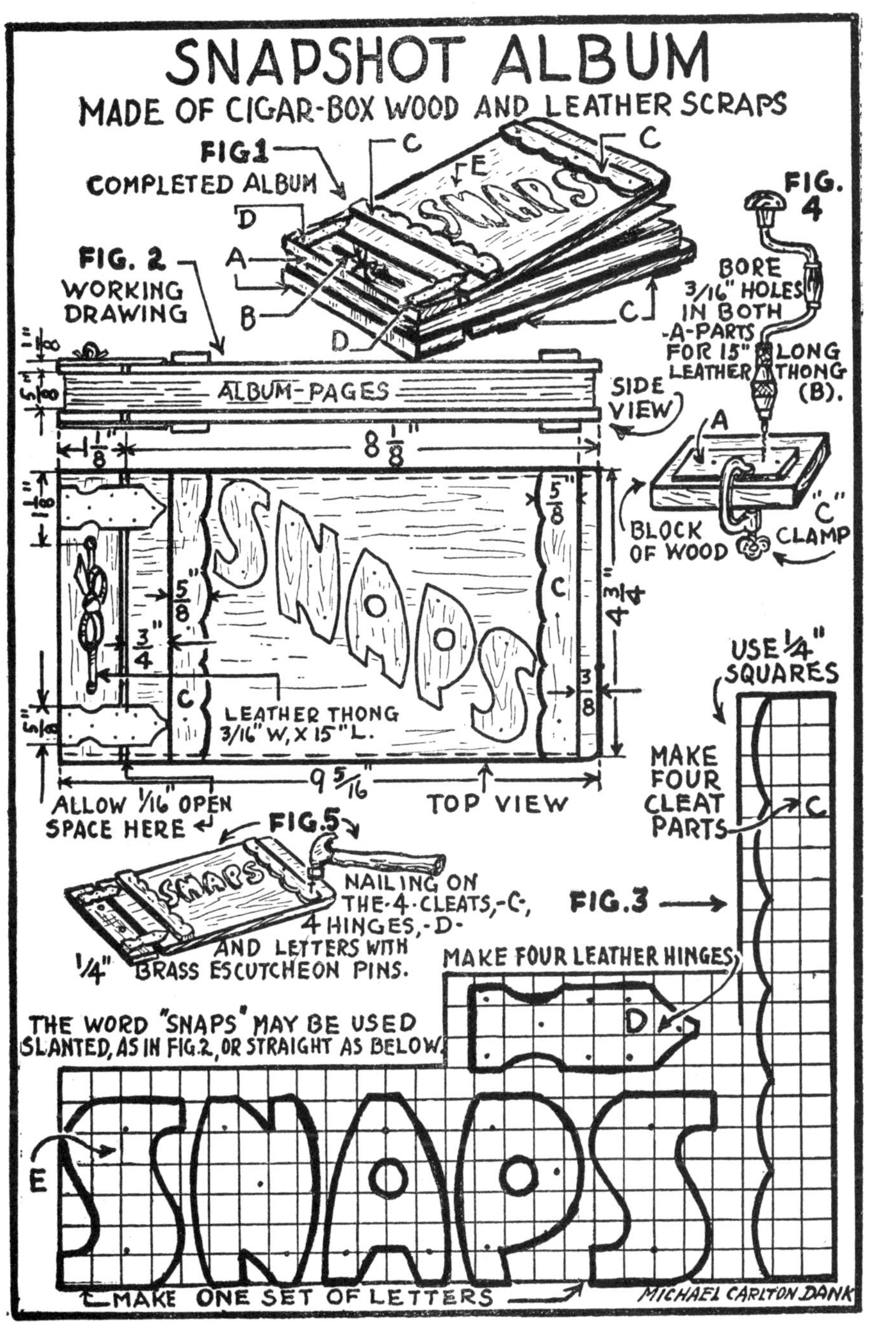
SNAPSHOT ALBUM
MADE OF CIGAR-BOX WOOD AND LEATHER SCRAPS
FIG 1
COMPLETED ALBUM
FIG. 2
WORKING DRAWING
ALBUM-PAGES
SIDE VIEW
TOP VIEW
LEATHER THONG 3/16" W, X 15" L.
ALLOW 1/16" OPEN SPACE HERE
FIG. 4
BORE 3/16" HOLES IN BOTH -A-PARTS FOR 15" LONG LEATHER THONG (B).
BLOCK OF WOOD
"C" CLAMP
USE 1/4" SQUARES
MAKE FOUR CLEAT PARTS
FIG. 3
FIG. 5
NAILING ON THE 4 CLEATS, -C-, 4 HINGES, -D- AND LETTERS WITH 1/4" BRASS ESCUTCHEON PINS.
MAKE FOUR LEATHER HINGES
THE WORD "SNAPS" MAY BE USED SLANTED, AS IN FIG. 2, OR STRAIGHT AS BELOW.
MAKE ONE SET OF LETTERS
MICHAEL CARLTON DANK

Illustration 5

gether by small leather hinges. The smaller members of these two-part wooden covers, as represented in Figure 2, Illustration 5, measure 1-1/8 inches, while the larger members measure 8-1/8 inches in length. The overall measurements of the album are 4-1/2 inches wide by 9-5/16 inches long.

The two scalloped cleats used across the width of each of the larger parts of the cover are 5/8 inch in width. In addition to their decorative value, these cleats serve to reinforce the thin wood cover parts considerably.

A leather thong or lace is used as a tie bow to hold the pages and the wooden covers of the snapshot album tightly and securely in place, as represented in Figure 1, Illustration 5.

The word "SNAPS," used on the top cover of the album, is sawed out in separate letters and mounted in applique fashion.

Aside from the leather hinges and tie bow, the covers of this album are made entirely of cigar box wood. In this connection it should be noted that although cigar boxes made of composition board material can also be used for the construction of this project, only cigar boxes made of real wood, especially cedar wood, will produce the best results.

Only a few simple tools and working procedures are required to make this cigar box snapshot album. Thus it is an appropriate project for arts and crafts shops of schools, summer camps, and recreational centers.

The album may also be used as a small size scrapbook to mount clippings, greeting cards, and other small items. When used for this purpose the word "SCRAPS" can easily be substituted for the word "SNAPS."

I. Materials

A. The wood of a single cigar box, preferably of the red cedar grade.

B. A few scraps of brown leather suitable for cutting out four small hinges and the tie bow thong or lace, the latter measuring 3/16 by 15 inches.

C. Any good grade of liquid glue.

D. Brass escutcheon pins of 1/4 inch length.

E. Nos. 0 and 1/2 sandpaper.

F. Burnt umber oil stain.

G. Turpentine.

H. Clear white shellac.

I. Fine grade steel wool.

J. Polishing wax.

K. From 36 to 48 sheets of drawing paper of a fairly heavy grade cut to 4-1/2 inch by 9 inch, for use as inside pages for the album. Good colors are tan, brown, grey, green or black.

II. Tools

A. The coping saw equipment shown in Figure 3, Illustration 10.

B. Medium size smoothing plane.

C. Try square. See Figure 2, Illustration 1.

D. Boring brace and 3/16 inch drill or bit.

E. Scratch awl or any similarly pointed tool.

F. Small size nailing hammer.

G. Sharp knife suitable for cutting leather and paper.

H. Flat type brushes suitable for staining and shellacking work.

I. Soft cloth for use in connection with the staining and waxing procedures.

J. Metal rule for use in measuring and cutting album pages.

III. Directions

A. Taking cigar box apart

The first step in converting the discarded cigar box into a snapshot album is that of taking the cigar box apart into its separate wood pieces. This can easily be done as follows:

1. Using a pair of scissors or a single edge razor blade, cut through the paper or cloth hinge which holds the cover in place, thereby separating the cover from the box.

2. Turn cigar box so its bottom faces upwards. Then, using a screw driver, pry up the bottom of the box at a few places, causing the bottom of the box to loosen and rise a little.

3. Using a claw-type nailing hammer, remove nails carefully without injuring wood parts of box. As a result of this step the bottom board will be completely detached from the box.

4. Repeat these "prying-up" and "nail-pulling" procedures at each corner of the cigar box, causing the ends and sides of the box to come apart into separate wood boards.

B. Removing paper wrappers

Since cigar box surfaces generally come covered with various types of advertising matter in the form of paper wrappers and direct-to-the-wood printing, it is important that this be completely removed before the separated boards are put into work. A simple procedure for removing the paper wrappers is as follows:

1. Place the paper-wrapped cigar box boards, now in separated form, into a basin of suitable size filled with hot water. Allow the boards to soak for a few minutes.

2. Following this procedure, and after you feel the boards have soaked sufficiently, remove the first board and scrape off its paper wrappers, using either a knife or a single edge razor blade. You will find that the paper wrappers, already loosened considerably by the soaking treatment, will come off easily, requiring only a little scraping here and there. It is best to use the scraping instrument in the direction of the grain only.

3. Place the board, now scraped but still wet, on a double layer of blotter sheeting. Then place a heavy broad-surfaced weight, such as a marble or metal slab, or several large books, on top of the board which is now in proper position for drying.

4. Repeat this drying procedure for the rest of the soaked and scraped cigar box boards, placing one board over the other with a blotter sheet inserted between each two boards, and with the same weight used on top.

As a result of this drying process the boards will soon be free of all moisture and, what is also very important, they will dry in a perfectly straight form without warping.

C. Removing printed-to-wood advertising matter

To remove advertising matter from cigar boxes where the wood boards themselves have been directly imprinted, all you need to do is to plane such wood pieces a little and then rub the planed surfaces with a piece of medium grade sandpaper wrapped around a small wood block. In both these planing and sandpapering procedures it is important to work only in the direction of the grain of the wood. For complete details in connection with these smoothing operations, see text under Project No. 1, Cheese Box Wall Shelf, Section IV, C.

D. Preparation of working patterns for snapshot album

The only patterns which you will require for the construction of this snapshot album are a pattern for the cleat parts used across the widths of the top and bottom covers of the project represented as C in Figure 3, Illustration 5; a pattern for the word "SNAPS" which is to be cut out of wood into separate letters and appliqued to the top cover, shown in Figure 3 as E; and a pattern for the leather hinges, Figure 3, D.

The rest of the album parts can easily and conveniently be made without the aid of patterns by working directly from the working drawing represented in Figure 2, Illustration 5. This is because these parts are straight and square and can be marked off on the wood in preparation for cutting out, simply by the use of such laying out tools as the ruler and try square.

To prepare patterns C, D and E, first draw a grill of 1/4 inch squares, using the same number and arrangement of squares as shown in the reduced form pattern grill in Figure 3. Any light colored drawing paper is good for this purpose. Then copy pattern parts C, D and E exactly as represented in Figure 3. This will produce these same parts in their actual full size. When finished with the drawing of the patterns, cut each paper pattern out carefully with scissors. The word "SNAPS" should be cut into separate letters, since each letter must be individually traced and sawed out. When finished cutting the pattern pieces apart, place the patterns in an envelope labeled "Patterns for Snapshot Album," until they are ready to be used.

E. Tracing and sawing out album parts

As you will note from the working drawing in Figure 2, Illustration 5, the top and bottom covers of our snapshot album are each built in two parts to provide for the hinged construction shown. The larger member of each cover measures 4-3/4 inches by 8-1/8 inches while the smaller part measures 1-1/8 inches by 4-3/4 inches.

Since the larger part of each cover section is in the approximate size of the cover and bottom parts of the average cigar box, all you need to do to lay out these parts is to mark off the 4-3/4 inches by 8-1/8 inches measurement on both the top and bottom boards of the cigar box, using a ruler, try square and pencil, as instructed earlier.

The smaller members of the two-part album covers, measuring 1-1/8 inch by 4-3/4 inch, may be laid out in similar fashion on one of the end boards of the cigar box. When laying out these smaller cover parts, however, be sure that the grain runs in the direction of the larger dimension, just as shown in the drawing. This will assure greater strength of the part and better appearance of the whole project when completed.

Following the marking off of the main cover parts of the album, trace parts C and E to the wood, using for these parts one of the end and one of the side boards of the cigar box. As you will note from Figures 1 and 2, Illustration 5, you will need four cleat parts C, and one each of the letters of the word "SNAPS."

In tracing these wood parts, use the previously prepared paper patterns and be sure to keep the grain always in the direction of the larger dimension of each wood part. Since these particular parts are in simple silhouette form, no carbon paper is required in this tracing step. Just mark around the edges of each part with a very sharp pencil, using the other hand to hold the paper pattern firmly in its place on the wood.

After laying out or tracing all wood parts, use pattern D to trace four hinge parts on any scrap piece of leather. Brown or tan leather of a flexible type is best.

Now cut out the traced wood parts, using the coping saw and other equipment suggested in the text under Project No. 1. Refer also to Figure 3, Illustration 10, which gives a diagrammatical explanation of this process.

Following the sawing out of the small sections of the two-part covers, bore two 3/16 inch holes in each of these parts, 1-1/8 inches in from each end, to accommodate the leather thong which is used to bind together the album sheets and the wooden cover sections. This is described in Figure 4, Illustration 5.

After the wood parts are carefully cut out, file and sandpaper all edges, ends and faces of the parts until clean, smooth and uniform. The filing and sandpapering are also discussed in the text given under Project No. 1.

To cut out the traced leather hinge parts, simply place the piece of leather on any scrap piece of wood or composition board as a working foundation. Then, using a sharp pointed knife, carefully cut around the traced outlines of each of the four hinges. Be sure the cutting is done in a smooth, neat fashion.

F. Assembling cut out album parts

This phase of our project is as easy as the steps previously described. For best results proceed as follows:

1. Fasten scalloped cleat strips C in their correct locations, to the outer surfaces of the larger cover parts. You will note from the top view of our working drawing in Figure 2 the left cleat strip is placed 3/4 inch in from the left end of the larger cover part, while the right cleat is placed 3/8 inch in from the right end of the cover. Use liquid glue and three 1/4 inch brass escutcheon pins for the attachment of each of the four cleats. Do not use more glue than actually necessary as excess glue will ooze out and spoil the work. A small, claw-type nailing hammer is best for this assembling step. It is also a good idea to punch little holes with a pointed awl before nailing since this makes it much easier to drive the nails properly into place. See Figure 5, Illustration 5.

2. Glue and nail the cut-out letters of the word "SNAPS" to the central section of the upper surface of the top cover, employing the same fastening procedure as used in the nailing on of the cleat strips. Use two escutcheon pins for each letter and arrange the letters on the cover in diagonal form, as shown in Figure 2. However, if you wish, you may arrange the letters in a semi-circular fashion, or in the horizontal manner shown in Figure 5.

3. Glue and nail the leather hinges in place, allowing a 1/16 inch opening between the left and right members of each cover section. Place the hinges about 1/8 inch in from the cover edges. Also use eight 1/4 inch escutcheon pins for the attachment of each of the four hinges, as shown in the top view of Figure 2.

Before the paper sheets and assembled wooden covers of the album can be fastened together with the 15 inch long leather thong used for this purpose, the cover parts must first be colored and finished.

G. Coloring and finishing the cigar box snapshot album

Since most of the better grade cigar boxes are built of attractively grained cedar wood, it is a good idea to finish the album parts with some suitable color of transparent stain which will show up the natural wood grain markings to advantage. Proceed as follows:

1. Using a small pointed-style brush, apply a coat of clear, white shellac over the top surfaces of the wooden letters which form the word "SNAPS". Allow the shellac to dry thoroughly.

2. Following this step, and using a flat brush of about 1inch width, apply a coat of mahogany or walnut stain (either water or oil stains are satisfactory) over all wood surfaces of the album covers, including the shellacked letters.

3. Immediately after the stain has been applied, wipe off all excess stain with a soft cloth, permitting the wood grain to show up clearly. After the stain has been wiped away, you will find that the word "SNAPS", having been "protected" by the previously applied stain-resisting shellac coating, will show up in a light natural-wood color, while the rest or bulk of the project will appear in the dark, contrasting color of the stain.

4. As a final finish apply a coat of clear white shellac over all surfaces of both cover sections, including the lettering. When this overall shellac coating is completely dry, smooth the surfaces with fine steel wool, and polish all parts with either liquid or paste-form wax.

Now bind the covers and paper sheets together with the leather thong. The paper sheets should be cut a little smaller all around than the outside measurements of the top and bottom covers. This will not only look well, but will also assure protection for the sheets when the album is in use. Any sturdy drawing paper, brown and grey will be satisfactory. Use from 24 to 48 sheets, depending upon individual requirements.

Following the preparation of the sheets, bind them inside the covers, using for this purpose either a leather thong (3/16 inch by 15 inches is a good size), or a medium size leather shoe-lace. Of course, two holes must be punched through the paper sheets at the left end to correspond exactly with the holes previously drilled through the smaller section of the two-part covers. The leather strip may be tied at the top of the album in a bow-tie fashion, as shown in Figure 1, Illustration 5, or simply by knotting.

The completed cigar box snapshot album is sure to be of use in every home.

RELATED CIGAR BOX PROJECTS

Based upon the working procedures just described. In these related models, just as in our key project, the cigar box provides the essential construction material.

Project No. 9, Cigar Box Letter & Stationery Rack

See Figure 1, Illustration 6

I. DESCRIPTION

Like the snapshot album shown in Figure 1, Illustration 5, this letter rack can also be made of the separate parts of a single cigar box. Since an opaque coloring medium is used which completely covers the surfaces of all parts, this model can be built satisfactorily of cardboard or composition board cigar boxes, as well as of wooden ones. As a general rule most lower priced cigars come in boxes made of these substitute materials. Because of their toughness they can be sawed, nailed, filed, sandpapered and drilled like wood.

This letter and stationery rack can also serve as a holder for paper pads, blotters, rulers, erasers, pens and pencils, and so forth. It can also be employed as a small card filing cabinet.

Because of the simplicity of its construction, this makes a good project for children's arts and crafts classes at schools or camps. Since the working procedures involved are similar to those described under Project No. 8, the general directions which follow are briefly presented.

II. MATERIALS AND TOOLS

In addition to the boards of a single cigar box, the only other materials needed are tempera paints, white shellac, medium grade sandpaper, liquid glue and 1/2 inch wire brads.

The tools required are the coping saw equipment shown in Figure 3, Illustration 10, a smoothing plane, a pointed awl, a small size nailing hammer, and a few water-color brushes of different sizes.

III. DIRECTIONS

A. Preparation of patterns

In the working drawing of our project, given in the lower section of Illustration 6, three views are shown, viz., top, front and side views. By carefully studying these you will find that our project consists of the following separate parts:

Part A—Side .... Two required .... Size 5-1/2 in. by 9-3/4 in.
Part B—Back ...... One required ...... Size—2-1/2 in. by 5-1/2 in.
Part C—Middle .. One required ...... Size 4-3/4 in. by 9-3/8 in.
Part D—Front .... One required ...... Size 2-1/2 in. by 9-3/8 in.
Part E—Bottom .. One required ...... Size 3 in. by 9-3/4 in.

To make a paper tracing pattern for each of these parts simply mark off each of these sizes on a large sheet of sturdy drawing paper, using a sharp pencil, a ruler, and either a small carpenter's square or a right angle triangle of the type commonly used in mechanical drawing. Next divide each laid out part into 1/2 inch

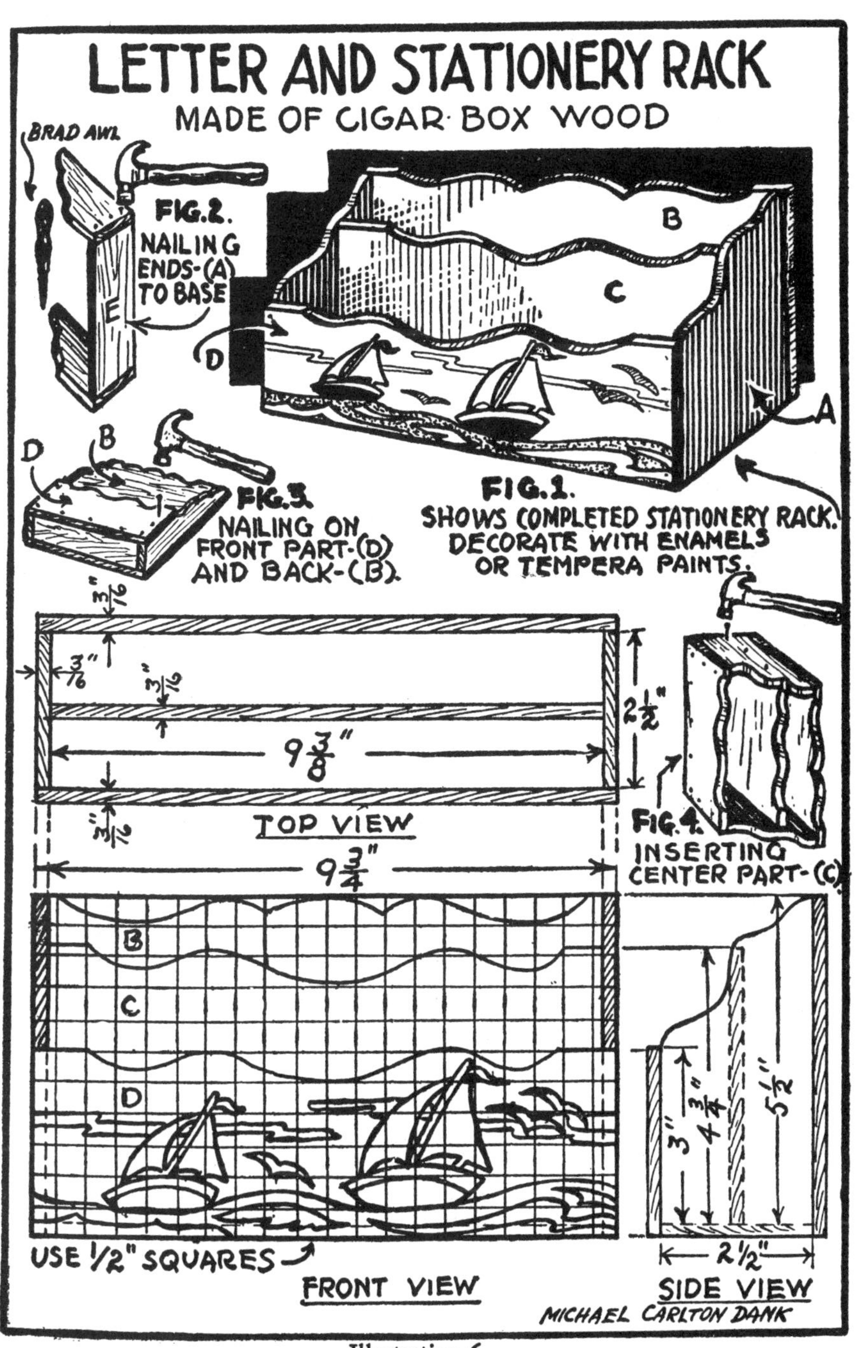
LETTER AND STATIONERY RACK
MADE OF CIGAR BOX WOOD
BRAD AWL
FIG.2.
NAILING ENDS-(A) TO BASE
E
B
C
D
A
FIG.1.
SHOWS COMPLETED STATIONERY RACK. DECORATE WITH ENAMELS OR TEMPERA PAINTS.
FIG.3.
NAILING ON FRONT PART-(D) AND BACK-(B).
3/16"
2 1/2"
9 3/8"
TOP VIEW
9 3/4"
FIG.4.
INSERTING CENTER PART-(C)
3"
4 3/4"
5 1/2"
2 1/2"
USE 1/2" SQUARES
FRONT VIEW
SIDE VIEW
MICHAEL CARLTON DANK

Illustration 6

squares to form a grill of squares, one for each of the outlined rectangles. Now mark off the curved top edges of all the parts except the base. Carefully reproduce the ship design which appears on part D. This done, you will have a full-scale pattern of each separate part of the rack, including all design effects.

When all project parts have been laid out as directed, cut out each separate paper pattern using a sharp pair of scissors. Here again it is suggested that the cut out pattern be placed in a labeled envelope for safe keeping until needed.

B. Tracing patterns to the wood boards

Before tracing the patterns to the cigar box wood boards, it is necessary, of course, to remove all printed matter and to sandpaper all broad surfaces of the boards. These procedures are described in the text under Project No. 8, Cigar Box Snapshot Album.

To mark off pattern parts A, B, C, and E, trace around the edges of these patterns with a sharply pointed pencil. However, for transferring front part D you will require a piece of carbon paper underneath the pattern because of the ship decoraton here involved. When transferring all of these patterns, it is important to keep the grain of the wood always in the direction of the larger dimension of each part.

C. Sawing out wood parts

Having traced all the patterns to the wood boards, saw out each separate part, carefully following the traced outlines. Complete directions for sawing out small size irregularly shaped wood parts of this kind are given in the text under Project No. 1. Refer also to the diagrammatical sketch of this sawing process in Figure 3, Illustration 10.

D. Assembling cut out parts of the rack

Before the cut out parts can be fastened together it is necessary to file or sandpaper all sawed edges and ends as well as all faces of each part, following the directions given under Project No. 1. Then go ahead with the assembling of the rack as follows:

1. Join end parts A to base part E, using liquid glue and three 1/2 inch wire brads at each end joint. See Fig. 2, Illustration 6. Here

again you are referred to the text under Project No. 1 which explains how to use a pointed awl such as seen in Fig. 2, Illustration 6 to make little holes where the brads are to be located, in order that the brads may be driven into place more easily and with less danger of cracking the wood. Be sure to place a little glue on both contact surfaces of the joint rather than just on one. Remember, too, to keep all edges and ends of the jointed parts flush and even all around.

2. Using the same gluing and nailing process described above, nail on front part D and back part B, using three 1/2 inch wire brads at each end of the front part, and four brads at each end of the back. See Fig. 3, Illustration 6.

3. Now nail into place the last member of the rack, middle part C, being particularly careful that this part is placed in a perfectly straight position, just as indicated in the top and side views of our working drawing in Illustration 6. For this middle part use glue and three 1/2 inch wire brads at each end, as shown in Fig. 4, Illustration 6.

E. Coloring and finishing letter and stationery rack

After the parts of the rack have been properly assembled, round off all edges and corners with fine sandpaper. The rack is now ready for painting and finishing.

The coloring medium suggested for this particular model is tempera, which is easy to apply, is opaque and dries quickly in a strong though dull finish.

The directions for painting the rack with tempera are as follows:

1. Select a color scheme which will blend with the general decorative scheme of the room in which the rack is to be used. Or match it with the color of the desk on which it is to stand. A good idea is to use one overall color, and then one or two additional colors for trimming the edges and for painting the ship design on the front part of the rack.

2. Mix the first overall coat of tempera and apply it evenly over all surfaces, using a large size water-coloring brush, such as Nos. 8 or 10. Allow this coat to dry thoroughly before proceeding.

3. Mix another, harmonizing color and apply it neatly with a smaller size brush (Nos. 3 to 5 are good) around the edges of the rack parts as a trim.

4. Using this color and some other suitable one, paint in the parts of the ship design, following the sketch in Figure 1, Illustration 6.

5. After all paints have dried thoroughly, apply a coat of clear white shellac over the entire rack, and allow it to dry.

6. Rub shellacked coating with fine steel wool, and then polish with either liquid or paste-form wax.

Project No. 10, Cigar Box Doll Cradle

To construct a doll cradle from cigar box wood, proceed as follows:

1. Separate the cigar box into its individual parts and clean the boards of all advertising matter, as in Project No. 8.

2. Nail the boards together again into their original form, but leave the cover unattached. Use liquid glue and 1/2 inch wire brads. Before the parts are assembled, however, it is a good idea to saw the top edges of the sides and ends into ornamental curves such as are generally used in manufactured doll cradles. For shaping, use the coping saw equipment shown in Figure 3, Illustration 10. Smooth all sawed edges with sandpaper.

3. Following the completion of the upper section of the cradle, cut out two rocker parts, fashioning them like the lovely low cradles of colonial days. Use the top or cover of the cigar box for these rockers.

4. Nail the rockers to the upper section of the cradle, again using glue and small wire brads.

5. Color the assembled doll cradle with walnut or mahogany wood stain, as in Project No. 8, or with tempera paints as in Project 9. With either form of coloring, however, use clear white shellac, followed by a polished coat of wax as the final finish.

Project No. 11, Cigar Box Handkerchief or Glove Chest

See Project No. 4, Illustration 22

This useful project is easy to make. Simply retain the original form of the cigar box and cover its inside and outside surfaces with some appropriate material as described later in connection with Project No. 60, which is shown in Figure 4, Illustration 22.

Suggested covering materials for the chest are colorful prints, percale, chintz, felt, leatherette, cork, crepe paper and wall-paper. If either crepe paper or wall-paper is employed as a covering material, it is advisable to finish the covered surfaces of the chest with one or two coatings of varnish or shellac.

THIN PLYWOOD

By plywood we mean thin layers or veneers of wood glued tightly together to form a so called "laminated type of construction." Each ply or veneer sheet is arranged so that its grain runs at right angles with that of the sheet next to it. Thus, in three-plywood, for example, the grain of the inner ply runs at right angles with that of the veneers or thin wood layers above and below it. This cross-grain, laminated form of construction is responsible in great measure for the strength and durability as well as the non-warping quality of the wood.

Plywood may be purchased in large panels which vary in size from 2 to 4 feet in width and from 4 to 10 feet in length. The most commonly used varieties are fir, poplar, basswood, pine, and gumwood. The most practical thicknesses for craft work are 1/8 inch to 1/4 inch. Plywoods are widely used for the construction of office partitions, doors, inexpensive grades of furniture, and in the manufacture of a large variety of toys, games and novelties.

Scrap pieces of plywood of the types described above can always be found about the house, usually in the garret or basement. Odds and ends of plywood suitable for the construction of many projects, several of which are presented below, are also obtainable from such sources as broken toys and games, old furniture, parts of dismantled office partitions, and from woodworking shops or concerns who specialize in the manufacture of all types of plywood products. You will find additional sources for obtaining large amounts of scrap plywood listed in Chapter Two, under Scrap Lists 1 and 2.

Since plywood is characterized by its strong, non-cracking and non-warping qualities, it is especially suitable for the construction of projects requiring large dimensioned but thin parts. Thus, to make a wooden scrapbook cover, which requires thin wood of considerable size, plywood should be employed. Regular thin woods would, sooner or later, crack up or warp out of shape. Other uses of plywood are in the construction of the Bean Shooter shown in Figure 1, Illustration 7, and the Bingo Bango Paddle, Figure 2, Illustration 9.

Still another important use for scrap plywood is in the making of small novelty lapel pins, such as the "Laughing Clown" and "Blinkie-the-Fish" ornaments shown in Figures 1 and 2 respectively, in Illustration 10. In these small items the parts are mostly of an irregular breakable character. For this reason it is practical to use plywood stock, rather than regular thin wood.

The more you use plywood, the more you will enjoy working with it. After you have made the key models, try your hand at some of the other articles which can be built so successfully of plywood, such as ornamental wall plaques in which the background is completely cut away, wall shelves, piperacks, tieracks, and so forth.

Project No. 12, Plywood Bean Shooter

See Figure 1, Illustration 7

This popular toy can be made of any kind of thin scrap wood, but it is most practical when made of three-plywood material.

By referring to the sketch of the bean shooter in Figure 1, Illustration 7, you will observe that the shooter frame is built of three separate wood parts, a 12 inch long rubber sling, and a piece of leather, size 3/4 inch by 1-1/2 inch, which serves as the bullet or bean holder. A strip of rubber of required size cut from a discarded auto tire inner tube, will serve as the bean shooter sling.

To make the bean shooter, first make a cardboard pattern of the main or larger section of the wooden frame, a pattern of the handle part, and another of the leather bullet holder. You will find these three items represented as parts 3, 4 and 5 respectively in the pattern grill shown in Illustration 8. To reproduce these parts in full size, use a pattern grill of 1/4 inch squares, in the same arrangement as in Illustration 8.

After the patterns are completed, trace them to scrap pieces of plywood, making one tracing of part 3 and two of part 4, and being certain to arrange the patterns on the wood with their longer dimensions in the direction of the grain. Next trace the pattern of part 5 to a small piece of leather.

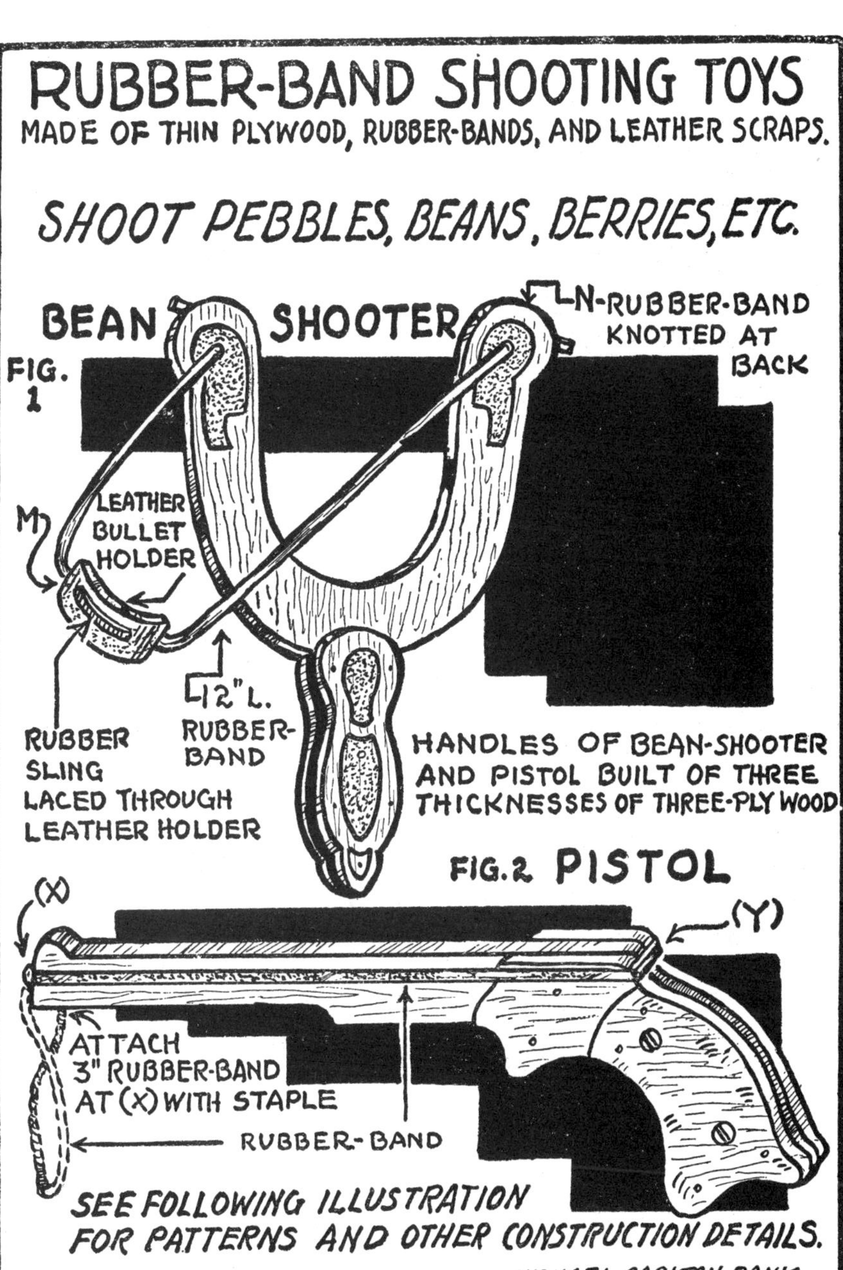
RUBBER-BAND SHOOTING TOYS
MADE OF THIN PLYWOOD, RUBBER-BANDS, AND LEATHER SCRAPS.
SHOOT PEBBLES, BEANS, BERRIES, ETC.
BEAN SHOOTER
FIG. 1
N-RUBBER-BAND KNOTTED AT BACK
M
LEATHER BULLET HOLDER
12" L. RUBBER-BAND
RUBBER SLING LACED THROUGH LEATHER HOLDER
HANDLES OF BEAN-SHOOTER AND PISTOL BUILT OF THREE THICKNESSES OF THREE-PLY WOOD
FIG. 2 PISTOL
(X)
(Y)
ATTACH 3" RUBBER-BAND AT (X) WITH STAPLE
RUBBER-BAND
SEE FOLLOWING ILLUSTRATION FOR PATTERNS AND OTHER CONSTRUCTION DETAILS.
MICHAEL CARLTON DANK

Illustration 7

Following the tracing of the project patterns, cut out the wooden frame and handle parts with a coping saw, using the equipment and process shown in Figure 3, Illustration 10. Clean and sandpaper all cut out wood parts neatly with medium grade sandpaper. Also drill 1/8 inch diameter holes at points R and S shown in part 3 of the pattern grill in Illustration 8. Following the cutting out of the wood parts, cut out the leather bullet holder, using for this purpose any sharp knife and a steel rule.

After both the wood and leather parts of the bean shooter are cut out, assemble as follows:

1. Nail one handle part 4 to each side of frame part 3, using liquid glue and 1/2 inch wire brads.

2. Paint the bean shooter frame with any two appropriate colors of tempera or enamel. If tempera colors are used, finish with an overall coat of white shellac or clear, quick-drying varnish. Be careful to apply both the paint and finishing coats evenly and neatly.

3. Punch two small holes in the leather bullet holder (see part 5, Illustration 8) and through these holes insert the 12 inch long rubber sling, as indicated at M, Figure 1, Illustration 7. Then thread the ends of the rubber sling through the holes previously drilled at the top ends of the shooter frame and make a tight knot at each end of the sling on the forward side of the frame. See N, Figure 1, Illustration 7. The "bullets" for this bean shooter may be pebbles, 1/2 inch lengths of 1/4 inch diameter dowel rod, paste-hardened paper balls, beans, hard berries, and so forth.

Youngsters who play with this bean shooter must be warned never to use it against people, birds, animals, or public property. Crafts teachers presenting the project to children should make a special point of this matter.

It is really best, and lots of fun too, to use the bean shooter against shooting targets, just as in the sports of archery and riflery.

Project No. 13, Rubber Band Pistol

See Figure 2, Illustration 7

This rubber band pistol, like the bean shooter just described, can be built of any kind of thin scrap wood, though three-plywood, because of its extra strength and ease of manipulation, is best.

PATTERNS FOR
PISTOL AND BEAN-SHOOTER
RUBBER-BAND ACTION TOYS
PISTOL PARTS-NOS. 1 AND 2
BEAN-SHOOTER PARTS-NOS. 3,4,5
CUT OUT AND ASSEMBLE PARTS AS INDICATED
USE 1/4" SQUARES
1/8" HOLE
PART 4
MAKE TWO
R
S
TIE 12 IN. RUBBER BAND AT R AND S
-PART 5- LEATHER MAKE ONE
1/8" HOLES
PART (2)
MAKE TWO
NAIL PARTS-3 TO EACH SIDE OF PART-3 AT (N)
PART (3)
MAKE ONE
(N)
PART 1
MAKE ONE
(M)
NAIL PARTS-4 TO EACH SIDE OF PART-1 AT (M).
MICHAEL CARLTON DANK

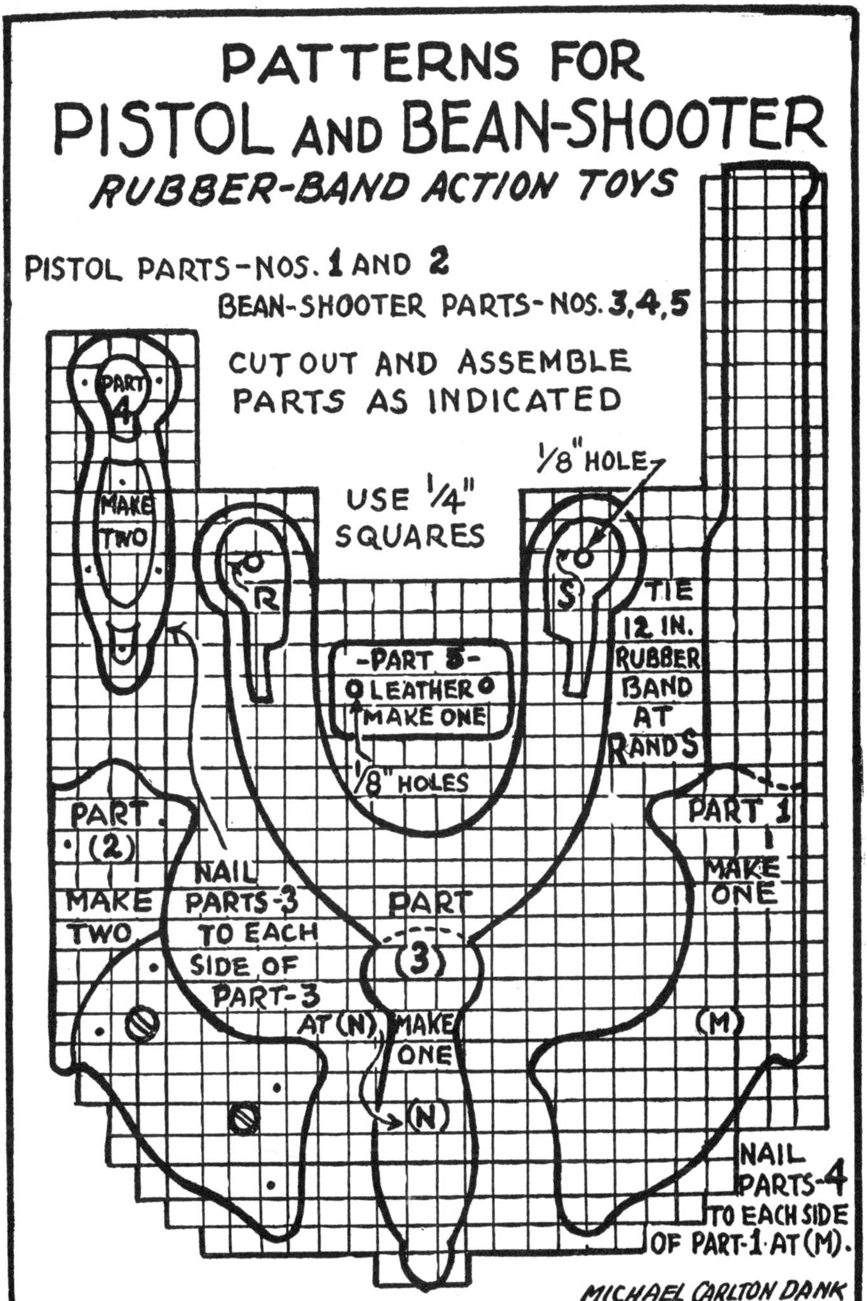

Illustration 8

This toy pistol is made of three separate wood parts and a long rubber sling. Beans, pebbles, short lengths of 1/4 inch dowel rod, paste-hardened paper balls and small darts can be used as "bullets."

To build the pistol, proceed as follows:

1. Make a full size cardboard pattern of main gun part 1, and handle part 2, as represented in the pattern grill in Illustration 8.

2. Using any sturdy grade of thin wood stock, especially three-plywood, make one tracing of part 1 and two tracings of part 2, arranging the patterns with their longer dimensions in the direction of the grain of the wood.

3. Saw out these three wood parts carefully, using the coping saw equipment suggested in Figure 3, Illustration 10.

4. Sandpaper the cut out parts carefully and then fasten one handle part 2 to each side of part 1, in the manner shown in Figure 2, Illustration 7. Use liquid glue and 1/2 inch wire brads, and be sure the three wood parts are exactly even or flush with each other before they are nailed together.

5. Color all wood parts of the assembled pistol with any two appropriate colors of tempera or enamel paints. Black and grey provide a good combination of colors for this purpose. If tempera colors are used, finish the gun with a coat of white shellac or clear quick-drying varnish. If enamels are used, apply a priming coat of shellac over the whole pistol before brushing on the enamel colors.

6. After pistol has thoroughly dried, attach a three or four inch rubber band or sling to its front end, using a small metal staple as a fastening device, as shown by X, Figure 2, Illustration 7.

To shoot the pistol, simply "load" the rubber sling or band with a "bullet", pull rubber band with the "bullet" placed into position, to the back of the gun "barrel" (see Y, Fig. 2). Take a good aim at the target and "fire".

Here again children must be warned against using this toy carelessly or in any way which may endanger the safety of people, birds, animals, or public property. As in the case of the bean shooter, it is best to employ regularly prepared shooting targets.

Project No. 14, Bingo Bango Game

See Figs. 1 and 3, Illustration 9

Boys and girls everywhere enjoy the Bingo Bango Game. As shown in Fig. 1, the equipment for this game consists of a plywood paddle with a long strip of rubber attached to the center of its forward surface, with a small rubber ball fastened to the other end of the rubber strip.

A suitable rubber strip can be prepared by cutting a 1/4 inch width of rubber about a yard long from a discarded auto tire inner tube. It can also be built of a series of strong rubber bands tightly tied together.

Every time the ball is hit by the plywood paddle it will bounce back to the paddle again because of the action of the outstretched rubber strip. The idea of the game is to keep the ball in play in this manner as long as the player's skill permits.

As you will observe from Figs. 2 and 3, the paddle is built of three separate pieces of 1/4 inch thick, three-plywood; one main part and two small handle-reinforcement pieces. The forward side of the upper broad section of the central paddle board has a covering of felt or sandpaper glued to its surface, as shown in Fig. 3, while at the back of this part of the paddle a picture of a ship is painted on for added decorative effect. In place of the ship, the words BINGO BANGO in a neat simple style of lettering may be used.

Directions for making the plywood paddle.

1. Make a grill of 1/2 inch squares on a sheet of drawing paper and then draw full size patterns of parts 1 and 2, just as represented in the reduced form grill in Fig. 2, Illustration 9.

2. Cut out the paper patterns and then, on any scrap piece of 1/4 inch thick plywood, make one tracing of part 1 and two tracings of part 2. As in all previous tracing procedures, be sure to arrange the patterns so that their longer dimensions run in the direction of the grain.

3. Cut out these three plywood parts, using the coping saw equipment shown in Fig. 2, Illustration 10.

4. Sandpaper all cut out wood parts until clean and smooth.

5. Using liquid glue and 1/2 inch wire brads, nail a handle piece, part 2, to each side of the handle end of part 1.

6. Employing a small brush and any single color of tempera or enamel paint, such as blue, red, or green, paint ship decoration on the back face of broad section of the paddle, exactly as in part 1, Fig. 2. With this color also paint the small handle-reinforcement pieces, part 2.

7. Line the forward side of the paddle with a covering of felt or medium grade sandpaper. This covering grips the ball as it shoots back, and prevents it from slipping off the paddle at the moment it is struck forward again. For fastening on covering, use any good glue or cement, applying it uniformly over the entire surface of the paddle. Then press covering to paddle firmly, to assure a neat esult.

8. Apply two coats of white shellac or clear varnish over all wood parts of the completed paddle, except the part covered by the felt or sandpaper.

Directions for making the rubber ball:

If you have a small rubber ball, simply punch a tiny hole at its center, make a knot at one end of the rubber strip and insert the knotted end of the rubber strip into the hole. However, if a ready-to-use rubber ball is unobtainable, one can be made as follows:

1. Make a small ball of absorbent cotton, over which wrap as many small rubber bands as are required to cover it completely. When applying the rubber bands try to produce as round a ball as possible.

2. Using any small brush apply a coat of rubber cement over the rubber-band-wrapped ball, brushing on the cement evenly and neatly. After the first coat has dried, brush on a second coat of cement. These applications of rubber cement will make the ball solid and will also hold the rubber bands tightly in place.

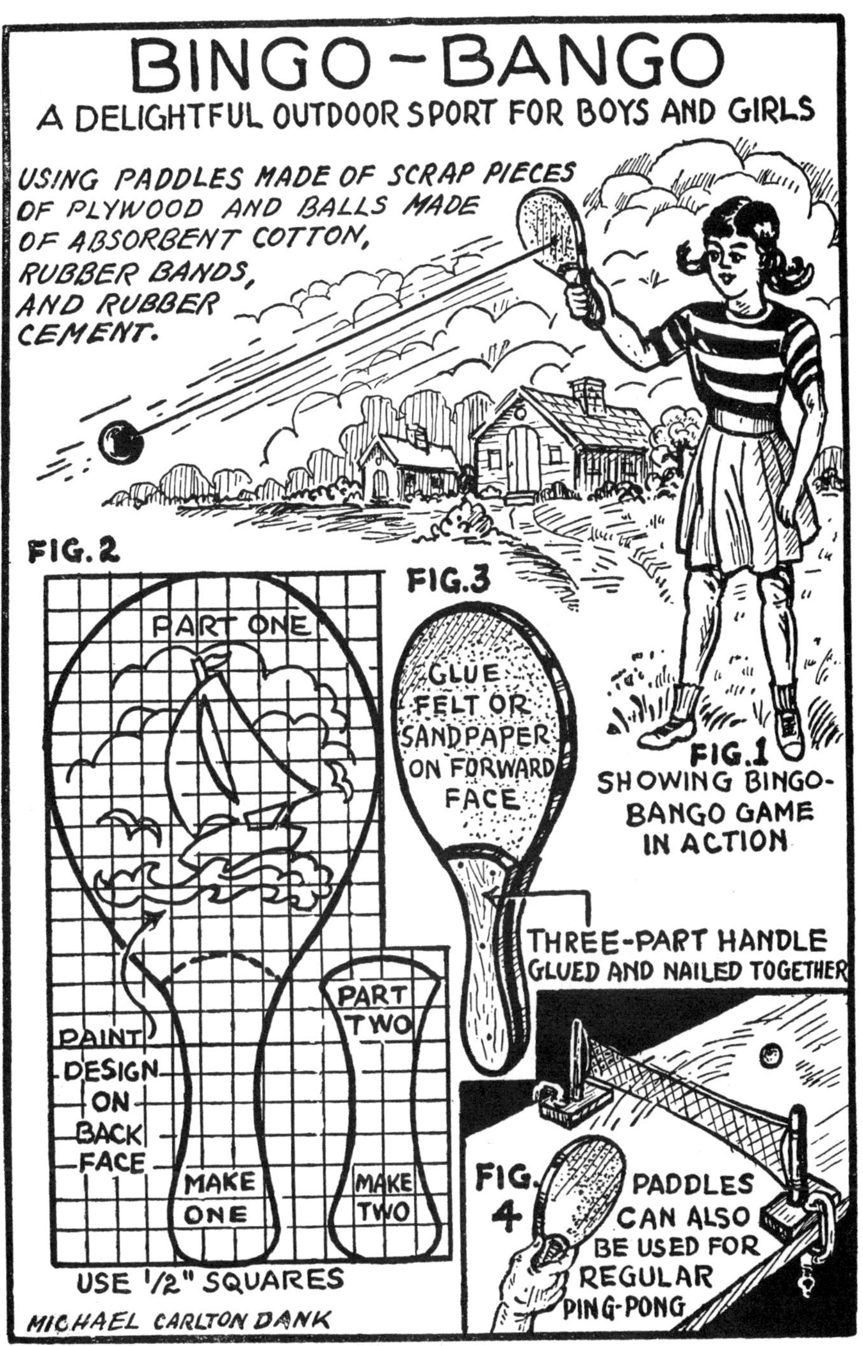
BINGO-BANGO
A DELIGHTFUL OUTDOOR SPORT FOR BOYS AND GIRLS
USING PADDLES MADE OF SCRAP PIECES OF PLYWOOD AND BALLS MADE OF ABSORBENT COTTON, RUBBER BANDS, AND RUBBER CEMENT.
FIG. 2
PART ONE
PAINT DESIGN ON BACK FACE
MAKE ONE
PART TWO
MAKE TWO
USE 1/2" SQUARES
MICHAEL CARLTON DANK
FIG. 3
GLUE FELT OR SANDPAPER ON FORWARD FACE
THREE-PART HANDLE GLUED AND NAILED TOGETHER
FIG. 1
SHOWING BINGO-BANGO GAME IN ACTION
FIG. 4
PADDLES CAN ALSO BE USED FOR REGULAR PING-PONG

Illustration 9

3. Using any pointed instrument, such as an awl or a nut-pick, force the knotted end of the long rubber strip into the center of the ball, after which apply an extra drop of rubber cement at the spot where the ball and the rubber strip are fastened together.

To attach the other end of the rubber strip to the forward face of the paddle, simply use a stapling machine or any ordinary hardware type of staple.

In addition to using the plywood paddle for Bingo Bango, it can also be made in pairs and used in the nationally popular game of ping-pong. In this game a celluloid ball is hit back and forth over a small net, clamped to a table, as demonstrated in Figure 4, Illustration 9.

Incidentally, the net and table used in ping-pong can be made of scrap materials as easily as the paddles. However, as we cannot concern ourselves with the construction of these items at present, we will ask the reader to use his own ingenuity in designing and working them out for himself.

Project No. 15, Laughing Clown Lapel Pin

See Figure 1, Illustration 10

This little lapel pin can be made entirely of thin plywood, or it can be made partly of wood and partly of leather materials. In either case it is most effective when made in two separate parts, one the clown's head and one his collar, rather than in a single piece.

When constructing this pin entirely of wood, simply make a full size pattern of Parts A and B, shown in reduced form grill in Fig. 6, Illustration 10. Reproduce the head and collar of the clown in full size, make a pattern grill on a sheet of drawing paper, using 1/4 inch squares. Then copy both parts exactly as represented in Fig. 6.

Following the reproduction of the full size patterns, cut them out and then trace them to 1/4 inch thick, three plywood, and then cut them out with a coping saw in the manner shown in Fig. 3, Illustration 10. In this illustration N indicates the coping saw, P the wood board in work, M the sawing support board, and O the small metal clamp which holds the support board firmly to the table.

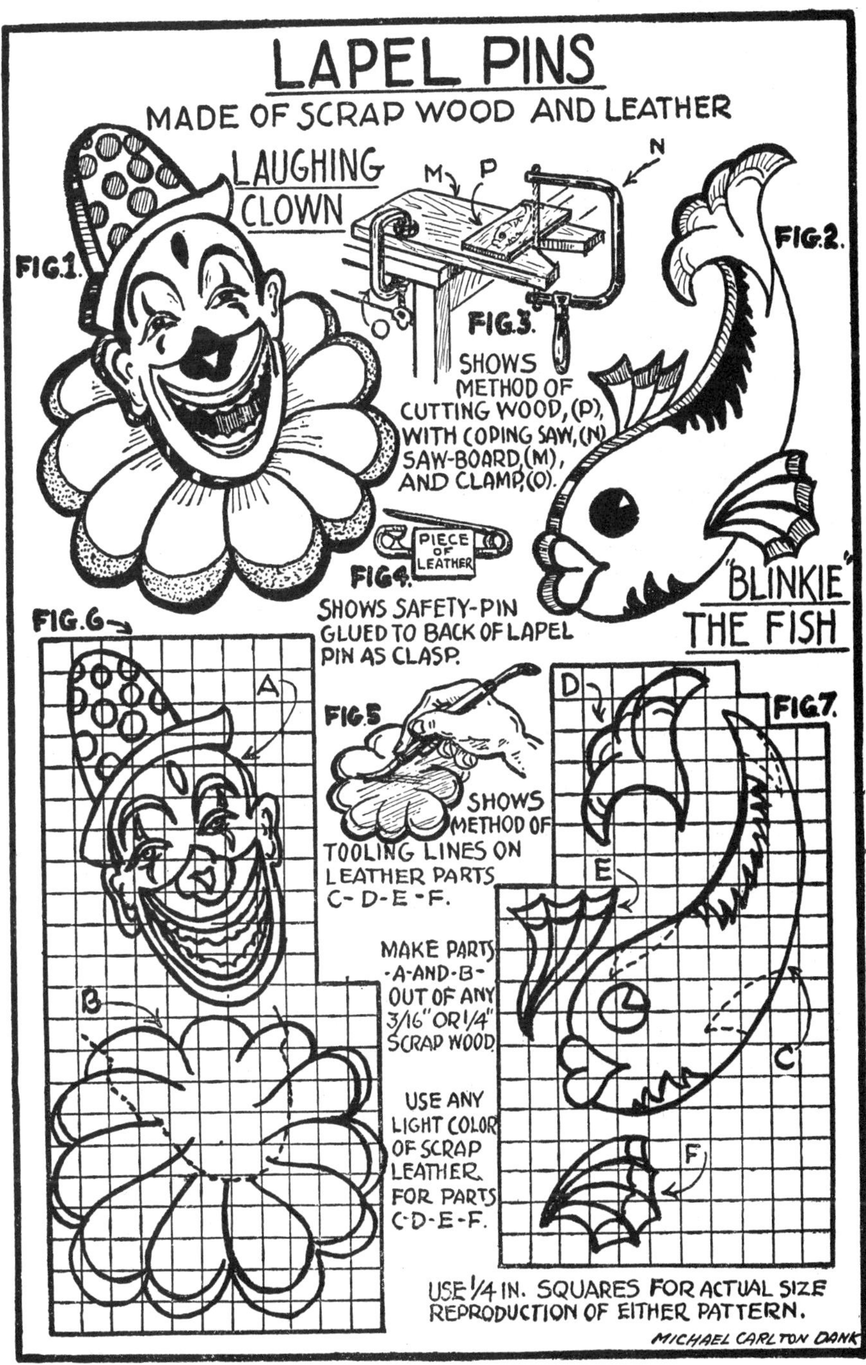

LAPEL PINS
MADE OF SCRAP WOOD AND LEATHER
LAUGHING CLOWN
FIG.1.
M
P
N
FIG.2.
FIG.3.
O
SHOWS METHOD OF CUTTING WOOD, (P), WITH COPING SAW, (N) SAW-BOARD, (M), AND CLAMP, (O).
PIECE OF LEATHER
FIG.4.
SHOWS SAFETY-PIN GLUED TO BACK OF LAPEL PIN AS CLASP.
"BLINKIE" THE FISH
FIG.6
A
FIG.5
SHOWS METHOD OF TOOLING LINES ON LEATHER PARTS C-D-E-F.
D
FIG.7.
E
MAKE PARTS -A-AND-B- OUT OF ANY 3/16" OR 1/4" SCRAP WOOD.
B
C
USE ANY LIGHT COLOR OF SCRAP LEATHER FOR PARTS C-D-E-F.
F
USE 1/4 IN. SQUARES FOR ACTUAL SIZE REPRODUCTION OF EITHER PATTERN.
MICHAEL CARLTON DANK

Illustration 10

After the wood parts are cut out, sandpaper all edges smoothly and glue the head A to the collar B, following the dotted line indicated on part B in Fig. 6 for correct location of the parts.

You may now color the wood parts of the clown with bright tempera or enamel paints. After applying the paint, use a very thin brush for small details, as well as a hairline outline between the colors. If tempera colors are used, finish pin with a coat of white shellac.

To complete this lapel ornament, attach a safety pin clasp to the back of the clown's head. This is easily done by gluing a small piece of leather over the lower bar of the pin and then by reinforcing this glued-on leather strip with small carpet tacks or 1/4 inch brass escutcheon pins which are nailed through the leather and into the wood. See Fig. 4, Illustration 10. For best results use two tacks or pins on each side of the leather strip.

Should you desire to make the clown's head of plywood and his collar of leather, first cut out and paint the head as earlier directed. Then trace the collar pattern to a scrap of tan-colored leather and cut out the collar with a sharp knife. Following this, moisten the back of the cut out leather collar with water, then tool the radiating lines of the collar deeply with a regular leather-modeling tool, in the manner shown in Fig. 5. It is a good idea to color the outer edge of the collar in some suitable color of the same paint medium employed for the head.

The leather collar, now tooled and colored, can be glued beneath the clown's head, following the dotted lines in Part B of Fig. 6. The safety pin clasp may then be attached to the back of the clown's head, using the leather strip as a holding device.

Project No. 16, Blinkie-the-Fish Lapel Pin

See Figure 2, Illustration 10

This little lapel ornament, like the laughing clown shown in Fig. 1, same illustration, can also be made entirely of scrap plywood, or of a combination of plywood and leather materials.

If made entirely of plywood, use 1/4 inch thick plywood for the body part C, and 1/8 inch plywood for the tail D and the fins E and F. See Fig. 7, Illustration 10.

After preparing a set of full size paper patterns of these parts of the fish, again using a grill of 1/4 inch squares, trace the parts to their respective thicknesses of plywood and then cut them out with a coping saw in the manner shown in Fig. 3. After the parts are cut out, be sure to smooth all edges neatly with sandpaper.

Following the sawing and sandpapering, glue the tail and fins of the fish to its body, and color all wood parts with tempera or enamel paints. Use a very small brush and black paint for all detail and trimming effects.

To complete "Blinkie" attach a safety pin to the back of his body, at about the center, using the same method for attaching the clasp as used for the laughing clown, shown in Fig. 1, and as in Fig. 4.

To construct "Blinkie" out of a combination of wood and leather materials, first cut out and color the body part, following the procedure described above. Then, trace the patterns for the tail and fins to a scrap of tan leather and cut them out neatly with a sharp knife. Following this, moisten the leather parts with water, and tool all detail lines with a modeling tool as shown in Fig. 5. When the tooled leather parts have completely dried, use a suitable color of the same paint medium employed for the body section, around the outer edges of each of the leather parts, as in Fig. 2. Complete the project by attaching a safety pin to the back of "Blinkie" in the manner just described.

This ornament, as well as the laughing clown, may also be used for window shade pulls, party name cards, or decorations for calendars, book-ends, scrapbook covers, memo-pads, and so forth. These designs may also be worked out in other materials such as copper foil, cardboard, cork, felt, and plastics.

DISCARDED MOP AND BROOM HANDLES BROKEN CHAIR RUNGS, AND OTHER ROUND WOOD SCRAPS

Discarded wooden sticks, rods, poles, chair and ladder rungs, dowels, and so forth can be used in the construction of many toys, games and novelties. In most cases, these sticks and other round wood scraps are combined with flat-shaped boards of various widths, lengths and thicknesses to produce the ring-toss game shown in Fig. 1, Illustration 11, or the novelty photo-frame shown in Fig. 1, Illustration 12. However, round sticks, poles, and so forth, of various lengths and diameters, can also be employed as the sole material of construction to make a large number of useful articles such as walking sticks and canes, children's swings, bird houses, novelty plant boxes, rustic garden fences, log cabin models, woven top foot stools and taborets.

Another application of discarded wooden rods of various types and sizes is in the preparation of different kinds of wheels, useful in the construction of toy carts, toy wagons, pull-toys, novelty buttons, checkers, costume jewelry such as lapel pins, bracelets and necklaces, and checkers, costume jewelry such as lapel pins, bracelets and necklaces. The novelty sport belt, Project No. 81, shown in Illustration 31, represents one such application of small wooden discs which can easily be made out of round sticks, poles, and rods.

In addition to the two main projects discussed in this unit, several other related projects are included in order to give the reader as wide a perspective as possible in the use of these commonly discarded wooden articles.

It is suggested that you begin with a simple project such as the ring-toss game, shown in Fig. 1, Illustration 11. Later, when you are more experienced in the handling of this kind of scrap wood, you may try a more advanced form of construction, such as the photograph-frame, seen in Illustration 12.

And now, let us proceed with the discussion of our first key project, the ring-toss game made of wooden-rod material combined with flat-shaped wood.

Project No. 17, Ring-Toss Game

See Figure 1, Illustration 11

I. Description

This ring-toss game is of especial interest because of the unusual combination of scrap materials employed in its construction. Its post is prepared from the rung of a broken chair (See Fig. 4, Illustration 11); its base from the thick wood bottom of a vegetable crate (See Fig. 2); and its rings from the wire of old clothes-hangers (Fig. 3), pieces of cord, and clothes-line rope. It is easy to make and lots of fun to play with.

II. Materials

A. A round, thick-wood base of a vegetable crate, from 8 inches to 12 inches in diameter. See Fig. 2, Illustration 11.

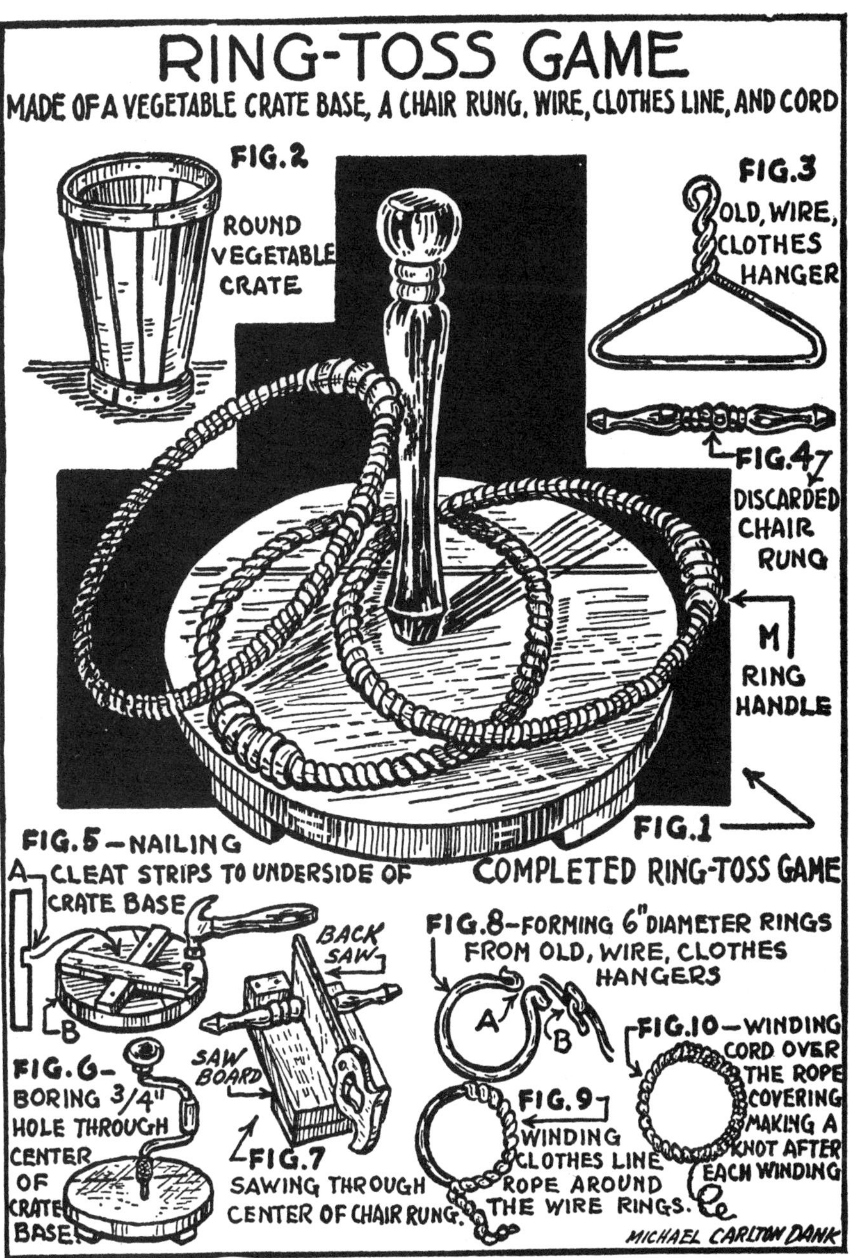
RING-TOSS GAME
MADE OF A VEGETABLE CRATE BASE, A CHAIR RUNG, WIRE, CLOTHES LINE, AND CORD
FIG. 2
ROUND VEGETABLE CRATE
FIG. 3
OLD, WIRE, CLOTHES HANGER
FIG. 4
DISCARDED CHAIR RUNG
M
RING HANDLE
FIG. 1
COMPLETED RING-TOSS GAME
FIG. 5—NAILING CLEAT STRIPS TO UNDERSIDE OF CRATE BASE
A
B
BACK SAW
SAW BOARD
FIG. 7
SAWING THROUGH CENTER OF CHAIR RUNG.
FIG. 6—BORING 3/4" HOLE THROUGH CENTER OF CRATE BASE.
FIG. 8—FORMING 6" DIAMETER RINGS FROM OLD, WIRE, CLOTHES HANGERS
A
B
FIG. 9
WINDING CLOTHES LINE ROPE AROUND THE WIRE RINGS.
FIG. 10—WINDING CORD OVER THE ROPE COVERING MAKING A KNOT AFTER EACH WINDING
MICHAEL CARLTON DANK

Illustration 11

B. Two strips of wood, 1/2 inch to 3/4 inches thick and about 1-1/2 inches wide.

C. A rung of a broken chair or ladder. See Fig. 4.

D. Two old wire clothes hangers. See Fig. 3.

E. About 3 yards of any grade of heavy cord.

F. About 3 yards of old clothesline.

G. A few 1 inch wire brads or nails.

H. Three appropriate colors of enamel paints. Also white shellac and clear varnish.

III. Tools

A. A small nailing hammer.

B. A boring brace, fitted with a 1/2 inch auger-bit (No. 8).

C. A back-saw or a coping saw.

D. A pair of pliers.

IV. Directions

A. Preparation of base and post parts

1. Remove the circular base board from a vegetable crate and any nails which may be found in the thick wood part.

2. Prepare two wood cleat strips, to measure from 1/2 inch to 3/4 inch in thickness, 1-1/2 inches in width, and as long as the diameter of the crate base.

3. Cut these cleat strips at their centers as shown in Fig. 5, A, Illustration 11, to form a half-lap type of construction. To produce this half-lap joint, first use a back saw and then a 1 inch chisel and a mallet.

4. Glue both cleat strips together, at right angles to each other, and then nail the strips to the underside of the ring-toss base, using wire brads or nails. See Fig. 5, B.

5. Using a hand brace fitted with a 1/2 inch auger bit (No. 8), bore a hole entirely through the center of the base board and the cleat strips below. Bore half-way from the top and half-way from the bottom of the base to avoid cracking the wood. See Fig. 6.

6. Using a back-saw or a coping saw, cut a broken chair rung in half, in the manner shown in Fig. 7. This will produce a post about 8 inches or 9 inches long, suitable for the requirements of this project. If a chair rung is unavailable, cut a broom-stick handle to this same size and round off the top end to give the post a finished appearance.

7. Make a small shoulder at the bottom end of the post, using a knife or a back saw and chisel, so that the tenon thus produced will fit exactly in the 1/2 inch hole, previously drilled in the center of the base board.

8. Sandpaper all sections of the base and post parts until smooth and clean.

9. Glue post into base and then reinforce this joint by inserting two or three wire brads of suitable size into the bottom end of the post from the underside of the ring-toss base. Insert the brads in a slanted or "toe-nail" fashion.

B. Preparation of rings

1. Using a pair of pliers, straighten out the wire of two old discarded wire clothes-hangers. This wire is to be used as foundation in the preparation of the ring-toss rings. About 5 feet of this wire or any other similar kind of wire are required for the construction of the rings.

2. Cut three strips of the wire to 18 inch lengths and then, using a pair of pliers, form a small hook at each end of each wire strip.

3. Bend each of the three wire strips into a circular shape as at A, Fig. 8, and then join and clinch their hooked ends together

as at B, Fig. 8. Next, tighten jointed ends of wire ring together securely with pliers.

4. Fasten the end of a yard long piece of clothes-line rope to the jointed section of the wire ring, using for this purpose a small piece of thin, milk bottle wire. Wind the rope tightly around the wire, in the manner shown in Fig. 9. Also use the milk bottle wire to fasten the finishing end of the rope securely to the wire foundation. Repeat this procedure for all three rings.

5. Over the clothes-line rope coverings wind any fairly heavy grade of cord, string, or twine, making a tight knot on the outside section of the ring, after each wind. See Fig. 10. Be sure to fasten the finishing end of the cord securely in place with an extra knot or two.

6. Make two or three extra layers of the knotted cord windings over that section of each ring where the clinched ends of the wire ring foundations are located. This will produce a sort of handle for conveniently holding the rings when they are in play. For this handle effect, see M, Fig. 1.

C. Coloring and finishing the ring-toss game

1. Apply a priming coat of white shellac over the post and base sections of the game as well as over the three cord-wound rings. Allow the shellac to dry thoroughly.

2. Paint the post and base parts in two contrasting colors of enamel.

3. To finish the rings, use either a third color of enamel that will harmonize with the other two, or a coat of clear varnish which will reveal the original color of the knotted cord-windings.

It is understood, of course, that any other suitable thick wood may be employed for the base board of this ring toss game, in place of the vegetable crate bottom. Instead of the chair rung employed for the post, any other round stick material from 3/4 inch to 1 inch in diameter may be used satisfactorily. Also, there are many other practical ways of making the rings. No matter what materials are used, however, the working procedures will be practically the same as those just described.

Project No. 18, Modern Photograph Frame

See Figure 1, Illustration 12

This photograph frame, like the ring-toss game, features round-stick wood in combination with flatwood and other materials.

For the posts you may use broom-stick handles, curtain-rods, or any other similarly shaped, round-stick stock. The foot-rests are made from discs cut from the same round-stick material used for the posts. The base is built of any neatly grained wood from 1/2 inch to 5/8 inch thickness. In addition to these two types of wood, you will also require for this project two pieces of glass, size 4 inches by 6 inches. As this is a standard size of picture-frame glass, you will have little trouble finding two pieces of this size somewhere about the house. However, you can also cut two pieces of glass to the required size by following the directions for glass-cutting given in Chapter Four, Section II, H.

In addition to the essential materials mentioned above, you will also need for the construction of this photograph frame two 1 inch flat-head screws, a little fine and medium grade sandpaper, mahogany or walnut oil stain, some clear white shellac or clear quick-drying varnish, and polishing wax.

The necessary tools include a smoothing plane, a try-square, a marking gauge, a back-saw, a hand drill, a 1/4 inch chisel, and a mallet.

A. Preparation of wood parts

1. Using a back-saw and a bench-hook, cut two lengths of any round-stick material of from 3/4 inch to 1-1/4 inches in diameter, such as a discarded broom-stick handle or curtain rod. For this process see Figs. 2 and 3, Illustration 12. Cut one length 3-1/2 inches and the other 5 inches. These round pieces are to be used as the posts which support the two glass sheets and the photograph, in the manner represented in Fig. 1, Illustration 12.

2. Round off or bevel the top ends of the posts neatly. The bottoms should be cut and left perfectly square.

3. Make a full-length groove in each of the two posts 1/4 inch deep and 1/4 inch wide. These grooves are to hold the photograph and glass sheets securely in place. The grooves can be made by placing the post in a vise; by making two full-length, 1/4 inch wide cuts with the back-saw; and then by cutting away the wood between the back-saw cuts with a 1/4 inch chisel and a mallet to a depth of 1/4 inch. See Figs. 4 and 5, Illustration 12.

4. Drill a hole, 1/8 inch in diameter and about 1/4 inch deep in the center of the bottom of each post. These holes are required to attach the posts to the base of the frame. See Fig. 6, which shows drilling in operation. The post should be clamped in a vise, either in a vertical or horizontal position, and the hole should be drilled perfectly straight.

5. Using the back-saw and bench-hook again, cut two 1/2 inch thick discs from the same round wood material as used for the posts. Then, cut these discs exactly in half to form four semi-discs. These semi-discs are to be the foot-rests seen at the bottom of the photograph frame in Fig. 1.

6. Make the base of the photograph frame from any neatly grained stock 1/2 inch to 5/8 inch in thickness. The completed dimensions of the base are 3-1/2 inches wide by 7 inches long. Start by making a working edge with a smoothing plane, being sure the edge is straight, smooth, and square. Then, gauge 3-1/2 inches from the working edge and plane excess wood away, working right up to the gauged width line. Test this edge also for straightness and squareness. To square up the ends of this piece, first try-square a line a little in from one of the unfinished ends, and then carefully cut along this line with a back-saw. Use a bench-hook for support and guide as demonstrated in Figs. 2 and 3. From this first squared-up end, measure the required 7 inches length, try-square a line across the width of the board at this point, and then carefully back-saw across this line as before.

7. Measure 1-1/2 inches in from the end and edge of each of the two front corners of the squared-up base piece, and draw a slanted line between each set of measurements. Using the back-saw and bench-hook again, cut off these two front corners to form the two slanted corners observed on the front section of the base of the photograph frame in Fig. 1.

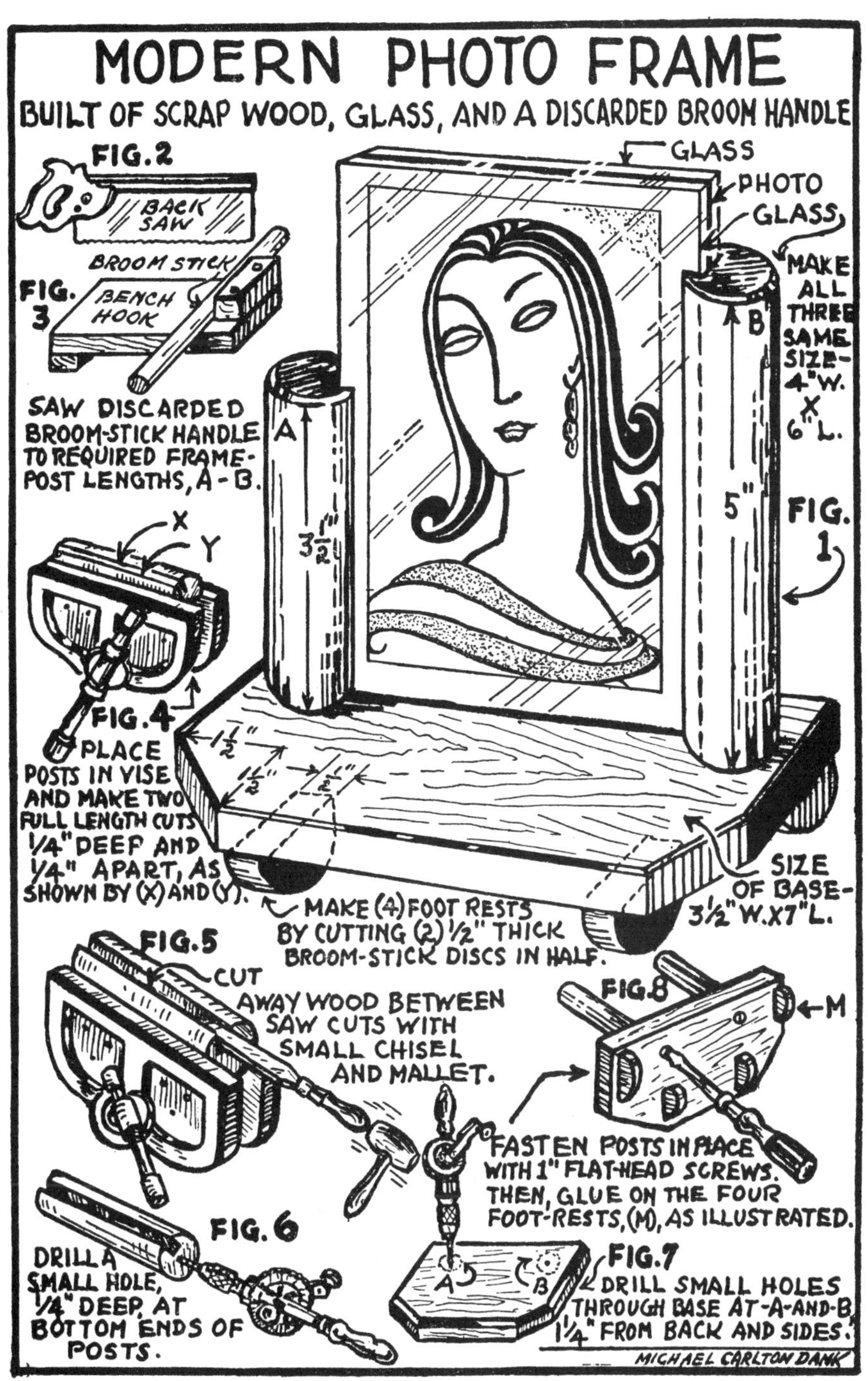

MODERN PHOTO FRAME
BUILT OF SCRAP WOOD, GLASS, AND A DISCARDED BROOM HANDLE
FIG. 2
BACK SAW
BROOM STICK
FIG. 3
BENCH HOOK
SAW DISCARDED BROOM-STICK HANDLE TO REQUIRED FRAME-POST LENGTHS, A - B.
GLASS
PHOTO
GLASS
MAKE ALL THREE SAME SIZE- 4"W. X 6"L.
A
B
$3\frac{1}{2}$"
5"
FIG. 1
X
Y
FIG. 4
PLACE POSTS IN VISE AND MAKE TWO FULL LENGTH CUTS 1/4" DEEP AND 1/4" APART, AS SHOWN BY (X) AND (Y).
$1\frac{1}{2}$"
$1\frac{1}{2}$"
MAKE (4) FOOT RESTS BY CUTTING (2) 1/2" THICK BROOM-STICK DISCS IN HALF.
SIZE OF BASE- 3½"W.X7"L.
FIG. 5
CUT AWAY WOOD BETWEEN SAW CUTS WITH SMALL CHISEL AND MALLET.
FIG. 8
M
FASTEN POSTS IN PLACE WITH 1" FLAT-HEAD SCREWS. THEN, GLUE ON THE FOUR FOOT-RESTS, (M), AS ILLUSTRATED.
FIG. 6
DRILL A SMALL HOLE, 1/4" DEEP, AT BOTTOM ENDS OF POSTS.
FIG. 7
A
B
DRILL SMALL HOLES THROUGH BASE AT-A-AND-B 1¼" FROM BACK AND SIDES.
MICHAEL CARLTON DANK

Illustration 12

8. Using a piece of sandpaper wrapped around a block of wood, slightly bevel off the edges of the base part at its upper face in Fig. 1.

9. Employing a hand-drill, fitted with a 1/8 inch drill bit, bore two holes through the base part, each located 1-1/4 inches in from the back edge and from the end of the base. These holes are later to be used for fastening the base to the two round frame posts. For this step see Fig. 7.

B. Method of assembling wood parts of frame

Before assembling the prepared wood parts of the frame, be sure they are neatly smoothed and finished. Then proceed as follows:

1. Fasten the base to the two round posts with 1 inch flat-head screws, inserting the screws from the underside of the base through the holes previously drilled in the base and and at lower ends of the posts. See Fig. 8. Be sure that the grooves, previously cut along the full lengths of the posts, face inward as in Fig. 1.
2. Glue the four semi-disc foot-rests to the underside of the base, arranging them in the manner shown in Fig. 8 and in Fig. 1.

C. Coloring and finishing the photograph frame

The most effective and simplest way to color and finish this photo-frame is to use an appropriate shade of oil stain over its base and to leave the round posts and foot-rests in a natural wood finish. The directions for this process are as follows:

1. Be sure all wood parts of the frame are thoroughly clean and smooth.

2. Mix a walnut or mahogany oil stain and with a small size flat-type brush, apply the stain over the whole base. Be careful not to tint any other part of the frame. Rub off the excess stain with a soft cloth.

3. After allowing the stain to dry overnight, apply a coat of clear white shellac or quick-drying varnish over both the stained and natural wood parts.

4. The following day, rub the shellacked or varnished surfaces with fine steel wool and polish the frame with any good grade of floor or furniture wax until a smooth, lustrous finish is produced.

To complete the frame and to put it to use, place the selected photograph between two sheets of glass, size 4 inches by 6 inches. Then, slide the glass sheets with the photograph inserted between them into and along the 1/4 inch grooves previously cut along the full length of the short and long frame posts. If all previous directions have been carefully followed, the photograph and glass sheets will fit exactly, as in Fig. 1.

This modern photograph frame can easily be made to hold two photographs by enlarging the base and by adding another 3-1/2 inch post at the right of the 5 inch post, placing the additional post the same distance from the longer post at the center as the 3-1/2 inch post at the left.

For a twin photograph frame, of course, it is necessary to have two grooves cut along the full length of the 5 inch post at the center instead of one to accommodate the extra photograph and glass sheets. It is also necessary to make the base of the frame about twice as long as the base used for the single-photograph frame. The same four foot-rests can be used as in the single frame, locating them the same distances from the ends and edges of the base.

THICK WOOD SCRAPS

Scrapwood in thickness of 1/2 inch to 1-1/2 inches and in various lengths and widths offers craftsmen of all ages unlimited possibilities in interesting woodworking projects.

The models shown in Illustration 13 are only a few typical projects which can be built of thick scrapwood, always easily obtainable, such as odd pieces of shelving, discarded bookcases, and other odd pieces of furniture. After you learn how to construct these key projects satisfactorily, you will have no difficulty in building innumerable other articles of your own design and planning for your home and for your friends.

It is interesting to note that in the construction of these heavier models, the tools and equipment needed are, with a few exceptions, the same as those required for making things of thin grade woods. However, a high quality of workmanship in this kind of woodwork can be produced only through the use of better grade tools. A few additional tools may even be necessary. With such equipment your work will be greatly facilitated.

It is suggested then, that you acquire as part of your working equipment such additional tools as a set of chisels and a mallet, one or two strong clamps, a good smoothing plane, a marking gauge, a rip-saw, and a cross-cut saw. A good sharpening stone is also an important item for your shop equipment to keep your tools in good working condition at all times. Besides these you will need the other tools, mentioned in connection with thin woodwork construction, such as a coping saw, back saw, try-square, hammer, boring brace, an assortment of different sizes of bits, and a fine and coarse type of file.

A good way to begin working with heavier grades of wood is to start with the construction of a simple, one-piece object, such as the bread cutting board shown in Fig. 1, Illustration 13. In this manner you will get the "feel" of heavier wood stock and also become acquainted with the basic procedures required in the forming and shaping of thick woods. Later, after you have acquired some experience, you will be ready to try your hand at more elaborate and complicated forms of woodwork in which two or more thick wood parts are joined together in various ways. A few such projects are the basketball game shown in Fig. 2, Illustration 13; the magazine and book rack shown in Fig. 3; the plant box shown in Fig. 4; and the shoe polishing stand shown in Fig. 5.

Because of its simplicity, we have selected the cutting board, Project No. 19, as our first key model in this construction unit. The basketball game, Project No. 20, will be our second key model; it combines thick wood with thin plywood and round wooden rods. It also employs other interesting scrap materials such as cord, soda bottle caps, and metal strapping.

The author is confident that after you have built these two key models and the other related models shown in Illustration 13, you will be able to make many other equally useful thick wood projects of your own design.

Project No. 19, Bread Cutting Board

See Figure 1, Illustration 13

I. Description

In the construction of this practical article you will learn how to "true up" a board so that its edges, ends, and faces are perfectly

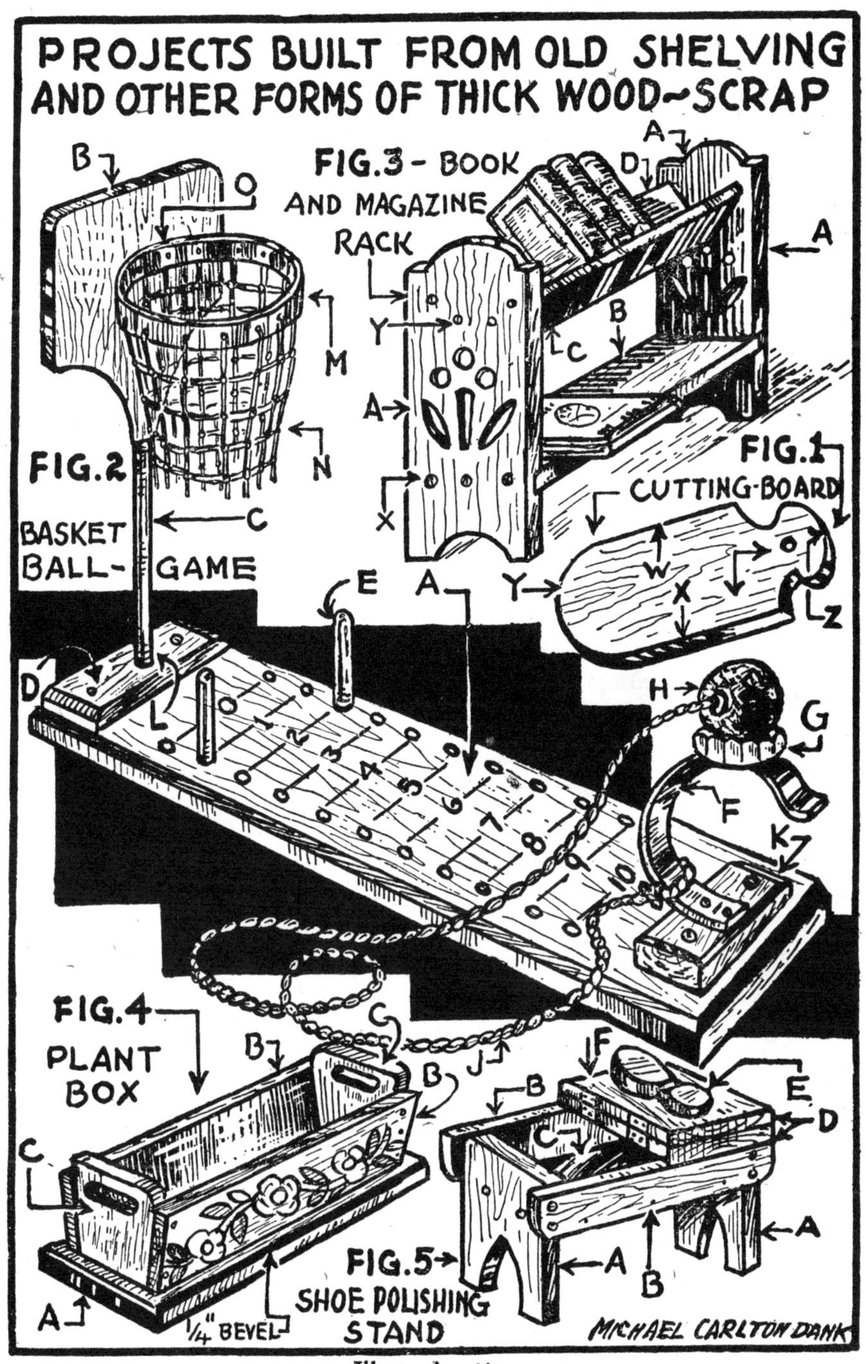

PROJECTS BUILT FROM OLD SHELVING
AND OTHER FORMS OF THICK WOOD-SCRAP
FIG.3 - BOOK
AND MAGAZINE
RACK
FIG.2
BASKET
BALL-GAME
FIG.1
CUTTING-BOARD
FIG.4
PLANT
BOX
1/4" BEVEL
FIG.5
SHOE POLISHING
STAND
MICHAEL CARLTON DANK

Illustration 13

square with each other. This important process is generally known in woodworking as "squaring up" a board.

After you have learned how to make this bread cutting board, you will have little difficulty in constructing any other more complicated articles of thick wood.

The bread cutting board may be built in various shapes and sizes, in accordance with individual taste and requirements. The one shown in Fig. 1, which was designed and built by the author for use in his own home, measures 3/4 inch thick by 7 inches wide by 12 inches long. This size board is very practical and is less likely to warp than larger cutting boards.

As for the best types of wood for this project, any scrap piece of fine-grain wood is satisfactory, although a hardwood board of fine-grain construction will provide a more serviceable cutting board than one made of soft wood.

This handy board may also be used for cutting fish, vegetables, meats, and so forth. A small hole is drilled at the top of the board so that it can be hung up when not in use.

II. Materials and Tools

1. A scrap board about 3/4 inch thick and a little larger than the required measurements of the finished project, 7 inches wide by 12 inches long.

2. Ruler.

3. Smoothing plane.

4. Try-square.

5. Marking gauge.

6. Coping saw equipment. See Fig. 3, Illustration 10.

7. Half-round, medium and heavy grade wood files.

8. Boring brace and a No. 6 auger bit.

9. Medium and fine grade sandpaper.

III. Directions

The first requirement in the construction of our bread cutting board is to "square up" the board to its correct measurements. Following this procedure, use the coping saw to produce the neatly curved contours at the top and bottom of the board.

The directions for these operations as well as the instructions for properly finishing the cutting board, are as follows:

A. "Squaring up" the board.

1. Place board (slightly larger in size than the required measurements of the project) upon the work bench top with one of the broad unfinished faces of the board turned upward. Prop board securely against a small wood-block or clamp it in place to one corner of the work-bench top.

2. Using a smoothing plane, clean, smooth and level off this first, broad surface of the board, using a ruler or try-square edge to test for "levelness." This first surface, now planed and trued, is known as the "working face."

3. With ruler, draw a guide line 1/4 inch from one edge of the board and then place the board in a work bench vise, with the marked edge of the board facing upward.

4. Plane this first edge until it is straight, square, and smooth, being careful not to work below the ruled guide line. Test planed edge with a try-square. Also test for straightness, using a ruler. When satisfactorily completed, this first edge is known as the "working edge." See Fig. 1, W, Illustration 13.

5. Placing handle of try-square solidly against the working edge, draw a guide line about 1/8 inch in from one of the unfinished ends of the board, and completely across its planed face.

6. Place board in vise with the marked off end facing upward. Then plane to the try-squared guide line, until the end is straight and square with the previously planed working face and working edge of the board. In order to avoid cracking the corners of the board during this step, work halfway in one direction and

halfway in the other. Or, you may first cut away a part of the corner of this end, at the unfinished edge side of the board, and then plane all the way across the end, working away from the working edge, toward the unfinished edge. Use try-square for testing. When satisfactorily completed, this end is called the "working end."

7. Using ruler, measure 12 inches from the working end and try-square a line across the working face at this point. Extend line across the working edge.

8. Place board in vise with the second or "length end" facing upward, and then plane exactly to the 12 inch length line. For this end-planing step use either one of the two methods described under 6 above. Also use try-square for testing.

9. Using rule, draw a line along working face exactly 7 inches away from the working edge, making certain that this line is drawn perfectly parallel with the working edge. Following this, place board in vise with the edge showing the 7 inch width line facing upward, and plane exactly to this line, testing with ruler and try-square for straightness and squareness. This "width edge" is indicated by X in Fig. 1, Illustration 13.

10. Using a marking gauge, set at a slightly smaller amount than the thickness of the board up to this point, and placing the head of the gauge tightly against the previously planed working face of the board, mark off a line all around the board's edges and ends.

11. Clamp board to bench top with the unfinished face of the board appearing upward and then plane to the gauged thickness line until this second face of the board is as clean, smooth and level as the first or working face. The work in this form is now "squared up" and ready for any further shaping or processing.

B. Forming curved ends with coping saw

Following the "squaring up" of the board, make a cardboard pattern showing both ends neatly designed and formed according to the general style used in our model, at Y and Z, in Fig. 1, Illustration 13. Then, place pattern on one face of the "squared up" board and trace around the pattern's outside edges, to purchase an exact replica of its shape upon the surface of the board.

For cutting out the curved shapes at both ends of the board, use the coping saw equipment shown in Fig. 3, Illustration 10. When using the coping saw for cutting thick wood such as employed in this project, however, it is a practical idea to use two small "C" clamps instead of just the one employed for thin woods. One clamp should be used to hold the "V"-notched sawing board in position on the work bench or work table, and another clamp should be employed to fasten the board-in-work to the saw board. The reason for this extra clamp is that more pressure is required to hold a thick board in place while it is being cut with the coping saw, than a thin board. Aside from the use of this extra clamp, the coping saw process for thick wood is just the same as for thin wood.

After the board is properly shaped, place it in a vise and file the cut out, curved edges and ends until they are uniform and perfectly square with the faces of the board. Use a rasp file first and then finish with a medium grade wood file. Use try square for repeated testing of filed edges and ends until a satisfactory result is produced.

Now place the board in the bench vise, in a vertical position, with top end upward, and bore a 3/8 inch diameter hole at point V, in Fig. 1, Illustration 13. Drill halfway from both faces of the board, to avoid cracking the wood.

The final step in the preparation of our bread cutting board is to sandpaper all edges, ends, and surfaces for a neatly finished product.

Because of the nature and purpose of bread cutting boards, no additional finishing treatment is to be employed. In other words, our bread cutting board with its sandpapered, natural-wood finish is now ready for use in the kitchen.

Project No. 20, Basket-Ball Game

See Figure 2, Illustration 13

This game, designed and developed in the au'hor's shop classes, is interesting because of the variety of scrap materials here employed in combination with several different sizes of thick wood parts. Although it is built of quite a few parts, requiring the use of several different kinds of materials, it is, nevertheless, very easy to build.

The simple directions required for building this table-type basket-ball game are as follows:

1. Using any scrap board of wood from 1/2 inch to 3/4 inch in thickness construct base of game, shown as A in Fig. 2, Illustration 13. The required measurements of this base are 7-1/2 inches wide by 14 inches long. For the preparation of the base use the "squaring up" process detailed under Project No. 19, bread cutting board.

2. After base is "squared up", plane a 1/4 inch bevel all around its edges and ends, at the top face only, as represented in the sketch of the completed project in Fig. 2, Illustration 13.

3. Drill a series of ten holes, 1/4 inch in diameter and 3/4 inch apart, at a distance of 1/2 inch from each edge of the base, just as shown in Fig. 2.

4. Make a cleat strip, D, size 3/4 inch by 2 inches by 5 inches, bevel its two ends at the top and fasten this part to base with two 1-1/4 inch round-head screws in the manner shown at D, Fig. 2.

5. Make a cleat strip, K, size 3/4 inch by 2 inches by 4 inches, bevel its two ends at the top, and fasten it to the base in the center of its width with two 1-1/4 inch round-head screws, as seen at K, Fig. 2. Note that this cleat strip, K, is located 1/2 inch in from the back or shooting end of the base, while cleat strip, D, is placed exactly at the beginning of the bevel of the forward end of the base.

6. Using 1/4 inch plywood, make a piece 6" square and shape the bottom end of this piece to form the basket support board, B. Also round its two top corners slightly, as shown.

7. Cut a 1/2 inch dowel rod to a length of 12 inches and fasten the top end of this dowel rod to the back of the lower end of part B. To make a strong joint of these two wood parts, it is best to cut a 2 inch shoulder of half thickness at the top end of the dowel and then fasten dowel support C to part B, using liquid glue and 1/2 inch wire brads.

8. Bore a 1/2 inch diameter hole at L, about 1 inch deep and in the center of part D. Then, into this drilled hole, glue dowel support C.

9. Cut a 1/2 inch wide strip of steel strapping (the kind commonly used for strapping wooden crates) to a length of 6 inches, to form the shooting spring indicated as F. About 1 inch in from the top end of this metal strip, fasten on a soda bottle, metal cap, such as G, using as a fastening device either a small rivit or a brass fastener. Bend metal strip into a "C" shape as shown by F in Fig. 2. and then fasten lower end of strip to cleat part K, using for this purpose two 1/2 inch round-head screws as shown.

10. Make a circular ring of a 10 inch length of the same 1/2 inch wide metal strapping as used for the shooting spring, and fasten the ends of the ring tightly together with a piece of milk bottle wire. Lace the wire through punched holes at ends of metal ring. See M, Fig. 2.

11. Punch or drill about eight 1/16 inch holes around the center of the width of the metal ring, locating the holes about 1 inch apart. From these holes suspend 4 inch lengths of white colored top cord, making a neat knot at the top of each cord length, inside of the band. Following this, attach pieces of the same cord from one suspended string to the other, making a neat knot at each joint, to form the knotted-cord basket shown at N, Fig. 2. Arrange the horizontal cords about 3/4 inch apart, as represented in the sketch in Fig. 2.

12. Attach completed basket securely to support board B, by fastening jointed section of metal ring M to the center of support board B, at point marked O. Use milk bottle wire as a fastening device by first drilling two small holes through B at point where basket is to be attached. Tiny round head screws may be used in place of the wire, if desired.

13. Cut two 1-1/2 inch lengths of 1/4 inch dowel rod and neatly round off their tops and bottoms to form the score posts E. Place one post in the left No. O hole and one in the right No. O hole, where they must always be placed at the start when playing this basket-ball game.

14. Cut a 24 inch length of the same white cord as used for the construction of the basket to form the ball-retrieving cord J. Fasten one end of the cord to the lower part of the metal shooting spring F, and to the other end of the cord attach any kind of small ball such as shown by H, Fig. 2. Satisfactory balls for this game, may be had through the use of discarded golf-balls, old hand-balls, small size toy balls, or even homemade balls, constructed of paper and string, held tightly together by means of a coating of rubber cement.

15. After all parts of the game have been properly prepared and assembled, apply a coat of light oak or walnut oil stain over all wood parts of the game. After stain has dried, use a small, pointed brush and black enamel for applying the small straight lines and numbers seen in Fig. 2, between each set of scoring post holes, on upper surface of base part A. For a neat, satisfactory result, it is important to first mark these details in with a sharp pencil and a ruler, before they are finally executed in the black enamel paint. As a final finish, and after the enamel work has dried, apply two coats of white shellac or clear, quick-drying varnish over all wood parts. Allow first coat to dry thoroughly before the second one is applied. When shellac or varnish finishing coats have dried, the game will then be complete and ready to be put into play.

To play this table-type basket-ball game, first place ball H into shooting cup G. Then, using right index finger, press down the handle part of shooting spring F to a distance of about 1-1/2 inches, carefully aim for center of basket, and suddenly release finger from shooting spring. The ball will quickly shoot upward in the direction of the basket, either to "score" a point or to make a "miss." If the player who is up has succeeded in scoring a point, he is entitled to move his scoring post from No. O hole to hole No. 1. The same player may then continue shooting the ball until he makes a "miss." The opposing player now proceeds to try his skill in this same manner.

This entertaining game may be played by opposing teams of from one to four players. Girls and boys as well as adults will find it most enjoyable.

Project No. 21, Book and Magazine Rack

See Figure 3, Illustration 13

This useful and attractive book and magazine rack can easily be built of old shelving boards or of the boards of discarded, broken furniture. As shown in the sketch in Fig. 3, Illustration 13, it can hold a good number of books and magazines and is designed for use in a home library, in a boy's or girl's room, den, or work room.

To build this thickwood project, proceed as follows:

1. Make two vertical end parts, A, by first squaring up two boards to measure 3/4 inch thick, 10 inches wide, and 28 inches high. For this "squaring up" process see text under Project No. 19, Bread-Cutting Board.

2. Make a cardboard pattern in the form of a stencil like the decorative design shown on parts A, then trace this pattern to one of the surfaces of each part A.

3. Since this flower decoration is to be cut or perforated right through these vertical parts A, it will be necessary to first bore holes with a brace and 1/4 inch auger bit, and then proceed to cut out the flower, stem and leaf sections of the design with a coping saw. See text for using coping saw when working with thick woods, as given under Project No. 19, Bread-Cutting Board.

4. After the decorations are properly cut out, make cardboard patterns for top and bottom ends of parts A, trace the patterns to these boards and then proceed to cut along the traced outlines to produce the gracefully formed contours shown in the sketch of the completed project, in Fig. 3. To complete these end boards, use file and sandpaper as required, on edges, ends, and faces.

5. Make one lower horizontal shelf, part B, to measure 3/4 inch thick, 10 inches wide, and 30-1/2 inches long. (Allowance of 1/2 inch is here made in the length for dado joint construction to be explained below). Be sure faces, edges, and ends are carefully squared up, just as in the case of vertical parts, A.

6. Join vertical parts, A, to lower, horizontal shelf part, B, by first cutting 3/4 inch wide dados or grooves across the full widths

of the inside surfaces of end parts A. Locate these grooves 8 inches up from the lower ends of parts A and make the grooves exactly 1/4 inch deep. A good method for preparing these grooves in the preparation of this dado-butt joint form of construction is as follows: First try-square carefully measured pencil lines across the widths of the boards in accordance with dimensions indicated above. Make 1/4 inch deep cuts along these lines with a back saw, using small, straight strips of wood as sawing guides. Cut away the wood between each pair of back saw cuts, using for this purpose a 3/4 inch chisel and a mallet. Chisel grooves from each edge of the boards to avoid cracking the wood. Also, cut the grooves carefully and refrain from using any sandpaper.

After grooves are cut, bore three 1/4 inch diameter holes through the end boards, A, locating the holes exactly in line with the center of the thickness of horizontal board, B, and bore from the outside surfaces of end boards, A. Drill one hole at the center and one hole 1-1/2 inches in from each edge of vertical parts A. See X, Fig. 3. Following the boring of the holes, brush liquid glue over the grooved sections of parts A and over the ends of lower shelf, B. Then, fasten the three wood parts together, using three 1-1/2 inch round head screws at each joint as shown at X, Fig. 3. Be sure parts are joined evenly and securely and have the cuts in the screw heads all face in the same direction.

7. Make upper horizontal shelf boards C and D, to form the "V"-shaped shelf construction seen in Fig. 3. The measurements for shelf part C are 3/4 inch thick, 6 inches wide, and 30 inches long. Those of shelf part D are 3/4 inch by 5-1/4 inches by 30 inches. The difference in the widths is explained by the fact that part D is to be joined under the edge of part C, making both parts appear as having the same width when fastened together. For joining C to D, use liquid glue and about five 1-1/2 inch wire brads. Round head screws may be used in place of the brads if desired.

8. After shelf parts C and D are fastened together, to form the "V" or angular type upper shelf construction seen in Fig. 3, screw them into place between vertical parts A. Locate the top edges of this upper shelf section about 3 inches down from the top ends of vertical end boards A. You will note that no grooves or dados are required for the assembling of this upper shelf section, as a

simple screwed-butt joint for this part of the project will be sufficiently strong and satisfactory. However, dados may be used in the assembling of this upper section of the rack if desired. After marking location of shelf parts C, D, on the inside surfaces of vertical boards A, drill four 1/4 inch holes through each vertical board A, arranging these holes as a Y, Fig. 3. Then, using four 1/2 inch round head screws at each end of the rack, fasten shelf section C, D securely in place. Be sure the screws are driven in straight and exactly into the center of the thickness of each of the ends of shelf boards C and D.

9. Having thus assembled the book and magazine rack, make sure all excess glue is carefully removed and that all edges, ends and faces of the project are neatly and smoothly sandpapered in preparation for coloring and finishing steps.

10. Apply a coat of mahogany, walnut, or oak oil stain over the entire rack, using a flat brush, about 1-1/2 inches wide. A few minutes later, wipe off all excess stain with a soft cloth and rub the stain well into the wood to show up the wood grain prominently and effectively.

11. After the stain has dried, apply a coat of white shellac over all stained surfaces and allow to dry thoroughly. Then, rub this first shellac coat with fine steel wool until surface is smooth. Following this, apply a second coat of the shellac and again rub and smooth the surfaces with steel wool.

12. As a final finishing treatment, apply a coat of paste or liquid wax over all shellacked wood surfaces and then polish the entire project with a soft cloth until an attractive, smooth, lustrous finish is produced.

The combination book and magazine rack is now complete. The reader is no doubt aware that the particular design and coloring treatment outlined above is only one of many different kinds of decorative treatments which may be employed. For instance, enamel may be used instead of oil stain, and the rack may be made larger or smaller than the particular size suggested above.

Project No. 22, Plant Box

See Figure 4, Illustration 13

This plant box, like most of the other thickwood projects represented in Illustration 13, may be built in various sizes and in a variety of styles, in accordance with individual taste and requirements. The plant box model represented in Fig. 4, is a good average size and is designed for the window sill of the average classroom or home, as well as outdoors, on the porch-ledge.

As you will note from the sketch in Fig. 4, Illustration 13, this plant box consists of one base, two sides, and two ends. The ends and sides taper inward a little from the top to the base. The ends are neatly rounded at the top corners and are provided with perforated hand-holes for convenience in lifting and moving the plant box as necessary. The edges and ends of the base extend 3/4 inch beyond the side-walls of the box and are neatly beveled at the top for added decorative effect.

All five parts of this plant box model are made of 3/4 inch wood; and any scrap wood of this thickness, either of the hardwood or softwood grades is satisfactory for its construction. You will find this plant box very easy to build, especially after you have become familiar with the method of "squaring up" a board as detailed in the text under Project No. 19. Here are the simple directions:

1. "Square up" one board for the base part, indicated as A, Fig. 4 to measure 7-1/2 inches wide by 30 inches long. Later, plane a 1/4 inch bevel at the top section of its edges and ends as shown in the sketch.

2. Square up two boards for the sides of the box, B, to measure 5-1/2 inches wide by 29 inches long.

3. Square up two boards for the ends of the box, C, to measure 6-1/2 inches wide by 6-1/2 inches long.

4. Round off the two top corners of each of the end parts, C, making certain also that the grain of these end parts of the box runs vertically or in the direction of the sides of the box, B. This is important since the perforated hand-holds will be weakly constructed if the grain is made to run in a horizontal direction.

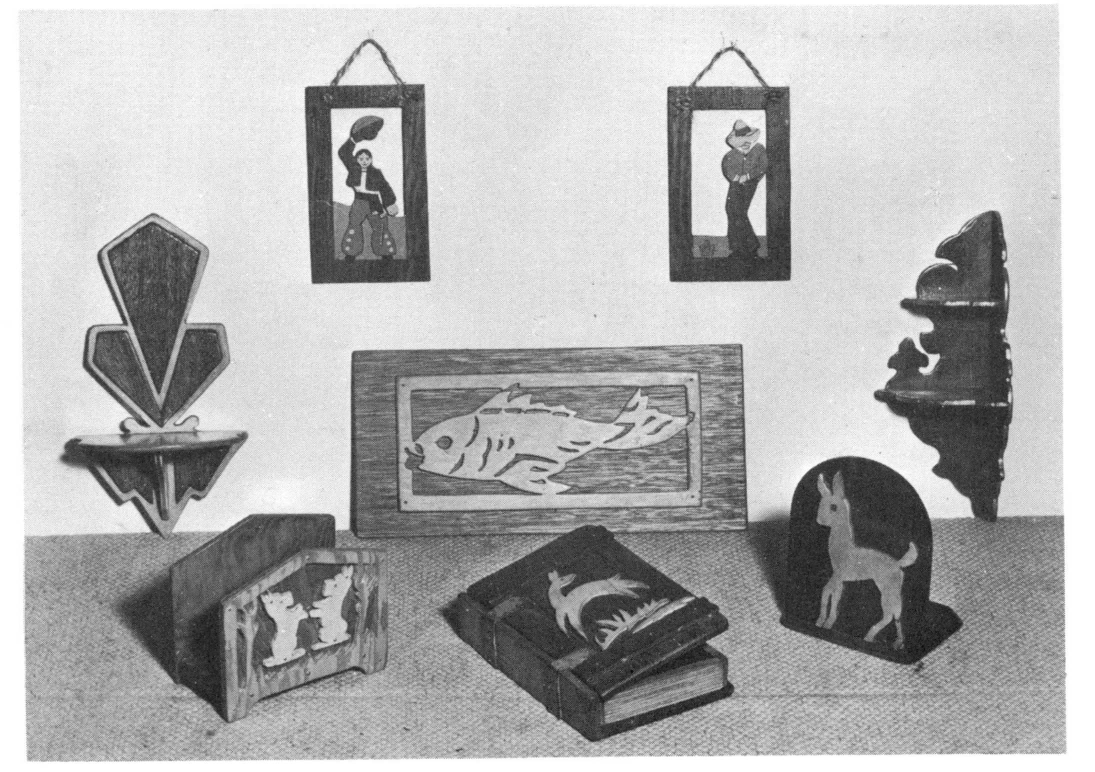

Plate 3. The wall plaques, cigarette box, shelves, book end and stationery rack shown above were all made entirely from scrap pieces of wood.

5. Measure in 1/2 inch from each lower corner of each end part, C, draw slanted lines from these points to the top corners of these end parts, and then saw along these lines with a hand-saw, to form the tapered or slanted sides of these ends, as shown in the sketch in Fig. 4. The slanted ends may be formed with a plane instead of with a saw, if preferred.

6. Lay out hand-holds on end parts, C, to measure 3/4 inch wide by 3 inches long. Locate top of each hold opening 1-1/2 inches down from the top of each end part, C. To cut out these hand-holds, first drill a 3/4 inch diameter hole at the left and right extremities of each hold layout. Then complete perforation either with a 3/4 inch chisel and a mallet, or with a coping saw and a file.

7. Drill three 1/8 inch holes 3/8 inch in from each end of side parts B, placing one hole at the center of the width and one 1 inch from each edge. Then, using 1-3/4 inch long, round-head screws, fasten side parts, B, to end parts, C, just as represented in Fig. 4. In this assembling step, it is important that each corner joint is made neatly and evenly.

8. Place the four assembled sides of the box in a vise, with their bottom edges facing upward, then plane the bottom edges of side parts, B, until they are perfectly level with the bottom ends of end parts, C. This planing step is necessary due to the tapered effect of the sides of the box.

9. With the assembled sides of the box still in the vise, in this upside-down fashion, place base part, A, over the upturned edges, making certain it is centrally and properly located, and then screw it down securely with 1-3/4 inch long flat-head screws. Use two screws at each end and four at each side section of the box. In this jointing step, it is important that the bevelled edges appear at the top of the base thickness and that the 1/2 inch margin or extension of the base appears evenly and uniformly all around the box, just as represented in the sketch of our project in Fig. 4.

10. Bore three 1/2 inch diameter holes through the base part, A, to provide a means of escape for surplus water when watering the plants, when the box is put into use.

11. Sandpaper all parts of the plant box carefully and paint it as follows: Apply a priming coat of white or orange shellac over all surfaces of the box. When dry, brush two coats of dark green enamel over all outside surfaces of the box, allowing an overnight drying period after each coat is applied. The inside sections of the box need no other painting treatment than the shellac coating since these surfaces will later be covered with earth. As a final decorative treatment, use two or three harmonizing colors of enamel for painting an appropriate decoration on the forward side section of the plant box. These colors must be carefully selected to contrast with the dark green overall enamel coat previously applied. A good method is to sketch the design with pencil or chalk and then paint it in. A floral design of the type employed in Fig. 4 is very effective. If the plant box is to be used outdoors, it is a good plan to apply a coat of spar varnish over the enamel as an added protection against the elements.

After the plant box has been completed it is practical to place risers or rests at the bottom of the box, locating them at the corners and central section of the box. These rests will raise the box from the window-sill or porch-ledge and prevent its bottom from rotting or soiling the foundation upon which it is placed. For indoor plant boxes, it is suggested that a metal tray or drain-pan be used underneath the box to receive the surplus water.

Project No. 23, Shoe Polishing Stand

See Figure 5, Illustration 13

For the construction of this useful article you will need eight separate wood parts, all made of 3/4 inch stock. Any thickwood scrap of suitable sizes will serve satisfactorily in the building of this project. The finished sizes of each of these shoe polishing stand parts are as follow:

Ends, A, make two, size 6 inches wide by 12 inches long.
Side rails, B, make two, size 3 inches wide by 14 inches long.
Bottom, C, make one, size 6 inches by 10-1/2 inches.
Top boards, D, make two, size 7 inches wide by 7-1/2 inches long.
Foot rest, E, make one, overall sizes 3 inches wide by 5-1/2 inches long.

The proper procedure for constructing this simply designed shoe polishing stand is as follows:

1. Square up two boards for the end parts, A, and then, using a coping saw, cut out the decorative notches at the lower section of these ends, as shown in Fig. 5.

2. Cut out two side rails, B, rounding up their lower corners as indicated in Fig. 5. After completing these side rails, fasten them to end parts, A, allowing the ends of the side rails to extend 1 inch beyond end parts A, just as observed in Fig. 5. In the assembling of these end and side rail parts of the stand, use two 1-3/4 inch round head screws, evenly arranged, at each jointed corner.

3. Square up bottom part C and then fasten it inside of the assembled side rail and end parts, using three 1-1/2 inch wire brads at each side and two at each end. See Fig. 5.

4. After squaring up the two top boards, D, hinge them together, using two suitable size brass hinges, in the manner shown in Fig. 5, F. Set the hinges into the edges of the top boards, so the tops of the hinges will be exactly flush with the wood.

5. Nail down the top member only of this two-part cover or top section, allowing the left member to open and close freely, after the fashion indicated in Fig. 5.

6. Using a coping saw and file, cut out foot-rest E, following the general pattern or form suggested by foot-rest E, as employed in our model. Make front section, or, sole, of foot-rest, 3/4 inch thick, and heel part at back, 1/2 inch thick.

7. Sandpaper all wood parts of stand until clean and smooth and then apply a coat of walnut or oak oil stain. Apply stain with a flat brush and then rub away excess stain with a soft cloth. As a result of this staining and rubbing, the wood grain should show up very effectively.

8. Finish shoe polishing stand with a rubbed down coat of clear white shellac, followed by a polished coat of wax.

When closed, the cover of the stand fits exactly over the full length of the side rail sections, and the stand assumes the form of a neat foot stool. The inside compartment of this stand provides ample room for all necessary shoe polishing tools and materials.

CHAPTER SIX

WORKING WITH SCRAP METAL

IN INTRODUCING this important and highly popular branch of handwork, and in order to make the discussion of it most helpful to craft enthusiasts everywhere, we intend to treat it in two distinct forms.

First, is the use of tin cans as a whole or in their original shape. Second, is the use of the cut-apart and flattened out tin cans as a source of sheet metal.

As our key project for the first of these two types of construction work, we are employing Project No. 24, tin can electric light shades, shown in Fig. 1, Illustration 14. As our key project for scrap sheet metal, we will use Project No. 38, hot pot stand, shown in Fig. 1, Illustration 17.

When you have made these representative projects, you will find it easy to build the many other metal articles which are presented as related projects and which employ similar construction.

Working with discarded tin cans and sheet metal obtained from tin cans, offers home craftsmen and arts and crafts teachers an unlimited field of activity in the production of toys, games, novelties, and various practical gifts for home use.

Working with inexpensive metals such as provided by all sizes and shapes of tin cans, is excellent preliminary training for work with more valuable metals such as copper, brass, aluminum, pewter, and silver. Another advantage of tin can crafts is the comparatively low cost of tools and equipment required for this branch of metal work.

It is of interest, too, that girls like this type of arts and crafts as much as boys do. And, why shouldn't they, when they can so easily and quickly make lapel ornaments, bracelets, barrettes, and other pieces of costume jewelry in this way?

We are devoting much space to the treatment of this scrap craft activity because of its importance in educational and recreational handicrafts and its general appeal.

DISCARDED TIN CANS

Project No. 24, Tin Can Electric Light Shades

See Figure 1, Illustration 14

I. DESCRIPTION

This novel electric light shade is most useful in summer camps, cottages, bungalows, and country clubs. Not only is it practical, but because of its neatly punched or pierced decorations in Mexican or Indian motifs, it is also unusual and attractive.

The handwork procedures required for the preparation of these tin can electric shades are easy to apply.

For these tin can shades you may use either a pint size or quart size can, depending upon the size of the room for which they are planned or the size of the electric light bulbs used. Tin cans in these sizes are discarded every day in large quantities by hotels, restaurants, food stores, home kitchens, and so forth.

After the reader has learned to convert discarded tin cans into electric light shades, he will have no difficulty in building any of the other projects of this type as shown in Illustrations 15, and 16.

II. MATERIALS

A. Empty pint or quart size tin cans, with tops removed.

B. Enamel paint.

C. Clear lacquer.

D. Fine and medium grade steel wool.

E. Medium grade emery cloth.

F. A spool of thin wire.

III. Tools

A. A metal working hammer, ball-peen style, from 12 oz. to 16 oz. such as shown in Fig. 2, A, Illustration 14.

B. Cold chisel with a 3/8 inch wide tip, of the type seen in Fig. 4, Illustration 14.

C. Nail set, with tip ground to a point. See Fig. 5, Illustration 14.

D. Either a woodworking or metal working vise.

E. An old, discarded baseball bat.

F. A 1 inch wide, flat-style, lacquering brush.

G. Nos. 3 to 5, pointed style paint brushes.

H. Small and medium size, half-round, metal working files.

I. A small, stiff bristled, scrubbing brush.

IV. Directions

A. Selecting and conditioning the tin cans

The first consideration in the construction of these home-made electric light shades is to determine how many and what size tin cans will be required for the particular job on hand. If we are making tin can shades for the social hall or dining room of a summer camp, we must first ascertain the number of lighting fixtures which are to be suspended from the ceiling and the manner in which they are to be arranged. We must also decide as to the size of electric light bulbs which are to be employed for the purpose, and as to the size and type of tin cans which will be most appropriate and effective.

We may find, for example, that pint cans will be most practical and satisfactory, especially if a more subdued form of lighting is desired. On the other hand, quart size cans may be used to produce a brighter light. Still another possibility, is to use pint cans for the side or outer sections of the ceiling, and quart cans for the center of the room.

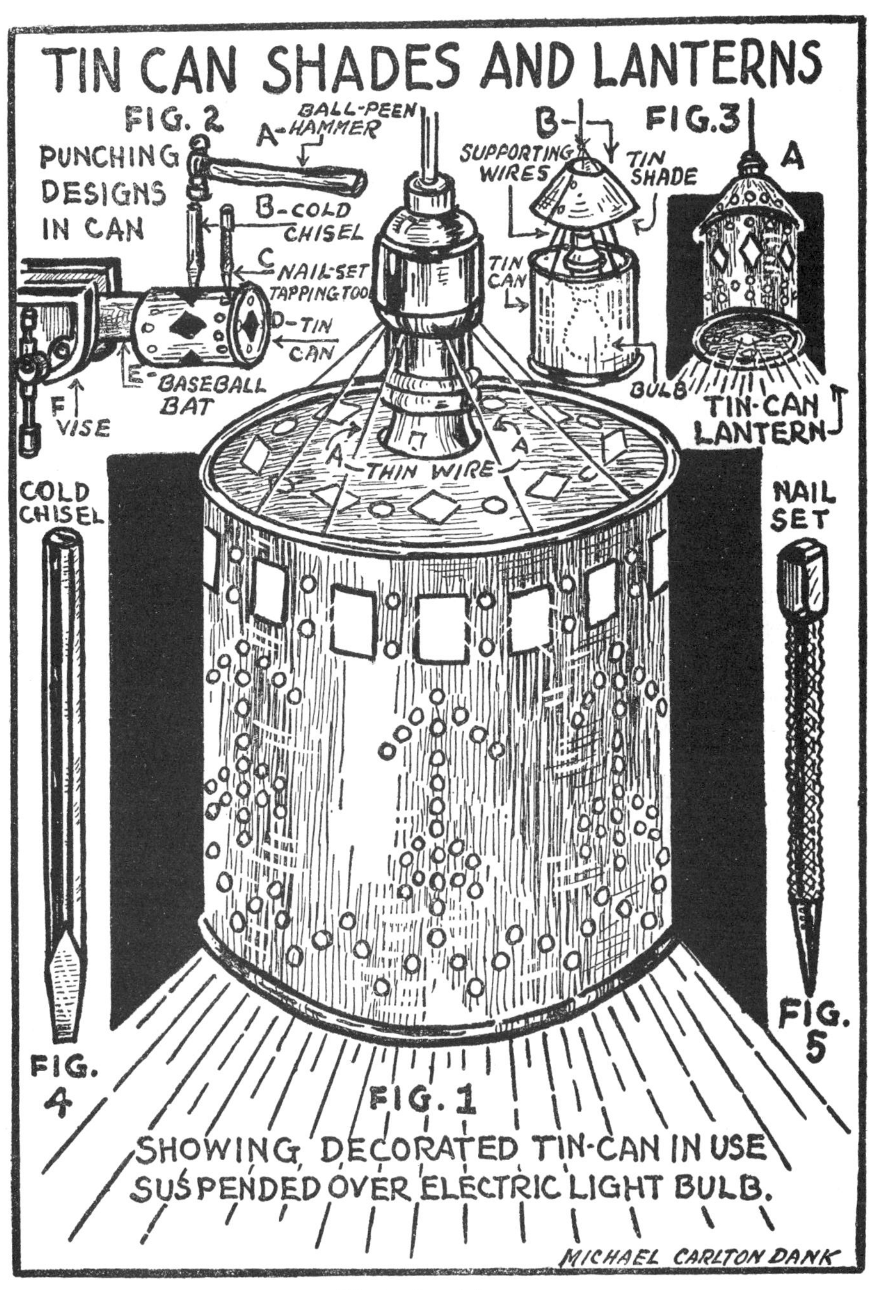

Illustration 14

Whatever the lighting plan may be there will be no trouble whatever in providing the necessary number and size of cans required for the job. It is important, however, that only those cans be selected which are free from dents, rust, or any other such imperfections. It is also essential that the tops of the cans be removed in a smooth, clean-cut fashion. Generally, those cans which are newly opened by means of a regular can opener, will be found entirely satisfactory for the purpose.

After selecting the proper tin cans, it is necessary to remove all paper wrappings and to clean the inside sections of the cans thoroughly of all food particles, odors, and so forth. This can easily be done by washing all parts of the cans in warm water and soap flakes, scrubbing them well with a stiff-bristled brush. The cans should then be thoroughly dried with an old towel or any scrap of cloth to prevent rusting.

The next step is to polish the inside and outside surfaces brightly with fine or medium grade steel wool. In this step, the steel wool may be used in a circular motion at first, but, at the end, should be used in a straight, up and down motion, in the direction of the length of the can. Polishing in this manner will prevent the appearance of unsightly scratches all over the outside surfaces of the cans, and will produce a smooth, bright finish.

The tin cans are now ready for the application of the punched or pierced decorations, such as shown in the drawing of the electric light shade, in Fig. 1, Illustration 14.

B. Preparing patterns for punched or pierced designs

The purpose of these ornamental apertures is twofold. First, they beautify the tin shades and disguise their lowly origin. Second, they enable some of the light to shine through the top and sides of the shade, in addition to the full beam of light which is emitted through the bottom. The size, shape and number of these decorative openings have a direct effect upon the lighting efficiency of the completed tin can shades.

The reader can now appreciate the need for a careful, systematic procedure in this phase of our project. The following method for preparing the working patterns for the pierced decorations on the tin can shades, will be found both practical and easy to apply.

1. Cut a piece of wrapping paper or any light colored drawing paper so it will fit exactly around the sides of the can like a wrapper. To determine the circumference of the can, simply wind a string around the outside surface of the container. This will give you the length of the pattern sheet. For the width, just measure the height of the can.

2. Next, cut another piece of this paper to fit the circular, end section of the can.

3. Fasten these two paper sheets on a drawing board, or on any smooth-surfaced wood board, and then begin to work out in light pencil some suitable arrangement or scheme for the design which is later to be pierced all around the can.

4. In planning the character and type of these ornamental units, it is important that they be of simple form and located sufficiently apart from each other, to make it easy and practical to punch them through the metal. Simple motifs which can be used in repeat fashion all around the can will be found most appropriate for this purpose. You may use Mexican designs, Indian designs, or geometric shapes with equally good results. The choice of a particular motif, however, should be in harmony with the general plan of the room for which the tin can shades are planned.

5. After determining the decorative schemes for the piercing designs, for both the end and side sections of the cans, lay them out carefully on the pattern sheets with a pencil and ruler. Be sure the units are arranged neatly and evenly. For the side pattern it is a good idea to start by drawing guide lines with the ruler for each series of repeat units. For the top pattern, it will be necessary to use a pencil compass as a means of properly drawing these guide lines. Then, following the guide lines, draw in all of the decorative units as planned. The reader will get a good idea of how these repeat motifs are arranged and laid out by referring to the sketch of the completed tin can electric light shade in Fig. 1, Illustration 14.

6. After the patterns have been carefully and completely drawn up, place them on the can to make certain that all the units have been arranged properly and that the general effect of the decorative scheme employed is entirely satisfactory. If correct, the patterns are then ready for our next step in which the decorative units are traced to the can.

C. Tracing piercing designs from patterns to tin can

One way to use the prepared piercing patterns is simply to paste the patterns directly to the end and side sections of the can and then punch out the ornamental units, working right over and through the pattern sheets.

This direct method of using the patterns, however, is suggested only for experienced and skillful craftsmen. Furthermore, this method should be used only when the design motifs or units are of a bold, simple character, and not too close together.

Should the decorative scheme employed consist of many small punching units or of a combination of different shapes and sizes of punching units, such as employed in the decoration of our model, Fig. 1, Illustration 14, it is wise to trace the design units from the pattern sheets to the tin cans, instead of piercing directly over or through the pattern sheets.

The proper procedure for transferring the piercing decorations from the pattern sheets to the surfaces of the tin cans is as follows:

1. Cut a piece of carbon, to exactly the same size and shape as the end and side pattern sheets.

2. Paste these carbon sheets with their carbon sides facing downward in their proper places over the outside surfaces of the can. Use only a few spots of paste, sufficient to hold the carbon sheets in place during the tracing step. Be sure to stretch the sheet tightly to avoid formation of wrinkles.

3. Next, and again using only a few spots of the adhesive, paste the pattern sheets in their proper places over the carbon sheets, having the side with the design drawings on top. Here also stretch sheet taut, to prevent formation of wrinkles.

4. Using a sharply pointed pencil, or the pointed end of a leather modeling tool, trace over all the outlines of the decorative units in each pattern. To produce a clear carbon reproduction of the various designs on the surface of the can, you must press firmly on the pencil or modeling tool point throughout this tracing procedure. It is also a good plan to go over the lines twice to make sure that all the outlines will show up clearly and in a well defined form.

5. After tracing the end and side patterns of the can, remove both the carbon and pattern sheets, being careful not to smear the carbon outlines.

6. With an ice pick, a scratch awl, or any other type of sharply pointed metal instrument, scratch over the carboned outlines of the designs, now appearing on the top and side sections of the can. This scratching, scribing or engraving step, must be done slowly and carefully, again taking every precaution against smearing or blurring the outlines before they have been scratched into the surface of the can.

7. Using any scrap of cloth, rub off all carbon lines and/or smears from the surfaces of the can, permitting the scratched lines which now outline the decorative units to show up in clean, distinct form.

Our tin can electric shade is now ready for the punching or piercing of the decorative apertures outlined on the surfaces of the can. It is this tooling procedure which really transforms the discarded tin can into a thing of beauty and artistic charm.

D. Piercing the ornamental apertures on top and side of can

The tools and equipment used in this tin can punching or piercing procedure consist of two types of punching tools, a ball-peen style of metal working hammer, an old baseball bat, and any form of metal or woodworking vise.

One of the punching tools used is sharply pointed and tapered at its end, and is employed for punching the small round holes, such as used for the arrows in Fig. 1, Illustration 14. For this tool you may use any sharply pointed metal instrument, such as a large size, common wire flat head nail, or pointed punches prepared from broken twist drill or auger bits. The best punching tools of this pointed type, however, may be provided by sharply pointing the tip of an old nail set. You will find this nail set punching tool represented in Fig. 5, Illustration 14.

The other of the two punching tools needed for this tin can piercing procedure, has a tapered tip which is flat and sharp at the end, resembling the tip of a screw driver, though, of course, much more sharply ground. This tool is known as a "cold chisel" and is used to "chop or chisel out" the square, rectangular, or diamond shaped openings, which have straight edges, rather than round. The reader will find this tool represented in Fig. 4, Illustration 14. Both of these tools are made of strong steel and will retain their sharply pointed working tips for a long time. However, should the tools become somewhat dull after a considerable amount of punching work, their tips can easily be resharpened and put in good working condition again, first by touching up on the grindstone, and then by rubbing the tip over a carborundum stone or any form of whetting stone.

The hammer used in this punching operation should be a strong ball-peen grade of metal working hammer of the type seen at A, Fig. 2, Illustration 14. Be sure the ball-peen hammer you select for this purpose has a large pounding surface at the flat end of the head.

Should a metal or woodworking vise be unobtainable, the baseball bat used for the working foundation in this piercing operation may be fastened securely to the top of the working table or work bench by means of any type of large size clamp.

The method for punching out or piercing the decorative apertures or light openings on both the top and side sections of the tin can shades, is as follows:

1. Piercing round holes

a. Fasten an old, discarded baseball bat securely in a vise or to the top of the work table with a clamp, allowing about one third of the thick end of the bat to extend forward from the vise or table edge.

b. Place the can over the extending thick end of the bat in the manner shown at D, Fig. 2, Illustration 14.

c. Using the metal working hammer, shown at A, Fig. 2, and a pointed instrument, such as the nail set shown at Fig. 5, start punching or piercing all the round openings in the design, such as the arrows and other round hole units seen in Fig. 1, Illustration 14.

d. Be sure that each punch is made directly over the top part of the bat to assure a solid working foundation. As the punching operation continues, simply turn the can as needed, and keep working directly over the top part of the bat, until all the holes used in the ornamental scheme are completely punched. See Fig. 2, Illustration 14.

e. In this step it is necessary to use a lesser amount of punching force for the smaller holes, and a somewhat greater degree of force when piercing the larger holes. Where the holes are of the same size, as in the case of the arrows used in the decoration of the shade in Fig. 1, every effort should be made to punch the holes uniformly and with the same amount of punching force.

2. Piercing square, rectangular, or diamond shaped holes

Punching these larger, straight-edged, ornamental openings will require a little more skill and care than round hole punching. This is explained by the fact that four or more separate punches of the cold chisel are needed for each opening and that each cut must be made neatly and uniformly, if good results are to be obtained. Another important consideration in this step is to make certain that the cutting edge of the cold-chisel employed is sufficiently sharp and free from nicks. A cold-chisel with a 3/8 inch wide cutting edge is most satisfactory for the requirements of this work.

For satisfactory results in this straight-edged piercing operation, proceed as follows:

a. Keep baseball bat securely fastened in vise, or to the top of the work-table, just as in round hole piercing.

b. Place can over thick, protruding end of the bat and then with the cold-chisel in the left hand, and the ball-peen hammer in the right, start punching out the first square, rectangle, or diamond shape, as shown by the previously scratched in outlines on the outside surface of the can. Work directly over top section of the bat.

c. For each punch, in this piercing step, it is necessary to place the edge of the cold chisel exactly over the scratched outline of the design unit, and then, while pressing the cold chisel firmly downward on the surface of the can, strike the top of the cold chisel quickly with the hammer. Use just enough pounding force to cause the sharp cutting edge of the tool to penetrate through the metal.

d. Following this first cut, move cold-chisel ahead to the next side of the square, rectangle, or diamond shaped unit, and then repeat same cutting or piercing action as in the first cut. Proceed in the same manner until the decorative unit is completely cut loose, and falls out of place.

e. Continue by this same procedure until all the decorative units of this straight edged type are cut out. In Fig. 1, Illustration 14, you will find square shaped units on the side of the shade and diamond shaped units on the top of the shade, which are cut out in this manner.

3. For piercing the round and straight edged holes on top of the cans it is necessary to place the baseball bat in a vertical position in the vise, instead of the horizontal position used before. If no form of vise is available, you can clamp the bat to the leg of a table or a chair with the end of the bat protruding upward and work in that manner very conveniently. Then, proceed as follows:

a. Place open end of can over projecting end of the bat, and then using the hammer and the pointed punch, pierce all round holes appearing in the decoration of this part of the shade. As each hole is punched, move can so that the middle section of the end of the bat is located immediately below, thus providing a solid working foundation for each punching action. As in piercing the round holes in the side of the can, use a smaller amount of punching force for smaller size round holes, and a greater amount of force for larger size round holes.

b. After piercing all the round holes appearing in the decorative plan at the end of the can, cut out all straight edged units. For this step, use the hammer and cold-chisel, just as directed previously for cutting out straight edged units on the side of the shade.

For both round hole piercing and straight-edged piercing, on the side and end sections of the shades, it is important to follow the scratched outlines of the decorative units very carefully, in order to produce a neatly and uniformly tooled effect. Irregular or careless piercing work will detract considerably from the appearance of the completed electric light shade. This matter cannot be over emphasized since the shades are always in the public eye, in full view, and all tooling imperfections are easily discernible.

E. Filing the edges of the pierced decorations

As a general rule, the round holes, after they are pierced with the pointed punch, appear sufficiently smooth and finished at their cut edges. These round openings, therefore, require no further smoothing treatment.

Square, rectangular, and diamond shaped openings, however, made with the straight edged cold-chisel, often do require a little touching up or finishing. Should you find such additional smoothing treatment necessary, simply run a small, metalworking file over those edges or parts of edges of the cutout design units which appear jagged, rough or irregular. In this edge-smoothing step, use the file carefully to avoid denting or distorting the shape of the can.

After this filing procedure is completed, rub the filed edges with a piece of medium grade emery cloth. This will leave the edges perfectly smooth and free of all filing burrs.

F. Coloring and finishing the tin can electric light shades

Properly coloring and finishing these tin can electric light shades is really a matter of individual taste. In many cases, too, the choice of a particular finish for the shades will be influenced by the type or style of decoration used in the rest of the room or interior in which the shades are to be hung.

One good way to finish the shades, is simply to polish each over brightly both on its interior and exterior surfaces, using a medium grade of steel wool. Then, apply an overall coat of clear lacquer as a final finish. The lacquer will act as a form of protection, prevent the formation of rust, and preserve the brightly finished effect of the shades for a long period of time. Finished in this simple manner, the shades will be attractive in the day time as well as at night.

Another good finish, a little more ornamental than the plain, lacquered finish, may be obtained by using an appropriate color of enamel paint in various decorative treatments, on the outside parts of the shades. It can be used as an overall covering on the outside surfaces of the shade, or just in certain spots.

A good idea is to use a thin line of the selected color of the enamel paint around each circular or straight-edged opening. For this coloring procedure use a small, pointed style brush to make it possible to apply the thin lines of color around the units in a neat manner. Thus, each cut-out unit trimmed with a thin line of enamel paint contrasts effectively with the original bright metal finish of the bulk of the can.

When using the enamel paint as an overall finish on the outside surfaces of the shades, it is a good plan to apply a coat of clear lacquer on the inside of the can only, to protect that part from possible accumulation of rust. However, when using the enamel just as a form of trim around the decorative cutouts, it is advisable to apply the lacquer finish over both surfaces of the shades.

G. Method of suspending shades

The simplest way to use the tin can electric shades is as follows:

1. Using the pointed nail set punch and the ball-peen hammer, make a hole of about 1-1/4 inch diameter, in the center of the top of the shade. Work over the end of the baseball bat, just as explained earlier in the discussion of this project.

2. Holding shade with open end facing downward, insert top of electric light bulb through the 1-1/4 inch hole in the center of the top of the shade.

3. Screw the light bulb into the socket which is suspended from the ceiling, and allow the tin can shade to hang from the neck of the bulb. See Fig. 1, Illustration 14.

For a more secure method of suspending the tin can shades, attach four thin wires to the top of the shade, through small punched holes, knotting the ends of the wires firmly inside the can. Then fasten the other ends of the wires to the narrow neck of the electric light socket, above. See Fig. 1, Illustration 14.

The advantage of these wire hangers is that the shades remain suspended when the bulbs are removed or changed. The shade also hangs more securely when suspended from the wires than when it is held up by the light bulb alone.

RELATED TIN CAN PROJECTS

In which the tin can, in its entirety or original form, is used as the essential construction material.

Project No. 25, Tin Can Lanterns

See Figure 3-A, Illustration 14

This project is built in very much the same manner as the tin can electric light shade, shown in Fig 1, Illustration 14. It is also just as much fun to build and just as practical and attractive as regular lighting fixtures when completed.

The pierced decorations used in the construction of this lantern are produced in exactly the same fashion and with the same tools as the ornamental apertures used on the top and sides of the shade in Fig. 1, Illustration 14. Furthermore, the directions and methods required for coloring and finishing this lantern, are also identical with those employed for the tin can electric light project. The reader is accordingly referred to the text furnished under Project No. 24, for full particulars.

As you will note in Fig. 3-A, Illustration 14, the open end of the can in this lantern project, is located at the top, while the closed end is at the bottom. In the tin can shade project, however, as you will observe from Fig. 1, Illustration 14, the tin can is used in exactly the opposite manner, with the open end of the can located at the bottom, and the closed end at the top.

For the construction of these ornamental lanterns you may use discarded tin cans of either the pint or quart size, depending upon the size of the electric light bulbs which are to be employed inside the lanterns when they are completed. Another consideration in determining the proper size of cans to use in the building of these lanterns, is whether just one lantern is to be used, as a single lighting fixture, or whether several lanterns are to be employed as a group, in close proximity to each other. In the former case, it is best to use a large size can, with a suitably large size bulb to match, while in the latter case, the small size cans may be used to good advantage.

A distinctive feature of these tin can lanterns is their conically shaped hoods. See Fig. 3, A and B, Illustration 14. These hoods are made of scrap metal, obtained by cutting a tin can apart into sheet form. The upper part of the hood has an opening of about 1-1/2 inch diameter, or a little larger than the diameter size of the neck of the electric light socket which is inserted through it. The diameter of the lower part of the conical hood, must be made a little larger than the diameter of the can used, to provide the required overlapped form of construction shown in Fig. 3-A, Illustration 14.

To construct the lantern hood, first make a pattern in thin cardboard of the required shape of the hood and then fasten its ends together with paste or brass fasteners to produce the cone shape of the hood. When completed place the cardboard pattern over the can, to make certain that it fits right and looks well. If satisfactory, the cardboard pattern may then be used as the guide for the construction of the hood in the sheet tin. The ends of the metal hood may be fastened together with small size, tinner's rivets, or can be joined by soldering. See Fig. 3, B, Illustration 14.

To suspend the tin can lanterns properly, attach four thin wires to the top rim, at the open end of the can, then fasten the other ends of the wires to the electric cord just above the metal neck of the light socket. This will permit the conical hood to rest right over the top, open end of the can with the suspension wires acting as a form of support beneath. The hood may thus be left unattached, to be raised or lowered into position as required. Should it be necessary to change the bulb, after the lantern is in use, simply raise the loose, conical hood, lift up the socket and make the necessary change of bulbs. Then, lower the hood so that it just touches the top rim of the can.

By referring to the sketch of the finished tin can lantern, in Fig. 3-A, Illustration 14, you will note that this articular lantern model is equipped with ornamental light apertures on the side and bottom sections, as well as on its conical hood at the top. Constructed in this manner, and neatly painted with enamels or finished in a bright lacquer, these tin can electric light lanterns are most attractive, especially when used as lighting fixtures for a cottage or bungalow porch, for a camp social hall, and so forth.

Project No. 26, Tin Can Bank

See Figure 1, Illustration 15

This savings bank, designed in a military motif, has an especial appeal for little boys and girls and may inspire them to save their pennies, nickles and dimes.

This novel savings bank in the form of a drum is realistically fastened to the drummer boy, who, in turn, is suspended from the wall within easy reach of the young depositors of the household. The drummer boy is built of 1/4 inch three-plywood, although he can also be made of any kind of pressed composition board, or even

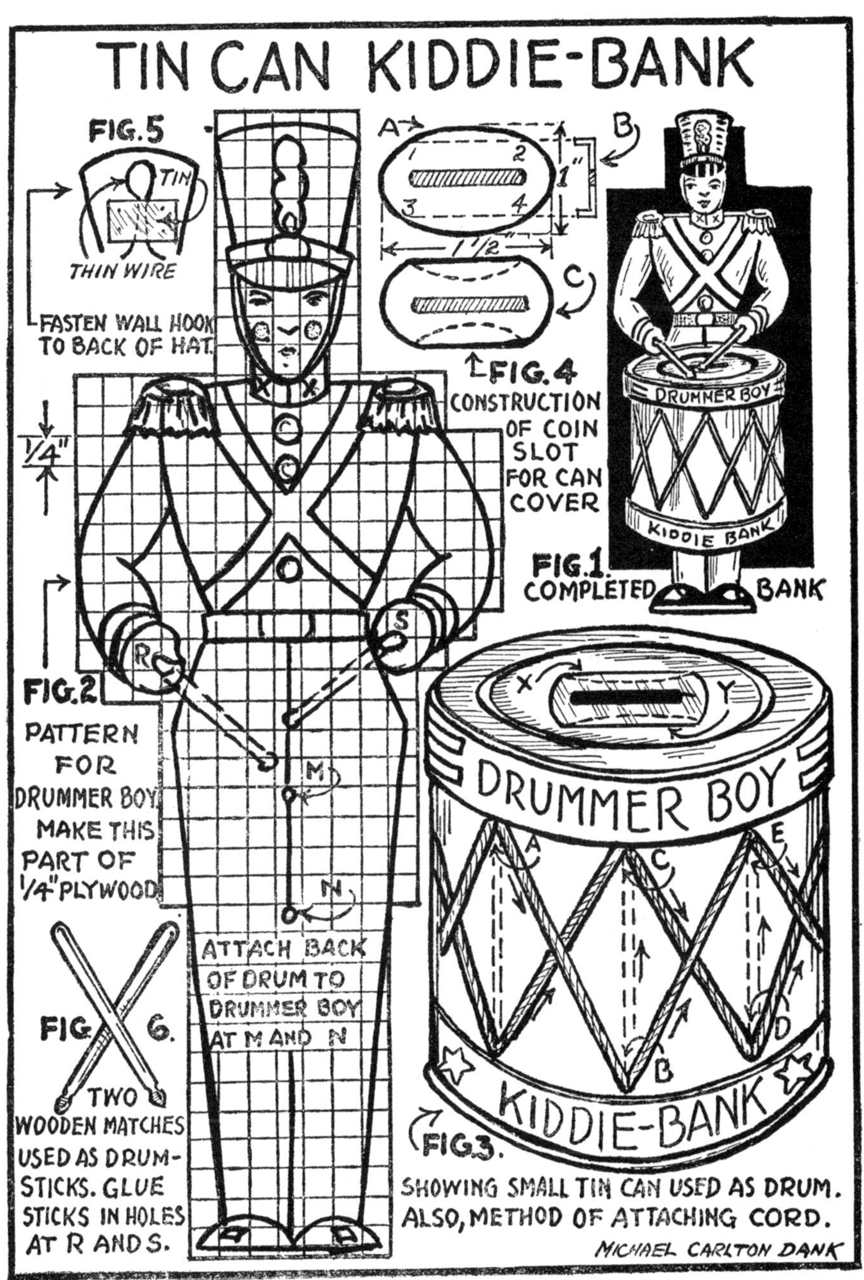
TIN CAN KIDDIE-BANK
FIG.5
TIN
THIN WIRE
FASTEN WALL HOOK TO BACK OF HAT.
A
B
1
2
3
4
1"
1 1/2"
C
FIG.4
CONSTRUCTION OF COIN SLOT FOR CAN COVER
DRUMMER BOY
KIDDIE BANK
FIG.1. COMPLETED BANK
1/4"
FIG.2
PATTERN FOR DRUMMER BOY. MAKE THIS PART OF 1/4" PLYWOOD
R
S
M
N
ATTACH BACK OF DRUM TO DRUMMER BOY AT M AND N
FIG 6.
TWO WOODEN MATCHES USED AS DRUM-STICKS. GLUE STICKS IN HOLES AT R AND S.
X
Y
DRUMMER BOY
A
C
E
B
D
KIDDIE-BANK
FIG.3.
SHOWING SMALL TIN CAN USED AS DRUM. ALSO, METHOD OF ATTACHING CORD.
MICHAEL CARLTON DANK

Illustration 15

scrap tin, with equally satisfactory results. In addition to providing a convenient, practical savings bank with which to teach children the virtue of thrift, it also serves as an attractive wall decoration for a nursery or playroom.

The directions for building this tin can bank, are as follows:

I. To Make the Drum

A. Procure any small size tin can which has a removable cover, with an overlapping rim, commonly furnished with such products as baking powder, peanuts, spices, and so forth. A good size for the tin can required is about 3 inches high by 3 inches in diameter. See Fig. 3, Illustration 15.

B. Clean and polish the can brightly, in the manner described under Project No. 24.

C. Using a pointed-tip punching tool, of the nail set variety, shown in Fig. 5, Illustration 14, or any similarly pointed, metal instrument, punch small holes, about 3/32 inch in diameter at points A, B, C, D, E, F, etc. all around the can. Space the holes 1 inch apart, and have the holes at the top exactly opposite or over the holes at the bottom, just as shown in Fig. 3, Illustration 15. Punch the holes over the thick end of a baseball bat, securely fastened in a vise, in the manner described under Project No. 24.

D. Next make the coin slot part of the bank, by cutting a piece of tin to the shape of an ellipse, size 1 inch wide, by 1-1/2 inches long, just as represented in Fig. 4, Illustration 15.

E. Using a cold-chisel, of the type shown in Fig. 4, Illustration 14, and working over any form of thick, scrap board as a foundation, punch out a narrow slit in the center of this coin slot piece, about 1/8 inch wide by 1 inch long. See shaded area in Fig. 4-A.

F. Using a file and a piece of emery cloth, rub outside edges and slit edges of coin slot metal part until smooth and uniform all over.

G. Bend coin slot piece on lines 1 to 2, and 3 to 4, indicated in Fig. 4-A, working over the edge of a hard wood block. The flaps should be about 1/8 inch wide and should be folded down at right angles to the top of the coin slot piece, as at Fig. 4-B.

H. With a cold-chisel of the type seen in Fig. 4, Illustration 14, punch two narrow slits, 3/4 inches apart and 1 inch long, in central part of the cover of the can. Work over the thick end of a baseball bat fastened in a vise in a vertical position.

I. Through these slits in the cover of the can, insert the two folded flaps of the coin slot piece, and then bend the flaps back underneath, as shown at Fig. 4-C. The coin slot will now be fastened securely to the can cover, as at X and Y, Fig. 3.

J. To color the can, use bright shades of enamel paints. A color scheme of red, white, and blue, is suggested as most appropriate for this purpose. First apply the overall colors, using a small size, flat type brush. Then, after the overall coat is dry, apply the lettering and the stars and stripes as shown in Fig. 3, Illustration 15. For this detailed work, use a small size, pointed style brush.

K. After all painting is complete and dry push a white cord or tape or ribbon through the punched holes at A, B, C, D, and so forth. You will have no difficulty in this lacing step, if you carefully follow the diagrammatical explanation of this procedure, as indicated in Fig. 3, Illustration 15. Start by knotting an end of the cord inside of the drum at any one of the top series of holes, as at A. Then, run the cord over the outside of the drum to B. Next run end of cord inside of can, straight up to C. From this point, proceed ahead toward the right following the arrows and working in the same manner as the first lacing stitch, just described. After completing this left to right lacing step all around the drum, repeat the same procedure, working this time from right to left. The result of this two-way lacing operation will be the same as that in Fig. 3. Be sure the cord is pulled taut as each stitch is made. Also remember to locate all beginning and finishing knots on the inside of the can.

II. To Make the Drummer Boy

A. Make a pattern on a piece of drawing or wrapping paper of the drummer boy shown at Fig. 2, Illustration 15. To do this correctly and to obtain the right size required for the construction of this project, draw the same number and arrangement of squares, as represented in Fig. 2, but use 1/4 inch squares instead of the reduced size squares employed in Fig. 2.

B. After completing the grill of squares in this manner, make a careful copy of the drummer boy figure, putting in all outlines and details, exactly as in Fig. 2.

C. Using carbon paper and a sharply pointed pencil, trace drummer boy pattern carefully to a scrap piece of three-ply wood, of sufficient size. Make sure, in tracing, that the grain of the wood runs in the same direction as the length or height of the drummer. See directions for proper tracing methods under Project No. 1, Section IV-D.

D. With a coping saw, cut out the drummer boy figure carefully, making certain that all outside sawing outlines are followed as represented. You will know which lines to follow when you saw out the drummer boy by referring to the sketch of the completed drummer boy bank, in Fig. 1, Illustration 15. For full details governing the use of the coping saw, see text under Project I, Section IV-E.

E. After drummer boy is cut out, drill drum-stick holes through hands at R and S, Fig. 2, Illustration 15. The holes should be about 1/8 inch in diameter. Following this, rub all sawed edges of the cut out drummer boy with medium grade sandpaper, until smooth and neatly finished.

F. Color drummer boy with enamel or tempera paints, using red, white, and blue for his uniform, and pink or flesh color for the face and hands. Yellow is a good color to use for the buttons and epaulets, while black may be used for the shoes, hat visor, and facial features. It is a good idea to paint in the extra small details, such as the facial features, epaulet lines, buttons, and so forth with black india ink, using for this purpose, an ordinary writing pen. If enamel paints are employed, no subsequent finishing coat is required. However, if tempera colors are employed, it will be necessary to apply an overall coat of clear, white shellac to provide a bright protective finish.

III. To Attach Tin Can to Drummer Boy

A. Bore two holes of about 1/16 inch in diameter through the drummer boy figure at points M and N, indicated in Fig. 2.

B. Then, bore two holes, the same distance apart as M-N, through the back of the drum. The top hole should be located about 1/4 inch below the cover of the can to make it possible to remove the cover easily as needed, without having to disconnect the drum from the drummer boy.

C. Fasten two lengths of milk bottle wire, braided together, through points M and N in the drummer boy, then connect drummer boy figure to drum by fastening the ends of the wire through the holes previously punched at back section of drum. Twist the ends of the wire securely inside of the drum to produce a strong joint of the two connected units. The top of the drum will now be located a little below the drummer boy's belt in the way that real drummers hold their drums.

IV. To Complete the Bank and to Hang It on the Wall

A. Fashion two drumsticks from wooden matches as in Fig. 6, Illustration 15. Sandpaper the match sticks until smooth and clean, then insert them in the holes previously drilled through the hands, fastening them securely in place with liquid glue.

B. Be sure the drum sticks extend forward in an inward direction or toward each other, just as they are held when really in use. See dotted indication for position of drumsticks in Fig. 2, Illustration 15.

C. To hang the savings bank properly on the wall, make a loop of milk bottle wire, using two lengths of the wire braided together and fasten this loop-hanger to the back of the drummer-boy's hat. This can easily be done by nailing a small piece of tin over the ends of the wire loop, using four 1/4 inch brass escutcheon pins or two screws of the same size. See Fig. 5, Illustration 15. A small piece of leather may be used in place of the tin, if desired, in which case glue, in addition to the nails or screws, may be used as a fastening aid.

Project No. 27, Drinking Mug

See Figure 1, Illustration 16

This tin can drinking mug is not only attractive, but practical as well. It is especially useful on scouting, camping, or picnicking trips.

The mug is made of a pint size tin can, of the variety known as "gilt-lined" or "keglined" cans because of their brass-colored lining. This "gilt-lined" finish on the inside of the can is a certain kind of lacquer which prevents rust and makes the mug sanitary for drinking purposes. Beer and fruit juice cans are commonly manufactured with this protective inside finish.

The handle, which is attached to one side of the mug, is made of a scrap piece of tin, and has a folded flap at each edge for added strength and attractiveness. It also provides protection against possible injury to fingers when cup is used.

After formed into the shape seen in Fig. 1, Illustration 16, the handle is firmly attached to the can by means of strong white cord, such as used for spinning tops, or for the baskets used in basketball. The cord is wound around the can six to eight times in a close, tight manner, at the top and bottom of the can. This permits the bright metal surface of the can to show at the center.

Before each ring of cord is applied around the can, liquid glue is first brushed on the can where the cord is to be located. After winding on all the rings in this manner, and after the glue has thoroughly set and dried, the handle will be attached very securely. The cord windings applied in this fashion add considerably to the appearance of the mug.

The uncovered, original metal surface of the mug, between the two cord-wound sections, is neatly decorated with an appropriate design colored with enamel paints. The brightly colored floral design used in our model, in Fig. 1, is very effective in contrast with the plain polished surface of the can. A coat of clear lacquer is applied over all outside surfaces of the mug, as well as over the handle, as a bright protective finish. The lacquer also serves to reinforce and tighten the cord windings around the upper and lower sections of the can, thus causing the handle to be held even more solidly in place.

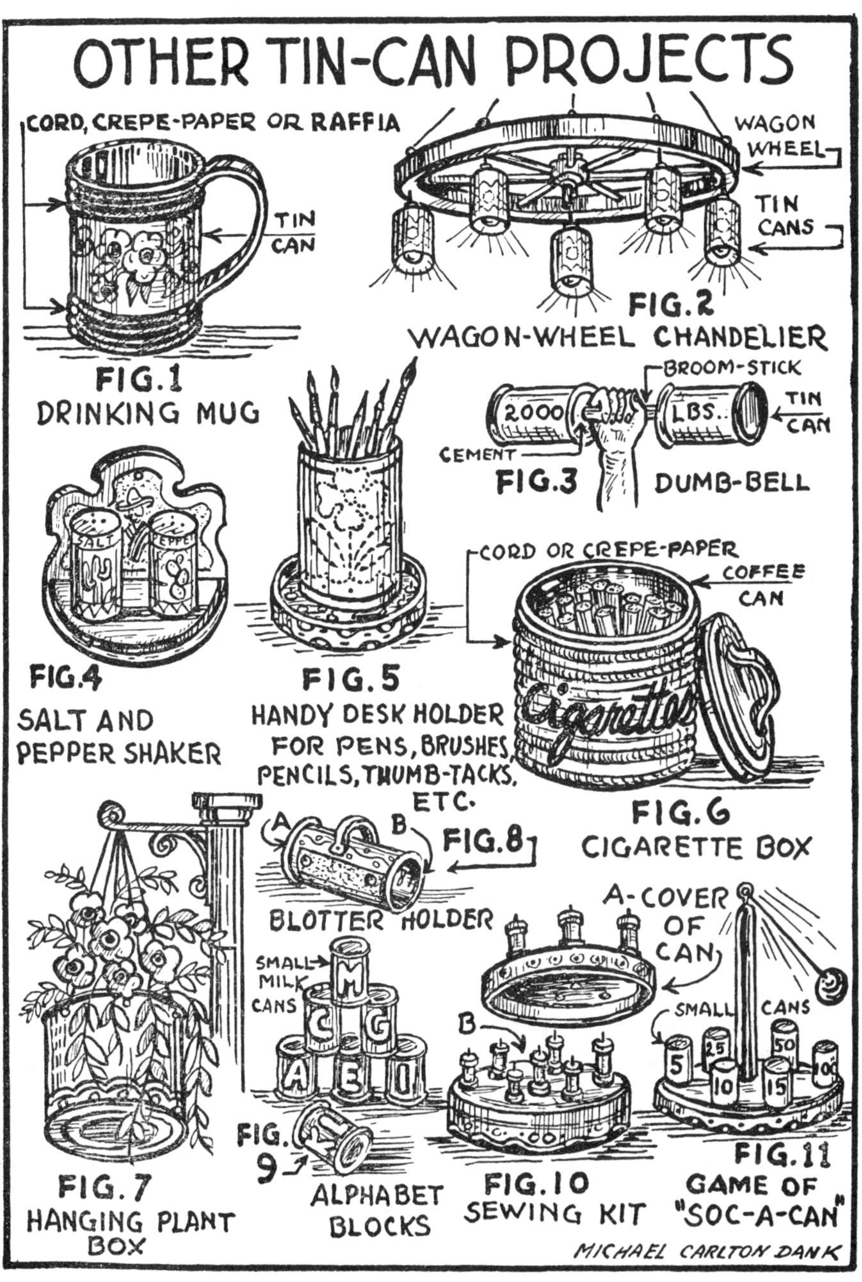
OTHER TIN-CAN PROJECTS
CORD, CREPE-PAPER OR RAFFIA
TIN CAN
FIG. 1
DRINKING MUG
WAGON WHEEL
TIN CANS
FIG. 2
WAGON-WHEEL CHANDELIER
BROOM-STICK
2000
LBS.
TIN CAN
CEMENT
FIG. 3
DUMB-BELL
SALT
PEPPER
FIG. 4
SALT AND PEPPER SHAKER
FIG. 5
HANDY DESK HOLDER FOR PENS, BRUSHES, PENCILS, THUMB-TACKS, ETC.
CORD OR CREPE-PAPER
COFFEE CAN
Cigarettes
FIG. 6
CIGARETTE BOX
A
B
FIG. 8
BLOTTER HOLDER
SMALL MILK CANS
M
C
G
A
E
I
FIG. 9
ALPHABET BLOCKS
A-COVER OF CAN
B
SMALL CANS
5
25
50
10
15
100
FIG. 7
HANGING PLANT BOX
FIG. 10
SEWING KIT
FIG. 11
GAME OF "SOC-A-CAN"
MICHAEL CARLTON DANK

Illustration 16

Instead of using enamel paint as a means of decorating the exposed, middle section of the outside of the can, such other decorative treatments may be employed as finger-painting the metal surface, tapping a suitable design around the can with a pointed nail or other metal instrument, or combining the tapping treatment with the use of enamel paints.

The bottom of the can, on the outside, may simply be finished with a coat of clear lacquer, or may first be given a coat of a suitable color of enamel and then lacquered.

When not in use, this home-made drinking mug can be displayed on a wall shelf, mantel, or book-case.

Project No. 28, Wagon-Wheel Chandelier

See Figure 2, Illustration 16

This project represents a novel and effective application of the tin can electric light shade, shown in Fig. 1, Illustration 14, and described in the text under Project No. 24.

The author had the pleasure, one summer, of supervising the construction of this unusual rustic chandelier for use in the lodge hall of a boys' summer camp.

The construction of this novel chandelier is very simple. The first step is cleaning and reconditioning a wagon-wheel, to rid it of accummulated dirt. This is easily accomplished by first polishing the metal rim of the wheel with emery cloth and steel wool. Then scrub and sandpaper the wooden spokes, hub and the round wooden frame of the wheel and finish with two appropriate colors of enamel paint.

Now fasten five strong screw eyes to the top part of the wagon wheel rim, in equidistant fashion. Strips of strong wire are then attached to these screw eyes, fastening the other ends of the wire strips securely to the ceiling, about two feet above the suspended wheel. The wires extend upward in an inward direction and are connected to the ceiling at the center where the light outlet is located. An electric wire is then extended from the central outlet along each of the diverging suspension wires. The ends of the electric wires are subsequently inserted through holes drilled in the wagon wheel rim and connected to the light sockets located just below the rim. The bulbs and tin can shades are then added to complete the chandelier.

Project No. 29, Tin Can Dumb-Bells

See Figure 3, Illustration 16

These dumb-bells, made in sets of two, provide adults as well as husky youngsters with an opportunity for developing their muscles.

A. To construct the tin can dumb-bells

All that you will need for a set of two, are two 12 inch lengths of an iron pipe or a broom stick handle, four pint size empty tin cans, and some hard setting plaster or cement.

After gathering these materials together, mix sufficient quantity of the cement or plaster, using for this purpose any available pail or basin. Employ proper amounts of the material and other required ingredients in accordance with the directions on the package or container. When plaster or plaster of Paris is used, add one part of the plaster to two parts of water, then stir thoroughly. If cement is used, add sand and water, using proper proportions of the materials as directed on package. Mix enough of the plaster or cement to fill completely each two or four of the cans.

After the cement or plaster is properly prepared, fill the tin cans with the mixture. Then, while the plastic material is still sufficiently soft, insert one end of the iron pipe or broom stick handle, into the exact center of each can, allowing at least 4 inches of each end of the rod to be inside of each can, and about 4 inches of its central part to remain outside to provide the handle of the dumb-bell. Make sure that the tin cans and handles are in perfect alignment with each other, and allow the cement or plaster to set until dry and solid.

B. To finish the dumb-bells

First brighten the cans with fine steel wool and then coat the cans and the handle with either black or gray enamel paint. A second coat of enamel will produce an even better finish. Neatly letter the left section of the dumb-bell to read "2000" and the right section "LBS.", as in Fig. 3, Illustration 16. This will provoke much merriment. The dumb-bells will, however, weigh enough to tax your muscles and to give you and your friends plenty of healthful exercise.

Project No. 30, Salt and Pepper Shakers

See Figure 4, Illustration 16

For this set of salt and pepper shakers you will need two empty small tin cans of the same size and shape. Good types of cans for this purpose are baking cans, peanut, hard candy, and spice cans.

The spice cans such as those in which cinnamon and paprika are ordinarily packed already come equipped with little holes at the top, and are therefore especially appropriate for this purpose. When using cans with covers, but without holes punched at the top, you will find it a very easy matter to punch about five little holes in the center of the cover, using any pointed metal instrument. A good tool to use for this is the nail set punch shown in Fig. 5, Illustration 14.

When punching the holes, use a small block of wood as a foundation to assure a neat job. Also be certain to locate the holes uniformly, placing one hole at the center and four holes in equidistant fashion, about 3/8 inch in from the circumference of the can cover.

To decorate the cans for use as pepper and salt shakers, first apply an overall coat of enamel paint, in some color which will harmonize with the general color scheme of the kitchen or breakfast-room in which the shakers are to be used. After this overall coat has thoroughly dried, paint some appropriate design with contrasting colors of enamel paints. Mexican designs, floral subjects, simple animals and figures, and sail boats may be employed.

The model in Fig. 4, Illustration 16, employs two different Mexican designs, repeated two or three times around the sides of the cans. Of course, the particular subjects used for these decorations, like the enamel colors employed, must conform to the general decorative scheme of the kitchen or breakfast-room. On the top rim of one of the cans, it is a good idea to letter the word "salt" and on the other can, the word "pepper" as in Fig. 4. For painting the designs, borders and lettering, use a small size pointed type brush. For applying the overall enamel coats, however, it is best to use a small size flat type brush.

These tin can salt and pepper shakers may, of course, be used independently of any rack or stand, by merely placing them, when not in use, on the kitchen refrigerator or in the china closet.

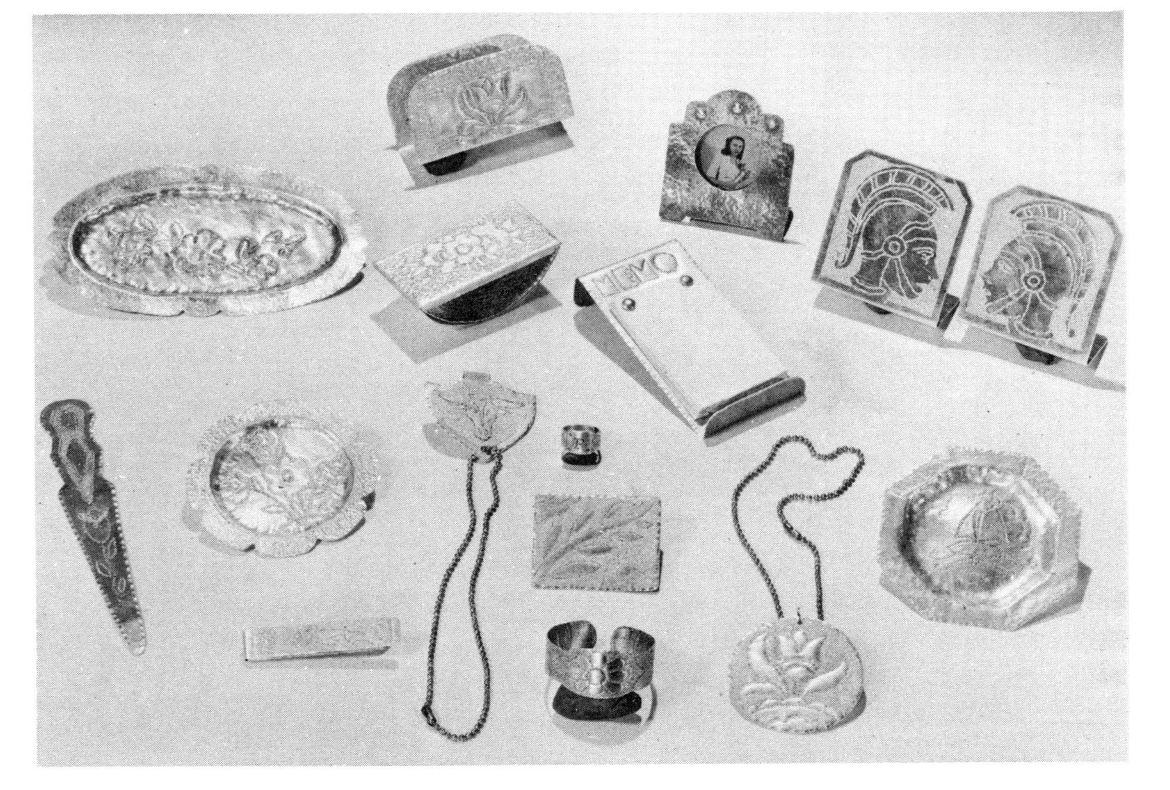

Plate 4. This illustration indicates the wide variety of attractive jewelry and gift items that can be made from scrap tin or aluminum.

Plate 5. Scrap aluminum, copper, brass or nickel silver can be made into ornamental bracelets and pins.

However, should you wish to build a little stand for the shakers you can get a good idea for one from our sketch in Fig. 4, Illustration 16.

The stand shown in the sketch may be made of any scrap plywood simply by cutting out the parts with a coping saw. You will find complete details for woodwork construction of this type in the text given earlier in this book, under Project No. 1. The rack illustrated in Fig. 4 is built of three separate parts, consisting of one back part and two base parts. The upper part of the base has two holes cut out, the same size as the diameter of the shakers, to hold the shakers neatly in place. This upper part is also slightly smaller in size, to produce a nicely finished, beveled effect around the front, circular edge of the stand.

When constructing the stand, be sure to sandpaper all edges and surfaces thoroughly before applying the paints. Use liquid glue and small wire brads for joining the parts together. For coloring the stand, use the same paint medium in harmonizing colors employed for the tin can shakers. Note that the back section of the stand in Fig. 4 is decorated in the same Mexican motif used for the decoration of the shakers. A small hole is drilled at the top of the back of the stand so that it can hang on the wall when not in use.

Project No. 31, Desk Holder

See Figure 5, Illustration 16

This project is very easy to make, requiring as material any empty pint-size tin can for its upper or vertical section and a rimmed cover of a larger size can for its base part. The can is securely soldered to the central part of the inside surface of the cover section, providing a neatly assembled single unit of the two tin can parts.

The decoration on the vertical section of the desk holder may be painted with carefully selected enamel colors or may be tapped or stippled with a wooden mallet and a pointed metal tapping tool. A good tapping tool for this purpose is the nail set punching tool shown in Fig. 5, Illustration 14. For this project, however, this tool is to be used as a denting tool rather than as a punch for piercing holes entirely through the metal. You will find detailed directions for this procedure in the text provided under Project No. 38. For tapping designs on the outside surface of a tin can it is best to tap the outlines only, using a closely applied, uniform arrangement of the dents throughout the work. Just as in Project No. 24, it is best to work over the thick end of a base ball bat fastened to a vise.

When planning the decoration for this project, it is essential to use the same types of design for the tray section at the bottom as for the vertical section. Thus, if the vertical container is decorated by the tapping method, the same form of treatment must be used for the tray section. The tray may be decorated around the outside of its rim section, as shown in the sketch, in Fig. 5, Illustration 16.

Another good idea in the decoration of this desk holder is to tap or dent the outlines of the decorations used, and then to apply enamel paints, in appropriate colors just inside the dented outlines. In this decorative procedure, it is best to leave the bulk or remaining metal surfaces of the tin can holder in the original bright metal finish, thus producing an attractive contrasting effect. It is wise to apply a thin coat of clear lacquer over the entire holder as a finish.

This desk holder serves as a convenient container for such frequently used articles as pens, pencils, brushes, rulers, and so forth.

Project No. 32, Cigarette Box

See Figure 6, Illustration 16

All you need to build this cigarette box is a discarded coffee can, a small tube of cement or glue, a small piece of scrap sheet tin, and some crepe-paper, cord or raffia.

A coffee can is suggested for this purpose because it has a removable cover and is of the proper shape and size. After the selected can is thoroughly cleaned, rings of cord, raffia, or twisted crepe-paper are wound around its entire outside surface. The rings are applied in a tight, close formation, just as in the construction of the Drinking Mug, shown in Fig. 1, Illustration 16.

Before each ring of the material is wound around the can, a little liquid glue is applied to the surface of the can to hold the ring securely in place. This same procedure is followed until the entire outside surface of the can is covered with the rings. It is a good idea to employ different colors of the material used to produce a more interesting decorative effect. This method of applying the rings is shown in our sketch of the cigarette box in Fig. 6. When applying the rings around the can, commence at the bottom and work upward. Remember to allow enough uncovered space at the top of the can to accommodate the rim of the cover.

As a final finish for this home-made cigarette box, apply a coat of clear varnish or white shellac over all inside and outside surfaces. This overall finish will not only add lustre to the general appearance of the completed article, but will also harden and secure the ornamental cord windings previously glued over its surfaces.

A convenient handle may be made for the cover by first forming a strip of sheet tin in the manner represented in Fig. 6. The metal strip should be about 1-1/4″ wide and should have 1/4″ flaps folded under at each edge to make it sturdy. After forming the handle to shape, wind the cord, raffia, or crepe paper used to decorate the rest of the cigarette box, all around the entire surface of the handle. Then fasten the handle in place by working the rings over it at the same time the rings are applied to the top surface of the cover.

By way of a final, practical suggestion, it is important that the cover of the cigarette box always be clamped tightly in place at the top of the container, and be removed only when cigarettes are to be taken out or put into the box.

Project No. 33, Hanging Plant Box

See Figure 7, Illustration 16

For this useful project you may employ almost any size or shape of can, provided it is not too shallow for the purpose here planned. The type of can used for our model in Fig. 7 is a quart size fruit juice can. The selection of the can should, of course, be determined by the type of hanging basket desired, and the nature of the place where it is to be hung.

To construct this tin can plant box, first punch four small holes in equidistant fashion around the top of the can, about 1/2 inch below the rim. Follow this step by polishing the entire outside surfaces of the can with medium grade steel wool.

As the next procedure, apply a suitable color of enamel paint over all exterior parts of the can, and allow it to dry thoroughly. Good colors are red, green, blue and yellow. With an appropriate contrasting color of enamel, add a few carefully chosen decorations. After the enamel paint has thoroughly dried, apply a coat of spar varnish over the entire outside and inside surfaces of the can and allow sufficient time for the varnish to dry completely.

In this form, our plant box is ready for the addition of the suspension wires which are the means of hanging the plant box securely on the front or back porch, in some suitable spot in the garden or perhaps inside the home, in front of a large window, where the sun always shines in. For these suspension wires you will need two strips of strong wire, the proper length of which must be determined by the place where the plant box is to be hung. Two strips, each measuring about 36 inches is a good average length for these wires. Fasten one end of the wire securely in one of the four previously punched holes, and then attach the other end of the wire to the hole opposite it. Repeat this step with the other strip of wire, using the other two punched holes.

The plant box may now be filled with earth and put to use.

After planting the seeds or flowers, hang the box neatly and securely in its designated place. A few strong screw-eyes fastened in place at the top is one simple way to support the suspension wires which are attached to the upper rim of the plant box. Another practical arrangement for hanging up the plant box is suggested by our sketch of this project, in Fig. 7. In this latter method of suspension, a neatly fashioned, band-iron bracket is employed which is equipped with a loop at its end, through which the plant box wires may easily be inserted. This bracket also permits the plant box to sway gracefully in the wind.

Project No. 34, Blotter Holder

See Figure 8, Illustration 16

For the construction of this simply built blotter holder you will need a small size can of the variety commonly furnished with soups, cooked vegetables and so forth.

The first step in the construction of the blotter holder is that of carefully removing both ends of the can with any good standard can opener. After the ends are cut away, finish off all cut edges with a piece of medium grade emery cloth to make certain that they are perfectly smooth and free from any jagged points or other such imperfections.

The next step is drilling six holes, all of 1/8 inch diameter. Two of the holes must be drilled at the upper section of the can for the attachment of the handle. Then, two holes are to be drilled at each side of the circular surface of the can for fastening on the blotter sheet. You will get a good idea for the proper location of these holes, by referring to our sketch of this tin can blotter holder in Fig. 8, Illustration 16. To drill the holes, first punch tiny or starting holes with any sharply pointed, metal instrument. Then working through these starting holes, use a hand-drill equipped with a proper size drill, to produce the 1/8 inch size holes here required. For this drilling procedure, it is a good idea to use the thick end of an old baseball bat as a foundation, clamping the bat securely in a vise.

After punching all the holes, tap a few simple appropriate designs around the upper section of the can like those represented in our sketch of this project. For this design tapping step, work over the thick end of a baseball bat or some similar hardwood foundation.

Our next step is to prepare the handle using a scrap piece of tin of the same color and texture as the can employed for the main part of the holder. This handle like that built for the Drinking Mug, represented in Fig. 1, Illustration 16, has a 1/4 inch flap folded under at each edge for extra strength and finished appearance. For attaching the handle to the holder it is necessary to drill a hole at each end of the handle, of the same size as those previously punched at the upper section of the can. After preparing the handle in this manner, attach it to the circular section of the holder. This may easily be accomplished by using small size, tinner's rivets, and fastening them in place with the round end of the head of a ball-peen hammer. In this riveting step, as in the drilling procedures, it is also best to use the thick end of a baseball bat as a working foundation.

Following the proper attachment of the handle, polish all metal surfaces of the blotter holder with medium grade steel wool. You may then proceed to add a few spots of color within the tapped design sections, using appropriate colors of enamel paints, and a small size, pointed style brush. If you prefer, however, you may rely entirely upon a bright original metal finish for the decorative effect. With either treatment, add an overall coat of clear lacquer to produce a permanent, bright finish for this practical little desk piece.

To complete the holder attach a suitably colored blotter, using a brass fastener through each of the four previously drilled holes. Keep the heads of the fasteners on the outside, and the ends on the inside. By means of this simple, practical arrangement, when the old blotter is used up, a new one can easily be substituted for it. For best results, however, use two blotters at once, placing one over the other.

Project No. 35, Tin Can Alphabet Blocks

See Figure 9, Illustration 16

These tin can alphabet blocks require very little time or work in their preparation, and afford small children many hours of healthful play. Not only can they roll these blocks freely in all directions, but they can also use them for building houses, bridges, castles, and other such constructions.

To make these alphabet blocks, thirteen small size condensed milk or evaporated milk cans, all of exactly the same size and shape, are needed. This particular type of can is suggested because once emptied of its contents, both ends of the can are still intact, with only two little holes punched through the top. Thirteen cans are necessary for this project because two letters of the alphabet are painted on each can. See Fig. 9, Illustration 16.

After collecting the required number of cans, give them all a thorough washing and scrubbing, both inside and outside, using hot water and soap. Later, wipe the cans until they are completely dry, and follow this by rubbing their outside surfaces with medium grade steel wool. As a final preliminary step, solder up the two small holes at the top of each can. For this use any good grade of already prepared liquid solder. Simply fill up the holes, allow the solder to dry solidly, and finally clean the surface with steel wool. Another method is to use a regular soldering copper, together with flux and bits of soft solder.

All that is needed to complete the blocks is to paint them in bright colors and apply the alphabet letters. For most effective results, first brush an overall coat of any good grade enamel paint over each can. Use a different color of enamel for each of the blocks, employing such bright hues as red, yellow, green and blue. Allow these overall coatings of enamel to dry overnight. The following day, apply the alphabet letters to the blocks, placing two letters on each, one at the front and one at the back, using contrasting colors. For this painting step use a small size, pointed type brush. Make the letters neatly in a solid block form, something like the letters used in our sketch of this project, in Fig. 9. Another good idea is to paint the top and bottom ends of the cans with colors which are complementary to the color used on the circular sides of the cans. Then paint the ends with a second coat of orange. If green is used for the sides, paint the ends with red, and so forth.

Finally apply a coat of bright spar varnish over all surfaces of the blocks. This varnish coating, which must be allowed to dry thoroughly will not only provide a strong protective finish for the completed blocks but will also add smoothness and lustre to their surfaces.

Project No. 36, Sewing Kit

See Figure 10, Illustration 16

For the construction of this serviceable sewing kit use any large size, circular-shaped tin can, equipped with an overlapping cover. Cans of this type are commonly furnished with better makes of candies.

The cover of the can provides a handy arrangement for holding different size spools. The bottom section serves as a container for needles, thimbles, buttons, pins and other sewing necessities.

As supports or posts for the spools of thread on the top of the cover of the kit, common-wire, flat-head nails of about 2 inches length are employed. The nails are solidly soldered in place through drilled holes, with the heads of the nails located on the inside surface of the cover. See Fig. 10-A, Illustration 16.

To insert and firmly fasten the nails into position, first punch tiny holes through the cover of the can, using any sharply pointed instrument, and working over any thick block of wood as a base. Locate one hole in the center of the cover, and six holes, equidistantly spaced around the cover, about 1 inch from its edge. See Fig. 10-B, Illustration 16. Then, using a hand-drill, fitted with a 1/8 inch drill point, bore through the tiny, punched holes, again using the wood block as a working foundation. The flat head nails may then be inserted through the drilled holes from the underside of the cover and soldered tightly into position. Make certain the nails are inserted and fastened into place in a perfectly straight, upright manner. Use any standard form of soldering copper, following the suggestions for general soldering work given in Chapter Four.

To complete the sewing kit, color all outside sections of the circular can with enamel paints. First apply an overall coat of enamel on all outside sections of the container, including the bottom.

When this initial coat has thoroughly dried, add a few designs using enamel colors which will effectively contrast with the overall coat. At the same time, color the shafts of the flat-head nails which extend upward from the cover of the can.

When completely dry, this novel kit may be equipped with a full supply of sewing materials.

Project No. 37, Soc-A-Can Ball Game

See Figure 11, Illustration 16

As you can readily understand by referring to our sketch in Fig. 11, "SOC-A-CAN" is an appropriate name for this toy.

All you need to do is to whirl the rubber ball in a circular direction, and when the tension on the cord slackens, the ball gradually lowers and socks which ever cans stand in its path, throwing them "head-over-heel" off the ball "field." The player who succeeds in throwing off the greatest total of points in accordance with the numbers indicated on the six small cans, previously placed into position on the field, wins the game of SOC-A-CAN.

To build this toy you will need the cover of a large size circular tin can of the common candy can variety, similar to that used for the sewing kit, shown in Fig. 10. You will also require six, small size baby food cans, a 12 inch length of discarded broom stick handle, a piece of strong string, and an old rubber ball or golf ball.

The directions for building this game of SOC-A-CAN are as follows:

Cut a 12 inch length from an old broom stick handle. Then, round off the top end of the stick neatly and make certain that the lower end is perfectly flat and square. Sandpaper the stick until it is smooth and clean and insert a good size screw eye into its top, rounded end, as seen in Fig. 11.

Drill a small hole in the center of the cover of a large size circular shaped tin can. Then fasten the prepared broom stick pole securely to the top of the can cover, using a proper size screw, driven into the lower end of the pole, from the inside surface of the cover.

With gay, harmonizing colors of enamel paints, color the pole and all surfaces of the tin can cover and set it aside to dry. Later, using black enamel, paint six 2 inch diameter circles on the top of the can cover, to indicate where the numbered "pins", (small cans) are to be located. See Fig. 11 for proper arrangement of the pins and the black circles.

Procure six small size baby food cans all exactly the same, clean them thoroughly and rub them wth medium grade steel wool. Following this, paint each of the cans with a different gay color of enamel paint. When dry, letter one of the cans with the number "5", another "10", etc. as shown in the sketch in Fig. 11.

As a final step, attach one end of a strong string, about 12 inches long to the screw eye located at the top of the pole. To the other end of the string, fasten an old golf ball or small rubber ball. A ball made of paper and glue (in papier-mâché fashion), will also serve satisfactorily for this purpose.

Prepared in accordance with the directions above, the game of SOC-A-CAN is now completed and ready for use. To play the game properly, set the differently numbered cans on the black circles around the "field", with the numbers on the cans facing outward and with the open ends of the cans located at the bottom. Then, whirl the ball around with a quick, fast motion, and suddenly let it go. The ball will soon slacken in its pace, will gradually lower itself, and then, SOCCO! some of the cans will be struck down and thrown from the field. Others, of course, may remain on the field, just as in bowling, depending upon the skill of each player. The player who totals the largest score after an establishd number of times "up" wins the game.

SHEET METAL SCRAP

In the proceding section we have treated in detail the wealth of projects which can be made from all shapes and sizes of tin cans in their original form.

In this discussion of metalcraft, we are going to treat the possibilities of the tin can as a source of sheet metal. In this manner, the vast and always available supply of tin cans may be utilized for the construction of a considerably larger scope of projects.

Thus, simply by cutting oil cans, soup cans, candy cans, and numerous other types into flat sheets, we have at our command an unlimited supply of valuable sheet metal of assorted shapes, sizes, and gauges. The possibilities for constructing toys, games and novelties out of sheet tin are really unlimited.

After you have built a number of simple projects in sheet tin, you will be ready to try your hand at more elaborate projects, employing more expensive sheet metals as construction materials. For the simple tooling procedures presented below may be applied equally well to such sheet metals as copper, pewter, nickel or silver.

As our key project, we have selected the hot-pot-stand, shown in Fig. 1, Illustration 17. After you become familiar with the working procedures required for its construction you will find it easy to apply the same methods to the creation of many other equally useful projects, several of which are later described in this scrap craft unit.

Project No. 38, Hot-Pot Stand

See Figure 1, Illustration 17

I. Description

We have selected this particular article as our representative project in sheet metal construction work, because it incorporates many basic tooling and decorative procedures. Among these techniques are methods of cutting metals, metal bending, use of sheet metal in combination with wooden foundations, methods of tracing and inscribing decorative designs on metal surfaces, design tapping and embossing procedures, methods of coloring sheet metals, and so forth.

This hot-pot-stand also lends itself well to decoration, because the ornamentation employed is an essential part of the article. The particular decorative scheme shown in Fig. 1, Illustration 17 is perhaps the most appropriate for this type of stand, since it is reminiscent of the charming tea-tiles of another day. It is also a fascinating craft technique and easy to apply.

A practical and distinctive feature of this hot-pot-stand is the interesting and effective use of ornamental upholstery nails, both at the top and side sections of the stand. See B and E, Fig. 1. Besides being a fastening device to hold the metal covering to its wooden foundation, they also enhance the attractiveness of the project. Those used on the top surface of the stand also act as elevating rests, which prevent injury to the tapped and colored decoration when a hot pot or plate is placed upon the stand.

II. Materials

A. A clean flat sheet of tin, a little larger in size than 7-1/2 inches square.

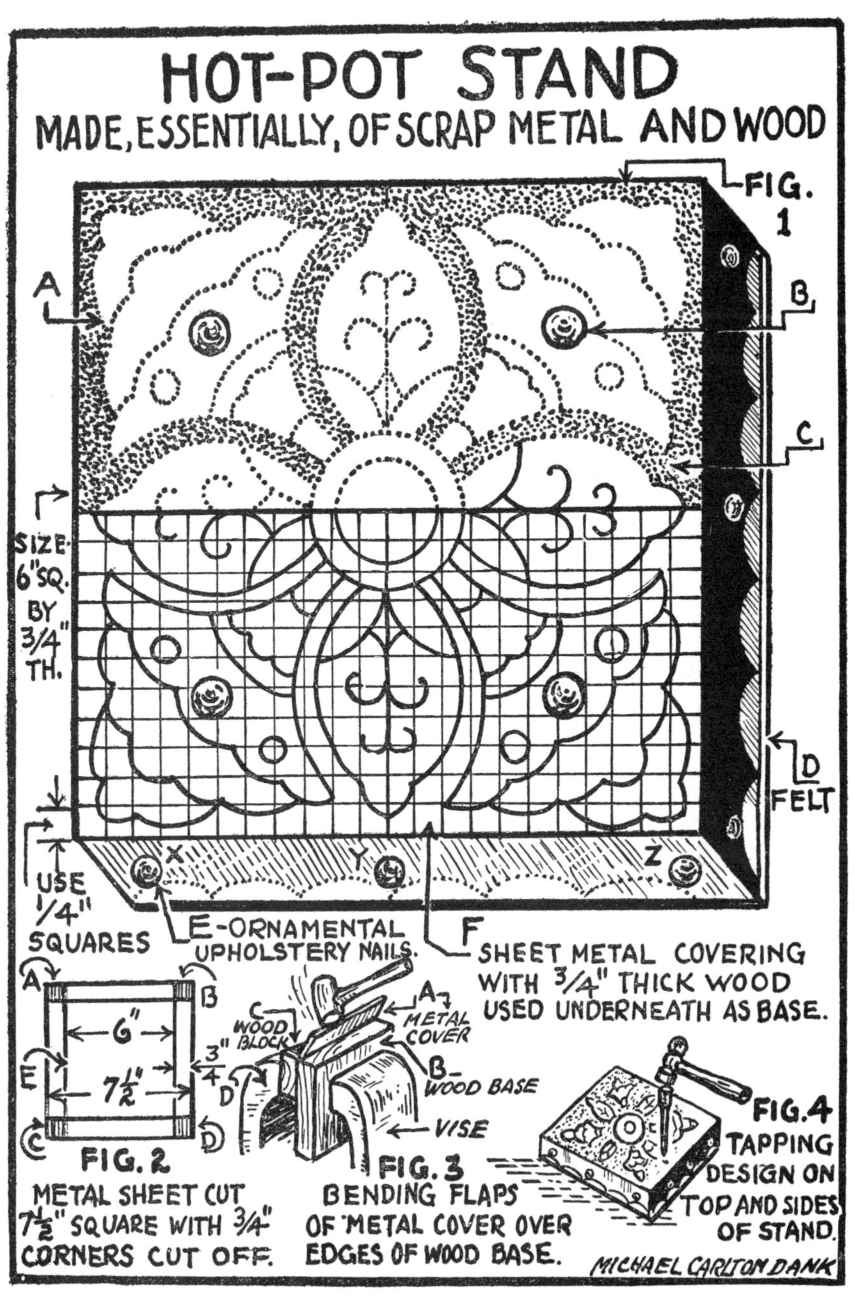
HOT-POT STAND
MADE, ESSENTIALLY, OF SCRAP METAL AND WOOD
FIG. 1
A
B
C
D
FELT
SIZE 6" SQ. BY 3/4" TH.
USE 1/4" SQUARES
X
Y
Z
E-ORNAMENTAL UPHOLSTERY NAILS.
F
SHEET METAL COVERING WITH 3/4" THICK WOOD USED UNDERNEATH AS BASE.
A
B
6"
E
7 1/2"
3/4"
D
C
D
FIG. 2
METAL SHEET CUT 7 1/2" SQUARE WITH 3/4" CORNERS CUT OFF.
C
WOOD BLOCK
A
METAL COVER
B
WOOD BASE
VISE
FIG. 3
BENDING FLAPS OF METAL COVER OVER EDGES OF WOOD BASE.
FIG. 4
TAPPING DESIGN ON TOP AND SIDES OF STAND.
MICHAEL CARLTON DANK

Illustration 17

B. Block of wood, such as pine, basswood, or poplar, 7/8 inch to 1 inch thick, and a little larger than 6 inches square.

C. Sheet of scrap felt or cork, at least 6-1/4 inches square.

D. Sixteen ornamental upholstery nails, all of the same style, and preferably with large, dome-shaped heads.

E. Any good grade of liquid glue.

F. Medium grade steel wool.

G. Medium grade emery cloth.

H. Enamel paints, quick-drying, in appropriate assortment of colors.

I. Clear lacquer, suitable for use as overall coatings over metal surfaces.

J. Pencil carbon paper, for use in tracing designs to metal.

K. Fine and medium grade sandpaper.

L. Scotch or gum tape. Cloth tape also satisfactory.

III. Tools

A. Metal cutting shears, medium size, with straight cutting jaws.

B. Pointed, metal instrument, not too sharp, suitable for tapping small dents in soft metal surfaces. The nail set punching tool shown in Fig. 5, Illustration 14, is excellent for this purpose.

C. Sharply pointed metal instrument such as a scratch-awl or ice pick, for scratching traced designs into surface of metal.

D. Medium size wooden mallet.

E. Smoothing plane.

F. Try-square.

G. Metal rule, preferably the 24 inch type.

H. Cross-cut and rip saws.

I. Woodworking bench, equipped with vise.

J. Assortment of brushes for enameling, gluing, and lacquering procedures.

K. Medium size pair of scissors.

L. Ball-peen metalworking hammer.

IV. Directions

A. Preparation of wooden base

For the construction of the wooden base of our hot-pot-stand, you will require some form of woodworking vise, a smoothing plane, a try-square, and a metal rule. A sheet of sandpaper, wrapped around a wood block, is also needed to do a good job. For best results in the preparation of this foundation board, proceed as follows:

1. Cut a scrap piece of wood, of 7/8 inches to 1 inch thickness, to about 6-3/8 inches square. Use a cross-cut saw for cutting the board across the grain, and a rip saw for cutting with the grain. See text in Chapter Four, Section I, A, 2 and 3.

2. Clamp board in vise with one edge facing upward, then with a smoothing plane, smooth and "square up" this edge carefully. Use try-square for testing the edge. When completed, this first edge is called the working edge.

3. Next, plane one end of the board, straight and square again, using the try-square for testing. This squared up first end is called the working end.

4. Using rule, measure 6 inches from the working end; then, at this point, draw a line across the board with the try-square, then plane to this 6 inch line, making this second or length end also straight and square.

5. Measure and mark off a line, 6 inches from the working edge, the edge which was planed first, and then plane to this line to produce the final or width edge. As a result of this procedure, our board will be true all around and will be 6 inches square as required for our project. When marking off widths from the working edge, it is good to use a so-called marking-gauge, although it is not absolutely essential, since a rule can also be used for this marking step.

6. Select the better of the two broad surfaces of the board, and from this surface draw a line 3/4 inch away, all around the edges and ends of the board. The marking gauge previously referred to is a good tool to use for this step if you have one on hand. Otherwise it can easily be drawn by the use of a rule, or by using the fingers as a guide.

7. Using a piece of medium grade sandpaper, wrapped around a small block of wood, carefully smooth all planed edges, ends, and broad surfaces of the board. The wood base part of our project is now completed and may be set aside for awhile.

B. Preparation of metal covering

The first step in the processing of the metal covering of our hot-pot-stand is to cut the sheet tin to its proper size and shape.

If a tin can of suitable size is employed as the source of the sheet metal, first cut away the top and bottom ends of the can, using any standard type can opener. Then, with a pair of straight-jawed, metal cutting shears, cut along the soldered seam of the can. As a result of these two simple steps, the tin will be flattened out in sheet form ready to be cut to the size required for the construction of our stand covering.

Having thus procured the metal, clean off all dirt and food particles, wipe dry with a cloth, and then proceed as follows:

1. Select a straight edge or mark off a straight line on the tin sheet, then with this edge or scribed line as a guide, measure and mark off a 7-1/2 inch square. Use a scratch awl to mark off the lines, as a pencil will not show clearly enough Be sure all corners of the marked off square are exactly at right angles, using the try-square to check the corners for squareness.

2. Using a metal rule and a scratch awl, scribe a 3/4 inch border all around the metal sheet, extending the lines from edge to edge. See Fig. 2 E, and corners A, B, C, D. This should leave a 6 inch square section in the center of the metal sheet.

3. With metal shears cut away all metal beyond the 7-1/2 inch section. Then, follow by cutting away corner sections A, B, C, D shown in shaded form in Fig. 2.

C. Nailing metal cover over wood base

1. Place prepared wood base exactly within the 6 inch square section marked off on the metal sheet, then, clamp both the metal and wood parts carefully in a vise. Place a scrap wood block, (C), between the outer surface of the metal cover, (A), and the vise jaw, (D), to protect metal against denting. See Fig. 3.

2. Using a wooden mallet, with a small piece of wood used between mallet head and metal flap, as a further protection against injuring metal surface, fold flap over, so it will be flush with the edge of the wood base. See Fig. 3.

3. Repeat this flap bending procedure for each of the four flaps of the metal cover.

4. Using mallet and any form of pointed metal instrument, punch three small holes through each of the four bent over metal flaps, now wrapped around the wood block base. Punch one hole at the center of each flap, and one 1/2 inch in from each corner indicated by X, Y and Z in Fig. 1, Illustration 17.

5. Through these twelve punched holes, on the edges of the stand, hammer in some attractive kind of dome-shaped, ornamental, upholstery nails. The nails are a means of fastening the metal flaps tightly to the wood, and are a decorative feature as well.

6. Hammer a similar type nail in each of the four corner sections of the top of the stand, locating them as indicated by E, in Fig. 1. These four nails, with their domed heads at a higher level than the surface of the metal covering, act as lifts, or rests, to prevent the tapped design on the top surface of the stand from being injured or soiled, when a hot plate or pot of any kind is placed upon the stand.

D. Tracing design to metal surface

1. The first step is to make a full-size reproduction of the design, given in somewhat reduced form in Fig. 1 To do this properly, first draw a grill of 1/4 inch squares, using the same number and arrangement of squares as given in the lower half of the design

used on the top of the stand in Fig. 1. Of course, to reproduce the design in its entirety, you will have to use exactly twice as many squares as represented in the drawing. If you wish, you may duplicate just half of the design just as given in Fig. 1 and then use this half pattern twice, on a separate piece of paper, to form the complete design. If done properly, the design should measure 6 inches square.

2. After the design is reproduced in full size, cut away all paper beyond the border of the design, thus making the design the same size as the 6 inch square measurement of the stand.

3. Cut a piece of pencil carbon paper to match the size of the pattern sheet and stand.

4. Using four small strips of scotch tape, fasten the design and carbon sheets evenly over the top metal surfaces of the stand. Be sure that the carbon sheet is placed between the pattern and metal surface with the carbon side of the sheet facing down.

5. Using a pencil, modeler, or stylus, trace over all outlines of the design, pressing sufficiently downward on the tracing instrument to assure a clear impression of the design on the surface of the metal.

6. When finished, lift up one corner of the pattern and carbon sheets, look under to make sure the tracing took well, and if satisfactory remove the sheets from the stand. It is suggested at this point that the pattern be mounted in some form of design scrapbook for future use or reference.

7. Using a sharply pointed metal instrument, such as a scratch awl or ice pick, carefully scratch over all the outlines of the design, now appearing in carbon on the top metal surface of the stand. When finished, wipe away all the carbon lines and smears, leaving only the scratched in outlines to remain and to show up clearly, in preparation for the metal tapping.

E. Tapping design on metal covering of stand

1. Using a ball-peen hammer and a pointed metal instrument such as a sharpened 3 inch long flat-head nail, or the nail set punch

shown in Fig. 5, Illustration 14, tap little dents, in uniform, close formation over all the scratched-in outlines of the decoration. In addition to applying the indentations in a close, uniform fashion, it is important to avoid making holes through the metal. See A, Fig. 1, and also the diagram in Fig. 4.

2. After completing the outline tapping, use exactly the same tools as before to tap similar dents, but in solid, mass form, over all background sections of the decoration, just as indicated by C, Fig. 1.

3. Polish entire metal surface with fine grade steel wool. As a result of the outline and background tapping steps just applied the design will stand out attractively in bold relief. It is a good idea to outline tap a neat border around all four edges of the stand, as shown in Fig. 1.

F. Coloring and completing the hot-pot-stand

For coloring the stand, use a carefully planned, harmonizing combination of enamel paints. Apply the colors to just a few important raised sections of the tapped decoration. No paint should be used over the closely tapped background areas at all, permitting these sections to appear in the original bright metal finish. Furthermore, keep the enamel away from the tapped outlines, applying the colors just along side of the outlines and inside the untapped design parts. For added decorative effect, use a little enamel paint within the tapped border around the four edges of the stand. When applying the enamel, use a small size pointed style brush, and be careful not to have too much paint on the brush at one time. A flooded brush will cause the colors to run and spoil the work.

Apply a coat of clear lacquer, in a suitably thinned form, over all metal sections of the stand. To complete our project, glue a covering of cork or felt to the bottom of the wood block, making certain that it is attached neatly and securely. This lining will protect the stand when it is placed upon the table.

RELATED PROJECTS IN SHEET METAL WORK

Utilizing sheet metal scraps and the tooling procedures described in Project No. 38, HOT-POT-STAND.

Project No. 39, Metal Tapped Wall Plaque

Metal tapping lends itself well to the construction of ornamental wall plaques of many shapes and sizes. A good wooden foundation for projects of this type is provided by the use of ordinary plywood from 1/4 inch to 3/8 inch in thickness. Dome-shaped brass escutcheon pins, long enough to be clinched at the back of the plaque, are most appropriate for use in nailing the metal parts to their plywood foundation or mount.

It is a good idea in most metal tapped plaques to allow a border of wood to show all around the metal decoration. A good finish for such wooden borders as well as for the other parts of the wooden foundation board, is provided by the use of oil stains, in such colors as burnt umber, burnt sienna, olive green, drop black, and so forth.

Neat leather hangers may also be prepared for the plaques in the form of leather thongs or strips or braided leather lacing. To attach the hangers, knot both ends of the hanger in the front of the plaque, one in each corner.

The tapped metal plaques may be enhanced with a limited use of enamel paints, as suggested for the hot-pot-stand, Project No. 38, or may just be polished brightly and finished with a coat of clear lacquer.

Such motifs as ships, flowers, animals, birds, Mexican settings, and so forth lend themselves excellently as decorative material for these metal tapped wall plaques.

Project No. 40, Metal Tapped Book Ends

A very attractive pair of metal tapped book ends can be made by following the directions given for the hot-pot-stand, Fig. 1, Illustration 17, with few modifications.

Instead of four metal flaps around the edges of the wood base, only three are used, eliminating the flap at the bottom. In place of the bottom metal flap, fasten on a sheet of sufficiently heavy gauge metal, preferably galvanized iron, to serve as a base support for the book end. A good size for the base, is 6 inches wide by 5-1/2 inches deep or long. To attach the metal base, use flathead screws and countersink them neatly so their heads are level with the under surface of the metal base. It is a good idea to have 1/2 inch of the base extend forward beyond the front face of the upright section of the book end.

Many other styles and shapes of book ends may be made in the metal tapped fashion in which the tapping covers only a part of the front section of the book end.

For coloring and finishing the book ends, use the procedures outlined for metal tapped wall plaques, Project No. 39. The metal bases of the book ends should be colored with black, or any other suitable shade of enamel. Also, the under surfaces of the book ends should be lined and finished neatlv with felt or cork, to prevent their scratching the furniture.

Project No. 41, Metal Tapped Wall Shelf

Like the wall plaque and book ends previously described, metal tapped wall shelves may be constructed in various shapes and sizes, in accordance with individual taste and creative ability. A popular wall shelf may be constructed as follows:

Saw out a vertical back part, measuring about 9 inches by 12 inches, using any soft grade of 1/4 inch plywood. You will find detailed directions for using the coping saw under Project 1, Section IV-E. Do not make the contours of the back too elaborate or ornate, since this would detract from the effectiveness of the metal tapped decoration later to be applied.

Following the cutting out and sandpapering of the back of the shelf, cut a piece of sheet metal, about 6 inches in diameter and mount it to the upper part of the back of the shelf, making certain that it is located in the exact center of its width. To mount the metal sheet, use about 3/8 inch long escutcheon pins, clinching the points of the pins at the back of the vertical, plywood mount, just as in the construction of wall plaques. After nailing the metal unit in place, proceed with the design tracing and tapping, employing the methods detailed in Project No. 38. Color the metal with enamel paints or leave it in its original bright metal finish, as desired.

Having thus completed the back of the shelf, saw out a semicircular piece of 1/4 inch plywood or regular 1/2 stock, for the shelf. The back edge of this part must be made straight and square while the front edge should be neatly arc-shaped or curved. When finished fasten this shelf piece to the back of the project with liquid glue the 3/4 inch wire brads, driving the brads in place from the back of the vertical part.

The last part required in the construction of our project is a small support piece which is used under the horizontal shelf for reinforcement. For this third wood part use 1/2 inch stock. The top and back edges of this part should be at perfect right angles with each other, while the front edge should be curved in harmony with the curved edge of the horizontal shelf. Fasten this support piece into place, using 3/4 inch wire brads, inserted from the back of the shelf and from the top surface of the horizontal shelf part.

After making certain that all wood parts have been neatly sandpapered, color them with an appropriate oil stain in the manner suggested for metal tapped wall plaques, Project No. 39.

As a wall hanger for shelf, insert two small screw-eyes at the back of the vertical part, and then fasten on a strip of picture frame wire. Arrange to have the top part of the wire hanger low enough to remain invisible when the shelf is hung up.

After working with sheet tin, it is suggested that the reader acquaint himself with other, even more interesting metals, such as copper, brass, aluminum, nickel, silver and pewter.

Plate 6. These wall plaques were made from odd moulding strips, scrap wood and small pieces of metal foil.

Plate 7. Pieces of scrap metals such as tin and aluminum can be worked into attractive designs, and then attached to polished or stained pieces of wood to make wall plaques, flower pot holders and book ends.

CHAPTER SEVEN

WORKING WITH SCRAP FELT

FELT which can be obtained in a wide assortment of colors from old felt hats and many other kinds of discarded wearing apparel is a comparatively new handicraft medium. It possesses excellent qualities as a construction material and offers many advantages to home needleworkers and teachers of educational and recreational arts and crafts everywhere.

Among the important features of felt is its distinctive texture. Moreover, it can easily be cut into any required shape or size with ordinary scissors; it can be pasted to other surfaces; it can be sewed and embroidered; it can be moulded, pressed and dry cleaned. Above all, felt can easily be manipulated and processed by young as well as experienced craftsmen. Things made of felt are durable. Like leather and many other handicraft materials, felt is manufactured in a variety of grades and thicknesses.

Felt crafts can produce a wide variety of useful articles such as table-mats, belts, suspenders, pillows, bags, rugs, mittens, boleros, lapel ornaments, necklaces, and so on.

Felt crafts help to develop in the child appreciation of design and color. They offer children a variety of simple, interesting handwork skills, such as cutting, pasting, applique work, sewing, embroidery, and so forth. Felt crafts can also be correlated with various academic subjects through the construction of puppets, marionettes, historical displays and posters. Finally, scrap felt is easily obtainable and the tools and materials required for working with it are so inexpensive.

As our key project in felt crafts, we are employing the table-mat, Project No. 42, shown in Fig. 1, Illustration 18. In the construction of this useful article, are embodied the essential handwork procedures used in general felt work. After you become acquainted with the simple methods required for its construction, you will be able to make many other things out of felt.

Most of the manipulative procedures used with felt can also be employed with other materials such as prints, gingham, percale, chintz, and other cotton goods. This is especially true in making cloth paintings, puppets, lapel ornaments, dolls, bean-bags, covered cardboard container knitting bags, and so forth.

Project No. 42, Felt Table Mat

See Figure 1, Illustration 18

I. Description

The outstanding features of this felt project are its simplicity of construction, its effective design and coloring schemes, and the comparatively short time required for its production.

This particular felt mat consists of a 6-1/2 inch circular base part, made of a heavier grade of felt, a 3 inch circular part fastened to the center of the 6-1/2 inch base, and four similarly fashioned ornamental units, appliqued around the edge of the base, which are made of a somewhat thinner grade of felt. See Fig. 1, Illustration 18, for identification of these parts.

Each of the four decorative flower units is made up in a multiple applique fashion, and consists of five separate felt pieces assembled in progressively higher layers. You will obtain a good idea of the construction of these layers by referring to the pattern grill of these flower units, in Fig. 2, Illustration 18.

It is important in the preparation of this table mat, to employ an appropriate and carefully selected combination of felt colors. Use colors that will blend with the general decorative scheme of the room in which the mat is to be placed.

This table mat may be built in several other sizes, larger or smaller, than the size shown in Illustration 18. All that is necessary is to prepare the working patterns in accordance with the particular size of the mat desired. Thus, if a 13 inch diameter base is desired instead of the 6-1/2 inch diameter base specified in our working plan of the mat, it will be necessary to employ a grill of 1/2 inch squares for a proper size reproduction of the four flower units, instead of the grill of 1/4 inch squares indicated in Figure 2.

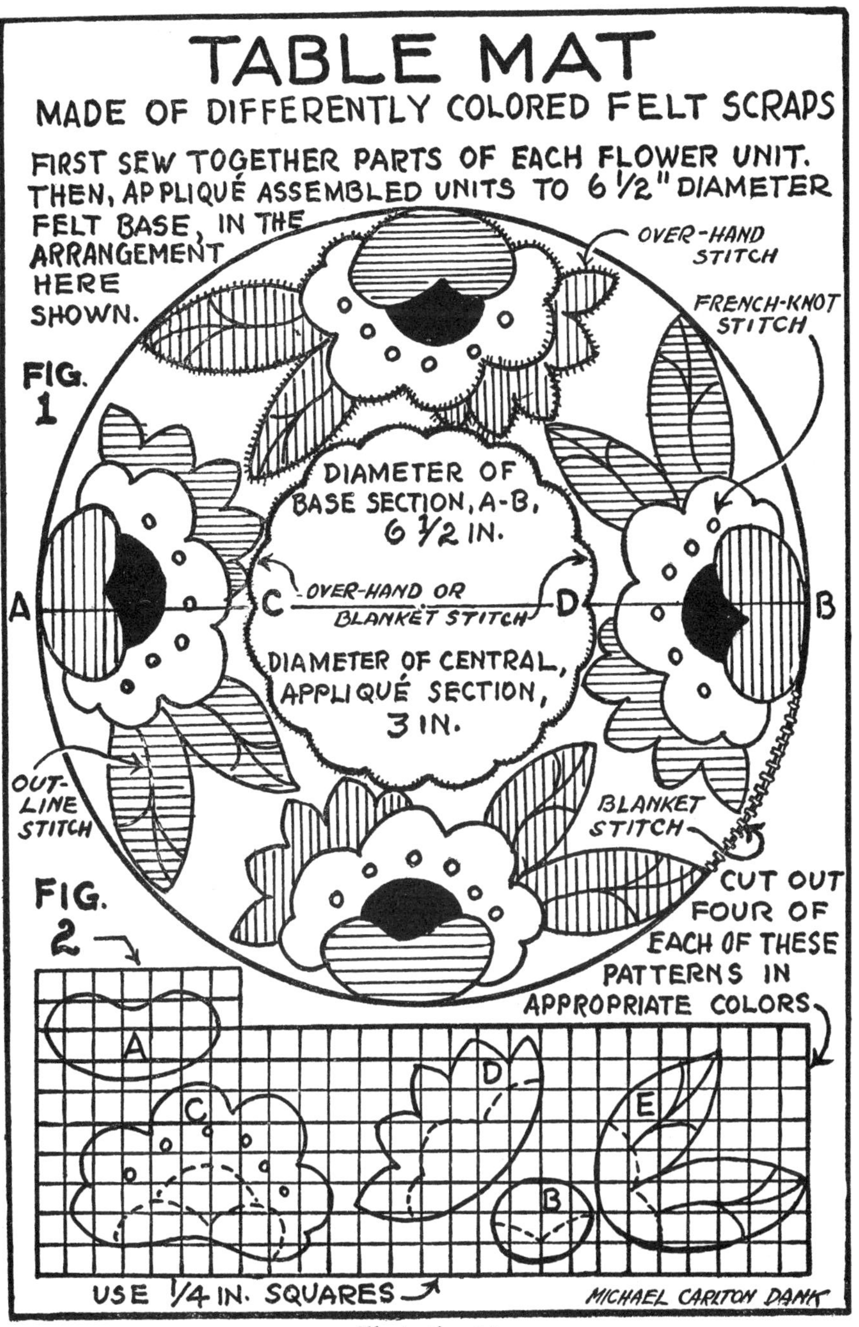
TABLE MAT
MADE OF DIFFERENTLY COLORED FELT SCRAPS
FIRST SEW TOGETHER PARTS OF EACH FLOWER UNIT. THEN, APPLIQUÉ ASSEMBLED UNITS TO 6 1/2" DIAMETER FELT BASE, IN THE ARRANGEMENT HERE SHOWN.
OVER-HAND STITCH
FRENCH-KNOT STITCH
FIG. 1
DIAMETER OF BASE SECTION, A-B, 6 1/2 IN.
A
C
OVER-HAND OR BLANKET STITCH
D
B
DIAMETER OF CENTRAL, APPLIQUÉ SECTION, 3 IN.
OUT-LINE STITCH
BLANKET STITCH
CUT OUT FOUR OF EACH OF THESE PATTERNS IN APPROPRIATE COLORS
FIG. 2
A
C
D
E
B
USE 1/4 IN. SQUARES
MICHAEL CARLTON DANK
Illustration 18

Before proceeding with the discussion of the table mat, the author wishes to explain that two different methods are given for attaching the applique floral units to the large, circular base of the mat. One is the pasting-on applique process, which is especially recommended for younger children. The more advanced method, suggested for older children and adults, is the sewing-on applique process. Both of these procedures may be used with satisfactory results although, of course, the sewing-on method produces a somewhat more elaborate finish and stronger form of construction.

II. Materials

A. A piece of felt large enough to make the 6-1/2 inch diameter base of the table mat. The felt used for this should be of a somewhat heavier quality than the other parts of the mat. Good colors for this base piece are black, brown, dark green, or grey.

B. A piece of felt of the same thickness as the large circular base, of sufficient size for cutting out the 3 inch diameter applique piece at the center of the mat in Fig. 1, Illustration 18. The color of this part may be a lighter shade of the color used for the large circular section, at the base of the mat. Or, it may be made in a harmonizing color.

C. Thin felt scraps, in a pleasing combination of colors, sufficient for cutting out the four complete flower units shown in applique form around the outer section of the table mat, in the sketch of our project in Fig. 1. You will find a set of patterns in representation of these flower units in Fig. 2.

D. Fairly strong thread in any appropriate contrasting color for sewing the applique pieces to the large circular base.

E. Any good grade of rubber or household cement. A good grade of liquid paste is also satisfactory as an adhesive in this work.

F. A sheet of oak-tag or any medium-weight, light-colored cardboard.

III. Tools

A. A large size pair of scissors for cutting large felt parts.

B. A small pair of scissors suitable for cutting the small felt parts, such as the applique flowers.

C. A small flat-style brush with stiff bristles for pasting on the felt parts.

D. A medium size needle.

E. Any suitable form of weight such as a cloth-covered brick, a fairly heavy block of wood.

F. Pencil compasses.

G. A 12 inch wooden ruler.

H. One light and one dark colored crayon pencil in either the wax-crayon or the water color crayon varieties. Good colors are black or blue and white or yellow. These pencils are used for tracing the contours of the table-mat patterns to the felt.

IV. Directions

First prepare an accurate set of working patterns; trace the patterns to the already colored felt material; cut out the outlined felt parts; and then, either paste or sew the project parts together, as the particular job may require. Be sure your hands are clean so as not to soil the felt.

A. Preparation of cardboard patterns

1. On a sheet of oak tag or any medium weight cardboard of a light color, draw a grill of squares consisting of the same number of squares and arranged in the same manner as the grill shown in Fig. 2, Illustration 18. When drawing your grill, however, use 1/4 inch size squares instead of the reduced size squares represented in Fig. 2. Use a well-sharpened pencil and a ruler.

2. Draw in the applique flower parts A, B, C, D, and E, exactly as shown in the grill in Fig. 2. If copied properly, the applique parts will appear in their correct, enlarged size, to fit the 6-1/2 inch diameter base of our project as planned in Fig. 1.

3. Be sure to include all detail lines exactly as shown on pattern parts B, C, D, and E.

4. Using a medium size pair of scissors, carefully cut out each of the five cardboard patterns as represented in your enlarged grill. Mark the patterns A, B, C, D, and E, just as indicated in Fig. 2.

5. Punch holes, about 1/16 inch in diameter, in the cardboard pattern C, to indicate the location of the French knot stitching later required for this felt part of the project. Pin holes should also be punched in cardboard pattern E, to show location of outline stitching of veins, required for this leaf part.

6. On a separate sheet of cardboard, and using compasses, draw a circle of 6-1/2 inch diameter. Below this, draw a circle of 3 inch diameter. Then, with scissors, cut out these two circular cardboard patterns. If a scalloped edge is required for the 3 inch diameter pattern part, divide the circle into 16 equal segments and then draw in the scallops in the manner seen in Fig. 1.

7. Place the completed cardboard pattern parts in an envelope of proper size, and mark the envelope, "Patterns For Felt Table Mat". This will prevent losing or misplacing the patterns, when not in use. It will also avoid the possibility of mixing these patterns with those of some other project. This is especially advisable when working with groups of children.

B. Tracing the patterns to the felt

1. Before tracing the cardboard patterns to the felt, mark on each one of the patterns the particular color of felt for which that pattern is to be used. Or paint each cardboard pattern in its intended felt color, using tempera paint. Plan the choice of colors carefully.

2. After coloring the cardboard patterns, put the pattern parts together, loosely, in the manner shown in Fig. 1. This will give you an idea of how the colors will look when the mat parts are placed into their proper positions. Having determined the final color scheme in this way, trace the patterns to the felt.

3. Place the pattern for the 6-1/2 inch circular base part on a sheet of felt corresponding in color to the color of that pattern part.

Plate 8. These hand puppets have heads made of papier mâché, decorated with bright tempera colors, and clothes made of scrap pieces of felt or cotton.

Plate 9. Bits and pieces of differently colored felt scraps can be used to make change purses, book marks and belts.

For this base of the mat, use felt of a fairly thick grade. Then, proceed to trace around the outside edge of the pattern with any contrasting color of crayon pencil. Either a water color or wax form of crayon pencil, well sharpened, may be used for this outlining step. Be sure the tracing outlines are made clearly and neatly.

4. Next, place pattern for the 3 inch circular applique part used at the center of the mat on a piece of felt of the same color as the pattern for this part, and trace around the outer edge of the pattern.

5. Make four outline tracings of each of the five applique flower part patterns. Here as before, use felt in colors which correspond to the colors of the pattern parts. Thus, you will need four tracings of pattern A, four of pattern B, etc.

6. When making the four tracings of pattern C, be sure to indicate with pencil the location of the French knot stitching required for this part by marking dots through the holes previously punched through this pattern part. When tracing pattern E, indicate stitching of leaf veins, by marking dots through the holes previously punched through this pattern part.

C. Cutting out traced felt parts

1. Using a medium size pair of scissors, cut out the large and small circular felt parts of the table mat. Work in a smooth, clean-cut fashion, following the traced outlines exactly as indicated. Edges cut in a jagged, irregular fashion, will detract from the appearance of the table mat.

2. Using a smaller pair of scissors, cut out felt parts A, B, C, D, and E, again following traced outlines carefully.

3. After all felt parts of the table mat are completely cut out, place the parts into a work envelope or work box to keep them clean and in good order until they are assembled.

D. Assembling cut-out table mat parts

As indicated above, we can employ two different methods for fastening on applique felt parts. One of these is simply to paste on the parts in their proper places, while the other is to sew on the parts with a needle and an appropriate color of thread. Directions for the former method follow:

1. Place the 3 inch circular part in its exact position on the 6-1/2 inch circular base and lightly indicate location with two or three pencil dots.

2. Using any good grade of rubber cement or household cement and a small, flat brush with stiff bristles, apply a thin coat of the adhesive to the underside of the 3 inch diameter felt piece. Brush the adhesive over the entire undersurface of this felt part, but do not use too much of it lest it ooze out and spoil the work.

3. Place moistened felt part carefully in its exact position on the center of the 6-1/2 inch circular base of the mat, press it down into place a little, and then remove it. This will cause some of the adhesive to adhere to and moisten the contact area of the bottom of the two parts being assembled.

4. A minute later, apply a second coat of the adhesive over the underside of the 3 inch circular piece only, and again place it into position over the central section of the 6-1/2 inch circular base. This time do not remove or disassemble the parts.

5. Press the two assembled parts together tightly, using a sheet of plain paper underneath the fingers, to keep the felt clean. Following this hand-pressing step, place any fairly heavy weight over the pasted parts and allow joint to set and dry.

6. After about 10 minutes remove weight. The two parts will now be fastened securely together.

7. Using this pasting-on procedure, assemble the five parts of each of the four separate flower units. Do this by first joining part A to part B. Then, join these two assembled parts to part C. Finally, join these three assembled parts to the leaf units D and E, thus forming the completed flower units shown in the sketch of our model, in Fig. 1.

8. After assembling all four flower units in this same manner, place the units loosely in their exact positions, on the 6-1/2 inch

circular base. For the correct locations of these flower units, see Fig. 1. After the felt flowers are correctly placed into position, make a few pencil dots around the outer edge of each flower unit to serve as pasting guides. Following this, paste each of the flower units tightly into place, employing the directions given above.

9. To produce the spots on flower parts C, and the veins on the leaf parts E, simply cut pieces of felt of appropriate colors and then paste them neatly in place. The spots and veins must necessarily be made a little larger and wider than they are seen in the drawing to make certain that they will hold strongly when the mat is in use. Of course, both the flower spots and the leaf veins may be disregarded entirely if desired.

When working with older children, it is best to assemble the felt parts of the table mat by sewing the parts together. The directions for the sewing-on method are as follows:

1. Place a little paste or cement on the center of the underside of the 3 inch diameter circular felt part, and press this part into its exact position over the central part of the 6-1/2 inch diameter base of the mat. The purpose of the adhesive here is to hold the parts securely in their correct positions while they are being sewed together.

2. Using a medium size needle and a suitable color of thread, sew these two circular parts together. Use for this purpose, any simple form of edging stitch, such as the "over-and-over" or "overhand" stitch shown in Fig. 1. Those who are adept in the use of the needle and thread may use some other more elaborate edging stitch, although the simpler stitch suggested is entirely satisfactory for this type of project. In any case, make very small stitches, and apply them in neat, close formation.

3. Next, paste and sew together the parts of each of the four flower units, using the procedure given in directions 1 and 2, above. First sew part A to part B. Then, sew these two assembled parts to C. Finally, sew the three assembled parts to leaf parts D and E.

4. After all the parts of the flower units are sewed together, sew each of these assembled flower units to the upper surface of the 6-1/2 inch circular base part of the mat as shown in Fig. 1.

5. To reproduce the spots of color on the flower parts C, use a French knot stitch, familiar to most needle workers. To reproduce the veins on the leaf parts E, use a simple outline stitch. See Fig. 1.

6. The outside edge of the 6-1/2 inch circular base part of the mat may or may not be finished by stitching in accordance with individual taste. However, for an attractive, well-finished appearance, it is a good idea to use a neat blanket stitch all around the outside edge of this circular base.

7. After all parts of the table mat are completely sewed and fastened together, place a few large books over it and allow them to remain there for an hour or two in order to press all parts neatly into place.

The table mat is now finished and ready to serve as a base for a flower vase, a table lamp, an ash tray, or a photograph. Dry-clean the mat, do not wash it. To press the mat, use a very hot iron, with a slightly damp cloth placed over the mat. Never use a wet cloth, as this will cause the felt to shrink.

The related felt craft projects presented below, are all constructed in accordance with the same general methods just outlined. Although specific directions are given below for each of these felt articles, you will have many opportunities for applying your own ideas as to design, color and arrangement of parts.

RELATED FELTCRAFT PROJECTS

Based upon the working procedures given in connection with the construction of Project No. 42, TABLE-MAT, shown in Fig. 1, Ill. 18.

Project No. 43, Felt Mittens

See Figure 1, Illustration 19

These stylish "fireside" mittens are appropriate for all winter sports. They can easily be made of scrap felt in a wide selection of colors by observing the following simple directions:

Cut a cardboard pattern a little larger than the hand size of the person for whom the mittens are intended. In the preparation of the pattern, follow the general shape of the mittens sketched in Fig. 1.

OTHER THINGS YOU CAN MAKE OF FELT SCRAPS
FIG.1
RUNNING STITCH
MITTENS
FIG.2
BOOK-MARK
A
B
HBD
PIN CUSHION
BLANKET STITCH
FIG.3
BUCKRAM OR SATEEN LINING
FIG.4
BLANKET STITCH
SPORT BELT
FIG.5 PICTURE
A
B
FIG. 6
BUTTON-BOX
USING REAL BUTTONS AT CENTERS OF FELT FLOWERS.
A
FIG.7
B
OVERCAST STITCH
LAPEL PINS
A
4 1/2"
2 1/4"
X
STRAP-5/8" X 9"
PURSE- 1 3/4" X 2 1/4"
FIG.8-WRIST COIN PURSE
MICHAEL CARLTON DANK

Illustration 19

Place cardboard pattern, with thumb finger located at the right, on a fairly heavy grade of felt of any suitable color. With a contrasting color of crayon pencil mark around the outside edge of the pattern. Then, on another part of the same felt material, make a second tracing of the mitten pattern, but this time with the thumb finger placed at the left. These two tracings will give you the top sections of the left and right mittens. For the bottom sections of the mittens, repeat these two tracing steps, using either the same material as employed for the tops, or any appropriate, harmonizing color of felt. After tracing the four separate mitten parts, cut them out carefully with a medium size pair of scissors.

The next step is the preparation of cardboard patterns for some simple decorative motifs to be cut out of felt and appliqued on the top sections of the mittens. For these decorations, it is a good idea to employ some winter theme such as the pine tree and snow flake motif used on our model in Fig. 1. Following the completion of these applique patterns, make tracings of them on gaily colored felt that will contrast with the mitten tops. Of course, it will be necessary to make duplicate tracings of each of the motif patterns, to take care of the left and right mittens. After tracing the patterns, cut out the felt parts carefully, then paste and sew them neatly in place on the mitten tops. You may darn the motifs on from the underside of the mitten tops, or you may sew them on with an appropriate color of thread, using small, closely applied overhand stitches. See text under Project No. 42, Table Mat, for complete details concerning this procedure in applique felt work.

To complete the mittens, sew the decorated "uppers" to the "lowers". A practical and attractive form of stitching for this purpose is the simple running stitch seen in Fig. 1. Use a contrasting color of strong wool yarn. Place the stitches neatly and uniformly around all edges of the mittens with the exception of their lower end sections which remain open for the hands. The edges of the open ends of the mittens should be separately hem-stitched, using the same yarn and running stitch employed for the closed edge sections.

Project No. 44, Felt Book-Mark

See Figure 2, Illustration 19

Felt makes good book-marks because of its softness and because of the many possibilities it offers in matters of design and color.

Felt book-marks can be made in a variety of styles and sizes. The one shown in Fig. 2 measures 2 inches by 8 inches, and is made entirely of thin felt scraps in gay colors. It is neatly fringed at the top by making scissor cuts 1/4 inch wide and 3/4 inch long, and then by cutting each separate fringe strip to a stubby point as shown. A 3/8 inch wide strip of felt is used at the upper section of the book-mark, (A), and at the lower section, (B), for added decorative effect and to help keep the book-mark in a neat, flat shape. These strips like the monogram used at the bottom of the project and the floral motifs along its central section, are simply pasted to the 2 inch by 8 inch base of the book-mark with rubber or household cement. For details concerning this pasting-on method in applique felt work, see text under Project No. 42, Felt Table Mat.

The three floral motifs used on this book-mark are made of two separate layers of felt. The central sections of the flowers, shown shaded in the drawing, have a 1/8 inch hole punched through at the middle, permitting the color of the petals or lower sections of the flowers to show through effectively.

All applique felt parts of this book-mark, other than the three flower units, are built in single layer fashion.

It is most important to use harmonizing colors of felt, and to do a neat, thorough job of pasting. A good general rule is to use a dark or neutral color for the base or foundation of the book-mark, and a tasteful combination of gay felt colors for the applique units.

Book-marks of this type make excellent projects for beginners in felt crafts.

Project No. 45, Felt Pin-Cushion

See Figure 3, Illustration 19

This useful sewing aid in the form of a fish is built of two perfectly round body sections of 4 inch diameter, two single layer fins, one single layer tail, and a few small applique pieces, representing the fish's eye, mouth, and scales, and the coloring of the fins and tail. Both the fins and tail are securely attached to the fish by being stitched between its two round body parts.

To be most practical and attractive, it is best to build the body parts of the pin cushion of a rather heavy grade of felt, using gay, contrasting colors of a lighter weight felt for the applique parts. The inside of the fish's body is stuffed high and solidly with absorbent cotton. No stuffing is used for either the fins or tail, however, since these parts are in single layers. To stuff the fish's body, first sew all around its circular edge, leaving an opening of about 2 inches just above its mouth for inserting the cotton. After stuffing the body, stitch the remaining open section of the body edge. Use a small blanket stitch. In sewing up the circumference of the body, sew the fins and tail into place as shown in Fig. 1. Because of this form of construction, allow an extra 1/2 inch at the assembling ends of both the fins and tail. It is a good idea to sew around the edges of the fins and tail as a finishing touch.

The fish's eye is made of two applique felt layers of such colors as black and white. All the other decorative features, however, are in single applique. It is best to use a simple overhand stitch around these applique parts in addition to pasting them on. The bottom of the fish is made of a plain piece of felt, without any ornamentation whatever.

Felt pin cushions may be made in other sizes and designs. Just prepare a proper set of working patterns in exact representation of the project as planned. You will find complete details in this connection in the text under Project No. 42.

This pin cushion may be kept ready for use on the vanity or dresser, or it may be hung on the wall by means of a cloth tape hook, sewed to the underside of the fish.

Project No. 46, Felt Pot-Holder

Serviceable and attractive pot holders may be made in practically the same way as the fish pin-cushion, shown in Fig. 3, Illustration 19.

The main difference is that the pot holders must be made a little larger than the pin cushions. A good size for the circular body of the fish, when meant to be a pot-holder, is 6 inches in diameter. Another difference is that only a very small amount of cotton stuffing is used inside the fish's body when it is to be a pot-holder.

A little cloth-tape loop fastened to the plain bottom of the fish will provide the pot-holder with a convenient wall hanger. As in the case of the pin-cushions, these pot-holders may be made in a variety of designs and colors.

When made in sets of three, using the same pattern and decorative motif, these pot-holders may be neatly suspended from a suitably fashioned rack, making an excellent gift for your mother or a friend.

Project No. 47, Sport Belt

See Figure 4, Illustration 19

This felt sport belt is most popular with girls and young women since it can be made in a wide variety of "catchy" styles and design treatments.

The belt shown in Fig. 4 was designed by the girls in one of the author's arts and crafts classes. The width of the belt may vary from 1-1/4 inches to 2 inches in accordance with individual taste. Its length is determined by the waist measurement of the person for whom the belt is made. The inner surface of the belt is made of a suitable form of lining material such as sateen or heavy white muslin. The outside surface of the belt consists of a strip of felt, made of a single, long strip of felt, or of several short strips sewn together, depending upon the amount and nature of the scrap felt on hand. This outside layer is attractively decorated with a series of gayly colored felt designs securely sewn on by simple overhand stitching. The inner lining and outer felt layer are neatly sewn together around their edges with a close blanket stitch. This stitching is also used all around the tapered end of the belt. An odd buckle, made of metal or plastic, is sewn to the other end of the belt by looping the end around the central bar of the buckle. See Fig. 4.

A good procedure for making this attractive sport belt is as follows:

1. Lay out and cut outside felt of strip belt to required size and to the particular shape desired. If this outside felt section of the belt is to be made of several short strips of felt, sew the strip neatly together. Use a finely applied running stitch and keep the ends of the strips on the inside. An interesting effect may here be produced by using a series of two or three different colors of felt which go well together. Have one end of the felt strip cut in a square cornered or straight manner, and the other one in a round, tapered fashion, as seen in Fig. 4.

2. Cut out and sew on a carefully planned and prepared series of applique felt motifs, something like those seen in Fig. 4. These decorative design units should be of a simple character and large enough to be handled easily. It is also important that the colors used for these applique motifs harmonize with the color used for the felt strip on the outside of the belt to which they are sewn.

3. Mark out and cut with scissors the sateen or muslin lining which is to be used on the inside of the belt. This lining strip should be made exactly the same size and shape as the previously cut outside felt strip.

4. Sew lining and felt layers together, using blanket stitching around the edges.

5. Sew on buckle, using a straight series of running stitches across width of belt, after looping 1-1/2 inches of straight end of belt around bar at center of buckle.

Teachers of arts and crafts should encourage each girl to create her own designs for the applique work here employed. They may even fashion interesting belt shapes, instead of the straight belt shown in Fig. 4.

Project No. 48, Felt Wall Picture

See Figure 5, Illustration 19

Painting with felt is a good way to describe this fascinating form of felt craft. The idea is to use scraps of felt, in a combination of colors, to make a landscape, a marine setting, or other interesting compositions. Good sizes for these pictures are 5 inches by 7 inches, 8 inches by 10 inches and 9 inches by 12 inches. When completed, these "painted" felt pictures are neatly framed under glass, and hung on the wall.

A good method of procedure in the construction of felt pictures of the type shown in Fig. 5 is as follows:

1. Determine size of felt picture to be made and then cut out a sheet of plywood, composition board or any heavy grade

of cardboard in this same size. This board is to serve as the backing or foundation for the felt picture.

2. Cover this foundation board with a sheet of black or royal blue felt material. Extend the ends of this felt covering over the edges and to the back of the foundation board, where the ends of the felt should be glued tightly in place.

3. Make a drawing on a sheet of paper, in exact representation of the proposed felt painting. Then, color this drawing with tempera paints, using such colors as you plan to employ for the final painting in felt. This tempera painting on the drawing paper is to serve as a design and color guide after which the felt picture may be intelligently and systematically fashioned.

4. After completing the color sketch, make cardboard patterns of all separate parts of the composition which are to be reproduced in felt. For instance, in the sailboat picture shown in Fig. 5, we will require separate patterns for the sail, flag, hull, waves; moon, birds, and so forth.

5. Trace the cardboard patterns of the proposed picture to such colors of felt as have been planned in the color sketch.

6. Cut out all felt parts carefully, following all outline tracings exactly as indicated.

7. Paste the cutout felt parts neatly in their proper respective places in the picture, in accordance with the tempera working plan. Remove any surplus paste.

8. Frame picture under a glass with a simple, narrow form of framing moulding, finished in maple, gold, or any other appropriate color, depending on the character and color scheme of the felt painting. Attach small screw eyes and picture frame wire to the back of the project for hanging on the wall.

Small size felt pictures, worked out in pairs or "twin paintings," is an especially fine way to apply this delightful form of feltcraft project.

Project No. 49, Felt Decorated Serving Tray

Another application of the "picture painting in felt" idea represented in Fig. 5, is to work out felt compositions or design arrangements in a horizontal form, and apply them for use as serving trays. Good sizes for felt decorated serving trays of this form are 7 inches by 12 inches and 9 inches by 16 inches. Mexican and peasant subjects, as well as simple floral arrangements, provide excellent design motifs for these trays.

All that is required to convert glass-framed felt "paintings" into serving trays is to add appropriate handles to the narrow ends of the frame, and rubber rests at the bottom. The rests are important since they prevent the tray from scratching the table or any other article of furniture. The handles may be plastic, wood, or metal, and can easily be attached to the ends of the tray with small screws.

Serving trays of this kind are not only attractive and unusual, but are most practical as well.

Project No. 50, Button-Box

See Figure 6, Illustration 19

Built of a tin coffee can or any similar tin can container, a few scraps of felt, and several ordinary buttons, this button-box makes an attractive and useful gift for any woman.

Although this project may be styled and built in various ways, the author has found the following method to be the easiest and most effective. It is especially recommended for children's arts and crafts groups.

1. Apply a coat of quick-drying enamel paint over all outside surfaces of the tin can container and allow to dry thoroughly. Apply the paint evenly, using a flat-style brush. Be sure to select a color which will provide effective contrast with the gayly colored felt decorations which are later to be applied.

2. Make cardboard patterns for a suitable form of trimming or border around the top and bottom edges of the can, similar to those seen at A and B, Fig. 6.

3. Trace these border patterns to appropriate colors of felt, cut out the felt strips, and glue them neatly and securely in place at the top and bottom edges of the container, in the manner seen in our sketch, at A and B, Fig. 6. Use a good grade of household cement or liquid glue.

4. Make a pattern for a simple flower such as the dogwood or daisy, and trace and cut out about seven of them in a suitable, gay color of felt.

5. Sew a black, brown, or dark green button to the center of each of these cutout felt flowers.

6. Glue the flowers with the buttons already sewn to their centers around the outside, enamel painted surface of the tin can, arranging the felt pieces in some attractive design such as employed in Fig. 6. Be sure each unit is glued tightly in place, using rubber bands or string as clamps during the drying period.

7. Make a pattern and a felt cutout of a similar flower to be used on the cover of the tin can. Then, glue it in place, as shown in Fig. 6.

8. Glue four small circles of felt to the bottom of the container to serve as protective rests.

When completed, this container makes a good receptacle for buttons and similar sewing supplies.

Other good decorative motifs for use in the construction of these button boxes are peasant figures, simple animal forms, Mexican subjects and so forth.

Project No. 51, String-Holder

This string-container is built in the same way as the button box, shown in Fig. 6, Illustration 19, except that no buttons are sewed to the applique felt flowers. Instead, small, dark-colored discs of felt are employed.

Another slight difference between the button-box and the string-holder is that the latter has a small hole drilled through the center of the cover of the tin can container, through which the string may be pulled as it is needed.

For complete particulars concerning the making of this convenient string-holder, see text under Project No. 50.

Project No. 52, Indian Doll Lapel Pin

See Figure 7-A, Illustration 19

This unusual felt project is particularly interesting because of its Indian motif.

To make this lapel ornament, first sandpaper the top and end sections of an odd clothespin and then coat the whole clothespin with white shellac. The next step is to cut out all the felt parts of the Indian doll. For these parts use appropriate, gay colors of felt, working out each part separately, and in correct proportions, in accordance with the size of the clothespin.

First cut out and prepare the doll's trousers and sew and glue them around the lower or pointed sections of the clothespin. Next, cut out and glue two or three thin strands of black felt over the top of the clothespin to represent the Indian doll's hair. Follow this by cutting out three small feathers, of different colors, and a narrow strip for the head-band. Glue the feathers inside the head-band and then glue the band over the hair and round the top section of the clothespin, as shown at Fig. 7-A. The last step is the preparation of the blanket. This is easily done by first cutting a piece of felt to the size and shape of the blanket seen in the sketch. Then glue small applique pieces of felt in gay colors and Indian designs to the front sections of the blanket. When the blanket is thus completed, glue or pin it around the shoulder of the clothespin, as in the sketch.

To complete the Indian doll lapel pin, draw simple features on the face of the doll with a pen and India ink, using two dots for the eyes, one dot for the nose, and a short, horizontal line for the mouth. Finally, sew a safety pin to the back of the lapel ornament as a clasp.

Clothespin lapel pins, constructed like our Indian doll model in Fig. 7-A can be made of other figures such as pirates, peasants, Mexicans, sailors, soldiers, and so forth.

Project No. 53, Felt Deer Lapel Pin

See Figure 7-B, Illustration 19

Except for the absorbent cotton used to stuff it, and the thread used to sew it together, this little deer lapel ornament is made entirely of scrap pieces of felt.

To make this "stuffed animal" lapel pin, proceed as follows:

1. Prepare a cardboard pattern of the shape of the deer, making the deer about 3 inches high. You can easily make a copy of the deer as represented in Fig. 7-B, by drawing a grill of proper size squares and then by reproducing the figure as shown in the sketch. You will need a separate pattern for the ears.

2. Make two tracings each of the deer and ear patterns, using any suitable colors of felt. Then cut out these four felt parts of the deer with small size scissors.

3. Sew the two deer sides together at the edges, using a simple overhand stitch, closely and neatly applied. Leave about two inches of the seam open until after the cotton stuffing is inserted.

4. Stuff deer tightly with absorbent cotton or any similar material. Then sew up the rest of the seam at the edge of the deer.

5. Sew an ear to each side of the deer's head as shown in Fig. 7-B.

6. Cut out and paste on black and white felt pieces to represent the deer's eye. Also a red piece of felt for the deer's nose, and a few round pieces in a proper color for the deer's spots.

7. Sew safety pin to back of deer as clasp.

Other good subjects for cotton-stuffed felt lapel ornaments are giraffes, elephants, rabbits, fish, squirrels, donkeys, camels, frogs, turtles and butterflies.

Project No. 54, Felt Bean-Bags

Bean-bags, in a wide variety of interesting subjects, may be built of scraps of felt in practically the same manner as the felt animal lapel pins shown in Fig. 7-B. You will find complete directions for this form of construction in the text under Project No. 53, felt deer lapel pin.

When making the bean-bags, however, the animals must be made about three times as large as the size required for the lapel pins. Also, instead of using absorbent cotton for the stuffing, employ pebbles or hard peas. Another requirement, when making the animal stuffed bean-bags, is to sew on the eye, nose, spots or other animal features, instead of just pasting them on. This is necessary because of the rough handling generally given bean-bags.

Project No. 55, Felt Coin Purse for Wrist

See Figure 8, Illustration 19

This trim little coin purse, designed to be worn on the wrist, is made entirely of gaily colored felt scraps, except for its buckle and button. It is sure to be popular with girls and young women everywhere, because it is fun to make and smart to wear.

As you will note from our sketch of this project in Fig. 8, it is made of two separate felt units, the purse and the strap parts. Though this project looks somewhat involved, it is really easy to make.

1. Cut a strip of a fairly heavy grade of felt for the wrist band, size 5/8 inch wide by 9 inches long. (Check this average length size with your own wrist or that of the person for whom the purse is intended, and change length size if necessary). Make one end of strip pointed and the other one straight or square, as shown in Fig. 8.

2. Punch three holes at pointed end of band for buckle tongue, using for this purpose any regular leather or paper punch.

3. Finish all edges of band with blanket stitching, neatly and closely applied.

4. Attach any odd metal or plastic buckle to straight end of band, either sewing it on, or, as shown in the sketch, using a small eyelet.

5. Cut a cardboard pattern for a simple applique design to be used along the length of the wrist band, like the tulip unit used on our model. Trace and cut out about five of these units, using for this purpose any suitable, contrasting color of felt. Then sew these applique felt units to the wrist band, with a simple overhand stitch. See sketch for arrangement of the applique decorations and method of sewing.

6. Make a cardboard pattern for the coin purse, size 2-1/4 inches wide, by 4-1/2 inches long, and shape one end neatly to serve as the purse flap. Also punch a small hole in the upper part of the flap to indicate location of button hole. See A, Fig. 8, for diagram of this purse pattern.

7. Trace purse pattern to appropriate color of felt, then carefully cut out this part. Punch hole at designed end for button fastener later to be used to hold flap in place. Cut two 3/4 inch long slits, 1 inch apart, at the back section of this purse unit, through which the wrist band is to be inserted.

8. Make cardboard patterns for felt decorations which are to be used on the top side of the purse. Then cut out these applique decorations carefully with small scissors, and either paste or sew them in place as desired. See locations and arrangement of these purse decorations in sketch. It is important that these applique design units be cut out of a suitable color of felt to contrast effectively with the color of the purse itself.

9. Fold felt purse piece into its proper purse form and then blanket stitch its edges together in the manner represented in Fig. 8. Also finish edges of button hole in this fashion. Complete purse by sewing on a fancy button to correspond with the location of the button hole in the flap. Use a plastic button if plastic buckle is used, and a metal one if a metal buckle is used.

10. Insert felt wrist band through the two slits previously cut at the back section of the purse. The purse is then completed and ready to be strapped neatly around the wrist.

Teachers of arts and crafts, presenting this gaily decorated wrist purse to girls, should allow them wide latitude in designing their own applique felt units. The design possibilities are unlimited.

There are many other articles besides those treated in this book which can easily be made of felt. Among these are book-covers, book-ends, picture frames, coasters and greeting cards. It is hoped that the reader will exercise his own ingenuity in designing and making these as well as many other attractive articles of scrap felt.

CHAPTER EIGHT

WORKING WITH CORRUGATED CARTONS AND SCRAP WALL-PAPER

As OUR next scrap craft, we are going to consider the wide range of projects which can be made out of stiff cardboard obtained from discarded corrugated cartons, and odds and ends of wall-paper sheeting.

The outstanding advantages of stiff cardboard are that it is easily obtainable, free of cost, and requires no cleansing or conditioning before being put to use.

A good source for wall paper sheeting is provided by the use of old wall-paper sample books which dealers, interior decorators, and paper hangers are always glad to dispose of, especially if the papers are obsolete or out of style. Also, most property owners generally have odds and ends of wall-paper in roll form lying about the attic or cellar for which they actually have no further use.

As for corrugated box cardboard the streets are full of it and most food stores will thank you to take it away. You will find many other sources for corrugated cardboard as well as other kinds of similar cardboard sheeting in the classified lists of scrap materials in Chapter Two.

Our key project in the use of corrugated box cardboard and wall-paper sheeting is the waste-basket, shown in Illustration 20. This article is not only useful and easy to build, but incorporates in its construction all essential procedures required in this form of handicraft. Among these procedures are (1) Methods of measuring and cutting corrugated cardboard and wall-paper sheeting, (2) Punching holes and lacing, (3) Methods of pasting and mounting printed paper sheeting, (4) Use and application of passe-partout or gummed cloth-tape trimming, (5) Methods of finishing applied printed paper surfaces.

After you have constructed this waste-basket, carefully following the methods and directions given below, you will have no difficulty in building the many other useful related projects which are presented below. These directions also apply to the use of metallic papers in silver, bronze, gold, and so forth, finger-painted papers, and novelty wrapping papers.

Project No. 56, Waste-Basket

See Illustration 20

I. Description

One can hardly believe that this attractive and sturdy waste-basket is made of commonly used corrugated box material, discarded everywhere as mere waste. Its decorative effect is produced by the use of gaily colored and designed wall-paper coverings on its tapered sides, by a neat arrangement of lacing at its corners, and by a trimmed finish at its top and bottom edges.

Although wall-paper is suggested here as the material for covering the corrugated cardboard sides of the waste-basket, other decorative treatments may be employed such as finger-painting or oil painting, or the sides may be covered with cotton goods, such as percale, chintz, gingham or cretonne. Crepe-paper, oil cloth, felt and cork may also be used. The choice of covering may, in most cases, be influenced by the type of scrap material available. Another factor in the selection of the proper material is its appropriateness. For instance, a decorative scheme which is suitable for a boy's room may not be appropriate in a girl's room.

Although specific sizes and patterns are given below for the construction of this waste basket, they may be modified to fit individual requirements.

In addition to providing amateur craftsmen with an interesting project for their home workshops, this waste-basket is also suitable for construction in school arts and crafts shops. It is easy to build, and involves such useful handwork procedures as designing, measuring, cutting, pasting, punching, lacing and trimming.

II. Materials

A. A corrugated box, large enough to provide four 12 inch square pieces from which to cut the sides of the basket, and a ten inch

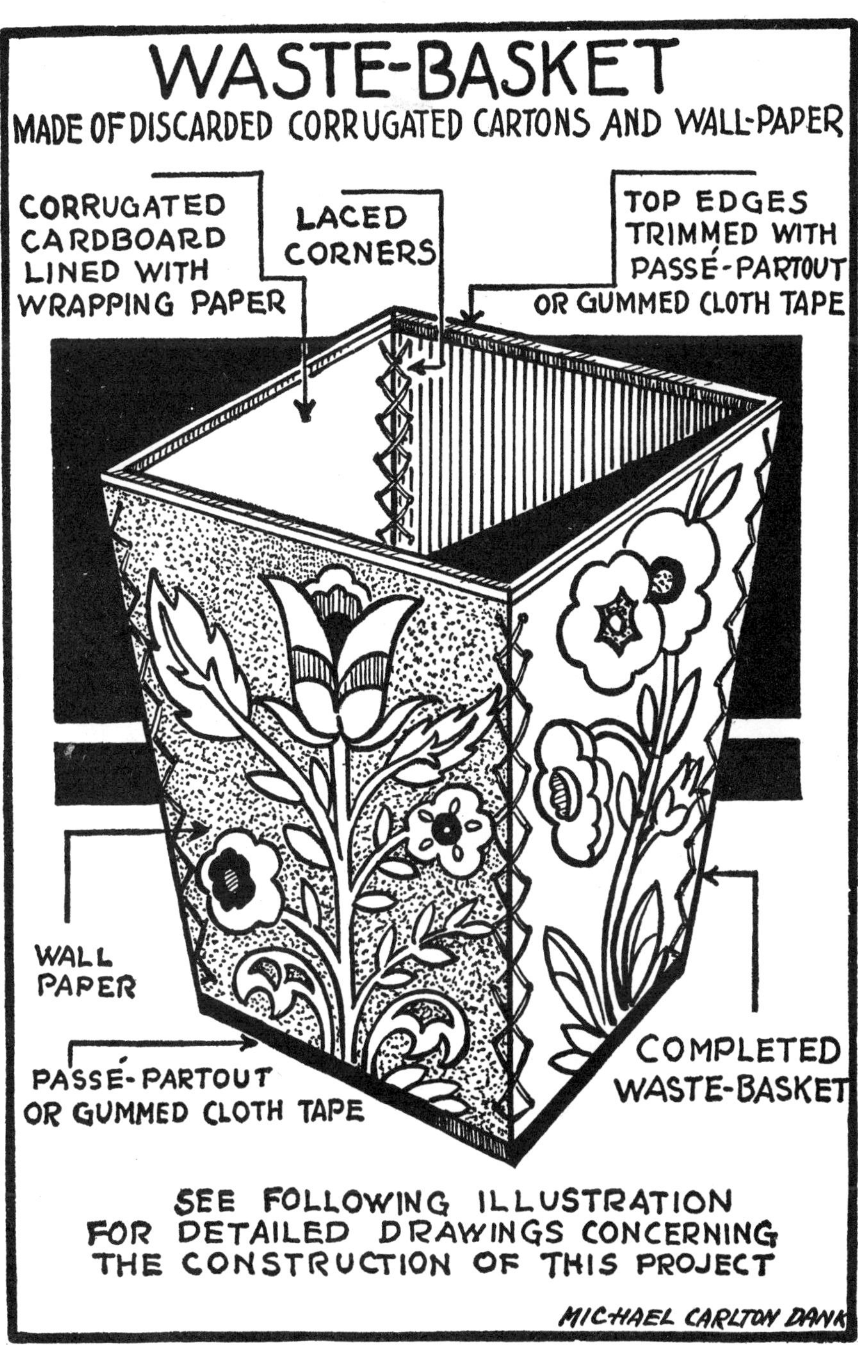
WASTE-BASKET
MADE OF DISCARDED CORRUGATED CARTONS AND WALL-PAPER
CORRUGATED CARDBOARD LINED WITH WRAPPING PAPER
LACED CORNERS
TOP EDGES TRIMMED WITH PASSÉ-PARTOUT OR GUMMED CLOTH TAPE
WALL PAPER
PASSÉ-PARTOUT OR GUMMED CLOTH TAPE
COMPLETED WASTE-BASKET
SEE FOLLOWING ILLUSTRATION FOR DETAILED DRAWINGS CONCERNING THE CONSTRUCTION OF THIS PROJECT
MICHAEL CARLTON DANK

Illustration 20

square piece, from which to cut the base. Use only smooth-surfaced, sturdy grade, corrugated board, unscratched and free from holes.

B. Scrap pieces of wall-paper in differently designed, bold, and gaily colored patterns. Both the sample book and roll forms of wall-paper are satisfactory.

C. About 5 yards of lacing, in the form of colored cloth tape, wide leather or leatherette lacing, or braided cord. Twisted strips of crepe-paper or raffia are also satisfactory lacing materials. Colors of lacing must fit the color scheme of the rest of the basket.

D. Approximately 1 square yard of scrap sheets of brown wrapping paper.

E. Passe-partout or gummed cloth tape in black or any other suitable dark color.

F. Flour paste and liquid glue.

G. Clear white shellac or clear quick-drying varnish.

III. TOOLS

A. Sharp knife, suitable for cutting cardboard.

B. Medium size pair of scissors.

C. Steel ruler, of at least 24 inch length.

D. Wooden mallet.

E. Leather or paper punch, capable of punching 1/8 inch diameter holes. A large-tipped nail set is also good for this purpose.

F. Cutting board, measuring about 14 inches by 16 inches, made of plywood, composition wall board, or any other smooth surfaced board stock.

G. Scrubbing brush or any other flat style brush, with fairly stiff bristles.

Plate 10. The waste basket illustrated was constructed of scrap corrugated cardboard, and the design was executed in finger paints on paper. Attractive book covers can be made of finger-painted paper or of wall-paper scraps.

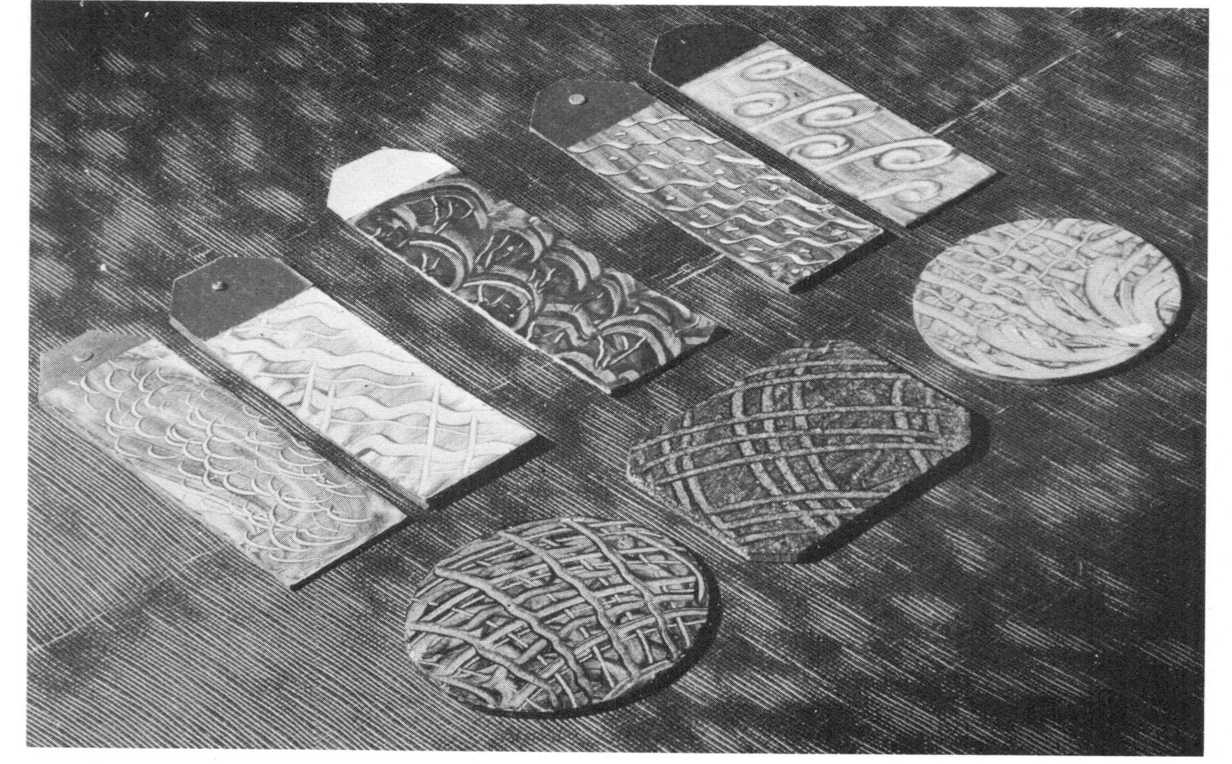

Plate 11. Cardboard decorated with scraps of wall-paper or finger-painted paper is useful in making coasters, trivets, memo-pad covers and blotter holders.

H. 1 inch wide, flat style brush, suitable for gluing and pasting operations.

I. 1-1/2 inch wide brush, suitable for overall shellacking or varnishing purposes.

IV. Directions

A. Cutting corrugated sides and bottom of basket.

This first step in the preparation of our waste-basket must be done very carefully as incorrectly or unevenly cut corrugated parts will detract considerably from the appearance of the basket. These corrugated parts form the foundation of our project, and all subsequent operations depend entirely upon the neatness and accuracy with which they are prepared. The correct procedure for cutting the corrugated sides and bottom of our waste basket is as follows:

1. Using a steel rule and pencil, lay out the first of the four corrugated sides of the basket, following the plan shown in Fig. 1-A. Illustration 21. Make the height 12 inches, the top edge 10 inches, and the bottom edge 7-1/2 inches.

2. Place corrugated sheet, thus marked off, on the cutting board. Then, using a steel rule and knife, cut off excess material (shown black in Fig. 1-A). While cutting, hold ruler firmly in position with left hand, keeping the fingers safely in back of the cutting edge of the ruler. Also, hold knife with its blade pointed forward and at right angles with the steel ruler. Working in this manner will produce clean-cut square edges. See Fig. 2, Illustration 21.

3. Using this first-cut corrugated cardboard side as a pattern, mark off remaining three basket sides in exactly the same shape and size. Lay out these three parts and cut them out carefully, employing the method described for the first basket side.

4. Lay out the bottom or base of the basket following the plan given in Fig. 1-B. Note that the inside measurement of this part is 7-1/2 inches square, the same as the bottom of the basket sides. Also note the 1 inch extra allowance required all around for the flap which is to be folded over and glued into the base of

the basket when the parts are assembled. The overall size of this bottom is thus 9-1/2 inches square.

5. Place corrugated sheet containing layout of bottom part on the wooden cutting board, and then cut around its 9-1/2 inches square measurement.

6. Using knife and ruler, score around the 7-1/2 inches square measurement of this part just enough to allow the 1 inch flaps to fold easily. Follow this by completely cutting out the corners, just as illustrated in Fig. 1-B, making it possible to form the tray arrangement of the bottom section as shown in Fig. 6.

B. Selecting, cutting and pasting on wall-paper coverings.

When selecting the wall-paper coverings for the basket, it is best to use bold, gaily colored patterns. If old sample books are used as the source for the wall-paper, you may employ a different pattern, though of the same general type, for each of the four basket sides. For example, you may use four different flower patterns, four different peasant subjects, and so forth, as in Illustration 20. If the roll form of wall-paper is used, you may employ the same subjects or patterns for all four sides of the basket.

After selecting the wall-paper material, use a sharp pair of scissors to cut the four wall-paper sheets to their proper shape and size. To do this correctly, simply trace the corrugated basket side to the back surface of the wall-paper, then add a 1 inch extra margin all around as a folding flap for the pasting. After laying out the four wall-paper sheets in this manner, cut them out. Cut the corners off at an angle as shown in Fig. 3-B.

Having thus cut the corrugated boards and wall-paper coverings to their proper shape and size, paste them together to form the basket sides.

1. Using flour paste and a 1 inch wide, flat brush, apply a coating of the paste over the entire surface of one side of the first corrugated board to be covered with the wall-paper. See Fig. 3-A.

2. Apply a coating of the paste to the underside of one of the wall-paper coverings. Use every precaution to prevent soiling the good side of the wall-paper with paste smears. This can

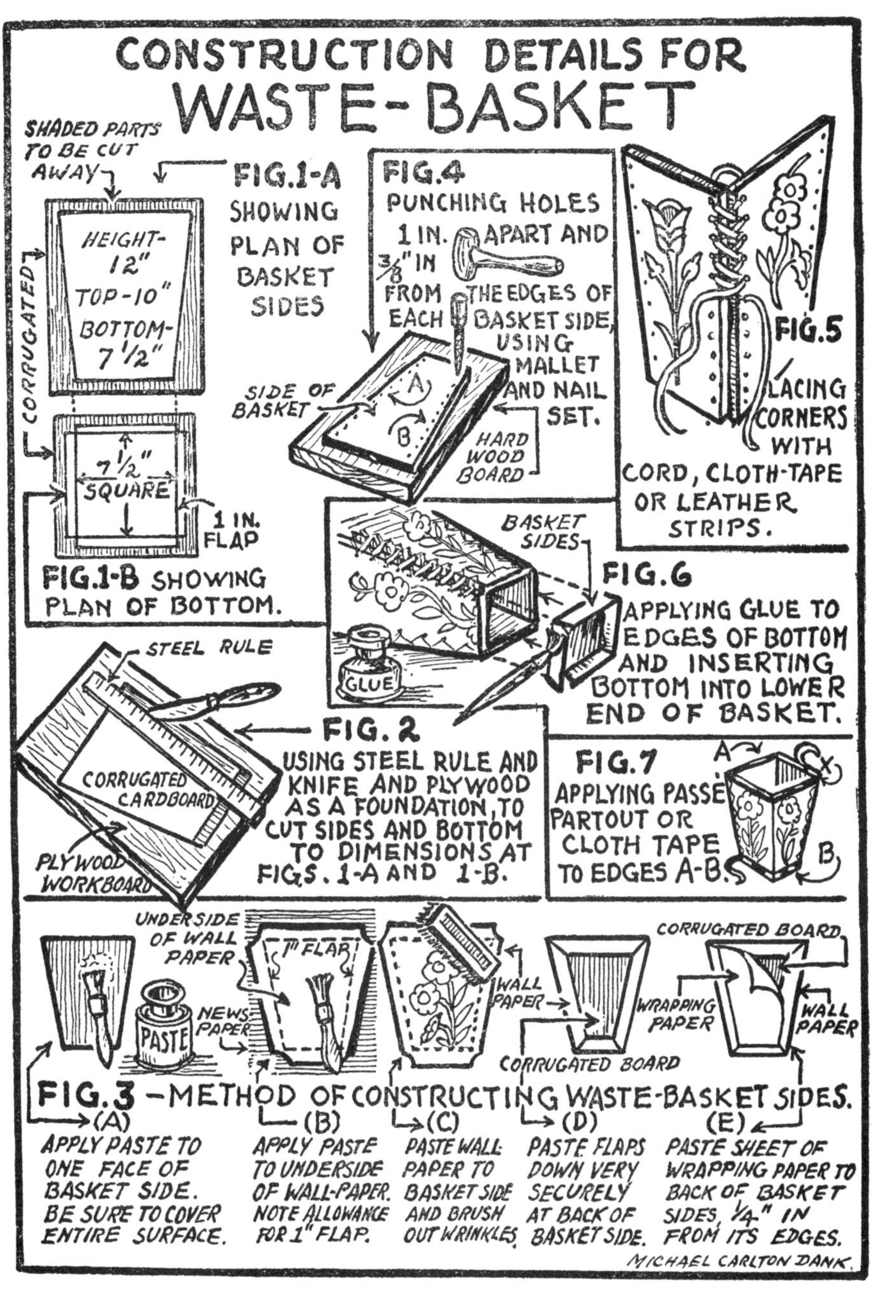

CONSTRUCTION DETAILS FOR
WASTE-BASKET
SHADED PARTS TO BE CUT AWAY
FIG.1-A SHOWING PLAN OF BASKET SIDES
HEIGHT-12"
TOP-10"
BOTTOM-7 1/2"
CORRUGATED
7 1/2" SQUARE
1 IN. FLAP
FIG.1-B SHOWING PLAN OF BOTTOM.
FIG.4 PUNCHING HOLES 1 IN. APART AND 3/8" IN FROM THE EDGES OF EACH BASKET SIDE, USING MALLET AND NAIL SET.
SIDE OF BASKET
HARD WOOD BOARD
FIG.5 LACING CORNERS WITH CORD, CLOTH-TAPE OR LEATHER STRIPS.
BASKET SIDES
FIG.6 APPLYING GLUE TO EDGES OF BOTTOM AND INSERTING BOTTOM INTO LOWER END OF BASKET.
GLUE
STEEL RULE
CORRUGATED CARDBOARD
PLYWOOD WORKBOARD
FIG. 2 USING STEEL RULE AND KNIFE AND PLYWOOD AS A FOUNDATION, TO CUT SIDES AND BOTTOM TO DIMENSIONS AT FIGS. 1-A AND 1-B.
FIG.7 APPLYING PASSE PARTOUT OR CLOTH TAPE TO EDGES A-B.
UNDERSIDE OF WALL PAPER
1" FLAP
PASTE
NEWS PAPER
WALL PAPER
CORRUGATED BOARD
WRAPPING PAPER
WALL PAPER
CORRUGATED BOARD
FIG.3 -METHOD OF CONSTRUCTING WASTE-BASKET SIDES.
(A) APPLY PASTE TO ONE FACE OF BASKET SIDE. BE SURE TO COVER ENTIRE SURFACE.
(B) APPLY PASTE TO UNDERSIDE OF WALL-PAPER. NOTE ALLOWANCE FOR 1" FLAP.
(C) PASTE WALL PAPER TO BASKET SIDE AND BRUSH OUT WRINKLES.
(D) PASTE FLAPS DOWN VERY SECURELY AT BACK OF BASKET SIDE.
(E) PASTE SHEET OF WRAPPING PAPER TO BACK OF BASKET SIDES, 1/4" IN FROM ITS EDGES.
MICHAEL CARLTON DANK

Illustration 21

easily be managed by working over a sheet of newspaper as a base. See Fig. 3-B.

3. Paste wall-paper to corrugated board and smooth out all wrinkles with a stiff-bristled brush, in the manner demonstrated in Fig. 3-C.

4. Place work with wall-papered surface of basket side piece facing down, on a clean sheet of newspaper; then apply paste to the 1 inch flaps and brush them down neatly to produce the result shown in Fig. 3-D.

C. Pasting wrapping paper to back surfaces of basket sides

1. With pencil and ruler lay out a sheet of wrapping paper in the same shape and size as the basket side, less about 1/4 inch all around.

2. With scissors, cut out this wrapping paper sheet as outlined, then paste it to the back surface of the basket side. In this step, as when pasting on the wall-paper coverings, both contact surfaces must be moistened with the paste. See Fig. 3-E.

3. Repeat these operations for each of the remaining three basket sides.

D. Punching lace holes

The holes which are required for lacing the four sides of the waste-basket together must first be laid out carefully with pencil and ruler. Otherwise, they will be uneven, irregularly spaced, and thus spoil the appearance of the complete article.

The holes must be punched along the full height of the basket side in a straight line 1/2 inch in from each long edge. Start punching the holes 1/2 inch from the top, and then continue with 1 inch spaces down the full length of the edge. The holes must be about 1/8 inch in diameter.

The holes may be punched with a regular leather punching tool, set for punching 1/8 inch diameter holes. Another and, perhaps, quicker and easier method, is to use a mallet and a 3/32 inch to 1/8 inch size nail-set, using any thick wood board as a working foundation. In this latter method, simply place the basket side piece with wall-papered surface facing upward upon the work board, then punch the holes with the nail-set, in the manner demonstrated in Fig. 4. The diameter of the holes punched should be determined by the width or thickness of the lacing material which is to be employed for assembling the sides.

E. Lacing basket sides together

To lace the sides of the basket together, you may use any one of a variety of scrap materials. Among these are colored cloth tape, wide leather or leatherette lacing, twisted raffia or crepe paper, and heavy braided cord. Of these lacing materials, the author has found 1/2 inch wide cloth tape, in an appropriate color, to be most suitable for this purpose.

For the lacing of each corner, you will need a strip of about 1-1/4 yards in length. This size may vary somewhat, depending upon the particular style of lacing employed. A good, simple lacing procedure for our basket corners is as follows:

1. Start lacing from the inside of the basket corner, inserting one end of the lace through the top hole of each of the two adjoining basket sides. This will form a loop at the inside of the corner, as shown in Fig. 5, Illustration 21.

2. Pull ends of lacing tightly until loop slack is fully taken up, then cross laces and insert ends through holes immediately below.

3. Continue lacing in an under-and-over crossed fashion, until the full length of the corner is completed. See Fig. 5, Illustration 21, and also completed basket sketch in Illustration 20.

4. Finish off at bottom, by gluing the ends of the lace on the inside surface of the basket.

Note:

There are several other lacing methods which may be employed successfully for assembling the basket sides, and it is a good idea for each builder of this project to work out his own lacing scheme.

Those familiar with the lacing procedures employed in leathercraft work, will find this phase of our project especially interesting.

F. Inserting basket bottom

To fasten the bottom section to the lower end of our basket, first fold the four flaps in right angle fashion as seen in Fig. 6. Then apply a coating of glue over the outer surfaces of the folded flaps and insert the base section inside of the bottom of the basket as indicated by the arrows, in Fig. 6. To be correctly inserted, the lower edges of the flaps of the base section must be exactly even with the lower edges of the basket sides. This will provide a strong, stable foundation for the basket.

G. Trimming top and bottom edges of basket

As you will note from the completed sketch of our project, in Illustration 20, the top and bottom edges of the basket are neatly finished with some form of decorative trimming material. This edging material may be passe-partout, which is a gummed paper, or it may be some kind of gummed cloth tape. A tape of 1 inch width is most suitable for this purpose.

Whether using the paper or cloth tape, it is important that the color used be in harmony with the rest of the project. Generally, however, black or any other suitable dark color will be found most effective.

The proper procedure for applying the tape trimming to the top and bottom edges of the basket is as follows:

1. Cut a strip of tape to a length of 8 inches or 1/2 inch longer than the top measurement of the basket sides.

2. Wet the gummed surface of this strip with a piece of cloth or sponge, then paste it over the top edge of one of the basket sides. Start pasting the strip exactly at the corner of the basket, and allow the other end of the tape to extend 1/2 inch around the top edge of the next basket side. Be certain that the tape is applied in a straight, even fashion, with half of its width appearing on the inside of the basket and the other half on the outside.

3. Cut next tape strip and paste it over the top edge of the next side, again starting exactly at the corner, but this time, covering 1/2 inch extension of the first applied strip.

4. Paste on the other two strips in this same manner, and then apply the strips over the bottom edges of the basket sides, following the same overlapping method of working.

5. If any glue smears appear on the taped edges, wipe them off carefully with a damp cloth.

H. Shellacking and finishing the waste-basket

As a final finish for our waste-basket, you may use either clear white shellac or clear quick-drying varnish. For a brighter and more protective finish, it is best to use two coats of the shellac or varnish, applying the second coat only after the first has thoroughly dried.

Coat both the inside and outside surfaces of the basket, using long, careful brush strokes, to produce a neat, uniform finish. Use a 1 inch wide, flat brush, and make certain that the shellac or varnish used is of a medium consistency. If too heavy, use alcohol as a thinning agent for shellac, and turpentine for varnish.

In addition to finishing the inside and outside surfaces of the basket sides, shellac or varnish both surfaces of the bottom of the basket. It is a good idea, too, to coat the tape trimming at the top and bottom edges as well as the lacing at the corners of the basket. When applying the finish over the laced sections, be especially careful to brush away any accumulated puddles or irregularities, to produce a smoothly shellacked or varnished appearance.

When applying these finishing treatments, it is important that the room be entirely free of dust or draft. This must also be the case when the varnished or shellacked basket is set aside to dry. For either finish it is a good plan to allow an overnight drying period before the completed project is put to use.

RELATED PROJECTS

Based upon the handwork procedures and the use of discarded corrugated cardboard and wall-paper sheeting, as employed in the construction of the waste-basket, Project No. 56.

Project Nos. 57 and 58, Scrap-Books and Photograph Albums

See Figures 1 and 2, Illustration 22

This useful project may be made in a wide variety of shapes and sizes. It may be made in a vertical form in such sizes as 10 inches by 12 inches or 12 inches by 14 inches, for use as a scrap-book. Or, it can be constructed in a horizontal form in such sizes as 6 inches by 9 inches, or 8 inches by 14 inches, for use as a photograph album. Another interesting application of this project is to use the figure of an animal, a ship, an airplane or a landscape, to form the actual shape of the book, instead of just straight sides. In all of these projects, the edges of both the top and bottom covers should be neatly laced with some suitable form of stitching such as the over-and-under or whip stitch. Another good stitch is the button-hole stitch, commonly employed in leathercraft. As for the selection of proper wall-paper patterns, it is best to use for this purpose subjects of a generally small character, and in close formation. Such subjects as ships, flowers, peasants, or even small abstract decorations are all satisfactory wall-paper selections for these scrap-books and photograph albums. For the tie-bows used to fasten together the sheets and covers of these books you may use the same material as employed for lacing the edges. Labels, reading "Photograph Album" or "Scrap-Book," may be separately lettered and pasted over the wall-paper covering on the top cover of the book. The books may be shellacked or varnished or even left unfinished, according to individual taste. The paper sheets used inside the covers may be wrapping paper, drawing paper, or any other suitable form of paper sheeting. The sheets should be cut in the same shape as the edges of the covers, though 1/4 inch shorter all around. A hinged effect for the top cover may be provided by the use of a strip of gummed cloth tape. See this hinged construction in Figs. 1 and 2, Illustration 22. If desired, the bottom cover of the scrap book or photograph album may also be hinged with cloth tape in this same manner.

Project No. 59, Photograph Frame

See Figure 3, Illustration 22

Good overall sizes for this novelty photograph frame are 3-1/2 inches by 5 inches, 5 inches by 7 inches, or 8 inches by 10 inches. Its edges, both outside and inside, may either be taped or laced.

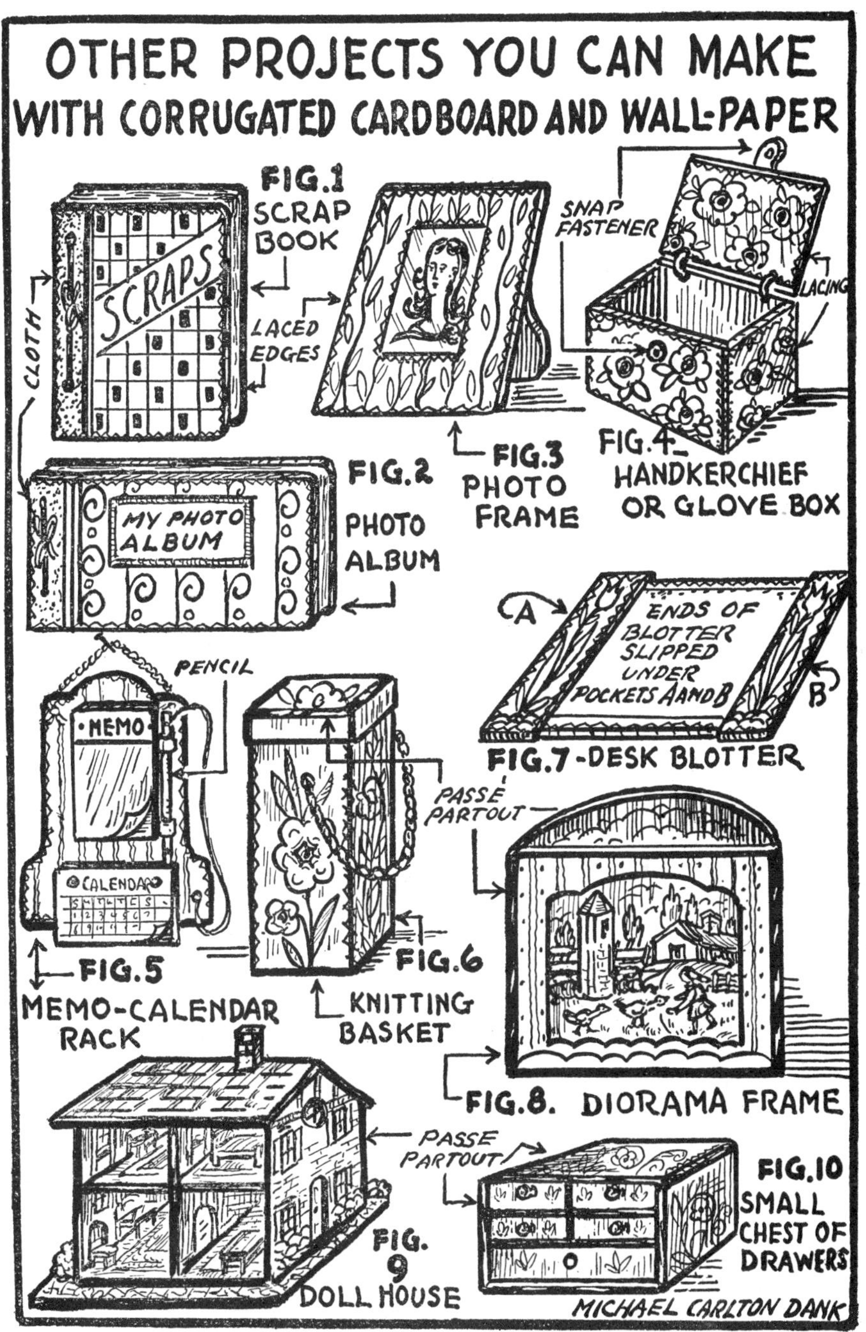
OTHER PROJECTS YOU CAN MAKE
WITH CORRUGATED CARDBOARD AND WALL-PAPER
FIG.1
SCRAP
BOOK
SCRAPS
CLOTH
LACED
EDGES
SNAP
FASTENER
LACING
FIG.2
PHOTO
ALBUM
MY PHOTO
ALBUM
FIG.3
PHOTO
FRAME
FIG.4
HANDKERCHIEF
OR GLOVE BOX
A
B
ENDS OF
BLOTTER
SLIPPED
UNDER
POCKETS A AND B
FIG.7 - DESK BLOTTER
PENCIL
MEMO
CALENDAR
PASSE
PARTOUT
FIG.5
MEMO-CALENDAR
RACK
FIG.6
KNITTING
BASKET
FIG.8. DIORAMA FRAME
PASSE
PARTOUT
FIG.
9
DOLL HOUSE
FIG.10
SMALL
CHEST OF
DRAWERS
MICHAEL CARLTON DANK

Illustration 22

Easel is attached to back of frame with 1 inch wide cloth-tape, and held in check at the bottom by a 1/4 inch wide strip of cloth-tape. Front of frame and easel should be covered with delicately patterned and colored wall-paper. Back of frame should be covered with wrapping paper or any other grade of brown paper. Pocket for holding glass and photograph may be made of 1/4 inch square strips of wood. Three scrap pieces of tin, measuring 1/4 inch wide by 3/4 inch long, may be nailed to the top of the strips in loose or swivel fashion to hold glass and photograph in place. The frame may be finished with an overall shellac or varnish coating, or, if desired, may be left in the original dull wall-paper finish. To be most effective, the coloring used for the tape trimming or lacing should be in harmony with that of the wall-paper.

Project No. 60, Handkerchief or Glove Box

See Figure 4, Illustration 22

Overall sizes of this practical box are 5 inches wide by 9 inches long by 4-1/2 inches high. Cloth tape is glued along top and bottom edges of box sides. The corners of the box and the edges of the cover are laced with cloth tape or leather lacing. The cover may be attached to the box with two metal or plastic rings, here employed as hinges. It may also be hinged to the box with two appropriately colored strips of cloth tape, neatly knotted on the outside of the cover with little bows. Both the ring or tape forms of hinges are fastened in place through small holes punched through upper part of back of box and lower part of cover, as in Fig. 4. Wall-paper covering in a gay pattern should be used on both the inside and outside surfaces of the box and cover sections. Buttons are sewed to bottom of box to serve as foot-rests, one at each corner. Entire project should be finished with varnish or white shellac In addition to being used as a convenient container for gloves and handkerchiefs, this box may also be employed as a sewing kit or jewelry box. A laced-in tongue piece on the front edge of the cover, and a small, fancy button sewed to the upper, middle part of the front side of the box, provide a convenient clasp to hold the cover neatly in place. A snap fastener may be used in place of the button and button hole form of clasp if desired. See Fig. 4.

Project No. 61, Toy Trunk

See Figure 4 (Handkerchief Box), Illustration 22

This toy trunk is constructed in exactly the same way as the handkerchief and glove box, shown in Fig. 4, except that a heavier grade of corrugated cardboard must be employed and a considerably larger size box is required. Use some juvenile pattern for the wall-paper covering of the trunk. A good size for this toy trunk is 18 inches wide by 24 inches long by 18 inches high. Mothers will find this trunk a very convenient container for toy blocks, dolls, pull-toys and various other playthings, and it will help the children to keep their playrooms in order.

Project No. 62, Combination Calendar and Memo-Pad

See Figure 5, Illustration 22

This project may be used in the kitchen or near the telephone. Its overall sizes are 6 inches by 9 inches. The calendar at the bottom of the rack may be in any suitable size, as shown. A good size for the memo-pad which is fastened to the upper section of the rack is 3-1/2 inches by 5 inches. Both the memo-pad and calendar are attached to the rack with round-headed brass fasteners. The pencil, seen at the right of the pad, may be conveniently held in place by two loops of cloth tape or tin inserted through the front side of the rack and fastened tightly at the back with strips of gummed cloth-tape. The edges of the rack may either be cloth-taped or laced with wool, leather or leatherette. The wall-paper covering used over the front surface of the rack should be of a delicate pattern, in subdued colors. A 12 inch long string is attached to the top of the pencil and to the lower part of the rack in the manner shown. A strip of braided cord or braided leather or leatherette lacing is attached to the top of the rack as a decorative hanger. The ends of the hanger are inserted through punched holes from the back of the rack and appear in front in a neatly fringed effect. No finish is required over the wall-paper covering as the dull, original wall-paper finish is more suitable and attractive for this particular project.

Project No. 63, Knitting Basket

See Figure 6, Illustration 22

The overall sizes of this neat and serviceable knitting or crocheting basket are 4 inches square by 12-1/2 inches high. The side pieces of the basket cover are 1-1/2 inches high. The top and bottom edges of both the cover and basket parts are trimmed with gummed cloth tape although passe-partout may also be used. The corners of the basket are laced with any suitable material such as cloth-tape or leather. A handle, 14 inches long, made of braided wool or braided cloth-tape, is fastened to two opposite sides of the basket. The ends of the handle are inserted through neatly eyeletted holes and securely knotted on the inside of the basket. The cover is made slightly larger than the 4 inch square measurement of the sides in order that it may fit snugly, as shown. Four buttons are sewn to the bottom of the basket, one at each corner, to serve as protective foot-rests. The wall-paper covering used for this knitting basket should be gaily and boldly patterned. The base of the basket is made in a separate piece in a folded flap arrangement, and is glued snugly in place at the bottom of the basket, just as in the construction of the waste-basket, shown in Illustration 20. See also Fig. 6, Illustration 21. All the outside surfaces of the knitting basket should be finished in one or two coatings of white shellac or clear varnish. Inside of basket should be left unfinished.

Project No. 64, Desk Blotter

See Figure 7, Illustration 22

This blotter may be made up in various sizes as required A good average size is 13 inches wide by 20 inches long. The four edges of the blotter pad are trimmed with gummed cloth tape in such colors as brown, green, or black, according to the general color scheme employed. The side strips, forming the blotter pockets are laced to the blotter pad in the manner shown with a suitable color of leather or leatherette lacing material. The inside edges of the pocket strips are trimmed with the same gummed tape as employed for the edges of the pad. The wall-paper covering used over the pocket strips should be neatly and simply patterned. Because of the long, narrow shape of these pockets, a pattern such as a long floral motif of the type shown in Fig. 7 is suitable. Wall-paper covering, in the same or in a similar pattern, should be employed over the top surface of the blotter pad, even though it is covered with the blotter sheet. The bottom surface of the pad should be covered with brown wrapping paper or any other suitable dark colored paper sheeting. The wall-paper covering of the pockets should be finished with a coat of white shellac or clear varnish to protect these parts against soiling.

Project No. 65, Diorama

See Figure 8, Illustration 22

Dioramas are useful as visual aids in various forms of educational work. They are also used a great deal in the planning and preparation of theatrical stage settings and in interior decoration. Dioramas can be constructed in various ways, depending upon the type of subject to be presented. The particular diorama shown in Fig. 8 consists of three parts or sections. These are the diorama frame, at the front, the background section, and the floor, or ground, section. The background section of this diorama is built in a circular form, since this arrangement is suitable for outdoor scenic displays. Interior displays are more effective with straight backgrounds. The three sections of this diorama are joined together securely with gummed cloth-tape as shown. The size of the frame at the front is 12 inches high by 16 inches long. The floor is 10 inches deep at the center, and is arc-shaped to fit exactly the curved arrangement of the background. The front of the frame is covered with simply patterned wall-paper. The back surface of the background is covered with brown wrapping paper. The inside surface of the background, as well as the upper surface of the floor, are covered with any plain white paper, such as white shelf paper, plain wall-paper, and so forth since these parts are to be painted with tempera colors.

The first step in the construction of the diorama is to paint the background. Next, the floor or ground section is painted. The third step is to join the background to the floor parts with gummed cloth-tape. The frame is then cut out, covered with the wall-paper, and joined to the background and ground parts, in the manner shown. The figures and other movable units used in the diorama display here shown are also constructed of corrugated cardboard with paper coverings. Tempera colors are used for these figures. All parts of the diorama frame, as well as the figures and scenic effects, are coated with two applications of clear white shellac. The same diorama may be employed for the presentation of other subjects or scenes simply by repainting the background and floor sections.

Project No. 66, Doll House

See Figure 9, Illustration 22

This doll house, like most of the projects in this group, may be built in various shapes and sizes in accordance with individual taste and requirements. It is constructed entirely of corrugated cardboard, wall-paper covering, and gummed cloth tape. The interior furnishings, seen in Fig. 9, are also built of these materials. The overall sizes of this doll house model are as follows: side elevation (shown as the long, open section in Fig. 9), is 12 inches high by 14 inches long; front elevation (showing windows and door, at the right), is 14 inches high by 12 inches long. The slanted roof section is built of two parts joined at the top with gummed cloth tape. The size of each of these two roof parts is 7-1/2 inches wide by 16 inches long. The chimney is first formed into shape and then glued to the roof in the manner illustrated. The ground section which is glued to the underside of the house floor extends 1 inch all around beyond the house walls. The inside partitions, representing the walls and upper story floor of this two story house, are built in half-lap jointed fashion. All other joints, such as the corners of the house, are glued together and then reinforced and neatly trimmed with gummed cloth-tape. The inside walls of the house are covered with wall-paper, using a different pattern for each room. The chimney, roof and exterior walls are covered with plain wall-paper, over which colored papers are pasted to represent the tiles, windows, doors, shrubbery, and so forth, shown in Fig. 9. The ground is covered with plain green wall-paper, although green crepe paper is also good for this purpose. All outside and inside surfaces of the doll house, as well as the movable furnishings used in each of the rooms, are neatly finished with a coat of clear white shellac. The edges of the roof, the partitions, and the ground section are carefully trimmed with gummed cloth tape.

Project No. 67, Small Chest of Drawers

See Figure 10, Illustration 22

This small chest of drawers may be placed on a desk to hold stationery, thumbtacks, paper-clips, and so forth, or on a dresser to hold gloves, handkerchiefs, pins, buttons and similar items. It may be built in various sizes and with any number of drawers to fit individual requirements. The model shown has four small and one large drawer. Wall-paper in floral or peasant motifs is used as a covering on all outside surfaces of the chest and drawers. Inside surfaces are lined with brown wrapping paper. All corners and edges are neatly trimmed and reinforced with gummed cloth-tape. The outside measurements of the chest are 9 inches high by 12 inches long by 7 inches deep. The four small drawers measure 3 inches by 6 inches. From these sizes must be deducted the thicknesses of the chest and drawer parts. The drawers are supported by two corrugated cardboard platforms, a little smaller than the top and bottom parts of the chest. These platforms are wrapped with wall-paper and trimmed with gummed cloth-tape. The platforms are securely glued to the back and sides of the chest, and reinforced with several medium size "U" shaped staples. Each drawer is built of a single piece of corrugated cardboard with folded up flaps forming its sides. All inside drawer surfaces are covered with wrapping paper, and the drawer corners are reinforced with gummed cloth-tape. The drawer knobs used here are plastic caps, commonly furnished with toothpaste tubes and other drugstore items. Brass fasteners are attached to the backs of the caps with their heads solidly imbedded in plaster of Paris. The two extending ends of the brass fasteners are inserted through the front sides of the drawers and securely clinched at the back. These improvised handles or knobs are attractive and practical. It is essential, of course, that the plastic caps used for this purpose be exactly the same. All outside and inside surfaces of the chest are finished with clear white shellac. All outside sections of the drawers are also coated with shellac. Four buttons, one at each corner, are sewn to the bottom of the chest as foot rests.

CHAPTER NINE

WORKING WITH NATURAL SCRAP MATERIALS

As YOU will note by referring to Chapter Two, Scrap List No. 3, nature is truly a storehouse of vast quantities of valuable scrap materials. These materials can be used advantageously in the construction of a wide range of handicraft projects, several of which are treated below.

Year after year, huge quantities of these natural products go through the same metamorphosis of coming to life, growing ripe, and then falling to the ground, to waste and decay with the dying season. A few examples of these products are acorns, pine-cones, certain varieties of nuts, cat-tails, fallen branches and sea shells.

Industrious and resourceful craftsmen who know how to convert these natural materials into articles of beauty and utility need only to gather as many of these supplies as they can use. For them there can never be a shortage of handicraft materials.

It is the purpose of this scrap-craft unit to show, by means of a series of representative or key projects, how easily you can utilize natural craft materials. Accordingly, in the pages which follow, you will learn how pine-cones and tree branches can be converted into a souvenir novelty in the form of an Indian peace-pipe. (See Fig. 1, Illustration 23.) You will also learn how birch bark and tree branches can easily be fashioned into a tie-rack. (See Fig. 1, Illustration 26.) You will be shown how acorns can be used in the creation of lapel ornaments, bracelets and necklaces. (See Figs. 1 and 4, Illustration 25, and Fig. 1, Illustration 24.)

In addition to these key projects, which are treated in detail, many other, equally interesting suggestions for the use of natural scrap materials are given later in this scrap craft unit. After building the projects discussed in this unit, it is hoped the reader will be able to devise projects of his own, for there is really no end to the possibilities of creative handiwork utilizing natural supplies. The author knows several creative business men who have profitably manufactured toys, souvenirs and novelties through the ingenious use of pine-cones, pine-needles, sea shells, pebbles, tree branches, tree bark, cat-tails, fish scales, and numerous other natural materials.

Let us proceed, then, with the discussion of our first key project in this absorbing scrap craft unit, in which pine-cones and tree branches are combined to fashion the Indian peace-pipe shown in Fig. 1, Illustration 23.

PINE CONES AND TREE BRANCHES

Project No. 68, Indian Peace Pipe

See Figure 1, Illustration 23

I. Description

Tree branches and pine cones, which are used in the construction of this Indian peace-pipe, are always easily obtainable wherever pine trees grow. In the latter part of August the pine cones fall to the ground in great numbers. If gathered soon after they have fallen from the trees, they are still alive, beautifully colored, and undecayed. In this form they can be used to make many attractive and useful articles.

Similarly, many pine, birch or other kinds of tree branches, required for the making of our peace-pipe, are also commonly found in the woods. These branches, like the pine cones, must be gathered from the ground while they are still fresh and sappy if they are to be of any real value in handicraft work.

The idea for this Indian peace-pipe was developed in a summer camp for boys, located in the White Mountains of New Hampshire. Owing to the scarcity of regular materials such as leather, plywood, metal and plastics, something had to be found to take their place. Some use was, of course, made of paper, cardboard, scrap lumber, tin cans, and so forth. But the problem of material shortages was not fully solved until one day when the author and his group of young craftsmen were tramping through the woods on their weekly hike. It was then, amid the giant pine trees, that the vast resources of nature's storehouse seemed to open to us. The ground was covered with great quantities of pine cones and variously shaped branches, shaken from the trees by the heavy winds of the day before.

One of the youngsters in the group brought a handful of the cones to the author and asked, "Isn't it a pity that these beautiful things must go to waste? Isn't there something we can do with them in our craft shop?" That question was all that was needed to point the way toward a real solution of our problem of material shortages through the use of nature's bountiful supplies.

The next day, the boys were sent out to the near-by woods to bring back piles of pine cones and tree branches of all shapes and sizes. Then the youngsters were encouraged to devise suitable projects which could be built of the newly discovered material. They had all seen the pine cones and tree branches ever so many times, but they had never thought of them as construction materials.

After a short period of planning the children were able to convert the cones and branches into many useful and attractive articles. Among these were tie-racks of all types, paper-knives, animals, games, hiking sticks, whistles, plant boxes, buttons, lapel ornaments, curtain pulls and dolls.

The project which proved most popular, however, was the Indian peace-pipe, because it involved interesting handwork processes, such as whittling, drilling, nailing, designing and coloring. Another reason for the success of this peace-pipe was that it symbolized Indian life and customs, fascinating to boys.

In addition to serving as excellent projects for work shops at summer camps, these Indian peace-pipes can also be made in quantity and sold at summer resort souvenir stores. When used for this purpose, the name of the particular resort can be lettered on the pipe stem.

Though primarily designed as a wall ornament, the peace-pipes may also be used as novelty tie-racks for boys. When used for this purpose, however, it is best to suspend the pine cones from each end of the pipe, instead of under the bowl, as pictured in Illustration 23.

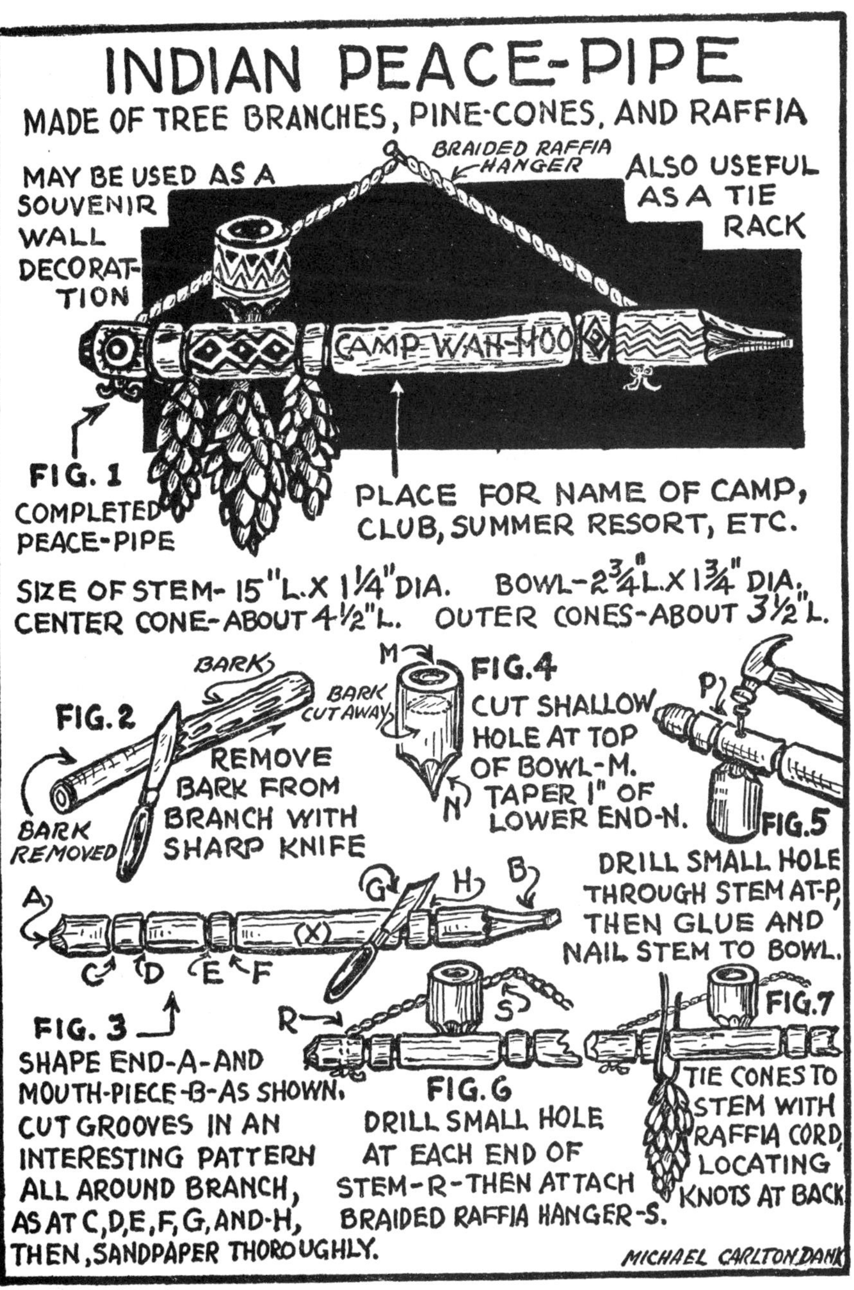

Illustration 23

II. Materials

A. A fairly straight tree branch, approximately 16 inches long, by 1-1/2 inches in diameter, to serve as the pipe stem. Also, a branch 3 inches long, by about 2 inches in diameter, to serve as the pipe bowel. Use only branches which are not dried out or decayed.

B. Three pine cones, two about 3-1/2 inches in length, and one about 4-1/2 inches long.

C. Three colors of raffia, leather lacing or leatherette lacing, for use in the preparation of the pipe hangers.

D. Tempera paints, in a gay assortment of colors.

E. Clear white shellac.

F. Liquid glue.

III. Tools

A. A sharp whittling knife. Any sharp pocket knife equipped with a long blade or a regular boy scout knife is entirely satisfactory for this purpose.

B. Medium size, pointed style, water color brushes.

C. A 1 inch wide, flat style, shellacking brush.

D. A boring brace, fitted with a 3/8 inch auger bit.

E. A medium size claw-hammer.

F. A medium-coarse, flat-faced file.

G. No. 1 and No. 0 sandpaper and a block of wood to serve as a sandpapering block. A good size of block is 4 inches by 2 inches by 3/4 inch.

IV. Directions

A. Preparation of pipe stem

The first step in the construction of our Indian peace-pipe is to make its long stem, or horizontal bar part. For this part of the pipe, we will need a sixteen inch length of tree branch, at least 1-1/2 inches in thickness, fairly straight, and without too many knots. It is also important to select a branch which is not dry or decayed, as, in that condition, it is too breakable.

The procedure for properly preparing the pipe stem is as follows:

1. Hold branch firmly in left hand, and with any long-bladed, sharp knife suitable for whittling, cut away the entire bark covering. Cut away from you, not toward yourself. Take every precaution against cutting fingers.

2. After the bark coating has been removed, whittle away any knots, large bumps, or other irregularities which may appear along the surface of the branch. Do not attempt to whittle the stem too smoothly, however, since a little ruggedness in its appearance adds to the desired rustic effect. It is important not to sandpaper the stem before all cutting, shaping, and grooving operations are completed. See Fig. 2, Illustration 23.

3. Cut forward or bowl end of stem in an irregularly tapered fashion, just as seen at A, Fig. 3.

4. Cut mouthpiece end so that it is flat-tapered at the top and bottom, and round-tapered at the sides. Make the mouthpiece about 2 inches long and whittle it in a uniform, extra smooth fashion. See B, Fig. 3.

5. Figure out a neat, well balanced arrangement of grooves and cut these grooves with the knife all around the stem, each about 1/8 inch wide and 1/8 inch deep. A good arrangement for these grooves is suggested by C, D, E, F, G and H in Fig. 3. When laying out the grooves, be sure to allow a space of from 4 inches to 5 inches at the center of the stem, for the resort or camp name, see X, Fig. 3. A good idea for spacing and arranging the grooves may be obtained by referring to the sketch of the completed peace-pipe, shown in Fig. 1, Illustration 23.

6. Using the edge of a flat-faced file, smooth the sides and the bottoms of the whittled grooves, making them neat and uniform all around. File may also be used to smooth long surfaces of stem.

7. As a last step in the processing of the stem part of our pipe, use sandpaper, wrapped around a block of wood, or around the file, to smooth and finish all the whittled and filed surfaces of the stem. The sandpaper may also be used without the aid of the block or file, in folded fashion, to smooth and neatly finish the sides and bottoms of the grooves. Special care should be given to the sandpapering of the mouth-piece and forward end of the stem.

B. Preparation of pipe bowl

For the bowl section of the pipe you will need about a 3 inch length of a 2 inch diameter tree branch. After cutting the branch to this size with the whittling knife (a back-saw or coping-saw may also be used for this purpose), proceed as follows:

1. Whittle away the outer covering of bark, then whittle sides of this bowl piece until all bumps or other irregularities are removed. Be sure that sides are fairly straight.

2. Using the pointed end of the knife blade, cut a shallow hole at the top of the bowl, about 3/4 inch in diameter and 1/2 inch deep. See M, Fig. 4.

3. Cut a 1 inch taper at the lower end of the bowl, in a neatly pointed fashion, in the manner seen at N, Fig. 4. The completed length of the bowl should be about 2-3/4 inches.

4. File and sandpaper all whittled parts of bowl until smooth and neatly finished.

C. Joining bowl to stem

1. Using a boring brace fitted with a 3/8 inch auger bit, drill a hole about 1/2 inch deep in the center and at the top of that part of the stem over which the bowl is to be attached. This section is shown between grooves D and E in Fig. 3.

2. Brush liquid glue over tapered tip of bowl and inside of drilled hole in stem, and then fasten bowl and stem together, as shown in Fig. 5. Although the glue is sufficient to hold these parts securely together, the parts may be further strengthened by being

nailed together with a 2 inch wire brad, driven into place from the underside of the stem, as shown in Fig. 5. A tiny hole, first drilled throught the stem with a brad-awl or icepick, where the nail is to be driven into place, will prevent possible cracking of the wood.

D. Designing and coloring pipe bowl and stem

In planning the decorative scheme for this peace-pipe, it is essential that only such ornamentation and colors be employed which are characteristic of the designs, symbols and color treatments commonly used by Indian tribes. A little research in this direction will help produce good results. The decorative symbols employed by the Indians are many in number, with some more commonly known than others. A few of these symbols have been incorporated in the decorative treatment used in the sketch of the completed model of our project in Fig. 1, Illustration 23.

Craft teachers, presenting this project to children, should encourage each child to create his own plan of decoration. The colors selected should be bright and well contrasted. Such colors as red, yellow, green, orange, white, and blue, used in proper combinations, are effective.

The coloring medium suggested for this work is tempera. In addition to these paints, you will need small and medium size water coloring brushes, some mixing pans, and a wiping cloth. For applying the finishing coat, you will need some clear, white shellac and a 1 inch wide, flat style brush.

The proper procedure for coloring and finishing the bowl and stem of our pipe is as follows:

1. Make a sketch of the completed peace-pipe on a sheet of white drawing paper, something like that shown in Fig. 1, Illustration 23. Make this drawing in full size, or as near full size as possible. After drawing the outlines of the pipe, add such Indian designs and symbols as you wish. Arrange these designs in interesting patterns and use them alike on the front and back surfaces of the pipe. See Fig. 1 for suggested Indian designs.

2. After completing the pencil drawing of the pipe, color this sketch gaily. Use this color sketch as a plan for the painting of the pipe itself.

3. Following these preparatory steps, draw the designs and symbols, as planned and worked out in the trial sketch, on the wooden stem and bowl of the pipe. Draw the designs and symbols carefully, as these outlines are to be used as guides when coloring the pipe.

4. Following the application of the pencil outlines, mix the required colors of tempera paint and color each section of the pipe according to the prepared sketch. Apply the colors evenly and neatly, brushing on the lighter colors first and the darker ones last. Do not allow any of the paint to enter into the sectional grooves of the pipe, as these are to remain in their natural wood color. Also be careful not to allow the colors to run together, permitting each applied color to dry completely, before brushing on an adjoining color.

5. Paint the central section of the stem in a light color, as this part of the pipe is to be used for the name lettering. Letter the name in a rustic fashion, using black or any other dark paint, and working with a very small brush. The name should be applied as the last coloring step.

E. Coloring and attaching the pine cones

As you will note from Fig. 1, Illustration 23, three pine cones are used as decorative accessories for our pipe. The cones, which simulate the feathers customarily employed by the Indians to adorn their peace pipes, are to be suspended from the stem of the pipe, directly below the bowl. The central cone should be about 4-1/2 inches long, while the two outside ones should be about 3-1/2 inches in length.

Paint the tips of the cone blades only, permitting some of their beautiful, natural coloring to show. The colors employed for painting the cones should be in harmony with those used for the pipe stem and bowl. A good idea is to use one color for the upper third of the cone, another for the lower third, and a third color for the central section of the cone. Each of the three cones should be painted in a different combination of colors, following the same plan.

After the cones are completely dry, finish them with two coats of clear white shellac. Later, when the shellac has dried, fasten the three pine cones to the pipe stem, using either raffia, leather lacing or colored cord, as tie strings. First attach the string to the top section of the cones, then tie them to their proper places on the pipe stem as in Fig. 1, Illustration 23. Tie the knots at the back of the stem, so that they will be out of sight when the pipe is hung on the wall.

F. Braiding and attaching hanger

The final step in the construction of our Indian peace-pipe is that of fastening a suitably decorative hanger to both ends of the pipe. The hanger may be made of different colored strips of raffia, leather or leatherette lacing, or heavy grade cord. Crepe paper is also satisfactory. After selecting your material, proceed as follows:

1. Cut three differently colored strips of the material to 24 inch lengths.

2. Tie the three strips together at one end and then braid the strips into a single cord, employing a neat, loose form of braiding.

3. Using a hand-brace, fitted with a 1/4 inch twist drill, bore a hole through the pipe stem 2 inches in from each end of the stem. Drill slowly and carefully to avoid chipping the wood.

4. Insert the ends of the braided hanger through the drilled holes and knot each end neatly at the bottom of the stem, just as shown in the sketch in Fig. 3.

ACORNS

Project No. 69, Acorn Necklace

See Figure 1, Illustration 24

I. Description

Making costume jewelry of natural acorns is a most gratifying and profitable handicraft activity. In addition to providing housewives with a fascinating form of handiwork, it provides an inexpensive and highly absorbing type of handicraft for children's arts and crafts shops.

In this acorn necklace, as well as in the acorn bracelet and lapel ornament projects shown in Figs. 1 and 4, respectively, in Illustration No. 25, natural acorns are used in combination with oak leaves made of scrap pieces of leather. Another scrap material, employed to advantage in the construction of acorn costume jewelry, is milk bottle wire, used for various forms of connecting devices, later described.

Included in the construction of this easy-to-make acorn necklace are such interesting processes as cutting and tooling leather, punching holes in leather, wire bending, assembling parts with liquid glue, shellacking, and so forth.

II. Materials

A. At least eight well-grown acorns of approximately the same size.

B. A scrap piece of medium brown leather, suitable for tooling and sufficient for making the leather neck-band and seven oak leaf forms shown in Fig. 1, Illustration 24.

C. A few strips of milk bottle wire.

D. A short length of brown cotton thread.

E. Liquid glue.

F. Clear, white shellac.

III. Tools

A. A 12 inch long metal rule.

B. A pair of long round-nose cutting pliers.

C. A sharp pointed knife, suitable for cutting leather.

D. A piece of masonite board, about 6 inches by 9 inches in size, for a working base for cutting leather.

E. A leather modeling tool.

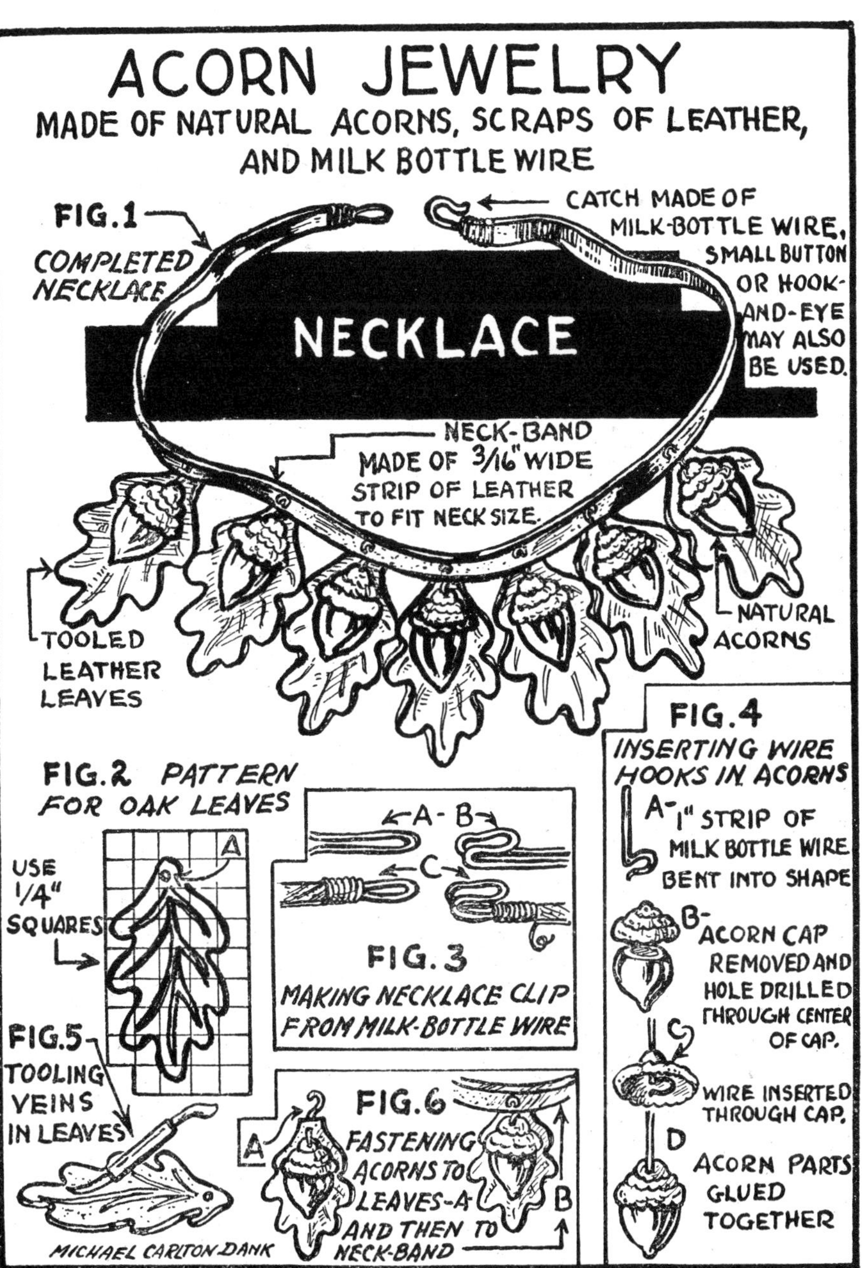
ACORN JEWELRY
MADE OF NATURAL ACORNS, SCRAPS OF LEATHER, AND MILK BOTTLE WIRE
FIG.1
COMPLETED NECKLACE
NECKLACE
CATCH MADE OF MILK-BOTTLE WIRE, SMALL BUTTON OR HOOK-AND-EYE MAY ALSO BE USED.
NECK-BAND MADE OF 3/16" WIDE STRIP OF LEATHER TO FIT NECK SIZE.
TOOLED LEATHER LEAVES
NATURAL ACORNS
FIG.2 PATTERN FOR OAK LEAVES
USE 1/4" SQUARES
A
A- B
C
FIG. 3
MAKING NECKLACE CLIP FROM MILK-BOTTLE WIRE
FIG.4
INSERTING WIRE HOOKS IN ACORNS
A- 1" STRIP OF MILK BOTTLE WIRE BENT INTO SHAPE
B- ACORN CAP REMOVED AND HOLE DRILLED THROUGH CENTER OF CAP.
C
WIRE INSERTED THROUGH CAP.
D
ACORN PARTS GLUED TOGETHER
FIG.5 TOOLING VEINS IN LEAVES
FIG.6
FASTENING ACORNS TO LEAVES-A AND THEN TO NECK-BAND
A
B
MICHAEL CARLTON DANK

Illustration 24

F. A leather punching tool, capable of punching 1/16 inch holes.

G. A small piece of sponge or cloth for moistening leather.

H. A small brush suitable for gluing.

I. A flat brush, about 1/2 inch wide suitable for shellacking small surfaces.

IV. Directions

A. Using the masonite board as a working foundation, a 12 inch metal rule, and a sharp, pointed knife, cut a strip of soft leather for neckband, to measure 3/16 inch wide by 18 inches long. This neckband will, of course, vary in accordance with the particular neck size of person for whom the necklace is intended.

B. Using a letter-punching tool, punch eight 1/16 inch holes along the center of the width of the neckband, placing the holes 1 inch apart and in the center of the length of the band. See Fig. 1, Illustration 24.

C. Using wire cutting-pliers, cut a piece of milk-bottle wire about 2 inches long and then bend it into the form of a loop or "eye," such as seen at A, Fig. 3.

D. Cut a piece of wire 3 inches long and bend it into the shape of a hook in the manner shown by B, Fig. 3.

E. Using thin brown thread, fasten hook B to one end of the leather band and loop A to the other end of the band. After winding the thread neatly around the ends of the wire in the manner shown by C Fig. 3, fasten the thread windings securely in place with a little rubber cement.

F. Make a paper pattern of the oak leaf form represented in pattern grill, Fig. 2; for proper size reproduction of this leaf form, use 1/4 inch squares.

G. Using a sponge or small piece of cloth, wet underside of a scrap piece of medium brown tooling leather. Then make seven tracings of this leaf form on the top or right side of the leather, us-

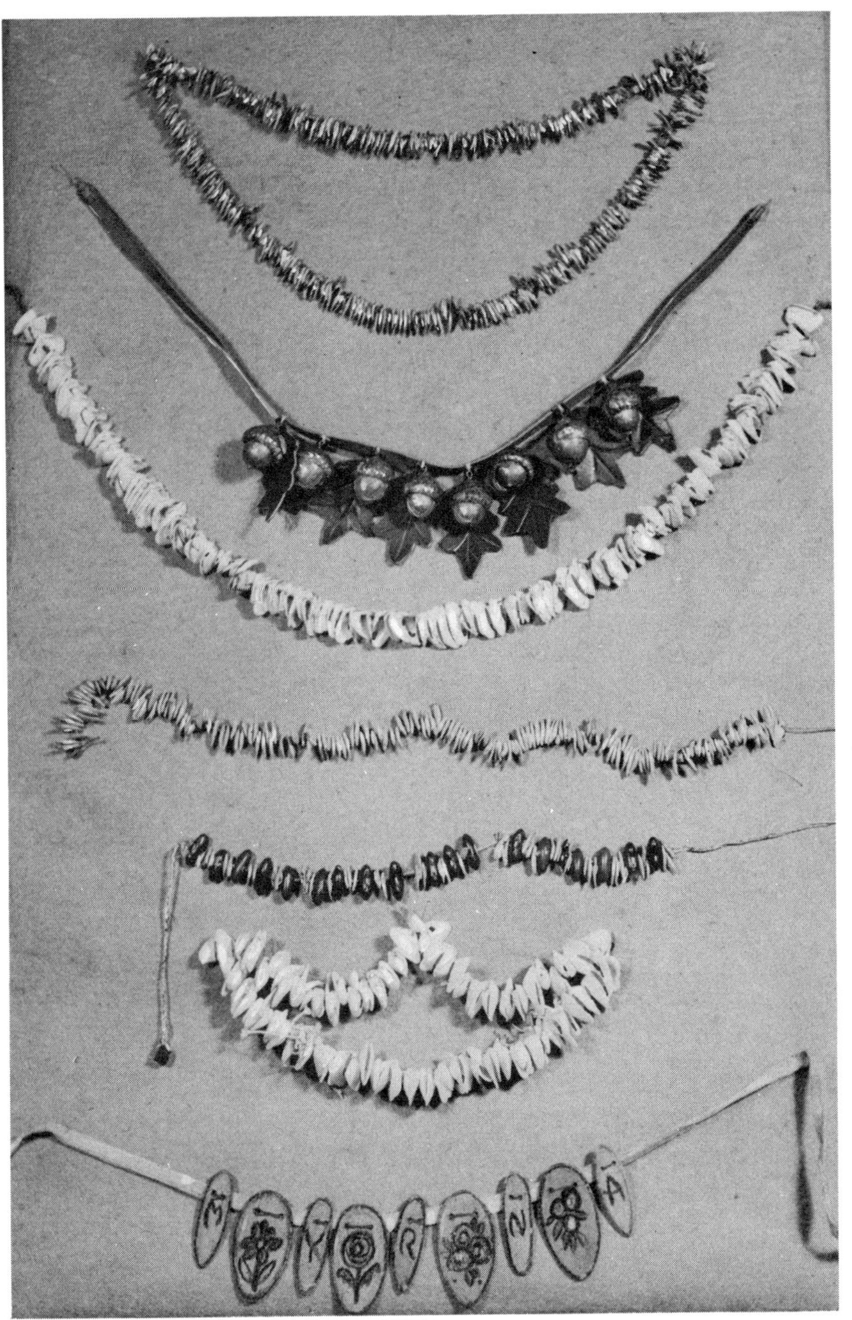

Plate 12. A display to indicate the many different styles of necklaces that can be made from such natural materials as squash seeds, acorns, kidney beans, watermelon seeds, leather strips, sea shells, and so forth.

ing either a pencil or the pointed end of a leather modeling tool. Be sure to trace vein markings on each leaf, just as indicated in Fig. 2.

H. After making the tracings of the leaves, cut them out.

I. Wet undersides of cut-out leather leaf forms, and tool all vein lines sharply and clearly, using the pointed end of the modeler in the manner demonstrated in Fig. 5. Be careful not to scratch the leather with the point of the modelor while tooling.

J. Using leather-punching tool, punch 1/16 inch holes at the top section of each leaf. See A, Fig. 2.

K. Remove caps from the acorns, being careful not to break or crack them, then drill 1/16 inch holes through the center of each cap. See Fig. 4, B.

L. Cut seven 1 inch strips of milk bottle wire, then form a hook at the bottom end of each wire in the manner shown by Fig. 4, A.

M. Insert pointed end of wire strips through the holes previously drilled in the center of each acorn cap, so that the looped end of each wire remains on the inside or underside of the cap as shown by Fig. 4, C.

N. Using liquid glue or rubber cement, fasten caps (with wires inserted) in their original position over the top of the acorn bulb, as indicated in Fig. 4, D.

O. Apply a coat of clear white shellac over all sections of the acorns and allow the shellac to dry thoroughly.

P. Insert the pointed ends of the wires, now protruding from top of each acorn, through the holes previously punched at the top section of the leather oak leaves. Then, using round-nose pliers, make a slight hook at the top of each wire, as indicated by A, Fig. 6.

Q. Next, insert semi-hooked wire ends through the holes previously punched in the leather neck-band, and then, with pliers, clinch each hook securely so each acorn and oak leaf unit will hang freely from the band. See Fig. 6, B. Do not clinch the hooks too tightly as they will distort the shape of the band and cause the acorn and leaf parts to hang too rigidly.

The acorn necklace is now complete and ready for wear. Simply place the leather band around the neck and then join its hooked end to its looped end. If neatly and properly made, your acorn necklace will be as attractive as that shown in Fig. 1; and no one will believe that it is home-made.

Project No. 70, Acorn Bracelet

See Figure 1, Illustration 25

After you have made the acorn necklace shown in Fig. 1, Illustration 24, you will find the construction of this acorn bracelet very simple indeed. The materials used in the preparation of this bracelet are just the same as those used for the necklace, and the craft skills here employed are similar to those employed in the preparation of the necklace. Because of their use of real acorns, leather oak leaves, and leather bands, these two costume ornaments make a smart companion set.

For the bracelet you will need ten small acorns, some medium brown scrap leather, brown cotton thread, a few strips of milk bottle wire, and a little clear white shellac. The tools needed are the same as those listed under Project No. 69.

The directions follow:

1. Make a pattern of the two-piece oak leaf unit shown in the pattern grill in Fig. 3. Use 1/4 inch squares for correct size reproduction of this leaf unit.

2. Wet underside of a scrap piece of medium brown tooling leather with a small sponge or piece of cloth, soaked in water. Then, make five separate tracings of the double leaf unit pattern on the top surface of the leather, showing also the leaf veins and location of holes, indicated as Y and Z, in Fig. 3.

3. Using a sharp knife and a masonite board as a foundation, cut out all five leather oak leaf units, working neatly and carefully.

4. With leather punching tool, punch two 1/6 inch diameter holes at the center of each pair of oak leaves, at point marked Y, Fig. 3.

5. Using leather modeling tool, tool all vein lines in leather oak leaves, first wetting underside of the leather as in the tracing step. Tool sharply and neatly.

6. Remove caps from the acorns, then join two caps together, top to top, by forming a loop at each end of a 1-1/4 inch strip of milk bottle wire. Locate the loops of the wire strip inside of the acorn caps, so that they will remain unseen when the caps are later glued to their acorns. Repeat this operation for each of the five units of this bracelet. See X, Fig. 2.

7. Attach acorns securely to their caps with liquid glue, then apply a coat of clear white shellac over all sections of the acorns.

8. Using a needle and brown thread, sew each pair of acorns to a pair of tooled and punched leather oak leaves working through the holes in the leaves (see Y, Fig. 3) and over the wire connectors between each pair of acorns. See X, Fig. 2.

9. Cut a leather wrist band to measure 1/4 inch wide and about 17 inches long and then punch 1/16 inch holes along the center of the band's width, placing the holes 3/4 inch apart, and in the center of the length of the leather band.

10. Using brown thread again, sew each of the five twin leaf and acorn units to the leather wrist band, working through the holes previously punched in the band.

Now the acorn bracelet is complete and ready to wear. Simply place the bracelet around the wrist and tie it securely in place with a neat bow-tie made of the ends of the wrist bands as shown in Fig. 1, Illustration 25.

Project No. 71, Acorn Lapel Ornament

See Figure 4, Illustration 25

This charming acorn pin matches the other two acorn ornaments, and can be worn effectively with the acorn bracelet shown in Fig. 1, Illustration 25. However, this lapel pin also makes a smart dress accessory when worn alone.

The acorn lapel pin is really very easy to make, since it consists only of five similarly constructed acorn and leaf units, neatly tied together with a small leather ribbon as shown in Fig. 4, Illustration 25. After you have already made the necklace and bracelet, you will certainly have no difficulty with this lapel ornament. The directions are as follows:

1. Make a pattern of the oak leaf form shown in the pattern grill in Fig. 5, Illustration 25. Use 1/4 inch squares for correct size reproduction. Be sure to include holes M and N and the leaf vein lines which are part of this pattern.

2. Make five separate tracings of this oak leaf pattern on a scrap piece of medium brown tooling leather.

3. Carefully cut out the leaves, using a sharp knife and a masonite working board foundation.

4. Punch 1/16 inch diameter holes M and N in each leather leaf.

5. Wet underside of leather leaves and then sharply tool the vein lines shown in the pattern of the oak leaf in Fig. 5.

6. Detach caps from the acorns, then insert 1 inch long milk bottle wire strips through these caps making a loop at the bottom end of each wire strip and locating the loops inside the acorn caps, as shown in Fig. 6, A.

7. Glue caps with wires inserted, securely to their acorns, and then apply a coat of clear, white shellac over all parts of the assembled acorns.

8. Thread wires extending from acorn caps through lower leaf holes, N, then loop wires at the back of the leaves in the manner shown at B, Fig. 6.

9. Sew top ends of leather oak leaves together with brown thread, working the thread through the upper holes, M, Fig. 5. Do not sew the leaves together too tightly as they must be left loose

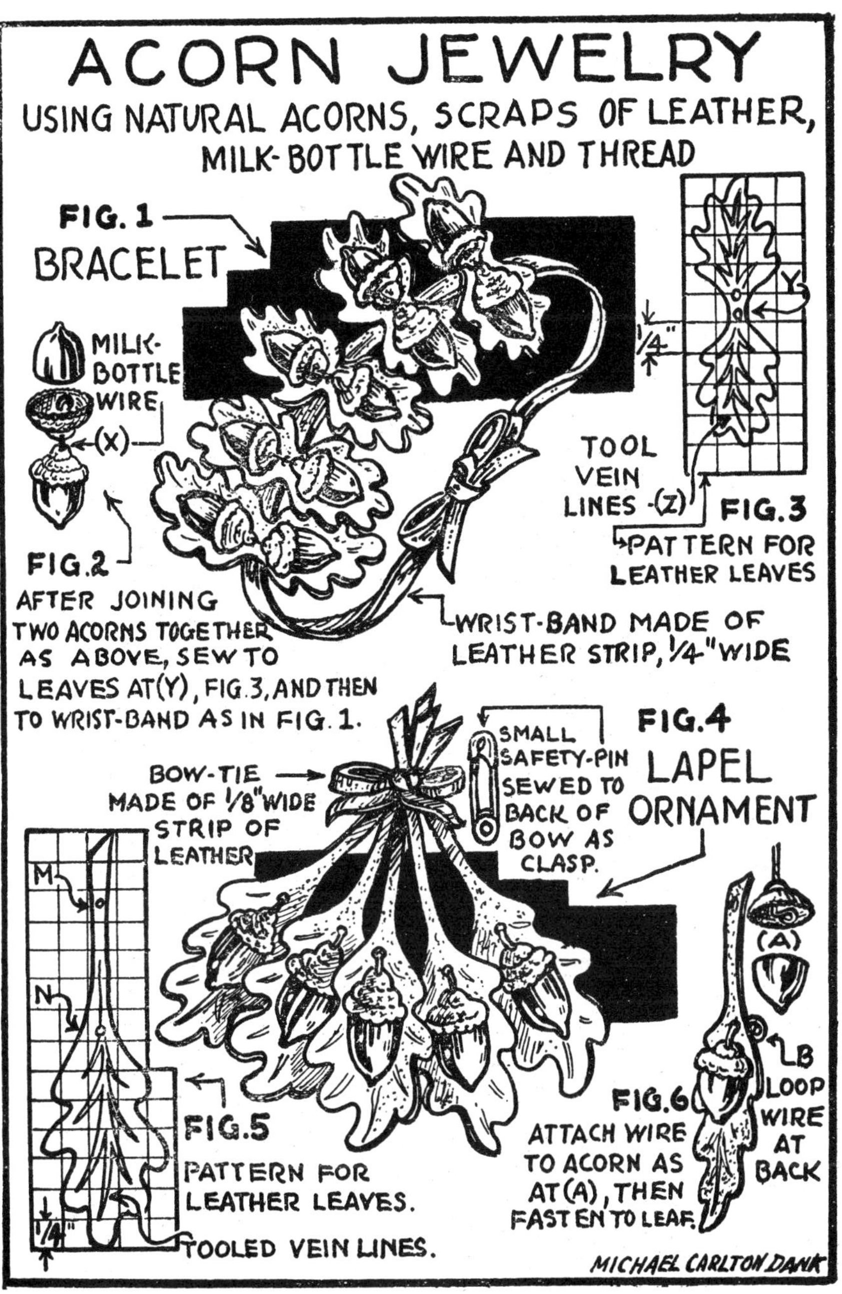
ACORN JEWELRY
USING NATURAL ACORNS, SCRAPS OF LEATHER, MILK-BOTTLE WIRE AND THREAD
FIG. 1
BRACELET
MILK-BOTTLE WIRE
(X)
FIG. 2
AFTER JOINING TWO ACORNS TOGETHER AS ABOVE, SEW TO LEAVES AT (Y), FIG. 3, AND THEN TO WRIST-BAND AS IN FIG. 1.
Y
1/4"
TOOL VEIN LINES -(Z)
FIG. 3
PATTERN FOR LEATHER LEAVES
WRIST-BAND MADE OF LEATHER STRIP, 1/4" WIDE
FIG. 4
LAPEL ORNAMENT
SMALL SAFETY-PIN SEWED TO BACK OF BOW AS CLASP.
BOW-TIE MADE OF 1/8" WIDE STRIP OF LEATHER
M
N
FIG. 5
PATTERN FOR LEATHER LEAVES.
1/4"
TOOLED VEIN LINES.
(A)
B
LOOP WIRE AT BACK
FIG. 6
ATTACH WIRE TO ACORN AS AT (A), THEN FASTEN TO LEAF.
MICHAEL CARLTON DANK

Illustration 25

enough to permit spreading out in the fan fashion shown in Fig. 4.

10. Cut a leather strip, using any soft, flexible grade of leather, to measure 1/8 inch wide and about 6 inches long. Then make a neat bow-tie with this leather strip, locating it right over the spot previously used for sewing the leaf and acorn units together. See Fig. 4.

11. Complete acorn lapel ornament by sewing a small safety pin as a convenient form of clasp, immediately in back of the leather bow-tie.

There are several other interesting ways in which you can use real acorns and leather oak leaves, such as in novelty window shade pulls, book marks, and decorative bow-ties for scrap books and photograph albums. The author is confident that the reader will have little difficulty in working out these acorn projects by himself.

Project No. 72, Tree-Trunk Wall Plaques

This natural scrap project involves the cutting off of a fairly thick section from a dead tree trunk or fallen branch by means of a hand-saw, cutting at a considerably slanted or acute angle. Thus an oval-shaped inner section of the trunk or branch is obtained, showing the beautiful annual rings of the tree. A very attractive rim or frame of bark all around the plaque is also produced by this "cross-section" sawing. Plaques varying in thickness from 1/2 inch to 1 inch, and in oval shapes which vary from 3 inches by 9 inches to 6 inches by 12 inches are most effective for this tree-trunk wall plaque.

If you should prefer a round or circular plaque, simply cut the trunk or branch in the desired thickness at right angles to its length instead of at a slanted or acute angle.

Oval or circular plaque boards cut from tree trunks or branches in this manner can be neatly and smoothly sandpapered, and then attractively decorated in various ways. Some appropriate picture or design may be painted on the central section of one of the broad faces of the plaque with oil, tempera or enamel paints. The entire plaque is then finished with two coats of white shellac or quick-drying, clear varnish.

Another effective way of decorating trunk or branch plaques is by first cutting a piece of thin copper foil, from 30 to 36 gauge, to the same shape as the plaque in work. Then, after tooling this copper sheet in some appropriate design subject, it is neatly mounted to the plaque with small, brass, escutcheon pins. The copper unit, displaying its artistically embossed decoration, may then be "antiqued" with a solution of liver-of-sulphur and finished with a coating of clear lacquer. This process is generally known as copper foil embossing or copper "repousse" craft.

Still another decorative possibility is that of pasting a decalcomania, or colored picture, on the central section of one of the broad surfaces of the plaque, followed by an overall coating of clear white shellac.

Finally, you can also produce a very attractive tree trunk plaque by cutting a piece of tin-can sheet metal to the same size as the particular plaque in work (just inside of the bark border), then mounting this metal sheet to the plaque and tapping some appropriate design unit on it. For this metal-tapping process, all you will need is a well pointed flat head nail and a hammer or mallet. When the tapping work is completed, the design may be attractively painted with one or more colors of enamel.

With all of these decorative processes, small pine-cones may be fastened to the top of the plaque.

A loop made of milk bottle wire may be attached to the back of the tree-trunk plaque with one or two thumbtacks to provide a convenient hanger for displaying the plaque on the wall. Two small screw-eyes and a piece of wire may also be used as a hanger.

Teachers of arts and crafts presenting this project to children should explain why it is wrong to cut such plaque boards from living trees. Only trees which have fallen to the ground or trees which are scrapped and actually dead should be used as a source of material.

SQUASH SEEDS AND KIDNEY BEANS

Project No. 73, Costume Jewelry

Lovely costume jewelry can readily be made through the use of a handful of squash seeds and kidney beans and a short strip of dental floss, any other form of strong string, or thin elastic cord. All you need to do is to string the seeds and beans on the thread or elastic cord in various interesting combinations in accordance with the following simple directions:

Using a sharply pointed metal instrument, such as a large needle, a scratch awl, or an ice pick, first punch small holes through the centers of the flat sides or surfaces of the kidney beans and squash seeds. Then, thread the seeds and beans on a suitable length of dental floss or elastic cord, using some interesting, alternating arrangement such as one bean followed by three squash seeds, or two beans followed by six seeds. Since squash seeds are of a light tan or maple color and kidney beans rich brown or burnt sienna, the combination of these two colors of nature, arranged in the alternating method suggested above, is most artistic and appealing.

For a pretty necklace, made in this fashion, use an 18 inch long string of dental floss, since a string of this length will fit the average neck size. As a convenient clasp for this necklace, make a loop of suitable size at one end of the dental floss, and at the other end fasten on a kidney bean. When inserted through the loop, the kidney bean will serve as a practical lock or clasp, to hold the necklace neatly and comfortably in place about the neck.

For a bracelet of squash seeds and kidney beans use brown elastic cord of proper length in place of the dental floss. Arrange the beans and seeds in the same alternating fashion as in the case of the necklace. If desired, a double string of kidney beans and squash seeds may be used in place of the single string.

In the construction of both the necklace and bracelet projects, an overall coat of white shellac may be applied over the seeds and beans for extra sparkle and protection although this shellacking treatment is not absolutely necessary.

Smart lapel ornaments can also easily be made of squash seeds and kidney beans in various decorative arrangements. One idea is to have three, four or five short strings of the seeds and beans suspended from a small twig. Another idea is to have the short strings of seeds and beans fastened together at the top with a leather strip bow-tie, just as in the case of the acorn lapel pin shown in Fig. 4, Illustration 25. In both of these seed and bean lapel models, a small safety pin may be sewed to the back of the project as a clasp. In the case of the twig model, the clasp should be sewed just in back of the twig, whereas in th leather bow-tie model, the clasp should be located in back of the bow.

BIRCH BARK

Project No. 74, Tie Rack

See Figure 1, Illustration 26

I. Description

Just as in the case of the Indian peace pipe shown in Fig. 1, Illustration 23, this birch bark tie rack and the other two birch bark projects which follow were created in a boy's summer camp craft shop, situated in the beautiful White Mountains of New Hampshire, where birch trees grow in abundance. In the construction of these birch bark projects, however, the bark was stripped from the trunks or branches of fallen or dead birch trees only. The children were strictly forbidden to strip any live birch trees of their covering.

Birch bark offers craft teachers and enthusiasts a wide variety of interesting handwork projects because of its natural beauty, strength, and adaptability. It is hoped that after the reader has built the useful and novel birch bark articles here presented, he will be inspired to make many other things with this material.

The birch bark tie rack shown in Fig. 1, Illustration 26, is appropriately designed in an Indian-in-a-canoe motif, in a typical White Mountain setting. Of course, various othere Indian motifs and designs can be employed in the decoration of this useful project, such as the Indian head design applied in the ornamentation of the memo-pad shown in Fig. 3, Illustration 26. Our tie rack can also serve appropriately as a holder for ribbons or belts.

This natural scrap project, apart from the four eyelets employed in its upper and lower corners is built entirely of material supplied by the birch tree. By referring to Fig. 1, Illustration 26, you will note that the large decorated section of the tie rack, indicated as A, is made entirely of a sturdy sheet of birch bark; that the hanger, B, is prepared from thin, braided strips of birch bark; that the two-tier bar supports, D, are built of narrow strips of birch bark; while the tie-bar, G, is fashioned from a 12 inch length of birch tree branch.

Another feature of this project is that the fascinating handicraft skill of electric burning is here employed as the method for applying its Indian design.

II. Materials and Tools

A. A sturdy sheet of birch-bark, sufficient for making decorative section A, measuring 7 inches wide by 6 inches high. See A, Fig. 1, Illustration 26. Also, a narrow strip of birch bark large enough for making braided hanger, B, and the tie-bar supports, D.

B. A fairly straight birch tree branch, about 1/2 inch in diameter and 12 inches long, completely covered with birch bark. See G.

C. Four medium size brown eyelets, having 1/8 inch centers. See C. and E.

D. An assortment of tempera colors.

E. Two pointed water color brushes, one of a small size such as No. 2 and the other larger, such as No. 6.

F. A sharp knife suitable for whittling.

G. A sharp pair of scissors of a fairly good size.

H. A leather-punching tool, capable of punching 1/8 inch holes.

I. An electric-burning pencil.

J. A heavy weight such as provided by two, regular building bricks, a marble slab, and so forth.

III. Directions

A. Using a good-size sharp pair of scissors, cut a piece of birch-bark, of a sufficiently stiff, heavy grade, to measure 7 inches in width by 6-1/2 inches in height or length, for decorative section A.

B. Moisten this cutout sheet of birch bark, preferably with hot water, place it between two pieces of heavy cardboard, and then place a heavy weight over the top sheet of cardboard to allow the birch bark to dry perfectly straight and flat.

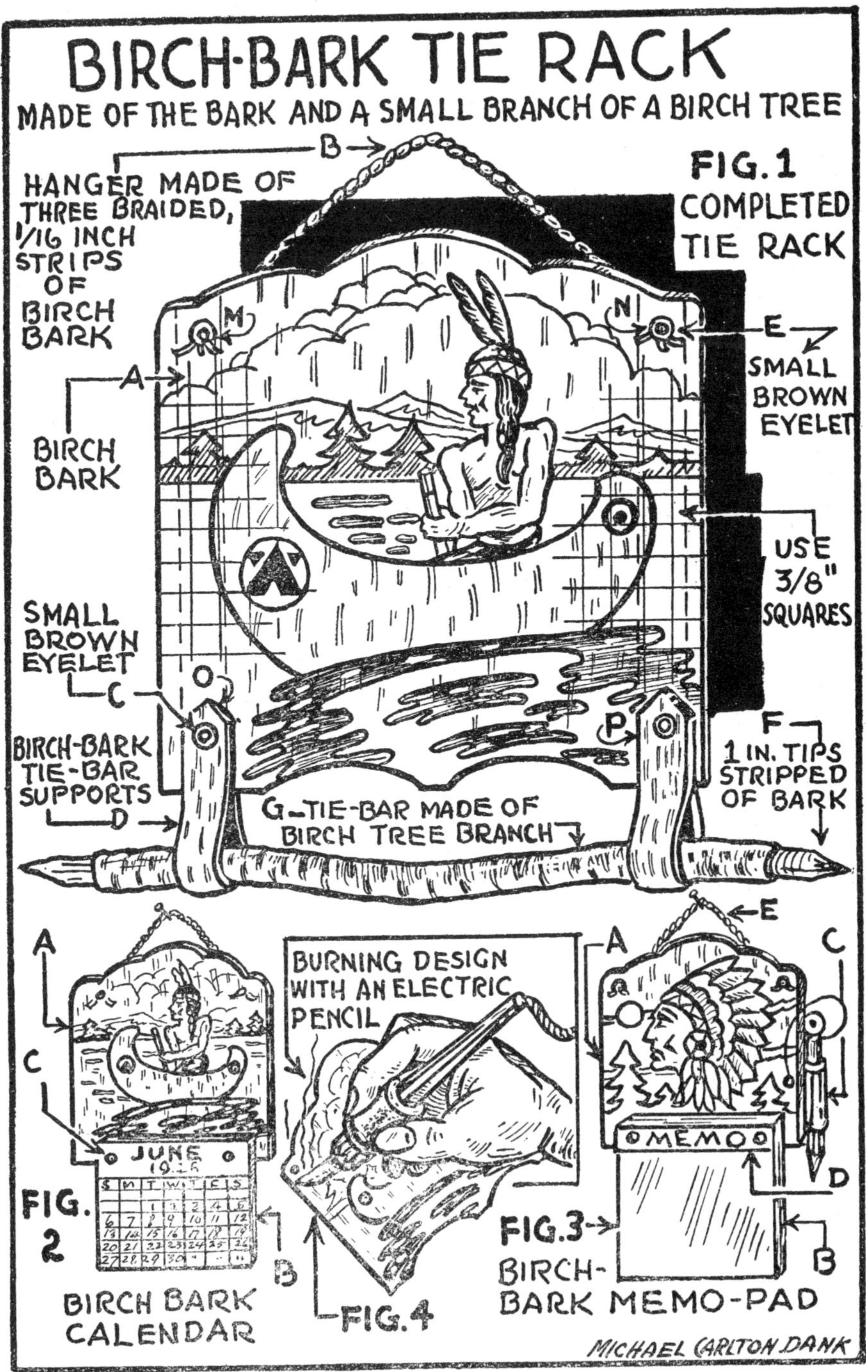
BIRCH-BARK TIE RACK
MADE OF THE BARK AND A SMALL BRANCH OF A BIRCH TREE
B
HANGER MADE OF THREE BRAIDED, 1/16 INCH STRIPS OF BIRCH BARK
FIG. 1
COMPLETED TIE RACK
M
N
E
SMALL BROWN EYELET
A
BIRCH BARK
USE 3/8" SQUARES
SMALL BROWN EYELET
C
O
P
F
1 IN. TIPS STRIPPED OF BARK
BIRCH-BARK TIE-BAR SUPPORTS
D
G–TIE-BAR MADE OF BIRCH TREE BRANCH
A
C
JUNE
FIG. 2
B
BIRCH BARK CALENDAR
BURNING DESIGN WITH AN ELECTRIC PENCIL
FIG. 4
E
A
C
MEMO
D
FIG. 3
B
BIRCH-BARK MEMO-PAD
MICHAEL CARLTON DANK

Illustration 26

C. While the birch bark sheet is drying, draw a 6-½ inch by 7 inch rectangle on a sheet of drawing or plain writing paper, then divide the rectangle into 3/8 inch squares, to form a pattern grill.

D. Carefully complete the rest of the squares shown in reduced form in Fig. 1, Illustration 26, then proceed to copy the Indian-in-a-canoe design here represented, on the full size grill of 3/8 inch squares, reproducing all details of the design as well as its ornamental top and bottom edges, exactly as represented in the reduced size grill.

E. After the moistened birch bark sheet, earlier placed under a weight, has sufficiently dried, remove it from the weight and then, using a sheet of regular typewriter carbon paper, trace the prepared full size pattern of the Indian design to the cleaner and more suitable of its two surfaces. Be sure also, in this design tracing step, to reproduce the neatly formed curves at the top and bottom edges of this decorative unit.

F. With a sharp pair of scissors cut top and bottom edges of the rectangular sheet of birch bark, carefully following the traced outlines for these sections.

G. Again using the scissors, cut two strips of birch bark for the tie-bar supports, B, to measure 3/4 inch wide by 4 inches long. Also cut the ends of these strips to form the pointed effect seen in the sketch at D.

H. Soak the two cutout tie-bar strips in hot water for a few minutes so they become pliable and non-breakable, and then fold them in half to form the tie-bar supports seen at D.

I. Using a 1/8 inch diameter, leather or paper punch, punch holes M, N, O, P, locating the top holes 1/2 inch down from the top edge of birch bark section A, and the bottom ones 3/4 inch up from its lower edge. Then, punch 1/8 inch diameter holes 1/2 inch from the pointed tips of the birch bark tie-bar supports, D.

J. Insert brown eyelets, having 1/8 inch diameter openings, at points M, N, O, P, using a regular eyelet setter or any similar conically shaped tool.

K. Cut a birch tree branch, of approximately 1/2 inch diameter, to a length of 12 inches to produce the tie rack tie-bar unit G. Then, using a sharp pocket or whittling knife, remove 1 inch of the bark at each tip of the branch and follow by pointing each branch tip neatly as shown at F, Fig. 1. When completed in this manner, insert the branch through the loops of the suspended tie-bar supports D, in the manner represented by G, Fig. 1.

L. Cut three birch bark strips to the size of 1/6 inch wide by 12 inches long, braid them together neatly and tightly to form hanger cord B, then fasten the ends of the hanger cord to the top section of the tie rack, through the eyeletted holes at M and N. For added decorative effect, make a neat little knot just in front of each eyelet, as seen in the sketch in Fig. 1.

IV. ELECTRIC BURNING AND COLORING THE DESIGN

To complete the novel birch bark tie rack, you may use any one of three decorative procedures. These are the following:

A. Color the design in a harmonious selection of tempera paints, using the paints sparingly and allowing a good part of the original natural birch bark surface to show through.

B. Burn in the outlines of the design with an electric burning pencil in the manner demonstrated in Fig. 4, Illustration 26.

C. First electric burn the outlines of the decoration, and then add a few spots of color, here and there, with tempera paints.

In each of these coloring treatments, be sure to allow as much of the original birch bark surface to show up as possible, for the color and texture of birch bark has a natural loveliness all its own.

If you wish, you may apply a coat of clear white shellac over both the front and back sections of the tie rack for extra gloss and finished effect. However, a dull natural finish, without the use of shellac, is equally artistic.

Project No. 75, Birch Bark Calendar

See Figure 2, Illustration 26

When you have completed the birch bark tie rack, shown in Fig. 1, Illustration 26, you will find the construction of this birch bark calendar a simple matter. This is because the decorated birch bark section of this calendar (See A, Fig. 2) is designed in the same Indian-in-a-canoe motif as the tie rack. It is also cut in the same shape and in exactly the same dimensions as the tie rack in Fig. 1.

To construct this birch bark calendar, first prepare the ornamental birch bark unit indicated as A, in Fig. 2, applying the same methods and directions for preparing the braided-cord hanger, for punching the holes, for inserting the small brown eyelets, and for coloring and electric burning the Indian design as given in the text under Project No. 74.

Upon the completion of the ornamental, birch bark part, instead of using the eyeletted holes at the lower section of the unit for attaching a tie bar, use them for attaching a suitable calendar, as represented by B, Fig. 2. To attach the calendar, insert a 3/4 inch long brass fastener through each of these two eyeletted holes, keeping the round heads of the fasteners at the front of the project and clinching their ends at the back, in the manner seen at C, Fig. 2.

A new calendar can be substituted for the old one each year by removing the brass fasteners, changing the calendars, and then inserting the fasteners into position again.

In this birch bark project, just as in the tie-rack shown in Fig. 1, clear white shellac may be employed as a final overall finish. Any other appropriate Indian design may be employed in place of the Indian-in-a-canoe motif represented in Fig. 2. The Indian head design which was selected as the decoration for the memo-pad seen in Fig. 3, for instance, would be just as effective in the decoration of the birch bark calendar, in Fig. 2, and vice versa. In this connection, arts and crafts teachers would be wise to arrange for the use of a number of different Indian designs in the decoration of the birch bark unit, rather than having all their pupils use the same design. This same principle, of course, applies equally to the other birch bark projects treated in this scrap-craft unit.

Project No. 76, Birch Bark Memo Pad

See Figure 3, Illustration 26

This last project in this series of natural scrap-craft projects employs the same size and shape of birch bark for its ornamental unit as used in the tie rack and calendar shown in Figs. 1 and 2 respectively. It also uses the same kind of braided cord hanger, made of strips of birch bark. This birch bark model features a neatly designed, practical memo-pad and pencil, fitted into a convenient pencil-pocket.

Like the calendar project in Fig. 2, the decorated birch bark part of this memo-pad remains as a permanent fixture, while the memo pad, attached with brass fasteners to its lower section, may be conveniently detached and replaced when used up.

Although an Indian head design is employed in the decoration of the birch bark unit of our memo-pad, the Indian-in-a-canoe design may also be employed. Any suitable Indian design is satisfactory.

For the proper construction of this birch bark, memo-pad project, proceed as follows:

1. Cut a piece of birch bark to measure 7 inches wide by 6-1/2 inches high. Then cut the top edge of this birch bark sheet in some appropriate design such as represented by the top edge of A, in Fig. 3, Illustration 26. See text under Project No. 74, Indian Tie Rack, for complete details regarding proper methods of conditioning and cutting of birch bark.

2. Make an enlarged copy of the Indian head design, using 3/8 inch squares, then trace this design to the cutout birch bark unit using carbon paper.

3. Color traced design with tempera paints, burn it with an electric pencil or both, as desired.

4. Punch eyelet holes at the top corners of the colored birch bark unit, insert small brown eyelets, and then attach braided cord hanger, made of narrow strips of birch bark. For this step see text under Project No. 74, Birch Bark Tie Rack.

5. Cut a piece of birch bark, 2 inches square, fold it around a pencil, then fasten this pencil pocket unit to the right side of section A, using a brown eyelet as a fastener, in the manner shown at C, Fig. 3.

6. Cut a piece of birch bark 3/4 inch wide and just as long as the width of the memo-pad planned for use in this project. See D, Fig. 3. Drill a 1/8 inch hole 1/2 inch in from the left and right ends of his birch bark strip and then electric burn or letter with

India ink, the word "MEMO", locating this word just in the center of the strip, as shown in the Illustration.

7. Drill 1/8 inch holes through memo-pad, B, exactly opposite those previously drilled in the birch bark pad-strip, D.

8. Drill similarly spaced holes through the lower section of decorated, birch bark unit, A, and then insert small, brown eyelets through these holes.

9. Following these hole drilling and eyelet inserting procedures, connect birch bark pad strip, D, and memo-pad, B, to decorated birch bark section, A, using two 1 inch long brass fasteners as connectors. Allow brass fastener heads to show in front of pad and clinch fastener ends at back of section A, to hold all three parts neatly and securely in place.

As each page is used, it can easily and neatly be torn off the pad, along the lower edge of birch bark strip, D. When the pad is completely used, remove the brass fasteners, substitute a new pad, and then insert the fasteners into proper position again, as before. Always keep the pencil, when not in use, in its birch bark pocket, C. A string may be attached to the top of the pencil if desired. The other end of the string may be fastened to the same eyelet which holds the pencil pocket in position.

This practical and attractive birch bark memo-pad may be used appropriately in the home, in the school classroom, or in a business office.

CHAPTER
TEN

WORKING WITH ROUND CARDBOARD CONTAINERS AND CARDBOARD TUBES

ROUND cardboard containers and cardboard tubes of various diameters and lengths are another popular form of scrap material which challenges the ingenuity and skill of amateur craftsmen, teachers, and students of arts and crafts everywhere.

As you will note in Chapter Two, Scrap List No. 2, round cardboard boxes or containers may always easily be obtained in the form of discarded oatmeal boxes, salt boxes, pint and quart size ice cream or coffee containers, various types of cosmetic boxes, hat boxes, and so forth. You will also note in Scrap List No. 2 that various kinds of discarded cardboard tubes may also easily be obtained from such common sources as box makers' paper roll tubes, mailing tubes, paper towel tubes, toilet tissue tubes, and so forth.

To make this scrap craft unit as helpful as possible to the reader, we are presenting below detailed discussions of several typical or key projects, each representing the construction possibilities of some popular kind of cardboard container or tube. For example, Project No. 77, Maraccas, shown in Fig. 1, Illustration 27, is our key project in the use of discarded ice cream or coffee containers. Project No. 78, Crocheting or Knitting Bag, shown in Fig. 1, Illustration 28, is presented in explanation of the arts and crafts possibilities in the use of discarded oatmeal or salt containers. Similarly, Project No. 80, Pot Holder Rack, shown in Fig. 1, Illustration 30, is included in this scrap craft unit to show the uses of discarded mailing tubes, and Project No. 79, Modern Flower Vase, shown in Fig. 1, Illustration 29, is intended to inform the reader of the project possibilities of paper towel and toilet tissue rolls.

In addition to these key projects, several other suggestions are given for the use of these standard round cardboard containers and cardboard tubes. Suggestions are also given for decorating these cylindrical materials with various coloring media and applique treatments, to produce artistic results.

The great advantage of these discarded cardboard containers and tubes is that they seldom require much, if any, cleaning or conditioning before they can be used. In most cases the tubes and containers are as good as new and can be stored away until you are ready to use them.

Other important advantages are that the cardboard tubes and containers can easily be cut to any required size, they can be attractively colored with crayons, tempera, or enamel paints, and they can be effectively decorated by being covered with such appropriate craft materials as crepe paper, oilcloth, cork, felt, or some suitable cotton print.

It is hoped the projects discussed below will guide the reader in making a successful use of these materials. Also that the key models selected for this scrap craft unit will inspire the creation of many other toys, novelties, games, and practical articles.

Let us proceed with our first key project, Maraccas, shown in Fig. 1, Illustration 27, in which we will learn how discarded ice cream and coffee containers can be converted into various articles. In this particular model a broomstick handle and a handful of pebbles are used in combination with the cardboard container.

Project No. 77, Maraccas

See Illustration No. 27

I. Description

These gaily colored rattles were created as the result of an actual need, in a children's summer camp, for some Latin-American rhythm instruments, popularly known as maraccas. They were to be used by the children in several dances in the camp's musical, "Festival to Our Good Neighbors."

The arts and crafts shop, conducted by the author, was asked to provide twelve of such maraccas, and only a week was allowed for their construction. The completed instruments or "Rhythm Rattles,"

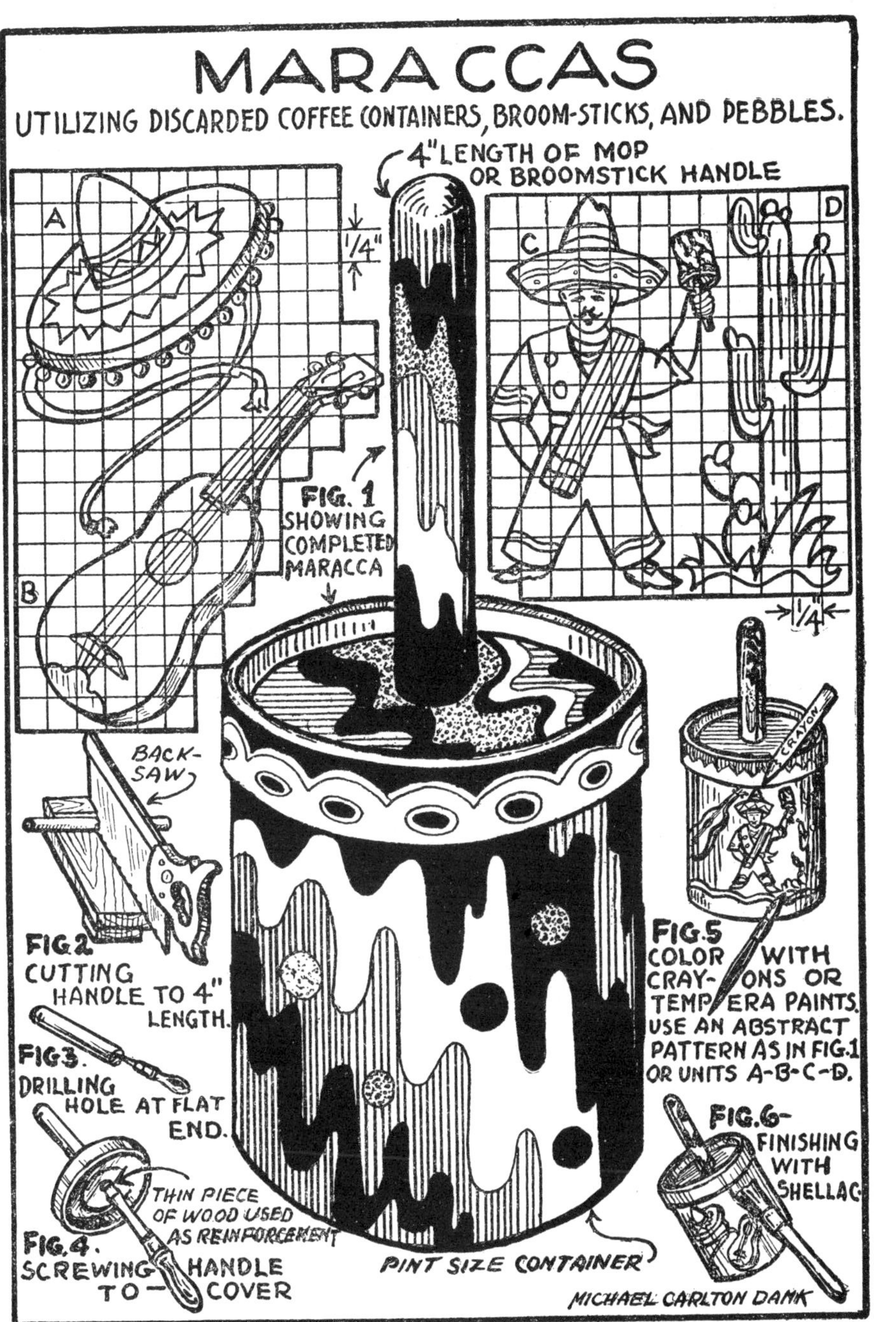
MARACCAS
UTILIZING DISCARDED COFFEE CONTAINERS, BROOM-STICKS, AND PEBBLES.
4" LENGTH OF MOP OR BROOMSTICK HANDLE
A
B
C
D
1/4"
1/4
FIG. 1 SHOWING COMPLETED MARACCA
BACK-SAW
FIG. 2 CUTTING HANDLE TO 4" LENGTH.
FIG. 3 DRILLING HOLE AT FLAT END.
THIN PIECE OF WOOD USED AS REINFORCEMENT
FIG. 4. SCREWING HANDLE TO COVER
PINT SIZE CONTAINER
CRAYON
FIG. 5 COLOR WITH CRAYONS OR TEMPERA PAINTS. USE AN ABSTRACT PATTERN AS IN FIG. 1 OR UNITS A-B-C-D.
FIG. 6 - FINISHING WITH SHELLAC
MICHAEL CARLTON DANK

Illustration 27

as the children like to call them, were built entirely of discarded materials found about the camp. They were fashioned exactly like the models represented in Illustration No. 27.

Six of the maraccas were built by younger children, using crayons as the coloring medium, and the gay abstract pattern shown in Fig. 1, Illustration No. 27, as the decorative scheme. The other six were made by older children using tempera paints as the coloring medium, and the design units A, B, C and D, as decorative motifs, applied as in Fig. 5.

In addition to being used as maraccas for rhythm dancing, these attractive instruments may also be employed in amateur rhythm bands and as babies' rattles.

II. Materials

A. Discarded pint size round cardboard container, such as used for packaging cocoa, coffee, and ice cream.

B. A round stick, 1/2 inch to 3/4 inch in diameter and at least 4 inches in length. Old broomstick and mop handles are excellent for this purpose.

C. Small pebbles or peas.

D. A thin piece of wood about 3 inches square. This is easily obtained by the use of a cheese or cigar box.

E. Crayons or tempera paints.

F. A 1-inch flat or round head screw.

G. Glue, clear shellac, and sandpaper.

III. Tools

A. Back saw and bench-hook.

B. Brad awl.

C. Screw driver.

D. Nos. 1 and 3 pointed water color brushes and a 1-inch, flat varnishing brush.

IV. Directions

A. Construction of handle

1. Using a bench hook and back saw, as in Fig. 2, Illustration No. 27, cut a 4 inch length of any round stick, 1/2 inch to 3/4 inch diameter. See II above for sources of sticks for this purpose.

2. Round off one end of handle, using first a medium grade rasp file, then a piece of sandpaper wrapped around a small wood block. See methods of sandpapering wood parts, Chapter Five, Section IV F.

3. Bore a hole, about 1/8 inch diameter and 1/4 inch deep, at exact center of the flat end of handle. Use either a brad awl as in Fig. 3, or a hand drill equipped with a suitably sized drill point.

B. Fastening handle to container cover

1. Cut a piece of thin cheese or cigar box wood to approximately 3 inches square.

2. Cut off 1/2 inch corners at each of the four corners of this piece, and then bore a 1/8 inch hole through its center.

3. Detach cover from cardboard container and bore a similar hole through its center.

4. Using a 1 inch flat or round head screw and a screw driver, join handle to cover by placing liquid glue on the end of the handle and on the inside surface of the thin wood piece. The wood piece, placed on the inside of the container cover, reinforces this joint. It also prevents the screw from tearing through the cardboard container cover.

C. Decorating the maraccas

1. Use a good grade of pressed wax crayons or opaque water color paints. The water color paints may be either the tempera or show card varieties.

2. To color the wooden handle, first draw a free hand pencil outline of the pattern seen in Fig. 1, directly over the handle. This abstract design may, of course, be modified in accordance with one's own taste. The lined, dotted, white and black sections seen on the handle in the drawing, indicate the use of carefully selected, gay, harmonious colors in the particular coloring medium employed.

3. Color the wooden handle with the crayons or tempera paints, carefully following the pencil outlines. See Chapter Five, Section IV, H for suggestions for the proper use of these coloring media. A good selection of colors for the handle are the following: lined sections—yellow orange; black sections—blue; dotted sections—red orange. Any other combination of colors may be used.

4. Draw a free hand pencil outline on the top and sides of the cover of the cardboard container only, of the pattern seen in Fig. 1.

5. Using the same coloring medium and the same combination of colors employed in the painting of the handle, decorate the cover of the container, following the previously drawn pencil outlines.

6. Cut a piece of white drawing paper to fit exactly around the body of the cardboard container. The width of this strip should be the full height of the container, less the 3/4 inch overlapping rim of the cover.

7. On this strip draw the pattern which is to be employed in the coloring of the body of the container. If the abstract pattern is used, as in the sketch of the completed model in Fig. 1, make a free hand outline drawing of this pattern on the white strip of paper. This pattern can also be rearranged if desired.

8. Cut a piece of carbon paper of the typewriter variety to the same size as the strip of white drawing paper.

Plate 13. Cork-decorated oatmeal boxes make useful and attractive knitting containers. Cork is used alone to make coasters, and with wood to make book ends, trays and card boxes.

9. Wrap the strip of white drawing paper, with the carbon sheet under it, around the body of the container. The pencil outline of the pattern must, of course, appear at the top of the white strip and the carbon paper must be placed with its carbon side facing downward, ready for tracing the design to the container. Use two rubber bands, one at the top and one at the bottom, to hold the two sheets in place. Small strips of scotch tape may also be used for this purpose in place of the rubber bands.

10. With a well-sharpened pencil, carefully go over all the outlines of the abstract pattern, using a medium amount of pressure.

11. After tracing, remove pattern and carbon sheets. If properly done, a clear carbon duplicate of the pattern now appears around the body of the cardboard container.

12. Using the same coloring medium and the same combination of colors as employed for the handle and cover, color the body of the container, carefully following the outline tracing of the pattern. Also follow coloring suggestions as shown in Fig. 1, Illustration 27, by the white, black, dotted and lined sections.

13. If design units A, B, C and D are used for the body of the container in place of the abstract pattern, simply trace these units to the white strip of drawing paper. The units should be arranged and spaced so they will show to best advantage around the container body, as in Fig. 5.

14. Wrap white strip of drawing paper together with carbon paper around container, and transfer the four decorative units in the same manner as described in 8, 9, 10 and 11 above.

15. Color the four design units now traced around the surface of the container body, using the same coloring medium as employed for the handle and cover.

16. Decorate the background in some appropriate color which will display the four design units to advantage.

D. Assembling and finishing the maraccas

1. Place a handful of small pebbles or peas inside the container body.

2. Brush a little liquid glue around the top edge of the container body and inside the rim of the cover and fasten the cover securely in place over the container body.

3. Using a small flat varnishing brush, apply a coat of clear white shellac over the entire project, including the wooden handle. The shellac coating should be used for both the crayon and tempera forms of coloring. See Fig. 6 in Illustration No. 27 and refer to Chapter Five, H for directions in the proper use of shellac.

RELATED PROJECTS

In which round cardboard containers such as oatmeal boxes, mailing tubes, paper towel tubes, ice cream and coffee containers, and so forth, are employed as the essential material of construction.

Project No. 78, Crocheting or Knitting Tube

See Figure 1, Illustration 28

I. Description

Like the maraccas shown in Fig. 1, Illustration 27, the crocheting or knitting tubes which we are about to discuss may be constructed and decorated through the application of a variety of craft materials and techniques, producing different though equally satisfactory results. For instance, the oatmeal box here employed may be decorated simply by a combination of tempera or enamel colors; it may be covered with wall-paper, crepe paper, corrugated paper, winding raffia, or cotton cloth; or it may be finger painted.

The adaptability of this crocheting or knitting tube to all of these easily obtained and inexpensive scrap materials and simple craft procedures, makes this a good project for craft shops in schools, camps and recreational centers everywhere.

In order to determine which craft process or material was most suitable for the construction of this project, the author built a

CROCHETING OR KNITTING TUBE
USING AN OATMEAL BOX, CORD, AND WALL-PAPER OR CLOTH SCRAP
FIG. 1
SHOWING COMPLETED OAT-MEAL BOX KNITTING TUBE
FIG. 2
USING KNIFE TO CUT HOLE IN CENTER OF OAT-MEAL BOX COVER
A
FIG. 5
SHOWING ENDS OF CORD HANDLE KNOTTED INSIDE TUBE.
A
B
C
M
OAT-MEAL BOX
PASTE
N
WALL-PAPER OR PRINTED CLOTH COVERING
FIG. 3
PASTING COVERING TO OATMEAL BOX
CARDBOARD BASE
WALL-PAPER OR CLOTH COVERING
BASE-B-GLUED TO BOTTOM OF OAT-MEAL BOX
FIG. 4
METHOD OF CONSTRUCTING BASE SECTION OF KNITTING TUBE
MICHAEL CARLTON DANK

Illustration 28

different model employing each decorative material and technique mentioned above. The project was also presented to his craft students in these different forms. It was found that each method of fashioning the crocheting or knitting tube proved entirely satisfactory.

Of course, as the reader will readily understand, it is impossible to treat each of these decorative processes in detail. Although we are employing scrap wall-paper or printed cotton cloth to decorate the oatmeal box, a few practical suggestions are also given with respect to the other scrap materials and decorative treatments which can advantageously be employed.

In the building of these tubes such craft procedures are involved as pasting wall-paper or printed cloth material on cylindrical cardboard containers, simple cord braiding, punching holes in cardboard, cutting cardboard, and shellacking wall-paper or cloth surfaces. Should empty oatmeal boxes be unobtainable, a quart size round ice cream or coffee container can also be used satisfactorily for this purpose.

As you will note in Fig. 1, Illustration 28, a hole is cut in the lid or cover of the oatmeal box to accommodate the tall knitting needles and to permit the yarn to be pulled through.

Because of the universal popularity of crocheting and knitting, these attractive tubes or bags are always useful.

II. Materials

A. One empty oatmeal box of the type shown in Fig. 1, Illustration 28.

B. A scrap piece of wall-paper or printed cloth, about 18 inches square, preferably in a bold flower or figure pattern to cover the oatmeal box.

C. Flour-paste or any good commercial paste, suitable for mounting wall paper or cloth material to cardboard surfaces. A little liquid glue is also required.

D. Heavy cotton cord for use in the preparation of the braided cord handle of the tube. See Fig. 1. Any form of heavy cord will be satisfactory. If white cord is used, it can easily be dyed to harmonize with the coloring of the oatmeal box wrapper. Tufted-rug cord, raffia, discarded stockings, and heavy grade cotton or wool yarn are also good materials for the braided handles. About 7 feet of the material are required.

E. A color of enamel paint which matches the color combination of the wall-paper or printed cloth material used as a covering for the oatmeal box.

F. A scrap piece of cardboard, such as used for laundry shirt supports.

III. Tools

A. A sharp medium size pair of scissors.

B. A sharp pointed knife, such as seen in use in Fig. 2, Illustration 28.

C. A good size flat style pasting brush. See Fig. 3. Also a 1 inch wide flat style shellacking brush.

D. Clear white shellac.

E. A leather or paper punch, capable of punching 1/4 inch diameter holes.

IV. Directions

A. Cut a scrap piece of gaily printed wall-paper or cotton cloth material (chintz, percale, and cretonne are especially good for this purpose) about 1/2 inch longer than the length and 3/4 inch larger in width than the circumference of the oatmeal box. Use a sharp pair of medium size scissors and cut the material straight, square and neatly at the edges. Also make certain that the printed patterns of the wall-paper or cotton cloth material will appear in their correct upright position when the covering is wrapped around the oatmeal box.

B. Using a good size flat pasting brush and any good grade paste, such as flour paste, wall-paper paste, and so forth, mount the printed wall-paper or cotton neatly around the circular sides of the oatmeal box. Locate the top edge of the wrapper immediately below the section occupied by the rim of the oatmeal box lid, as shown by M, Fig. 3. In this pasting step, it is best first to brush the paste evenly over the circular sides of the oatmeal box and then to mount the decorative covering gradually and tightly around the container, avoiding the formation of wrinkles or any other irregularities as you proceed. Make certain that the finishing edge of the covering is straight and tightly pasted down. It is also a good idea after pasting on the wrapper, to use an old clothes brush to smooth away all paste puddles and blisters. See Fig. 3, and note location of top and bottom edges of wrapper.

C. Brush some paste over the bottom of the oatmeal box and then fold over and paste down the surplus or extending end of the mounted wrapper over the oatmeal base. See Fig. 3, N and Fig. 4, A.

D. Cut a piece of cardboard to form a disc a little smaller in diameter than the diameter of the oatmeal base. Also, cut a disc from a piece of the same wall-paper or printed cloth used for the oatmeal box wrapper, and about 1 inch larger in diameter than the cardboard disc. Then, paste wall-paper or cloth disc over the cardboard disc, neatly folding over and pasting down extending edges of wrapper as shown in Fig. 4, B.

E. Fasten covered cardboard disc to bottom of oatmeal tube with any good grade of liquid glue, keeping the covered or finished side outward, as observed in Fig. 4, C. Place a weight, such as a few books, over the glued-on base section, allowing it to remain in place until the glue dries and the base is solidly attached.

F. With a sharp pointed knife neatly cut a 3/4 inch diameter hole in the center of the cover of the oatmeal box. See Fig. 2. If the edges are a little irregular or rough, they can easily be smoothed and finished with a small piece of fine grade sandpaper.

G. With a harmonizing or contrasting shade of enamel or tempera paint, color all outside and inside surfaces of the oatmeal box lid and allow it to dry. Or the outside and inside surfaces of the lid may be covered with the same wall-paper or cotton cloth used for the wrapping of the oatmeal box, in place of the tempera or enamel paint. You will find this latter method in the sketch of our completed project in Fig. 1, Illustration 28.

H. Using a 1 inch wide flat brush, apply two coats of clear white shellac over all outside and inside sections of the oatmeal box, including its covered or painted lid. This shellac coating is especially recommended when wall-paper is employed. However, it is practical to shellac cloth coverings also, to produce a bright, water-proof finish. Cloth coverings may be left unshellacked, if so preferred.

I. Braid together three two foot long strands of heavy cord or yarn to form the knitting tube handle shown in Fig. 1, Illustration 28. If only heavy white cord or yarn is available, you can easily dye it in any desired color with ordinary commercial dye.

J. Punch a 1/4 inch diameter hole at each side of the knitting tube, about 1 inch below the top edge of the tube. Use a regular leather punch, a paper punch, or any steel instrument such as a modeling tool or ice pick.

K. Insert ends of braided-cord handle through the punched holes in the side of the tube, and knot the ends on the inside of the tube as shown at Fig. 5, A. Constructed in this simple and inexpensive fashion, your crocheting and knitting tube is now complete and ready for use. If you have followed the directions given above, your model will be as attractive as the one in Fig. 1.

As suggested in the introduction, the oatmeal box may also be decorated in various other ways. Among these are fingerpainting and then shellacking the entire, outside surfaces of the oatmeal tube; covering the box with gay, harmonizing or contrasting colors of scrap felt; using corrugated cardboard as a covering and then painting on a few designs with enamel or tempera paints; using an overall covering of cork and then adding a few applique units of cork in a contrasting color; winding different colors of raffia, crepe paper cord, or other kinds of colored cord of a heavy grade around the container, followed by an application of a coating or two of clear shellac; or covering the box with an overall coat of enamel or tempera paint, pasting on some form of colored picture or decalcomania unit, followed by a coating or two of clear shellac.

Project No. 79, Modern Flower Vase

See Figure 1, Illustration 29

I. Description

While discarded cardboard paper towel tubes are the essential material in the construction of this modern flower vase, the main craft "trick" here involved, is to embed two tubes of different sizes and covered with corrugated cardboard wrappings in soft plaster, thus providing a solid base structure for the vase.

As you will note from the sketch of the completed vase, in Fig. 1, Illustration 29, a wooden doily or embroidery hoop is employed as a circular form or "fence", into which the plaster is poured in constructing the base of the vase. The corrugated cardboard here employed as decorative wrappings for the vase posts simulate marble columns and give the effect of porcelain or clay pottery vases. The type of corrugated cardboard suggested is regularly used to trim drug and stationery store window displays. Florists also use it to cover inexpensive flower pots and vases. This easily obtained scrap material is generally supplied and used in a single tone of white, yellow, green, and so forth. It is also made in a marbleized effect and in other neat patterns.

The fact that the two vase tubes used in the construction of this project are of different sizes is an interesting feature of this modern vase. These vase tubes may be used to hold any kind of artificial flowers which require no water. However, if you wish to use this vase for fresh flowers, all you need to do is to fit each of the two cardboard cylinders with glass test tubes or any similar receptacles capable of holding water.

As you will soon observe from the directions given below, this craft project lends itself excellently to a variety of decorative treatments and handwork skills. Among these are the use of enamel or tempera paints; marbleizing, oil painting process; the spraying technique; and the sand and glue method. Each of these decorative treatments simulates real pottery. Brief directions for each of these techniques are given below.

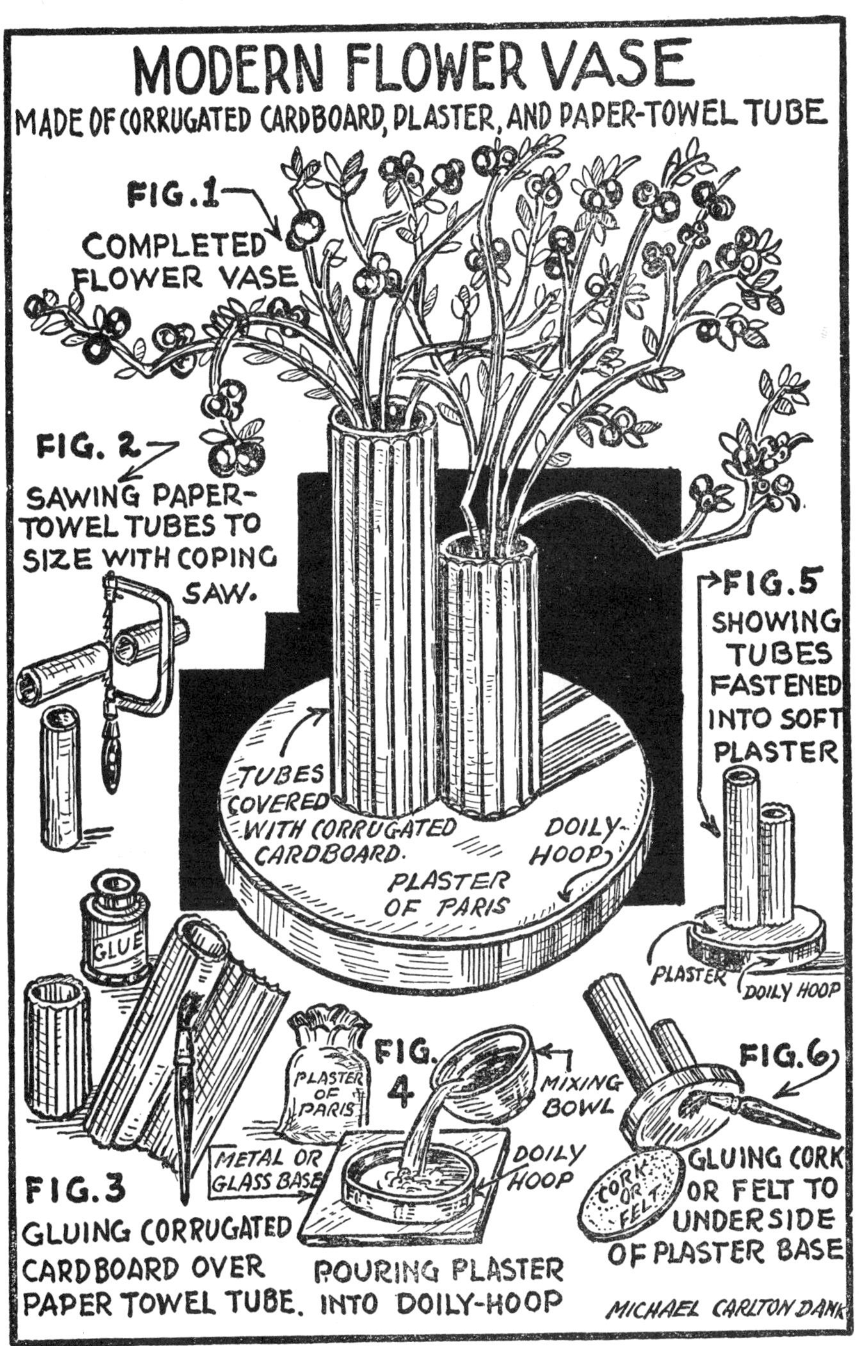
MODERN FLOWER VASE
MADE OF CORRUGATED CARDBOARD, PLASTER, AND PAPER-TOWEL TUBE
FIG. 1
COMPLETED FLOWER VASE
FIG. 2
SAWING PAPER-TOWEL TUBES TO SIZE WITH COPING SAW.
TUBES COVERED WITH CORRUGATED CARDBOARD.
DOILY-HOOP
PLASTER OF PARIS
FIG. 5
SHOWING TUBES FASTENED INTO SOFT PLASTER
PLASTER
DOILY HOOP
GLUE
PLASTER OF PARIS
FIG. 4
MIXING BOWL
FIG. 6
METAL OR GLASS BASE
DOILY HOOP
CORK OR FELT
GLUING CORK OR FELT TO UNDERSIDE OF PLASTER BASE
FIG. 3
GLUING CORRUGATED CARDBOARD OVER PAPER TOWEL TUBE.
POURING PLASTER INTO DOILY-HOOP
MICHAEL CARLTON DANK

Illustration 29

This useful vase can also be built with a single tube, larger in diameter, or with three tubes. Another effective application of this project is to build twin vases, each fitted with a single slender tube, constructed and decorated in exactly the same way.

II. Materials

A. Regular cardboard paper towel tubes. You will require two tubes for the model shown in Fig. 1, Illustration 29.

B. A wooden doily or embroidery hoop. A 5 inch diameter hoop is required for the model shown in Fig. 1.

C. A small quantity of plaster of Paris powder.

D. Discarded corrugated cardboard, large enough to cover the two paper towel tubes.

E. Any form of medium size mixing bowl, pan, or pot, suitable for preparing the plaster of Paris mixture.

F. Sheet of tin or glass about 7 inches in diameter or 7 inches square.

G. A little vaseline or mineral oil.

H. A good grade of liquid glue.

I. Several small rubber bands.

J. A piece of cork or felt to cover the base of the vase, a little larger than 5 inches square.

K. Clear white shellac.

L. A piece of fine grade sandpaper.

M. A plywood or pressed composition board, about 9 inches by 12 inches in size.

III. Tools

A. Coping saw, fitted with a fine toothed blade

B. A medium size pasting brush.

C. A 1 inch, flat style shellacking brush.

D. Sharp knife, suitable for cutting corrugated cardboard.

E. Steel rule or square.

IV. Directions

A. With a coping saw fitted with a fine blade or a sharp knife cut two lengths of paper towel tubes to required lengths. The shorter tube should measure 5 inches in length and the longer one 7 inches. These sizes include the 1/2 inch section at the bottom of each tube which is to be embedded in the plaster of Paris base section. Cut the ends of these tubes so they are square. After tubes are cut to size, smooth and true the cut edges with fine sandpaper. See Fig. 2, Illustration 29.

B. Cut a piece of corrugated cardboad to fit tightly and exactly around each of the previously cut paper towel tubes. The exact circumference size of the tubes may be determined by wrapping a plain paper sheet around the tube and then using this sheet as a pattern. After tracing the paper pattern to the corrugated cardboard, cut the corrugated material to required size, using a sharp knife and a steel rule or square. A good working foundation for this cutting step is provided by a sheet of plywood or pressed composition board.

C. Brush a coat of liquid glue over the outside surfaces of the tubes and over the inside or smooth surfaces of the corrugated cardboard wrappers. Be sure to cover all parts of both contact surfaces with the glue, but be careful not to get any of the glue on the outside surface of the corrugated wrappers. For this gluing step, use a 1 inch wide, flat style brush and apply the glue evenly throughout. After brushing on the glue, carefully wrap the corrugated sheets around the tubes, pulling the wrappers tightly as you proceed. Be sure that the beginning and finishing edges of the wrappers meet neatly and exactly, in order that the seam thus made may be as invisible as possible. Also make sure that the top edges of the corrugated wrappers are exactly even with the top ends of the tubes. See Fig. 3.

D. Place several small-size rubber bands around the full length of the newly corrugated-wrapped tubes, placing the rubber bands at intervals of about 1/2 inch. Applied in this manner, the little rubber bands act as clamps to hold the corrugated wrappers tightly around the paper towel tubes until the glue dries and sets, and the wrappers are securely and permanently attached. In place of rubber bands you can wind string around each tube tightly and then tie the ends of the string together to furnish the required clamping effect until the glue dries and the wrappers are securely attached.

E. Cut two heavy cardboard discs the same size as the outside diameter of the tubes. Then, glue one of these discs to the bottom end of each tube.

F. Place a 5 inch diameter wooden doily hoop on a sheet of metal or glass, measuring about 7 inches square or 7 inches in diameter. Then, apply a coating of vaseline or mineral oil over that part of the metal or glass base which is encircled by the rim of the embroidery hoop. Do not apply any of the vaseline or oil over any part of the wooden doily hoop.

G. In a bowl, pan, or any other suitable container, make a mixture of plaster of Paris, sufficient in quantity for filling up the area encircled by the wooden doily hoop up to its top edge. The idea here is to use the doily hoop as a "fence" and to produce a solid plaster of Paris base for the flower vase tubes. In this case, however, the doily hoop which is about 5 inches in diameter and about 1/2 inch high, is to remain attached to the hardened plaster base as a form of trim and protection against possible chipping. To prepare the plaster mixture, first pour about a pint of plain water into the bowl or other container used as the mixing dish. Then, sift powdered plaster of Paris into the water in gradual doses, stirring the mixture thoroughly as you proceed to eliminate formation of lumps. When the water seems to have absorbed a sufficient amount of plaster, and the mixture has assumed a uniform, heavy cream consistency, it is ready to be poured into the doily hoop form. At this point, pour the mixture into the doily hoop form until the top edge of the rim of the hoop is reached. See Fig. 4 for demonstration of this step.

H. Immediately after the plaster is poured into the circular form and while the plaster is still soft, place the two previously cut and corrugated-covered paper towel tubes in their exact positions, in the center of the plaster-filled form. Be sure the tubes are located exactly right as they cannot be moved or adjusted after the plaster hardens. The tubes must be embedded to the very bottom of the plaster or until the cardboard discs previously attached to the bottom ends of the vase tubes actually touch the metal or glass working base. With the two vase tubes thus properly embedded, allow the plaster to harden without moving or otherwise disturbing it. Following the hardening of the plaster, allow the wooden doily hoop to remain attached to the plaster base as a form of protective rim. See Fig. 5.

I. Cut a piece of cork or felt to the same size and shape as the outside diameter of the newly prepared base and then glue this circular disc to the bottom of the base section as shown in Fig. 6. Apply the glue evenly over all parts of both contact surfaces and later place weights around top of base to assure solid attachment of the felt or cork covering. Sandpaper outside edge of felt or cork covering until smooth and neatly finished. Also sandpaper around the top edge of the doily rim and over the top surface of the hardened plaster base.

J. Fill in the corrugated openings at the top edge of each vase tube with small bits of soft plaster further to simulate "solid pottery" and to disguise the corrugated cardboard.

K. Decorating the flower vase. There are several different methods which can be advantageously employed in the decoration of this vase. A short description of each of a few of the more popular of these decorative treatments follows.

1. Using tempera or enamel paints.

    a. Apply a thin coat of shellac (dilute shellac well with denatured alcohol) over all inside and outside surfaces of the flower vase with the exception of the cork or felt covering glued to the bottom of the plaster base. For this shellacking step use a 1/2 inch to 1 inch wide, flat-type brush.

    b. After the shellac coating dries, apply either tempera or enamel paints, using a pointed style brush of a medium size. You may use a single color of the paint over the entire project, such as pale yellow, pastel blue, and so forth, or you may use an appropriate, light color for the two vase tubes, and a contrasting dark color for the base section. You may also paint the insides of the vase tubes with a darker tone of the same color used on the outsides of the tubes.

    c. If you so desire, you may add a simple flower or marbleized pattern around different sections of the tubes for added decorative effect. This added coloring treatment is not necessary, however.

    d. After the paint has thoroughly dried, apply two coats of clear white shellac over all painted parts of the vase and allow to dry. The effect of this decorative treatment is that of highly glazed pottery.

2. The marbleizing technique.

    a. Apply a thin coat of shellac over all inside and outside surfaces of the flower vase with the exception of the cork or felt base.

    b. Fill a discarded gallon fruit-juice can with plain water. Then, allow a few drops of oil paint, of different though harmonious colors, to fall to the surface of the water.

    c. Stir contents of can with a small stick and then, holding vase with its tubes facing downward, slowly submerge the full length of the tubes into the paint-bespeckled water. After doing this, slowly withdraw the tubes from the water. As a result of this procedure the tubes will have an attractive, marbleized appearance.

d. After the decorated tubes have dried, paint the base section of the flower vase in a solid, contrasting color of enamel paint.

e. As a final finish apply two coats of clear white shellac over all sections of the vase and allow to dry.

3. The spraying process.

a. Apply a thin coat of white shellac over all surfaces of the vase and allow to dry.

b. Brush a coat of tempera or enamel in an appropriate color over all parts of the vase tubes and the base section.

c. Outline a few different small leaf shapes on drawing paper, and then cut them out with scissors.

d. Using only rubber cement (since no other form of glue or cement will be satisfactory) paste the paper leaf forms around the two vase tubes. Be sure the leaves are arranged in an interesting and pleasing manner.

e. Mix a contrasting color of paint in the same medium used for the overall coat, and place the paint in a small spray-gun such as is commonly used for spraying insects and clothes.

f. Spray all parts of the vase tubes as well as certain parts of the base section.

g. Remove paper leaf patterns from vase tubes and allow work to dry.

h. Apply a coat of clear white shellac over all sections of the vase and allow to dry. As a result of this rather tricky method of decorating the vase, the sections previously covered by the paper leaf patterns, will be left in the original overall paint color while the rest of the project will appear in the contrasting color of tempera or enamel paint applied with the spray-gun.

4. The sand-sprinkling technique.

   a. Cover all sections of the vase tubes as well as all parts of the base of the vase with a thin but overall coating of regular liquid glue.

   b. While the glue is still wet, immediately following its application, sprinkle any suitable color of ordinary sand over all glued surfaces of the vase tubes and base section. Use a discarded salt shaker, of a good size, or a suitable sugar dispenser, as a form of sieve.

   c. Apply the sand over the glued surfaces of the vase as evenly and uniformly as you can to form a light coating of the sand all over the vase tubes and base section, thus producing the effect of stone, and disguising the cardboard material underneath the veneer of the sand. For this sand sprinkling process, ordinary beach sand can be used in its original color. This same beach sand can also be dyed in various attractive colors suitable for this purpose. When working with dyed sand, one color can be used for the vase tubes and a harmonizing or contrasting color for the base section, with highly attractive results.

   d. If so desired, the sand-sprinkled surfaces may be left untouched to simulate the rough texture of sand or rock. However, the sand-sprinkled surfaces of the vase may be finished off with a coat or two of clear quick-drying varnish or shellac. This additional treatment will produce a bright, glazed pottery effect.

Finished in any one of these decorative treatments, this modern flower vase will be most effective.

Project No. 80, Pot Holder Rack

See Figure 1, Illustration 30

I. Description

In the production of this useful kitchen accessory, a single cardboard tube, commonly furnished with paper towel rolls, a scrap piece of printed cloth, some odd lengths of cord, and three small brass cup-hooks, are the few scrap materials required.

Among the simple operations involved are pasting printed cloth wrappers around cardboard tubes, braiding and attaching cord handles, screwing brass cup-hooks to the cardboard tubes, reinforcing the tubes with narrow strips of wood, plugging the open ends of the tubes with cloth-covered cardboard discs, and various fascinating techniques in the construction and decoration of suitable pot holder pads, used with the rack.

Although gaily printed cloth is the material employed for covering the paper towel tube, such other materials as wall-paper, corrugated paper, crepe paper, oilcloth, cork, or raffia, can also be used effectively for this purpose. In addition to these applique methods of covering and decorating the tubes, other ornamental schemes may be employed such as coloring the tubes with crayons, tempera paints, enamels, and finger paint. This holds true in regard to the preparation of the braided cord handle. In addition to white or colored cord, neat and practical handles can also be made of raffia, crepe paper, leather thonging, discarded milk bottle wires, real or imitation leather lacing, or heavy wool yarn.

As regards the decorations of the set of three pot holders made with the rack, flower, fruit, nursery and animal motifs are all suitable. These decorations may be painted, embroidered, or appliqued. Also, various interesting sewing stitches may be applied in finishing the edges and other sections of the pot holders. If you wish, you may use the same pattern for all three pot holders. Or, you may use an interesting set of different subjects as represented in the sketch of our completed model in Fig. 1, Illustration 30.

II. Materials

A. A single cardboard paper towel tube.

B. A scrap piece of gingham, percale, chintz, or cretonne. A piece measuring about 7 inches by 15 inches is sufficient for covering a single tube. Matching cloth material is also required for making three 6 inch square pot holder pads. Two 6 inch square pieces of the cloth are required for each of the three pads.

C. Any heavy cloth material such as an old, discarded blanket, a scrap piece of muslin, and so forth, for use as fillers for the pot holder covers. Cotton batting or asbestos padding may also be used as filling material.

D. A strip of wood, 1/4 inch thick, 3/4 inch wide and about 11-1/2 inches long or 1/2 inch shorter than the length of the paper towel tube used.

E. Three medium-size brass cup hooks.

F. Suitably contrasting colors of plain cotton thread and embroidery thread.

G. Flour paste or any good manufactured paste, suitable for pasting cloth to cardboard. Thinned-in-water liquid glue may also be used.

H. About 7 feet of 1 inch wide binding tape, in a suitable color to match coloring of rest of the material used for making the pot holders.

I. About 8 feet of heavy cord for use in the construction of the braided cord handle used to hang the pot holder rack on the wall. A harmonious combination of different colors of cord is best although plain white cord may be employed and dyed in any colors desired.

III. Tools

A. A good size pasting brush for pasting the cotton cloth around the tubes.

B. A medium size pair of scissors for cutting cardboard and cloth.

C. A medium size brad awl, a scratch awl or an ice pick.

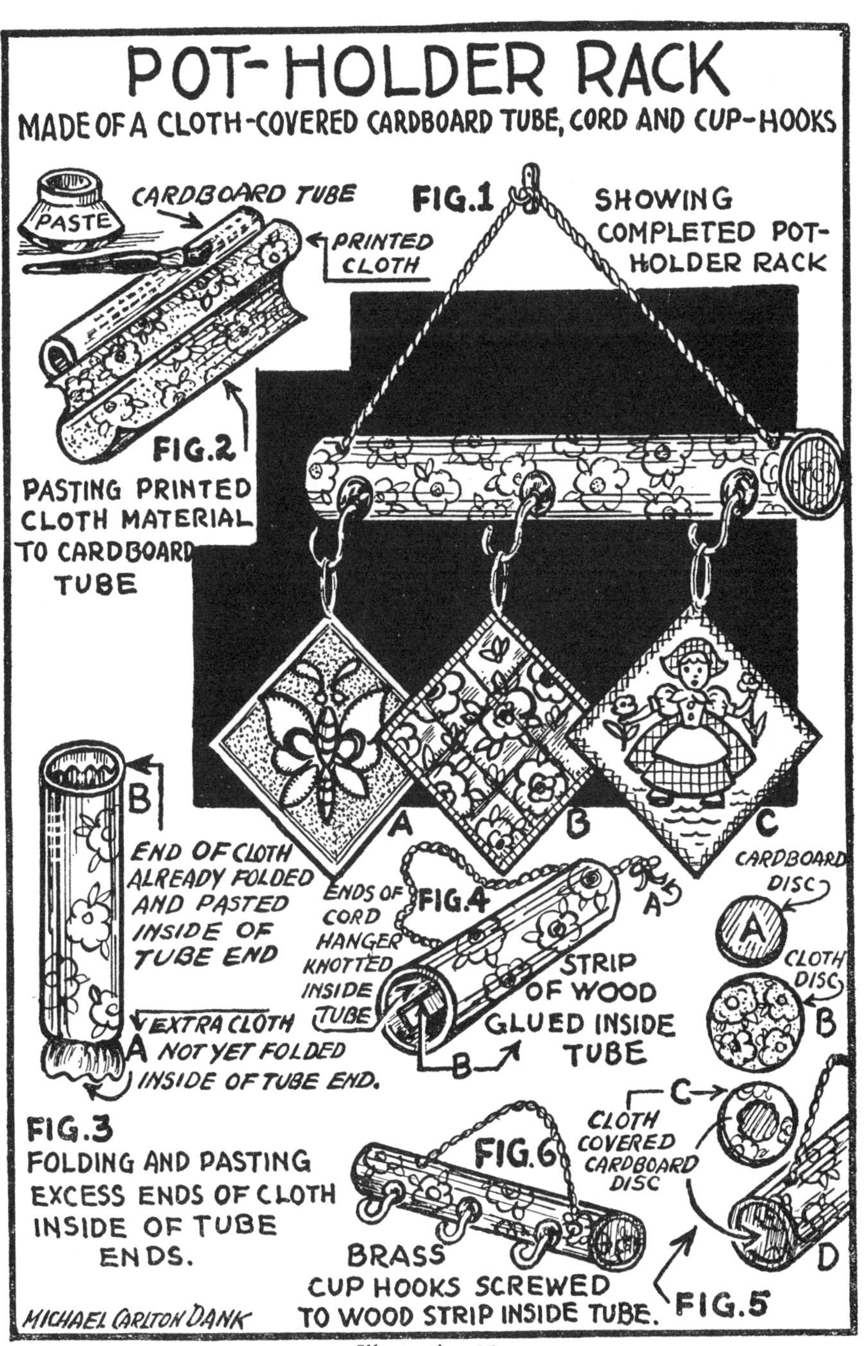
POT-HOLDER RACK
MADE OF A CLOTH-COVERED CARDBOARD TUBE, CORD AND CUP-HOOKS
PASTE
CARDBOARD TUBE
PRINTED CLOTH
FIG.1
SHOWING COMPLETED POT-HOLDER RACK
FIG.2
PASTING PRINTED CLOTH MATERIAL TO CARDBOARD TUBE
A
B
C
B
END OF CLOTH ALREADY FOLDED AND PASTED INSIDE OF TUBE END
EXTRA CLOTH
A NOT YET FOLDED INSIDE OF TUBE END.
ENDS OF CORD HANGER KNOTTED INSIDE TUBE
FIG.4
A
STRIP OF WOOD GLUED INSIDE TUBE
B
CARDBOARD DISC
A
CLOTH DISC
B
FIG.3
FOLDING AND PASTING EXCESS ENDS OF CLOTH INSIDE OF TUBE ENDS.
FIG.6
C
CLOTH COVERED CARDBOARD DISC
D
BRASS CUP HOOKS SCREWED TO WOOD STRIP INSIDE TUBE.
FIG.5
MICHAEL CARLTON DANK

Illustration 30

D. An old clothes brush or hair brush for use in the pasting step.

IV. Directions for Rack

A. Cut a piece of printed cloth (one with a small repeated pattern of flowers in gay colors is especially suitable) so that it will a little more than fit around the circumference of the paper towel tube and measure about 2 inches longer than the length of the tube used.

B. Using a good size brush, preferably a flat one about 1 inch wide, apply a coating of paste, or thinned liquid glue, over the entire outside surfaces of the paper towel tube. After applying the paste, remove all lumps or puddles with the brush to assure a smooth, even pasting result all around the tube.

C. Wrap previously cut printed cloth material tightly around the tube, making certain that no wrinkles or irregularities have formed. Be sure also that the tube is placed in the center of the 14 inch length of the cloth material to allow for folding 1 inch of the material over and inside of each end of the tube. See Fig. 2, Illustration 30.

D. After applying the cloth wrapper around the paste moistened tube, it is a good idea to use a small scrubbing brush or an old hair brush, well cleaned, to smooth out all remaining wrinkles or "blisters", and thus produce a neat, uniform, covering job around all sections of the tube.

E. Brush some paste on the inside of each of the ends of the tube and then fold over and fasten down the 1-1/2 inch of excess cloth material, allowed for this purpose, inside the tube ends. See Fig. 3, A and B.

F. Cut a strip of wood to measure 1/4 inch thick, by 3/4 inch wide and about 1/2 inch shorter than the length of the cardboard tube just wrapped with the cloth material. Then glue this wood strip inside of the tube, just in back of that part of the tube to which the brass cup-hooks are later to be fastened on. See Fig. 4,

B. Note:—Make a little mark on the outside of the tube, just in front of the wood-strip, to indicate location of brass cup-hooks after the holes are plugged up.

G. Cut three lengths of cord and then braid them together to form the braided-cord hanger shown attached to the tube in Fig. 1. Cord lengths of about 30 inches will produce a suitable size of braided hanger. See text under "Description," earlier in the discussion of this project, for suggested types of cord materials appropriate for making satisfactory braided hangers for this project, both in single and multicolor effects.

H. With a 1/4 inch paper or leather punch, a brad-awl, or an ice pick punch two small holes at the top section of the cloth-covered tube, one inch in from the left end of the tube, and one inch in from its right end. Then, thread the ends of the prepared braided-cord handle through the punched holes at the top of the tube, and knot the ends inside the tube. See Fig. 4, A.

I. Cut two cardboard discs to fit exactly inside of the tube ends. See Fig. 5, A. Following this, cut two circular discs of the same printed cloth material which was previously used as a wrapper around the tube. Make these cloth discs about 1-1/2 inches greater in diameter than the cardboard discs. See Fig. 5, B. Then, wrap the cloth discs around the cardboard discs, fold the extending edges of the cloth discs over the back surface of the cardboard ones, and paste the edges down securely as shown in Fig. 5, C.

J. Brush a little liquid glue or paste around the edges of the cloth covered cardboard discs, as well as inside the tube ends, and then plug the open ends of the tube with these discs in the manner shown in Fig. 5, D.

K. Screw three medium size brass cup-hooks into the front section of the cloth covered tube. Be sure the threaded points of the cup-hooks penetrate into the wood-strip, previously glued inside of the tube, in order that the hooks will be securely fastened on and will function satisfactorily as supports for the pot holder pads. See Fig. 6.

Having thus covered the construction of the pot holder rack, our attention is now to be directed to the preparation of the attractively decorated cloth pot holder pads. See Fig. 1, A, B, and C. As indicated in the introduction to the discussion of this project, these pot holders may be made in a variety of equally charming and practical styles. A brief description is given below of some of the more popular methods or techniques for making suitable types of pot holders, using a variety of scrap materials. The author has found each of these methods entirely satisfactory and suggests that the reader apply each of them in order to determine which is best for his purposes.

V. Directions for Pot Holders

A. Using same printed cloth material as used for pot holder rack:

1. Cut two 6 inch squares of the same printed cloth material as used for covering the paper towel tube, to serve as the top and bottom covers of the pot holder pads.

2. Cut a piece of cotton batting about 5-1/2 inches square, or a little smaller in size than the top and bottom covers of the pot holder to serve as stuffing or padding. In place of cotton batting as stuffing, you may use one or two layers of scrap felt or any heavy cloth. An old woolen blanket will serve excellently as padding material.

3. Place cotton batting or cloth layer padding between the top and bottom covers and then proceed to sew up the edges. For this edge sewing step, it is a good idea first to turn in the edges of the cloth covers about 1/4 inch all around, before sewing the covers together. Good edging treatments are the button hole or blanket stitch, represented in Fig. 1, B, or the cross stitch, shown in use in Fig. 1, C, using a contrasting color of thread or yarn. Another excellent scheme for sewing the edges of the pot holder covers, is that of using a suitable, contrasting color of binding tape as in Fig. 1, A.

4. Attach a loop of matching color tape to the top corner of the pot holder for hanging, before that particular corner is sewed up or bound.

5. As a finishing step, sew the middle section of the padded pot holder right through, from cover to cover, using four lines of running, basting, or outline stitches. Have two lines arranged at right angles to the other two, to form a tic-tac-toe effect as represented in pot holder model B, in Fig. 1. For this central section sewing step, use the same contrasting color of embroidery silk or colored yarn as employed for sewing up the edges of the pot holders. Place the four lines of stitches evenly apart, dividing the 6 inch pot holder square into nine 2 inch squares, as in the sketch at B, Fig. 1. By means of these four lines of stitches over the central section of the pot holder, the cotton batting or cloth padding inside the covers will be held neatly and securely in place, assuring longer and better wear.

Note: If desired, one of the four sides of the pot holder may be left open, neatly hemmed, and then fitted with two or three snap fasteners. By this arrangement, the padding inside the covers can easily be removed when the pot holder requires laundering. When applying this snap fastener method, it is necessary, of course, to refrain from using the four lines of running stitches through the central section of the pot holder covers, sewing only the edges of the covers.

6. Make the other two pot holders in exactly the same manner as the one just described, to produce a uniform set of three pieces. If you prefer, you may make the pot holders in a circular shape instead of the square shape just treated, applying the same directions as for the square shape, with equally attractive results.

B. Using solid color percale with novelty applique decoration made of same printed cloth material as used for pot holder rack:

1. Cut two pieces of solid color percale 6 inches square, selecting a color which will match or be in contrast with the printed cloth material used around the cardboard tube of the pot holder rack.

2. On a sheet of drawing paper, outline a simple bird, a flower, piece of fruit, and so forth, within a 6 inch square. This design may be drawn in a solid single-piece style or in a stencilled, multipiece fashion. The butterfly shown in Fig. 1, A, is a good example of the latter or stencilled form of design, while the peasant girl, shown at Fig. 1, C, is a good example of the former, or single-piece type of design.

3. Cut out the prepared paper pattern design unit and then trace around its outlines on the same printed cloth material as used for the covering of the paper towel tube.

4. Using a sharp pair of scissors, cut out traced design unit on the cloth. If design is of the multipiece type, you will have a set of several cloth shapes, such as the wings, eyes, antennae, body, and so forth, of the butterfly design used in model A, Fig. 1. If design is of the single-piece kind, you will, of course, have a single, solid cloth piece in representation of the entire design. This one piece design is much simpler and suggested for younger or inexperienced craftsmen.

5. Sew the cut out cloth decorative unit to the central section of the outside surface of one of the solid color, 6 inch percale squares, previously prepared. For this applique work use a small, tightly applied, overcasting stitch, or a tight buttonhole stitch, employing a contrasting color of colored yarn, embroidery silk, or heavy cotton thread. If design consists of two or more separate parts, as in the case of the butterfly motif used at A, Fig. 1, be sure the different parts are sewed on neatly and in their correct positions. After completing the outline sewing of the applique design unit, sew all detail lines of the design, using a running or outline stitch, and employing the same contrasting color of yarn or thread used for the outline sewing.

6. Prepare proper size padding of felt or cloth layers or cotton batting, and then sew the top and bottom covers of the pot holder together with the padding placed between them. Use either the buttonhole or blanket stitch as in Fig. 1, B; the cross stitch, as in Fig. 1, C; or the binding tape method represented in Fig. 1, A.

7. Attach a loop of a matching color of binding tape to the top corner of the pot holder to serve as a hanger, as shown in Fig. 1.

Note: In this method, as in method A, one of the four sides may be left open, neatly hemmed, and fitted with two or three snap fasteners, to make it possible easily to remove the padding from the inside, when the pot holder cover is laundered.

8. Construct the other two pot holders in the same manner as the one just described, using the same design unit for the applique decoration. Or, you may use a different though related, design motif for each of the three pot holders.

C. Using solid color percale or unbleached muslin with an embroidered decoration:

In this method, all directions for making the pot holders are the same as those given for Method B, just described, with the exception of the preparation of the decoration. In this plan, instead of appliqueing the ornamentation, it is embroidered. For the pot holder covers, use either a solid color percale or unbleached muslin, whichever best matches the color and pattern of the cloth material used to cover the paper towel tube. After cutting the pot holder covers to size, outline a design on a piece of drawing paper, selecting for this purpose any simple, appealing subject, and one which will be appropriate for embroidering. Use a design subject which is in harmony with the pattern of the cloth material used to wrap the cardboard tube of the pot holder rack. Thus, if the tube wrapper has a flower pattern, select some similar floral design for the pot holder decoration. If the design is of a peasant figure, use a motif such as shown in Fig. 1, C, and so forth. After preparing the design on the drawing paper, trace it to the upper surface of the top cover of the pot holder. A good method for tracing the design to the cloth material is as follows:

Punch small pin holes in close formation over all outlines of the design as represented on the drawing paper; place the punched paper pattern over the center of the top, cloth pot holder cover and then, using a sharply pointed pencil, make dots through each of the punched holes of the design as they appear on the paper pattern.

If done correctly, a dotted pencil tracing of the design will be produced on the cloth pot holder cover piece. After completing the tracing, embroider the design neatly, using one or several contrasting colors of embroidery silk, or any other suitable embroidery thread. Embroider the main outlines of the design first, using a running stitch, an outline stitch, a back stitch, or a long and short stich. This last stitch, which is applied at right angles to the design outline, produces an attractive, shaded effect. After you have embroidered the main outlines of the design, finish it up by embroidering the inside details of the design. For this detail sewing, you may work in other effective styles of embroidery stitches such as the weaving stitch, seen in the skirt and cap of the peasant girl in Fig. 1, C, the satin or solid stitch, the cross stitch, the loop stitch, the French knot stitch, and so forth.

When embroidering the design in this multistyled form of stitching, it is a good idea to work in different colors of thread to match the colors used in the cloth material employed for the covering of the paper towel tube.

D. Other good ideas for decorating the pot holders:

1. Using a linoleum block-printed decoration

Make a linoleum block of the selected or prepared design and then print this design on the upper covers of the pot holders, using any waterproof grade of printer's ink. For this decorative process, use unbleached muslin or a light, sold color of percale as the material for the pot holder covers.

2. Using a pressed, wax crayon decoration

Trace the design to the pot holder covers, which should be made of unbleached muslin; then color the design with appropriate colors of wax crayons. Following this, place two or three layers of a plain paper, such as wrapping paper, over the wax crayoned design, and press the cloth and paper sheets with a hot iron. This will cause the wax to dissolve and the crayon colors to be permanently absorbed by the cloth material.

3. Using scrap felt or oil cloth in applique style

Make pot holder covers of scrap oil cloth or felt, and an applique design of the same material, though in a suitable, contrasting color. Complete edges with any one of the decorative edging stitches described above.

In these three pot holder construction methods, use a cotton batting or folded cloth padding inside the covers. In these decorative schemes, too, it is a good idea to use corresponding materials, colors, and design motifs such as those used for the wrapper employed around the paper towel tube in the preparation of the pot holder rack.

The author trusts that the many decorative treatments presented above will enable the reader to be successful in this scrap craft project.

CHAPTER ELEVEN

WORKING WITH DISCS:

CARDBOARD AND METAL BOTTLE CAPS, AND CORKS

CIRCULAR disc materials in the form of cardboard milk bottle caps, metal soda bottle caps, cork discs, and similar types of discarded materials, can be put to excellent use in arts and crafts work in many interesting ways. All that is required is a few simple tools, a little time, and the application of the directions presented below.

Although, in this scrap craft unit, we are presenting only one key project, a number of practical project applications are also suggested.

Our key project is a novelty belt in which cardboard milk bottle caps artistically decorated are employed as a novel form of ornamentation. You will find this belt fully described in the text under Project No. 81, and shown in Illustration 31.

Although cardboard milk bottle caps are the main decorative feature of this sport belt, similar belts can be produced by using cork discs and metal caps, commonly used on soda bottles and similar containers. This same belt may be decorated with checkers, chips, odd buttons, and discs formed into shape from such scrap materials as linoleum, tin can and other metal sheeting, leather, or plywood

These related projects furnish arts and crafts teachers, students, and amateur craftsmen with many additional construction ideas in the use of discs. Once started in this branch of handwork, the reader will undoubtedly discover many other interesting applications of disc materials.

Project No. 81, Novelty Belt

See Illustrations Nos. 31 and 32

I. Description

This distinctive sport belt is easy to make, inexpensive, and attractive. Its outstanding feature is its colorful array of miniature decorative plaques made of discarded cardboard discs, commonly used as milk bottle caps. These plaques may also be used in other shapes than the circular form employed here. For instance they may be made in a series of squares, diamonds, rectangles, or in elliptical form. They can be used in a combination of shapes, such as circles and squares, circles and diamonds, and so forth.

The plaques can also be prepared from such scrap cardboard as shirt or shoe boxes, laundry shirt supports, and so forth. The milk bottle caps are suggested, however, because they are already circular and because they are made of a smooth, light colored cardboard stock which is easy to color. The plaques may also be constructed of such materials as tin, from discarded tin cans; leather, from old leather belts, boots, and so forth; from felt or linoleum scraps; from metal caps, commonly used on soda bottles; and from 3/16 inch to 1/4 inch thick plywood.

This novelty belt is particularly suitable for construction in arts and crafts shops because it involves such fascinating handwork procedures as sewing, leather-working, designing, and painting.

II. Materials

A. Cardboard discs, commonly used as caps for milk bottles.

B. Elastic, about 15 inches in length, and from 3/4 inch to 1 inch in width.

Such colors as brown, dark red, green, or tan are best. A striped pattern in these colors is also good. Discarded suspenders provide a good source of material for elastic bands suitable for this purpose.

C. Leather belting, from 3/4 inch to 1 inch in width, and about 12 inches in length. Discarded leather bookstraps, trunk or suitcase straps, or old belts are possible sources of this leather belting. Although cowhide belting is most suitable, other leathers such as suede, calfskin, steerhide, or patent leather are also satisfactory.

D. A belt buckle, of the kind commonly used for belts worn by girls and young women. Buckles made of metal, plastic, or those which come covered with leather, are all suitable for the requirements of this project.

E. Thin thread, preferably brown, for sewing. Also heavier grade thread, suitable for stitching the elastic to the belt parts.

F. Tempera colors, in paste or powdered form, and in a good assortment of colors. If preferred, enamel or oil paints may also be used, though these are somewhat more difficult to apply and require more time for drying.

G. Clear white shellac or clear quick-drying varnish, for use in supplying a bright protective finish to the painted plaques, used as decorations for the belt.

III. Tools

A. A sharp pointed knife, suitable for cutting leather.

B. Steel rule, used with knife when cutting leather.

C. A smooth-surfaced hardwood board, about one inch in thickness and measuring about 8 inches by 12 inches, for use as a base or working foundation for cutting leather and punching holes in the small decorative plaques.

D. A pointed brad awl or icepick.

E. A leather punching tool, capable of punching holes of 1/16 inch diameter.

F. Small size, pointed brushes, in Nos. 1, 2, and 3, for detaii coloring. Also a medium size flat style brush, suitable for shellacking and varnishing the painted plaques.

NOVELTY BELT

MADE OF MILK-BOTTLE CARDBOARD DISCS, AND SCRAP PIECES OF LEATHER AND ELASTIC AND AN ODD BUCKLE

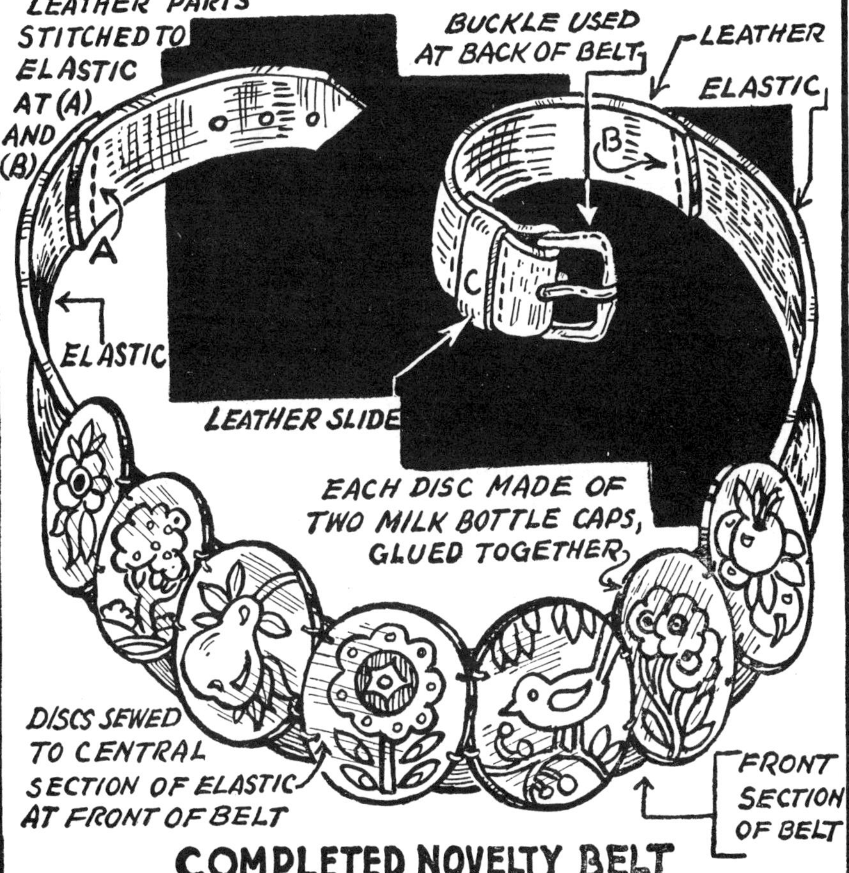

COMPLETED NOVELTY BELT

SEE FOLLOWING ILLUSTRATION FOR PATTERNS OF SUGGESTED DESIGNS FOR DISCS, AND FOR OTHER CONSTRUCTION DETAILS CONCERNING THIS PROJECT.

MICHAEL CARLTON DANK

Illustration 31

G. A sharp pair of scissors.

H. A medium size needle, suitable for use in sewing the cardboard discs to the elastic, and for sewing together the elastic and leather parts of the belt.

IV. Directions

A. Preparation of elastic for front section of belt

The front section of the belt is made of elastic band of any suitable color, width or pattern. Elastic band is suggested for this purpose since it assures a good, comfortable fit and is easy to obtain as scrap material from such sources as discarded suspenders, and odds and ends.

Elastic band in such plain single colors as brown, green, maroon or tan is best for the requirements of this belt. However, a striped pattern in these colors, or in a combination of subdued colors, is also satisfactory. A strip of such elastic material 15 inches in length, and from 3/4 inch to 1 inch in width, will be satisfactory for most belt measurements.

If the edges of the selected strip of elastic are in any way worn or frayed, it is a good idea to use a harmonizing color of thread or leather lacing to stitch or lace the edges of the elastic and thus produce a neat, decorative effect. If thread is used, an ordinary blanket stitch may be employed for this edging. If leather lacing is used, you may employ any one of such popular leather working stitches as the whip-stitch, cross-stitch, or button-hole stitch.

Having thus selected and prepared the elastic material for use in the front section of our novelty belt, proceed as follows:

1. Using a sharp pair of scissors, cut the elastic band neatly and squarely at the ends, to a length of 14 inches.

2. Fold back 1/2 inch of each cut end of the elastic and make a carefully finished hem by sewing across the width of the elastic with a needle and suitable color of thread. Use a simple running stitch, commonly used in belt construction, and make certain that the stitches appear straight and even, when viewed from the front side of the elastic. See Fig. 5, M, Illustration 32.

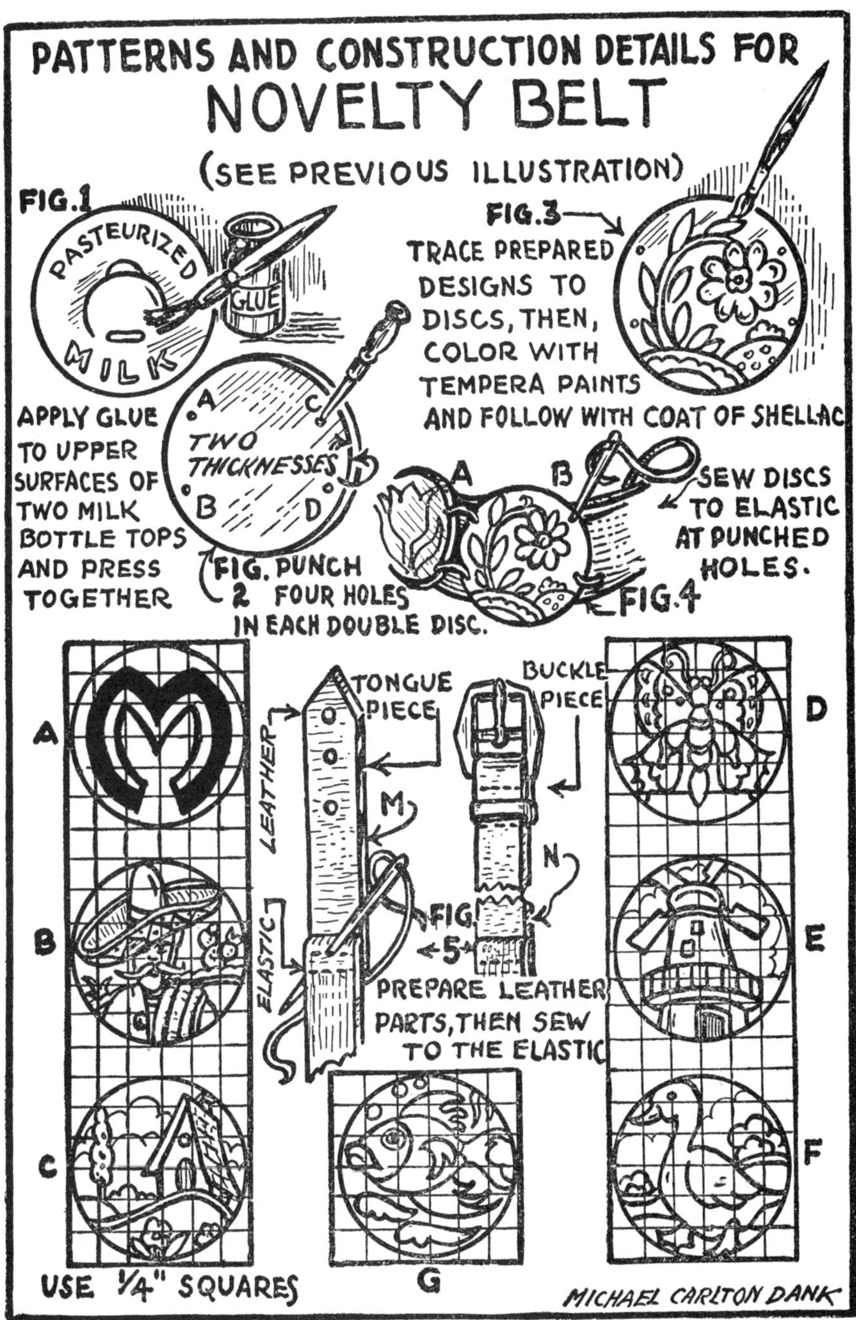
PATTERNS AND CONSTRUCTION DETAILS FOR
NOVELTY BELT
(SEE PREVIOUS ILLUSTRATION)
FIG.1
PASTEURIZED
MILK
GLUE
APPLY GLUE TO UPPER SURFACES OF TWO MILK BOTTLE TOPS AND PRESS TOGETHER
A
C
TWO THICKNESSES
B
D
FIG. 2 PUNCH FOUR HOLES IN EACH DOUBLE DISC.
FIG.3
TRACE PREPARED DESIGNS TO DISCS, THEN, COLOR WITH TEMPERA PAINTS AND FOLLOW WITH COAT OF SHELLAC
A
B
SEW DISCS TO ELASTIC AT PUNCHED HOLES.
FIG.4
A
B
C
TONGUE PIECE
LEATHER
M
ELASTIC
BUCKLE PIECE
N
FIG 5
PREPARE LEATHER PARTS, THEN SEW TO THE ELASTIC
D
E
F
G
USE 1/4" SQUARES
MICHAEL CARLTON DANK
Illustration 32

3. After completing the hems, set the elastic band aside until the leather parts have been prepared for the back section of the belt. The directions for constructing the leather parts are given immediately below.

B. Preparation of leather parts, for back section of belt

As the reader will observe from Illustration No. 31, the back section of the belt consists of two separate leather parts. These are the tongue part, shown at the left, and the buckle part, shown at the right. These leather parts may be used in the same width as the elastic band at the front of the belt, just as represented in Illustration 31, or they may be used in a somewhat smaller width. Thus, if the elastic band is 1 inch in width, the leather parts may be made in a width which may vary from 1 inch to 1/2 inch.

These leather parts may be cut to proper length and width from larger pieces of leather, or they may be already cut to proper width, if they are furnished by a discarded bookstrap, briefcase, trunk, or suitcase strap, or by any discarded belt. All that is necessary when using such discarded belts is to cut them apart and make a proper tongue and buckle section in accordance with the directions which follow. Any kind of leather material may be employed for these belt parts, provided it is not too thick and is sufficiently soft and flexible for comfort.

The proper procedure for preparing the leather parts of the belt is as follows:

If a ready-made, discarded leather strap or belt is used as the material for preparing the leather parts of our project, all that is necessary is to cut off proper size pieces from the pointed and buckle ends of the belt or strap. This is easily done in the following manner:

1. Place a smooth-surfaced, hardwood block or composition board on the worktable, as a foundation for cutting the leather.

2. Measure 8 inches in from the pointed end of the belt or strap, then draw a line across its width, making certain that the line is perfectly square. A try-square is a good tool to use for this purpose.

3. Place the marked off end section of the belt upon the cutting board, then, using a sharp, leather cutting knife, and a steel rule or try-square, cut off the 8 inch strip in a neat, clean-cut fashion. This pointed section of the belt should have from 3 to 5 holes, about 3/4 inch apart.

4. In like manner, measure 9 inches in from the buckle of the belt or strap and cut off that section, using the same procedure as directed for the pointed or perforated section of the belt. This buckle should be equipped with a leather slide-piece such as seen at C, Illustration 31.

The reader will find these leather parts represented in the upper section of Illustration 31.

If you prefer to make the leather parts from a scrap piece of calfskin, cowhide, steerhide, or any other suitable form of leather, they can easily be made as follows:

1. Place leather material selected for this purpose upon a smooth-surfaced, hardwood cutting board. Then, using a metal rule, measure two separate strips of the leather, one 8 inches long, for the pointed end of the belt, and one 10 inches long, for the buckle end. The width of these parts may be the same as the elastic band used at the front section of the belt, or, if preferred, may be cut somewhat smaller. Thus, if the elastic used is of 1 inch width, the leather parts may be cut to the same 1 inch width, or to such lesser widths as 7/8 inch, 3/4 inch, or 1/2 inch.

2. With a sharp leather-cutting knife and a steel rule, cut out the two marked off leather parts, being careful that the ends are perfectly square. This can be assured by marking off the ends with a try-square, before the strips are cut to their proper lengths.

3. To complete the 8 inch long, pointed end part, simply cut one of its ends to a point and punch from 3 to 5 holes, 3/4 inch apart, from this same pointed end, in the manner in which most belts are constructed. See upper left section of Illustration 31, where this pointed end part of our belt is represented in completed form.

4. To complete the 10-1/2 inch long leather strip, which is to be used as the buckled leather part of our belt, first cut a 1/8 inch wide slit, about 1/4 inch long, 1-1/2 inch in from one end of the strip. Then, insert the metal tongue of the buckle, which has been selected for this leather part, through the slit. Next, fold the 1-1/2 inch end of the strip completely to the back and stitch it securely in place. Use two rows of stitches, about 1/2 inch apart, as shown in the upper right section of the completed belt, in Illustration 31.

5. Cut a strip of the same leather material 1/2 inch wide and a little more than twice the width of the leather parts for use as the belt-slide piece.

6. Insert this slide part through the open pocket, formed by the two rows of stitches, stitch its two ends together, then turn it until the sewed seam is located inside the pocket and completely out of sight. See C, Illustration 31, for proper construction of this belt slide part.

Having thus completed the construction of the two leather parts of our novelty belt, we are now ready to join these leather parts to the elastic band which forms the front section of the belt.

C. Joining leather parts to the elastic band

As the reader will note by referring to A and B, in Illustration 31, all that is required in this assembling step is to sew the inside or squared ends of the prepared leather parts to the seamed ends of the elastic band with a simple running stitch.

It is important in this stitching step that the leather and elastic parts are in perfect alignment with each other, and that the joints are made neatly and strongly, so that they will hold securely together when the belt is worn.

The method for properly assembling the leather and elastic parts is as follows:

1. Using a try-square, draw a pencil line 1/4 inch in from the flat, inside end of each leather part.

2. With a leather punching tool, punch small holes, from 1/32 inch to 1/16 inch in diameter, and in close formation, along the entire lengths of these squared lines.

3. Using a needle and strong thread, sew the elastic and leather ends tightly together, permitting the ends to overlap about 1/4 inch. The color of the thread should either be the same color as the elastic, or any other color which will be in harmony with the elastic and leather parts. If so desired, leather or leatherette lacing 1/32 inch in width, may be employed to stitch the ends together, producing an even more decorative effect. Whether using thread or leather lacing to stitch the parts together, it is important that the ends of the lacing or thread employed are knotted at the back, with only the stitches, neatly placed, showing on the front side of the belt. This process of joining the leather parts of the belt to the elastic band, is shown in detail in Fig. 5, M and N, Illustration 32.

D. Preparation of onamental plaques from milk bottle caps

As explained in Section 1, the miniature plaques decorating the front of our novelty belt may be made of milk bottle caps, already shaped in circular discs, or may be cut into various interesting shapes from any sturdy scrap cardboard.

As shown in the drawing of the finished belt, in Illustration No. 31, seven plaques are required for this project. Since two milk bottle caps are required for the preparation of each plaque, a total of fourteen caps are needed for each belt. With this number of circular discs at hand proceed as follows:

1. Place two milk bottle caps on the work table with their printed cutout sides facing upward. Place a sheet of newspaper or cardboard underneath the discs to prevent soiling the table.

2. Using any good grade of liquid glue and a stiff-bristled gluing brush, apply a coating of the glue over the entire printed surfaces of the discs. See Fig. 1, Illustration 32.

3. Place both glued surfaces together, making certain that their edges are perfectly even all around, and then put a weight upon the assembled, two-piece disc, to press the two parts tightly together while drying. A heavy book, a paper-weight, or even a wrapped-in-cloth brick, will serve the purpose.

4. Repeat this same gluing process for each of the other six cardboard discs.

5. After the glued plaques have thoroughly dried, punch four tiny holes, of about 1/16 inch diameter, completely through each plaque, in the arrangement shown at A, B, C, and D, in Fig. 2, Illustration 32. Use either a pointed awl or ice pick for this purpose, working over a hardwood board as a protective foundation. The holes should be carefully centered and located about 1/8 inch from the edges of the discs, with the two upper holes placed about 5/8 inch apart from the lower ones.

E. Selecting and tracing plaque designs

The choice of suitable designs for the plaques depends entirely upon the ingenuity and taste of each craftsman.

It is, of course, fun to create your own series of designs for these decorative plaques. A number of suggested designs, however, are given in Illustration 32, from which the reader can make his selection.

One good idea is to have the plaques spell out the first name of the wearer of the belt, such as M-A-R-Y, utilizing some ornamental style of letters such as shown at A, Illustration 32. Another idea is to use a series of Mexican motifs or design subjects, such as seen at B, same illustration. Those who love and prefer natural subjects for use in decorating their belt plaques, will find several suitable design treatments represented at C, D, E, F, and G. Still other suggestions for good design subjects and motifs will be found in the drawing of the completed belt in Illustration 31.

After designing or selecting a suitable decoration for the plaques, make a careful drawing of each design in actual size, ready for tracing to the cardboard milk bottle discs. If you use the designs given in Illustration 32, it will be necessary to enlarge them a little to fit the 1-1/2 inch diameter size of plaques. If plaques are smaller, work accordingly.

To enlarge the designs to their full size, first use a compass to draw seven 1-1/2 inch diameter circles on a sheet of transparent tracing tissue. Next, draw a 1-1/2 inch square box around each circle and subdivide the box into 1/4 inch squares, in the manner shown at G, in Illustration 32.

After completing the seven 1/4 inch grills, copy each design and transform it to its full size. All you need to do is to locate each line shown in the reduced grill, in Illustration 32, in the same place and position on the grill of 1/4 inch squares as drawn on the tracing tissue. After the seven circular designs are enlarged in this manner, they are ready to be traced to the cardboard discs. This tracing procedure is performed as follows:

1. With a small pair of scissors cut out each circular pattern, previously drawn on the tracing tissue, so that it will be in exactly the same size as the cardboard discs.

2. Place the cutout tissue paper patterns on the table with their bottom surfaces facing upward. Then, using a soft lead pencil, blacken these bottom surfaces completely.

3. Place the first tissue paper pattern, with its blackened side facing downward, exactly over one of the cardboard discs. Then holding the pattern firmly in place with the left hand, go over all the design lines of the pattern with a sharply pointed pencil. In tracing, be sure to follow the pattern lines carefully and use a sufficient amount of pressure on the pencil to produce a clear impression of the design on the cardboard disc below.

4. Repeat this procedure for each of the remaining six circular plaques. After all the patterns are completely traced, the plaques are ready for coloring and finishing.

F. Coloring the plaques

As suggested above, any one of several different coloring media can be used for painting the pencil-designed plaques. Among these are crayons, oil paints, enamels, stains, and so forth. The author has found, however, that tempera colors are generally best for this purpose since they are easiest to apply, cheapest, and brightest.

1. Using a scrap piece of paper, make rough color sketches of the various color schemes which you plan to use on the plaques. Use small pans or metal covers of bottles for mixing the colors.

2. After determining the color schemes for the plaques, apply the colors to the first plaque, putting on the lightest colors first and the darkest ones last. Use pointed water-coloring brushes, in Nos. 3 or 4. Brush the colors on evenly and keep within the pencil outlines of each area colored. Allow each color to dry completely before applying another.

3. Repeat this coloring procedure for each of the remaining seven plaques, making certain that the same combination of colors is employed for each plaque to assure a harmonious color scheme.

4. Using a very small size brush, such as Nos. 1 or 2, paint a thin outline of black or any other suitable dark color around each color area.

5. After all the plaques have been colored and allowed to dry, apply one or two coats of clear white shellac over both the front and back surfaces of each plaque. This finish will make the plaques brighter and stronger, and will protect them against soiling. See Fig. 3, Illustration 32.

G. Attaching colored plaques to elastic

The completed plaques may now be attached to the elastic band at the front of the belt by any one of the following assembling methods.

One of these methods is to use extra small size brass fasteners. Pass one of these fasteners through each of the four holes of every plaque, and bend the protruding ends of the fasteners in an outward direction at the back of the elastic band.

Another method is to lace the plaques to the elastic with a suitable color of leather or leatherette lacing. In this method, the lacing is employed in two long strips, one for the top series of holes, and one for the bottom series. The lacing is done by connecting the corner of each of two adjoining plaques with each stitch in the manner shown in A, Fig. 4. Thus two stitches appear between each pair of plaques, one at the upper, and one at the lower holes.

The easiest and perhaps the most practical way is simply to sew the plaques to the elastic with a proper size needle and an appropriate color of thin thread. This method is shown in Fig. 4-B, Illustration 32. In this process, as in the lacing method, it is important that all resulting knots be located at the back of the elastic, so that they are entirely out of view when the belt is in use. It is also necessary that the plaques be attached tightly and that the stitches be arranged in neat, uniform fashion.

After completing this novelty belt in accordance with the directions given above, it is suggested that the reader make several other belts, employing some of the other materials suggested for making the plaques, such as plywood, metal, linoleum, composition board, leather, and so forth.

CHAPTER TWELVE

WORKING WITH SCRAP LEATHER

ALTHOUGH leather work is one of our oldest crafts, dating back as far as 5,000 years, it is today one of the most popular forms of educational and recreational handwork. It has always caught the imagination of craftsmen because of its fascinating development as a medium of artistic expression in the hands of the great craftsmen of olden times.

Historical records show that the ancient Egyptians used leather and regarded it as a sacred material, a worthy tribute to be offered to their kings and gods.

Leathercraft was introduced into Spain by the Moors during their occupancy and perfected in that country. The Crusaders brought back many of the methods employed by the Saracens. Modeled leather was introduced to the Venetians by the Oriental merchants and was used by the monks of the Middle Ages in their beautifully illumined manuscripts.

The Indians and the early American colonists accomplished much in the art of leather tanning, in the preparation of various essential articles such as foot gear, clothing, drinking vessels, blankets, and so forth. These articles were made from the shaggy sun-cured hides of animals that had been trapped or felled with clubs or arrows.

The popularity of leather work among modern craftmen is largely due to the ease with which skill in this work can be acquired. Leather work requires comparatively little and inexpensive equipment; and leather itself is a rich and durable handicraft material.

No special training or unusual skill is required for leather work although, as in most other crafts, the knowledge of a few basic principles and procedures is necessary. In order to become expert in leather work one must go about it systematically, making simple articles at first and then more and more complicated ones. Leather work can be as enjoyable and productive for children of six as for adults of sixty. It trains the eye and hand in perfect coordination, and helps to develop art appreciation and creative expression.

Articles made of leather can be tooled or not, as the individual craftsman prefers. Tooling leather articles, however, adds greatly to their beauty. This also applies to the procedure known as lacing. Both tooling and lacing are explained in detail below.

As the leather worker advances in his craft, he may develop many original designs. Or, he may obtain suggestions from illustrations in periodicals and from merchandise, not only leather, on display in store windows. Prepared designs can be purchased from handicraft dealers located in all sections of the country.

Handicraft dealers also have for sale many different kinds of leather kits, containing already cut-out project parts, instructions, diagrams and necessary accessories, requiring only tooling and lacing to be completed. In addition they can supply other useful items such as eyelets, belt buckles, metal ornaments, clasps, zippers, and all necessary working tools. Assorted colors of leather in hide or in scrap form, leather dyes, and so forth, are all available.

It is hoped that the few simple directions in leather work presented below will help to develop the reader's interest in this fascinating art.

Since scrap leather usually is obtainable in small pieces, and since it is the author's purpose to describe only the simplest and most basic procedures of this craft, the projects presented below are small and easy to make. In these popular leather projects, you will be instructed in such fundamental working procedures as cutting, tracing, tooling, lacing, and coloring. With these as a foundation you or your craft students will have no difficulty in constructing larger and more complicated leather craft projects.

Project No. 82, Leather Book Mark

See Figure 1, Illustration 33

I. Description

This ornamental book mark, designed in a bird and flower motif, is typical of the many book marks of various shapes and styles which can easily be made from odd or scrap pieces of leather. To produce

Illustration 33

book marks with tooled decorations, as in our model, use only leather of the tooling grade, preferably calfskin or steerhide.

If you have any difficulty in obtaining tooling leather in either of the kinds mentioned, you can also make book marks and many other leather articles of non-tooling grades of leather. This is done by decorating the work in some other way than by the tooling technique which we are about to describe. Among these other decorative treatments are burning the design into the surface of the leather with an electric pencil; painting on the design with an appropriate coloring medium, such as leather enamels; cutting out the design separately on a lighter or darker color of leather than used for the article itself, and then cementing it to the project in an applique form of construction.

We are presenting the book mark as our first project because it is a one-piece model, easily and quickly made, requiring for its construction only such basic leathercraft procedures as cutting, tracing, tooling, coloring, and finishing. Later in our discussion when we consider the construction of more advanced projects such as coin purses, comb and file cases, and so forth, the reader will learn how leather articles built of two, three, or more parts, can be joined by various attractive lacing techniques.

The book mark shown in Fig. 1, Illustration 33, is 1-3/4 inch wide by 7-3/4 inches long. However, as earlier indicated, it can be made in other, equally attractive sizes, shapes, and styles. Other appropriate sizes for book marks are 1-1/4 inches by 5 inches, 2 inches by 8 inches, and so forth. Good colors of leather for book marks are tan, brown, green, red and maroon.

The designs selected or prepared for use in the tooling of book marks, must be of a bold, simple character. The bird and flower motif used in the decoration of our model in Fig. 1, is a suitable design for this purpose because of its simple lines. Another good idea in designing book marks, also employed in our model, is the use of a monogram. Other good design motifs are tropical fish, cactus plants, Mexican figures, stylized trees, women's heads, scotties, deer, horses' heads, swans, Indian heads and geometric shapes.

In addition to the fascinating process of leather tooling, directions are also given below for multi-coloring and electric burning leather designs and decorations. Directions for appliqueing leather decorations of a simple character, when non-tooling grades of leather are employed, are also given.

II. Materials

A. A piece of tooling calfskin, sheepskin, or steerhide, a little larger than the 1-3/4 inch by 7-3/4 inch size required by our project. Good leather colors are tan, brown, red, maroon, green and black.

B. A small piece of sponge or soft cloth for dampening the leather.

C. A small pan containing plain water.

D. A sheet of thick glass or a slab of marble, about 9 inches by 12 inches in size, for use as a working foundation for tracing and tooling.

E. A fine-grained, hardwood board, about 9 inches by 12 inches in size, for use as a working foundation for cutting the leather. A plywood board of fine-grained, hardwood construction or a hard-pressed composition board, may also be used as working foundation boards for this leather cutting procedure.

F. A few medium-size paper clips.

G. An assortment of colors of waterproof inks, leather dyes, or leather enamels. Good colors are red, blue, yellow, brown, green, and black.

H. Saddle-soap or leather-polishing wax, used for finishing leather projects.

I. A clean, soft cloth for polishing waxed leather surfaces. A piece of felt or chamois is best for this purpose.

III. Tools

A. A leather modeling tool of the kind seen in Fig. 4, Illustration 34. A nut-pick may also be used as a modeler if a regular tool is unobtainable. Good modelers may also be made from ice-picks, scrap pieces of tooling steel, extra long, wire nails, and so forth.

B. A sharp knife, suitable for cutting leather, preferably of the style seen in use in Fig. 1, Illustration 34.

C. A 12 inch steel rule or steel square. See Fig. 1.

D. A medium-hard pencil for use in the preparation of the pattern, a pattern grill, and design. Also used for tracing the design from pattern to leather.

E. A few small watercoloring brushes.

IV. Directions

A. On a sheet of plain drawing paper, tracing paper, or architects' tracing cloth, draw a vertical rectangle, size 1-3/4 inches by 7-3/4 inches, then divide this rectangle exactly into 1/4 inch squares to form a full-size pattern grill, similar to the reduced-form pattern grill represented in Fig. 1.

B. Using reduced-form grill as a guide, copy all parts of the book mark plan on the newly drawn, full-size pattern grill, making certain to include all outlines and details of the design, the fringed or flapped section at the top of the book mark, and the curved effect and monogram section at the bottom. In place of the monogram seen in use in Fig. 1, substitute your own initials, or those of the person for whom the completed book mark is intended, using a similar style of lettering. If properly reproduced, the design and all other details of the book mark, will now appear in actual, required size.

C. Using a small pair of scissors, carefully cut around the outside contours or outlines of the full-size paper pattern of the book mark, so the pattern will now assume the same form in which the leather book mark will appear, when completed. In this pattern cutting step, it is best to cut out fringe-tips, X, but do not cut along the fringe-flap lines, Y. Also cut out curved section at bottom of pattern, such as indicated by Z.

D. Place selected piece of tooling calfskin, sheepskin, or steerhide, with its under or flesh side facing upward, on a marble slab or sheet of glass, about 9 inches by 12 inches in size. Be sure the leather is a little larger in size than the paper pattern of the book

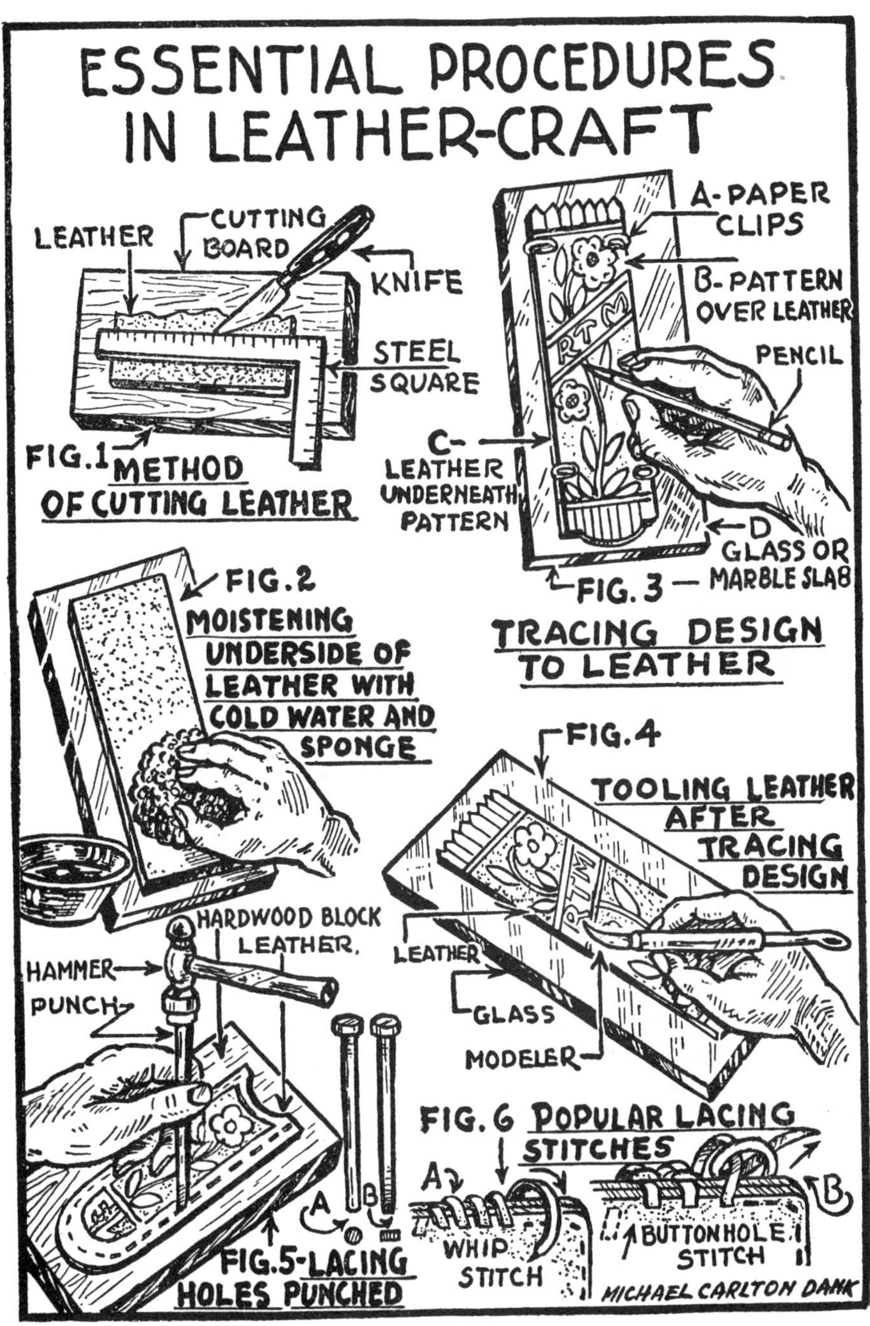
ESSENTIAL PROCEDURES IN LEATHER-CRAFT
LEATHER
CUTTING BOARD
KNIFE
STEEL SQUARE
FIG.1 METHOD OF CUTTING LEATHER
A- PAPER CLIPS
B- PATTERN OVER LEATHER
PENCIL
C- LEATHER UNDERNEATH PATTERN
D GLASS OR MARBLE SLAB
FIG. 3 — TRACING DESIGN TO LEATHER
FIG.2 MOISTENING UNDERSIDE OF LEATHER WITH COLD WATER AND SPONGE
FIG.4 TOOLING LEATHER AFTER TRACING DESIGN
LEATHER
GLASS
MODELER
HARDWOOD BLOCK
LEATHER.
HAMMER
PUNCH
A
B
FIG.5-LACING HOLES PUNCHED
FIG. 6 POPULAR LACING STITCHES
A
WHIP STITCH
B
BUTTONHOLE STITCH
MICHAEL CARLTON DANK

Illustration 34

mark. Then, using a small sponge or cloth, moistened in a pan of water, wet the entire underside of the leather. See Fig. 2.

E. Attach paper pattern, with designed side facing upward, exactly over the top or finished surface of the leather, using a medium size paper clip at each corner as a fastening device. Small strips of scotch tape may also be used. See Fig. 3, A, B, C.

F. Place moistened leather strip, with pattern now clipped over it, on the glass or marble slab. Then, using a fairly pointed pencil, trace over all the outlines of the decorative design and other book mark details appearing on the paper pattern. Do not press too strongly, as you may tear the pattern and injure the leather beneath it. Press just enough to produce a clear, uniform impression of the pattern lines on the upper surface of the leather. See Fig. 3.

G. After tracing, remove clips and paper pattern from the leather strip, and then place leather, top side up, on the plywood or hardwood board, ready for cutting.

H. With a sharp knife suitable for cutting leather, and a steel rule or steel square as a guide, cut around all outside contours of the book mark tracing on the leather, including the pointed fringe on top and the decorative effect at the bottom of the book mark. Also, cut apart the flaps of the fringe, cutting the leather along the indicated lines from A-B up to C-D. Curves such as the one at the bottom end of the book mark are cut with the knife only, without using the rule or square. When cutting the leather, hold knife firmly with the right hand, with the handle of the knife tipped backward at an angle of 45 degrees. It is important also, in this leather cutting step, to make certain that the knife is tipped neither inward or outward, lest the edges of the leather be cut in an undesirable, slanted fashion, rather than in the required square-edge manner of cutting. Make certain that the fingers of the left hand, which are used to hold ruler and leather securely in position, be located sufficiently in back of the cutting edge of the ruler or square, to avoid the possibility of a serious accident. See Fig. 1.

I. After all cutting has been done, place leather strip, with wrong or unfinished side facing upward, on the glass or marble foundation. Then, use sponge or cloth again to moisten the leather, this time in preparation for the tooling step.

J. After wetting underside of leather, place work on the glass or marble slab with the top or traced side of the leather strip facing upward. Then, holding modeling tool securely in the right hand, and supporting the work with the left hand, carefully go over all the traced outlines of the book mark decoration, monogram, and other details. For this outline tooling use the curved, pointed end of the modeler, holding the tool at an angle of 45 degrees to the work. See Fig. 4. As you proceed in this step, manipulate the work freely with the left hand, as necessary, to assure freedom and uniformity of tooling. Also, be sure the tip of the pointed end of the modeler faces upward and not downward, to avoid tearing and marring the surface of the leather.

K. After all outlines of the book mark design have been neatly and sharply tooled, use the larger or spoon end of the modeler to press or tool down all background sections of the design. Here, as in the outline tooling step, work in a clean, uniform fashion. You will find the background sections of the design indicated by dotted lines in Fig. 4. In this background tooling step the idea is to press down the background areas below the outline-tooled design sections, thus permitting the design or decoration to stand out beautifully in bold, artistic relief. In this step as in outline tooling, hold the modeler so its handle forms an angle of 45 degrees to the work. A final consideration, in background tooling, is to avoid distorting the previously tooled outlines of the design.

L. If you wish, you may leave the tooled background sections in this smoothly impressed form. However, it is often effective to stipple the background areas, after they are impressed, with the pointed end of the modeler. Another idea is to make short, horizontal, vertical, or diagonal strokes with the pointed end of the modeler. In some decorative schemes, a combination of plain, stippled and lined background treatments can be employed with highly artistic effect. You will undoubtedly discover these decorative possibilities for yourself as you progress in your work with leather.

M. As a final tooling step, go over all the design outlines with the pointed end of the modeler again, as in the first outline-tooling step, to assure a sharp, uniform, outlined effect around all sections of the embossed decoration.

N. Using a soft piece of cloth, apply a light coating of saddle soap or any other suitable form of leather-polishing wax, over the entire top surface of the tooled book mark. Let soap or wax coating dry for a minute or two and then polish with a fresh soft cloth until a velvety-smooth, bright finish is produced. Repeat this polishing treatment on all articles of leather work about every six months. This will assure long wear and attractive appearance.

In this simple, polished, natural leather finish, our book mark is now complete and ready for use. However, if you wish to color certain parts of the tooled design, you may do so by applying any one of the following coloring procedures:

Note: The coloring treatments which follow must be applied before any wax or saddle soap polish is used. In other words, the colors are to be applied subsequent to the outline and background tooling treatments and prior to the wax or saddle soap polishing treatment.

V. Coloring To Leather Decorations

A. Waterproof Inks.

These waterproof inks, which are really a form of transparent dyes, are obtainable in a variety of attractive colors, such as bright red, blue, orange, yellow, brown, green or black. Select an appropriate combination of colors and apply each separate color of ink with a proper size, clean watercolor brush. Do not "flood" the colors, but use sparingly, for they have a strong, penetrating quality. Apply each color carefully and neatly, keeping entirely clear of the tooled outlines of the design. Thus, if you are coloring a leaf with green ink, for instance, cover the entire area of the leaf just inside of its tooled or impressed outlines, without allowing any of the color to penetrate inside the outlines. For most artistic results, it is best to use the ink colors only over the raised or embossed areas of the tooled design and not over any part of the impressed background sections of the decoration. It is also a good idea, at times, to color only certain parts of the embossed design, depending on the character of the particular design employed. After coloring is completely finished, allow ink to dry thoroughly and then finish the book mark with saddle soap or leather polishing wax, as described above.

Plate 14. Tooled scraps of leather and wood scraps are used to make wall plaques, jewelry boxes and memo pads. The address book pictured is made entirely of scrap leather.

Plate 15. Decorative wall plaques, book ends and stationery racks made from tooled scraps of leather mounted on odd pieces of wood.

B. Coloring tooled designs with leather enamels

Leather enamels, in contrast to the subdued, transparent waterproof inks, are characterized by their gay, opaque quality. They are always effective in decorating leathercraft projects which are intended for the use of children. Just as in the case of waterproof inks, leather enamel colors should be applied sparingly and neatly, using suitable size water coloring brushes. Also, as in the waterproof ink coloring method, only the sections between the outline tooling grooves, and not the grooves themselves, should be colored. The idea of using just a few spots of color also applies to this coloring technique. Work colored with leather enamels may also be finished, when dry, with a polished coat of saddle soap or leather polishing wax.

It is suggested that teachers of leather work employ the single-tone, natural finishing process at the start, and later on present the multi-coloring techniques just described. Materials required for these coloring and finishing procedures may be obtained at most handicraft supply houses.

If you find it necessary to work with non-tooling leather scraps, you may use any one of the following decorative processes:

1. Coloring the original, plain surfaces of the leather with leather enamels or regular oil paints. After tracing the design to the leather, apply the colors and then polish entire project with saddle soap or leather polishing wax.

2. Burning the design into the surface of the leather with an electric pencil. Simply trace prepared design to the leather and then burn around the outlines of the design. Interesting shading effects may also be produced by this fine process. Also, waterproof inks may be added to the decoration after the design has been burnt in. Either the electric burning treatment alone or the combination electric burning and coloring technique is effective. This combination burning and coloring method of decorating leather is employed on a large scale in the manufacture of souvenirs and novelties.

3. Cutting decoration out of a separate piece of scrap leather and applying it to the book mark, change purse, file and comb case, and so forth, through the use of rubber or household cement. Using

a thinner grade of leather for the applique unit, preferably in a lighter or darker color than the color of leather used for the project itself, to produce a contrasting, silhouetted effect, is sure to bring very gratifying results.

Project No. 83, Comb and File Case

See Figure 3, Illustration 33

I. Description

In this useful and always popular leathercraft project the reader will learn another important skill, known as edge lacing. In this phase of leather work, two or more leather parts are joined together by means of various attractive styles of lacing stitches.

In the comb and file case, shown in Fig. 3, Illustration 33, we are to employ the easiest of all edge-lacing techniques, involving what is variously known as the over and over, spiral, or whip stitch. This elementary form of leather stitching is suggested for all beginners in lacing work, and especially for such small and simply constructed leather articles as the comb and file case.

By referring to the plan of the comb and file case in Fig. 3, you will note that it consists of two large parts, A, B, C, which form the comb pocket at the back, and a small part, D, E, C, which forms the pocket for the file, at the front. Those desiring to simplify the construction of this project, may eliminate small part D, E, C, and produce a single-pocket two-part case in place of the double-pocket, three-piece model here presented. When built in the single-pocket form, the tooled decoration shown in Fig. 3 on part D, E, C, may be employed on the front A, B, C member instead. The combination comb and file case is, however, more popular and, of course, serves a double purpose.

If a tooling grade of leather is unobtainable, and you find it necessary to work with embossed or other non-tooling leathers in the construction of this and other simple articles, you can produce equally attractive work by applying any of the other forms of ornamental treatments suggested below.

As in the case of the book mark, shown in Fig. 1, Illustration 33, teachers of leather work in children's craft shops will find that this file and comb case model provides an excellent opportunity for the development of originality of design.

II. Materials

A. Scrap tooling leather, sufficient in size for making two A, B, C parts and one D, E, C part. See Fig. 3. Although tooling calfskin is generally best for the construction of this project, tooling steerhide and sheepskin may also be employed with satisfactory results. Good leather colors are natural, light or dark brown, green, red, maroon, and black.

B. About 1-1/2 yards of regular goat lacing or imitation-type leather lacing in a color which will match or harmonize with the color of leather used for the project.

C. Items B, C, D, E, F, G, H and I, listed under "Materials" in the text given for Project No. 82, Book Mark.

III. Tools

A. Items A, B, C, D and E, listed under "Tools" in the text given for Project No. 82, Book Mark.

B. A regular single, two or three-prong thonging chisel, or a homemade, nail-type leather punch. See Fig. 5, Illustration 34.

C. A metal-working hammer of the type seen in use in Fig. 5.

IV. Directions

A. On a sheet of drawing paper, prepare a grill of 1/4 inch squares, employing the same number and arrangement of squares as used in the reduced form pattern grill of our project in Fig. 3, Illustration 33.

B. Make an exact copy of all details of the comb and file case plan as given in Fig. 3, including contours of all parts, location of punched holes for lacing, and the ornamental design. In place of the "T W" initials employed in our model, substitute your own initials or those for whom the comb and file case is intended, using the same style of lettering.

C. On another sheet of drawing paper, make a separate pattern of section A, B, C, showing contours and lacing hole locations of the two large back parts of the project which form the pocket for the comb. Then make a pattern of section D, E, C, showing contours, lacing holes, and outline of design of this front part, which forms the pocket for the file.

D. Using a small pair of scissors, cut around the outside contours of pattern parts A, B, C and D, E, C, so they can conveniently be traced to the leather material.

E. On a scrap piece of tooling calfskin, sheepskin, or steerhide, make two contour tracings of pattern part A, B, C, and one tracing of pattern part D, E, C. In this tracing step, trace only the outside forms of these parts and not the lacing holes or outlined decoration. Use either a sharp pencil or the pointed end of the modeler.

F. Cut out the three outlined leather parts, using a hardwood or plywood board as a foundation, a sharp leather cutting knife and a steel rule or steel square, in the manner shown in Fig. 1, Illustration 34. For additional particulars concerning this leather-cutting procedure, see text under Project No. 82, Book Mark. Be sure all leather parts are cut out accurately, with all edges appearing neat and square, rathei than irregular or slanted.

G. Moisten undersides of the cut out leather parts, attach the paper patterns with clips to the top or finished sides of the leather parts, and then make careful tracings of all details, including lacing holes, decorative design, and monogram. As you will note from Fig. 3, Illustration 33, you will need two separate tracings of part A, B, C, and one of part D, E, C. Use either a pencil or a leather modeling tool for this tracing step, and employ a sheet of glass or a slab of marble, about 9 inches by 12 inches in size, as a working foundation. See Figs. 2 and 3, Illustration 34, for diagrammatical explanations of these leather dampening and tracing procedures. After completing all tracing work, remove paper patterns from the leather parts, in readiness for the design-tooling step.

H. Dampen underside of leather part D, E, C again, place it on the glass or marble working foundation, with its top or traced side facing upward, and then proceed to tool all outlines of the design in the manner shown in Fig. 4, Illustration 34. In this outline-tooling step, use the pointed end of the modeler and hold the tool so its handle forms an angle of 45 degrees to the work. For complete details governing this outline-tooling step in leather work, see text given under Project No. 82, Book Mark.

I. After tooling the outlines of the decoration on part D, E, C, proceed to press down certain areas of the outlined decoration in order to produce an interesting, contrasting effect. For this background impressing operation, use the larger or spoon end of the modeler. A good scheme for the particular design employed in Fig. 3, Illustration 33, is to impress the dotted, outlined sections only, allowing the plain outlined sections of the decoration to appear in relief or embossed form. Should you so desire, you may further process the impressed sections by a stippling or short-line treatment, using for these procedures, the pointed end of the modeler. For further details governing outline and background tooling in leather work, see text under Project No. 82, Book Mark.

J. Place the three leather parts, right side up, on the hardwood or plywood board working foundation, and then punch all lacing holes previously marked off on the leather parts in tracing the pattern. For this hole-punching step, use either a regular, single, two- or three-prong thonging chisel or a homemade nail-type leather punch, together with a metal-working hammer, just as shown in Fig. 3, Illustration 33. Use enough hammer force over the head of the punch to produce uniform, clean-cut lacing holes throughout this phase of the work.

You can easily make a fine-working leather punch from a 3 inch long, flat-head wire nail as follows:

1. File the pointed tip of the nail until it is perfectly flat, as shown by A, Fig. 5.

2. File the sides of the lower end of the nail for a distance of about 1 inch up from its flat-filed tip, until the sides of the nail are flat instead of round, and thus form a square at the tip of the nail in place of the previous circular form of the tip.

3. File two opposite sides of the flat sided tip of the nail just a little, until the square-shaped tip of the nail assumes the form of a tiny rectangle. See Fig. 5, B, Illustration 34. A good, average size for the rectangular tip is 1/32 inch wide, by 3/32 inch long.

4. After forming the tip of the punch in this manner, rub the four filed sides of the working tip over an oil stone, to produce a smooth-edged, leather-punching tool.

K. After carefully punching all lacing holes of each of the three file-and-comb-case leather parts, place the parts in their proper position for assembling. Be sure the holes of all three parts are exactly lined up and matched. While they are in this position, place a few spots of rubber or household cement around the edges of the parts to hold them together and in place during the lacing procedure.

L. Start lacing by first cementing about 1/2 inch of one end of the lacing between the leather parts, in order that this beginning end may remain invisible, as shown by the dotted lines at B, Fig. 3. Use about 1-1/2 yards of either regular goat skin lacing or imitation leather lacing, in a color which will match the color of leather used for the project. After fastening the beginning end of the lacing in position, proceed lacing in an over and over fashion, as shown at E, Fig. 5, Illustration 33, and at A, Fig. 6, Illustration 34. Be sure the finished side of the lace is turned upward, as each lacing stitch is applied. Also, make certain the lacing is pulled tightly as each stitch is made, to assure neat, uniform stitching all around the project. This simple, though effective form of leather lacing is generally known as spiral or whip-stitch lacing. If the lacing should tear or should it be necessary to add a piece, you can easily join the ends of leather lacing together by first splicing or "skiving" the ends with a sharp knife and then fastening them together with rubber cement, by placing the bottom side of one end over the top side of the other end. The ends should overlap each other about 3/4 inch, and be pressed firmly together; the joint should be allowed to dry thoroughly before the lacing is put into work.

M. After all holes are properly laced all around the comb and file case, cut finishing end of lacing so about 1 inch is allowed to extend beyond the last-stitched hole. Then, cement this 1 inch end between or inside the leather parts just as we did for the starting end of the lacing, so that this end will also be invisible. See F, Fig. 3, Illustration 33.

N. If tooled decoration is to be left in its plain, natural-leather form, without using any kind of multi-coloring medium, finish by polishing all outside surfaces with saddle-soap or leather-polishing wax. If some form of coloring is desired, however, such as painting with different colors of water-proof inks, or leather enamels, apply the colors first and then finish the entire project with a saddle-soap or wax-polishing treatment. For further details concerning the multi-coloring and finishing of leather projects, the reader is referred to the text given under Project No. 82, Bookmark. Also see this same text for information concerning the methods for decorating projects made of non-tooling leathers, including oil color painting, electric-pencil burning, decorating with applique leather units, and so forth.

Project No. 84, Novelty Coin Purse

See Figure 2, A, B, C, Illustration 33

I. Description

In the construction of our third model, the reader will be introduced to a few additional skills which are also essential procedures in this handwork activity. Among these are a more advanced form of leather lacing, involving what is generally known as the buttonhole stitch, and the method of attaching metal snap-fasteners, important in the construction of coin purses, key-containers, and various other popular leather articles.

The particular style of coin purse which we are about to present has always proved popular in the author's craft classes in leather work because of its novel pocket-flap construction and its use of a tooled decoration on the back of the purse and a tooled monogram on the pocket flap at the front. See Fig. 2, A, Illustration 33.

By referring to Fig. 2, A, you will note that the tooled monogram on the purse flap appears upside down, and in reverse position to that of the tooled swan design on the back section of the purse.

However, when the flap is snapped into position, and the purse is closed, the monogram will assume an upright position on the front side of the purse. You will also note that the front section of the project, represented by B in Fig. 2, has no decorative tooling at all, since most of this part is covered by the monogrammed pocket flap, when the purse is closed.

The novel style and construction of this particular change purse, is only one of the many other equally attractive styles in which this popular little leathercraft project can be fashioned. It can be made in smaller or larger sizes in accordance with individual preferences; it can be fitted with two flaps in place of one, providing a two pocket form of construction; it can be designed in other attractive shapes such as circular, triangular, hexagonal, and so forth; and instead of being decorated by the tooling method, it can be enhanced by electric burning, oil painting, or by applying separately cut out design units.

After constructing the model coin purse shown in Fig. 2, Illustration 33, the reader is advised to try his hand at designing other types of coin purses, incorporating some of the ideas and features described in this chapter. Furthermore, after mastering the technique of making coin purses of different kinds, you will experience no difficulty in producing related leathercraft projects such as wallets, cigarette cases, key containers, picture frames, book-covers, bags, belts, knife sheaths, and so forth.

II. Materials

A. A piece of scrap tooling leather, preferably calf-skin, sufficient in size for making coin purse parts A and B, Fig. 2. Good colors are natural, tan, brown, red, maroon, green, blue, and black.

B. About 1-3/4 yards of regular, goat-skin lacing in a color which matches the color of leather used for the purse. In place of regular, goat-skin lacing, a substitute or imitation form of leather lacing may also be used.

C. A small size snap-button, for use in closing the coin purse flap. The snap used should match the color of leather employed for the purse.

D. Items B, C, D, E, F, G, H, and I, listed under Materials, in the text given for Project No. 82, Book Mark.

III. Tools

A. Items A, B, C, D and E, listed under "Tools," in the text given for Project No. 82, Book Mark.

B. Items B and C given under "Tools," in the text given for Project No. 83, Comb and File Case.

C. A snap-button-fastener set. This essential little combination tool can be obtained at most handicraft supply houses. There is a less expensive set at about fifty cents and a better grade at about one dollar. Since there is no other way for attaching snap fastener buttons than by using this device, all leathercraft workers and craft shops should have a set on hand as part of their working equipment.

IV. Directions

A. Make a pattern grill showing change purse parts A and B, Fig. 2, Illustration 33. Use 1/4 inch squares and copy all design matter, lacing holes, and other construction details, exactly as shown by back and flap section A, and front section B.

B. Cut apart pattern units A and B, then make only contour tracings of these two parts, on the scrap piece of leather selected for this project. When making contour tracings, do not trace the lacing holes, the outlined decoration, and so forth, but only the outside shapes or silhouetted forms of the parts. The leather used must be a little larger in size than the paper patterns, to allow for cutting. For this as well as all other tracing steps, in leather work use either a fairly sharp pencil or the pointed end of the modeler.

C. Cut out leather forms A and B, using the method diagrammed in Fig. 1, Illustration 34, and explained in the text given under Directions, for Project No. 82, Book Mark. Be sure to cut the edges in a neat, square fashion, as slanted or irregularly cut edges are unattractive and tend to spoil the work.

D. Clip patterns evenly over cut out leather parts of coin purse, and then trace all lacing holes, decorations, snap-button locations, and so forth, exactly as indicated. For more complete directions governing this detail tracing step, see Figs. 2 and 3, Illustration 34, and text given under Project No. 82, Book Mark. After completing this tracing step, remove patterns from leather parts.

E. Dampen underside of part A again and then proceed to outline tool the previously traced swan and monogram decorations, using the pointed end of the modeler. Following this outline tooling step, press down the background areas with the spoon end of the modeler. For details governing these outline and background tooling steps in leather work, as well as methods of stippling or short-lining impressed background sections of the designs, see Fig. 4, Illustration 34, and text given under Directions, for Project No. 82, Book Mark.

F. Punch all lacing holes as indicated on leather parts A and B. Then, punch a 3/16 inch or No. 7 hole on the flap section of the coin purse, part A, and a 1/16 inch or No. 0 hole on the front part B. These specially sized holes are required for inserting the snap button fastener. For properly punching these Nos. 0 and 7 holes, use either regular drive punches, in these particular sizes, or a revolving punch, equipped with these punching tubes. For details governing the punching of lacing holes, see Fig. 5, Illustration 34, and item J, under Directions, in the text given for Project No. 83, Comb and File Case.

G. Attach snap button at punched holes M and N, Fig. 2, Illustration 33, using a regular snap-button set, made specially for this purpose, and obtainable at all handicraft supply concerns. These concerns will be pleased to show you how easily you can use this important combination tool for all your projects requiring the attachment of snap-button fasteners.

H. Place coin purse parts A and B together in their proper positions, with all lacing holes in correct alignment, place a few drops of rubber or household cement around the edges, on the inside surfaces of the parts, and then proceed to assemble the parts, using the button-hole stitch shown at B, Fig. 6, Illustration 34. To assemble the coin purse parts in this slightly more advanced form of leather lacing, proceed as follows:

1. Cement beginning end of lacing (use about 1-3/4 yards of regular goat-skin lacing or imitation lacing), inside of leather purse, at holes Y and Y-1. See Fig. 2, A and B, Illustration 33.

2. Proceed to button-hole stitch around the purse, following the directions from Y to Z as indicated in Fig. 2, A, Illustration 33. Also, study diagrammatical explanation of this lacing step as given at B, Fig. 6, Illustration 34. After a little practice in button-hole lacing, you will have very little trouble producing a neat, satisfactory result. Be sure to pull the lacing tightly as you proceed, and make certain that the stitches are neat and uniform throughout.

3. After you reach holes X and X-1 (see Fig. 2, A and B, Illustration 33), proceed with the same button-hole stitch as before, even though you will be lacing along the edge of the pocket flap alone. Lacing the edge of the pocket flap, in this case, adds to the decorative effect of the completed purse.

4. After all punched holes are laced, finish just as you started, by cementing about 1/2 inch of the finishing end of the lacing inside of the purse, just as you did at Y, Fig. 2, A.

5. Using a wooden mallet, tap down the laced edges of the purse, to produce a flat, uniform effect. This tapping down treatment also tends to lessen signs of wear and tear when project is in use.

1. Finish tooled and laced purse with a polishing treatment of saddle-soap or leather wax. If you wish to use a multi-coloring form of ornamentation for the tooled decoration, color the parts first, using colored waterproof inks or leather enamels, and then apply the saddle-soap or leather-wax polishing treatment. For further details see text given under Project No. 82, Book Mark. Also refer to same text for methods of decorating projects made of non-tooling leathers. Among these ornamental treatments are using just oil colors, for painting on some appropriate form of

design or decoration; burning on a design with an electric pencil; decorating the project with a separately cut out, applique unit, and so forth.

Project No. 85, Puppy Lapel Pin

See Figure 1, Illustration 35

I. Description

This lapel pin, like the other novelty lapel ornaments described in this scrap craft project section, can easily be constructed from small pieces of odd or discarded materials, readily obtainable everywhere.

Although it is best to use for this puppy pin already colored calfskin or suede leather scraps, in the colors suggested below, it can also be built by using these same leathers in a single, light color, such as natural or light tan, and painted as required. Complete directions for painting the puppy are given below, under "Coloring."

Instead of leather, suitable colors of felt can also be used with equally good results.

In addition to its use as a lapel pin, the puppy head design unit may also be applied in various other interesting ways. For instance, it can appropriately be employed as a decoration for a hat or belt. For these purposes, the puppy may be made of leather or in felt in exactly the same way as the lapel pin, except that it may be sewn securely in place, rather than pinned. Other applications for this puppy design are as follows: decoration for the cover of a handkerchief, cigarette, or jewelry box; novelty bookmarks; a small leather or felt change purse; a decoration for a book jacket; a cover for a set of blotters, and so forth. For these purposes the puppy-head decoration should be constructed exactly as directed below for the lapel pin and then either pinned on, sewed on, or used unattached.

II. Materials

A. Calfskin or suede in a single color, preferably natural or light tan, or already colored calfskin or suede scraps, in the colors suggested later, in the directions for constructing this project.

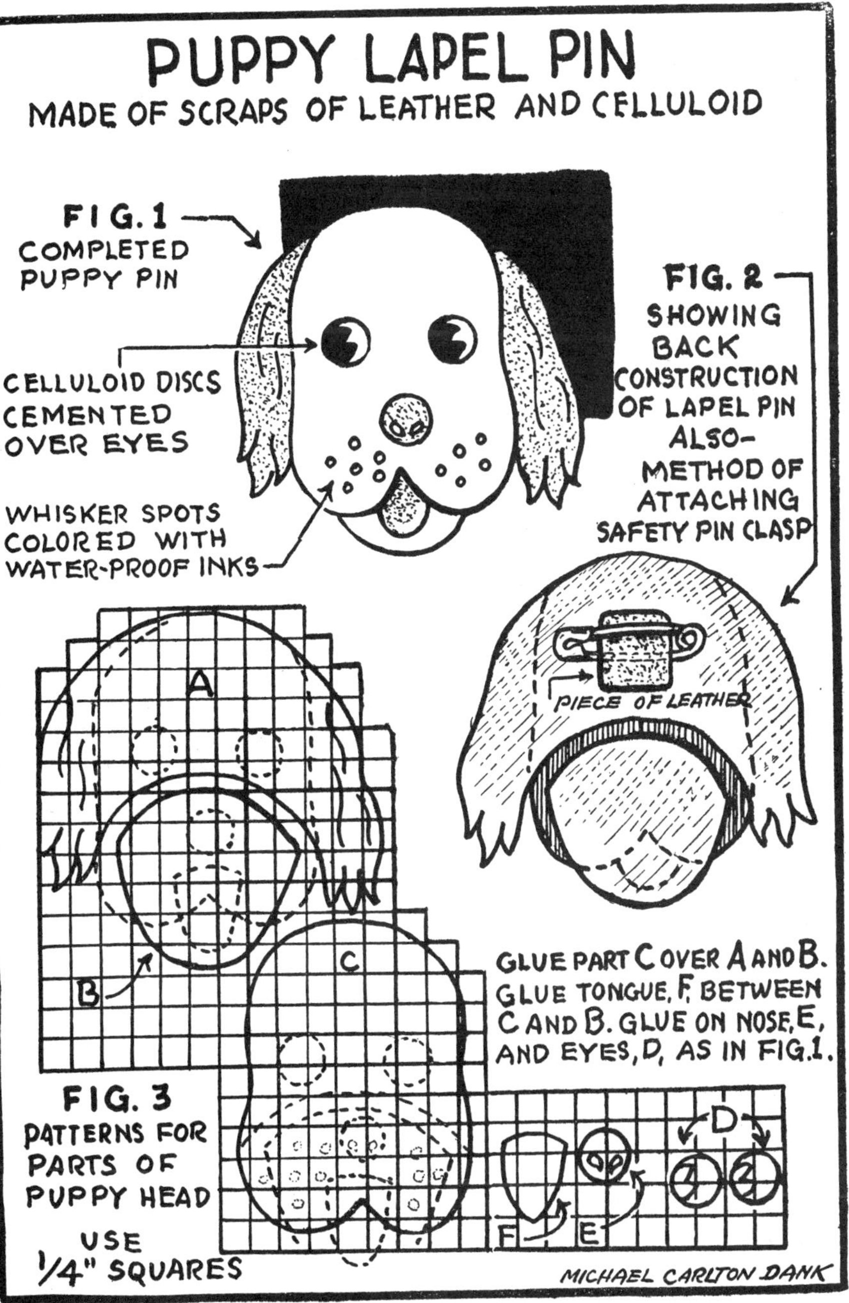
PUPPY LAPEL PIN
MADE OF SCRAPS OF LEATHER AND CELLULOID
FIG. 1
COMPLETED PUPPY PIN
CELLULOID DISCS CEMENTED OVER EYES
WHISKER SPOTS COLORED WITH WATER-PROOF INKS
FIG. 2
SHOWING BACK CONSTRUCTION OF LAPEL PIN ALSO- METHOD OF ATTACHING SAFETY PIN CLASP
PIECE OF LEATHER
A
B
C
D
E
F
GLUE PART C OVER A AND B. GLUE TONGUE, F, BETWEEN C AND B. GLUE ON NOSE, E, AND EYES, D, AS IN FIG. 1.
FIG. 3
PATTERNS FOR PARTS OF PUPPY HEAD
USE 1/4" SQUARES
MICHAEL CARLTON DANK

Illustration 35

B. Any light colored bond paper of medium weight.

C. Water-proof inks, in assorted colors.

D. A good grade of rubber or leather cement.

E. Small pieces of thin, transparent celluloid.

F. A small size sponge or a piece of scrap cloth.

G. A safety-pin 1 inch to 1-1/4 inches in length.

III. Tools

A. Sharp knife suitable for cutting leather.

B. Small pair of scissors suitable for cutting felt and paper.

C. Leather-modeling tool or nut pick.

D. A maple or any other hardwood block for use as a foundation for cutting and tooling leather. A smooth-surfaced, hard-pressed composition board is also good.

E. Small size, pointed style coloring brushes. Best sizes are Nos. 1, 2, and 3.

F. A pasting brush. A flat-tipped brush with short, stiff bristles is best.

G. Light or dark brown thread.

IV. Directions

A. Preparation of pattern.

1. On any light colored bond paper, draw a pattern grill, or set of squares, in the same arrangement as shown in Fig. 3, Illustration 35, except that 1/4 inch squares should be used, instead of the reduced size squares there represented.

2. After completing the grill, copy and draw in all the pattern parts of the puppy lapel pin, exactly as shown and arranged in the grill of Fig. 3.

3. You will note from studying Fig. 3, that six different parts are required in the construction of this pin. You will find these labeled as A, B, C, D, E, and F. The dotted lines seen in the various pattern parts indicate the construction or overlapping of the parts when joined together.

B. Transferring pattern parts to leather.

1. Using a small pair of scissors, cut apart pattern grill into the separate parts of the puppy.

2. Place natural or tan colored leather, either in a single piece large enough for all puppy parts, or in separate pieces, upon a smooth-surfaced, hardwood block, with the top or right side of the leather facing upward. If suede is used, have the rough side face upward, since, in this case, the rough side is the top or right surface.

3. Place pattern parts on the selected calfskin or suede in preparation for the tracing or design transferring step. If different colors of leathers are used, place the patterns on the leather in accordance with their proper colors. For instance, pattern A should be placed over a dark brown piece of leather; pattern C over a light brown piece of leather; part F over red colored leather, and so forth, in accordance with the color scheme planned for the puppy. Whether using natural colored leather or leather already dyed in the desired colors, it is a wise procedure to arrange the patterns on the leather so that a minimum amount of the material will be wasted.

4. Using a small piece of sponge or cloth, soaked in water, moisten the flesh or under-surface of the leather, especially where the pattern parts are located. As the leather under each paper pattern part is dampened, lift the pattern from the leather a little, then place it back again in approximately the same position as before. See Fig. 2, Illustration 34.

5. Holding the first pattern part to be traced firmly over the moistened leather with the left hand, use the other hand to trace over all the outlines and pattern details. For this tracing step, use either a well sharpened pencil, or the pointed end of a leather modeling tool or nut pick. Be sure each part is traced clearly and completely, before removing the pattern. Note: Small strips of scotch tape or paper clips may be used to hold patterns in place, if desired. For further details in regard to the proper methods of transferring project patterns to leather, see Fig. 3, Illustration 34. After all pattern parts of the puppy pin are traced to the leather in this manner, the paper pattern should be put aside (it is a good idea to paste them in a scrap book, for future use) in preparation for tooling.

C. Tooling design details on leather parts.

Although the details seen on the eyes, nose, cheeks, and ears of the puppy may simply be painted in, it is more effective to impress or tool these design lines neatly and clearly into the surface of the leather. This is easily done as follows:

1. Place piece or pieces of leather, containing the tracings of the puppy pin, on the smooth-surfaced, hardwood block, having the top or right side of the leather facing upward.

2. Moisten the under-surface of the leather with a sponge or cloth, as done, previously, in the tracing step.

3. Using the pointed end of a regular leather modeling tool, or a nut-pick, go over all the design details and outlines appearing on each of the traced puppy parts. Use a forward, steady tooling motion, pressing strongly downward, to produce a deep impression in the leather, of all the traced lines on each part. During this tooling step, use the left hand to manipulate the leather freely as required for each differently formed line. If necessary, moisten the leather again, and tool the outline and design lines more clearly and deeply. For a more detailed explanation of leather tooling see Fig. 4, Illustration 34. Also see text under "Directions," Project No. 82, Book Mark.

4. After all puppy parts are carefully tooled, allow them to dry, in preparation for the cutting step.

D. Cutting out project parts

1. Place the piece or pieces of leather with their tooled surfaces facing upward upon the maple block.

2. Hold leather piece firmly with left hand, and cut around the exterior outlines of each puppy part with a sharp pointed knife held securely in the right hand. If a regular, leather-cutting knife is unavailable, any other style knife, equipped with a sharp, pointed blade, such as a sloyd or pocket-knife, can be employed satisfactorily for this purpose. For best results, cut just outside of the tooled impressions of the exterior outlines of each part, rather than right over them. Also, be sure that the parts are cut out in a neat, careful manner, free of any jagged or irregular edges. For additional details concerning proper methods of cutting leather, see Fig. 1, Illustration 34.

3. The two small celluloid discs which are used as covernigs over the puppy's eyes, may be prepared by first making a paper pattern, the same size as leather part D. The paper pattern may be pasted to the celluloid material, and then cut out with a small pair of scissors.

E. Coloring

Note: These coloring directions apply only when using light tan or natural color leather. When using leather already dyed in the required colors, no further coloring, except for a few small details as in the eyes and on the cheeks, is necessary. For most effective coloring results in leather work such as in this project, it is best to use any good grade of waterproof ink in assorted colors. Solutions of powdered aniline dyes and hot water, mixed as directed on the package, are also satisfactory. The procedure for coloring the parts of the puppy lapel pin, is as follows:

1. Place the leather parts to be colored upon a sheet of glass, metal, marble, or oilcloth, to provide a protective working foundation.

2. Prepare a thin mixture of each over-all color which is to be used. If waterproof inks are employed, these may easily be diluted by adding distilled water to the ink as furnished in the bottle. If aniline dyes are used, simply add hot water. In each case, it is best to pour a little of the full intensity color in a small dish or pan, and then add the diluting agent, in the quantity desired. For the puppy project, the colors suggested are medium brown, bright red, black, and white.

3. Using a No. 3 water color style brush, first paint the whole top surface and edges of part A in a dark brown color. Be sure the color is applied evenly and neatly. Then, in similar fashion, paint part B in a light brown, and parts E and F in a bright red.

4. The eye parts, D, should be colored with a smaller brush, such as Nos. 1 or 2. For the light parts of the eyes, at the right, use white ink, and for the dark parts, at the left, use black ink. The nostrils on the red nose part, should be painted black.

5. Part C should remain unpainted, to appear in its natural leather color, except that the small circles at the lower part of the cheeks should be colored in light brown ink to suggest the puppy's spots or whiskers.

6. Allow all the colored parts to dry thoroughly before assembling.

F. Assembling and finishing the puppy lapel pin

For joining together pieces of leather as required in the construction of this project, it is best to use any good grade of rubber cement or household cement. Do not use glue, paste, or mucilage, as the work will be soiled and the assembling results will be ineffective. To put the parts of the puppy pin together, proceed as follows:

1. Place part C over part A, so that the tops of both parts are even, and lightly mark around the edges of part C with a sharply pointed pencil. Then, separate the parts, and using a

hard bristled brush, apply cement over the upper surface of part A and the under surface of part C, but only where these two leather parts are in contact. Allow the cemented surfaces to dry without being joined together.

2. Apply a second coat of cement to these same surfaces and then join them together in their exact positions. Any flat, heavy weight may now be placed upon the two cemented parts, for a period of about five minutes, until the cement has set and a tight joint is assured.

3. Using this same assembling procedure, cement the tongue in place underneath part C. Follow this by joining part B underneath parts C and F.

4. The eyes, D, and nose part, E, are next in this assembling procedure and these parts must be cemented in place with special care, in their exact locations on part C.

5. The last assembling step is that of cementing the celluloid discs over the eye parts, D.

6. To complete the puppy lapel pin, attach a safety-pin, 1 inch to 1-1/4 inches in length, to the back part of A, about 1 inch from the top. This may be done by using a needle and brown thread, or by cementing a small piece of leather over the lower part of the safety pin, and to the back of part A. Another and even more professional method is to cement a regular plastic pin to the back of part A, using any strong plastic or household cement as the adhesive.

7. For an extra finish for the puppy lapel pin, though not really necessary, carefully brush a little liquid wax over the entire pin. Then, after a minute or two, polish the entire surface of the pin lightly with a soft cloth, until a bright, soft finish is produced.

Note: If felt is used in place of leather for the construction of this puppy pin project, use appropriate colors of felt and assemble the parts in the same manner and with the same adhesive used for the leather material. Since no paint whatever can be used for coloring in the eyes, whiskers, and so forth, use small pieces of felt in the required colors for these details, which may be cemented in place in applique fashion. Thus for the black sections of the eyes and nostrils, use small pieces of black felt, for the lines in the ears and the whisker spots on the cheeks, use light brown felt, and so on. Otherwise, the construction of the puppy pin in felt is the same as it is in leather.

Project No. 86, Butterfly Lapel Pin

See Figure 1, Illustration 36

I. Description

This novelty pin, like the puppy pin No. 85, is constructed mainly of scraps of tooling calfskin leather. Like the puppy pin, too, this butterfly ornament may also be made of colored felt scraps if leather is unavailable.

Because of the bright colors required for the decoration of the butterfly, it is best to use natural or light tan leather. Using light colored leather for this purpose makes it easy to produce any elaborate color scheme with a variety of waterproof inks. When felt is used as the construction material, however, it is necessary to employ already colored felt scraps, since this material does not lend itself to painting, especially of a detailed nature.

Although the butterfly decoration is presented here in the form of a lapel ornament, it may also be employed in several other ways. For instance, it can be pinned or sewed to a hat or belt. A series of three butterflies can be mounted on the wall, arranged as if in flight, to decorate a child's room. The butterfly, made of leather or felt, may also be employed to ornament a sewing or crochet kit, a cigarette box cover, novelty book marks, the cover for a set of blotters, and so on. For these uses, the butterfly unit should be made up exactly as directed below for the lapel pins, then either pinned or sewed on, or used unattached, as an independent unit, in accordance with the purpose for which it is planned.

Since the butterfly design lends itself well to leather tooling, it can be used advantageously as a tooled decoration for a leather bookjacket, a pair of leather-covered book ends, a wallet, and so

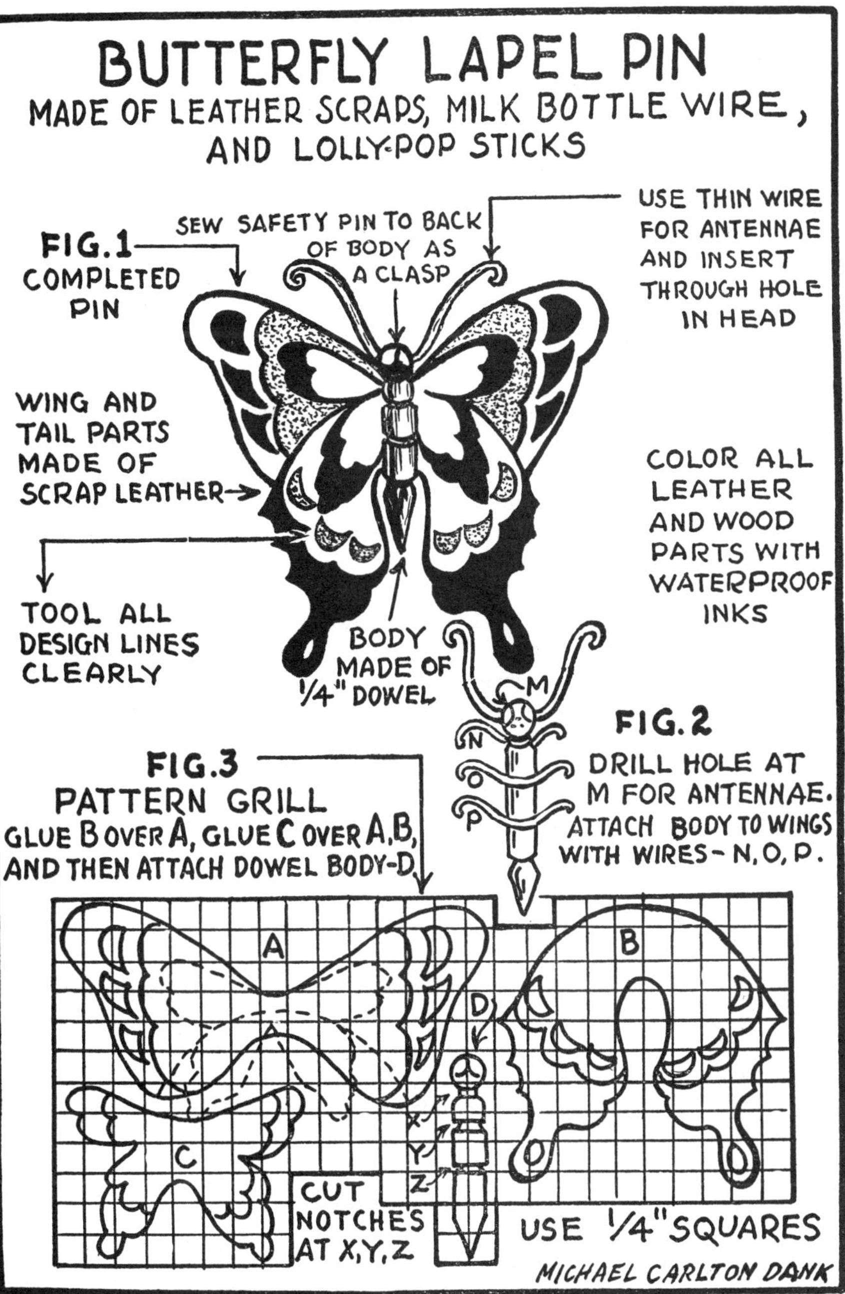

BUTTERFLY LAPEL PIN
MADE OF LEATHER SCRAPS, MILK BOTTLE WIRE, AND LOLLY-POP STICKS
FIG. 1
COMPLETED PIN
SEW SAFETY PIN TO BACK OF BODY AS A CLASP
USE THIN WIRE FOR ANTENNAE AND INSERT THROUGH HOLE IN HEAD
WING AND TAIL PARTS MADE OF SCRAP LEATHER
COLOR ALL LEATHER AND WOOD PARTS WITH WATERPROOF INKS
TOOL ALL DESIGN LINES CLEARLY
BODY MADE OF 1/4" DOWEL
M
N
O
P
FIG. 2
DRILL HOLE AT M FOR ANTENNAE. ATTACH BODY TO WINGS WITH WIRES - N, O, P.
FIG. 3
PATTERN GRILL
GLUE B OVER A, GLUE C OVER A, B, AND THEN ATTACH DOWEL BODY-D
A
B
C
D
X
Y
Z
CUT NOTCHES AT X, Y, Z
USE 1/4" SQUARES
MICHAEL CARLTON DANK

Illustration 36

forth. In these applications, the butterfly is simply used as a design unit and tooled directly on the leather, instead of being used in appliqued form.

II. Materials

A. Tooling calfskin leather in a natural or light tan color.

B. Any light colored bond paper of medium weight.

C. A good grade of rubber cement.

D. A few lengths of thin wire such as that furnished on milk bottle tops.

E. A small size sponge or cloth.

F. Water-proof inks in assorted colors.

G. A short length of 1/4 inch dowel or lollypop stick.

H. A safety-pin, 1 inch to 1-1/4 inches in length, or a plastic pin clasp of similar size.

III. Tools

A. A sharp knife suitable for cutting leather.

B. Hand-drill, fitted with a 1/16 inch drill point.

C. A small pair of scissors.

D. Modeling tool for leather work. Nut-pick can also be used.

E. Brad-awl with pointed tip.

F. A smooth-surfaced hardwood block, or hard-pressed composition board.

G. Pair of round-nose pliers.

H. Small, pointed-style coloring brushes. Best sizes are Nos. 1, 2, and 3.

I. A whittling-knife such as a sloyd or pocket-knife.

IV. Directions

A. Preparation of pattern

1. Draw a grill of 1/4 inch squares, using a light colored bond paper, and following the same arrangement and employing the exact number of squares, as shown in Fig. 3, Illustration 36.

2. Duplicate butterfly parts A, B, C, and D, in the same manner as represented in the reduced size grill in Fig. 3. You need not draw the dotted lines, as these serve only to show the method in which the different parts overlap each other.

B. Transferring pattern parts to leather

1. Using a small pair of scissors, cut out paper pattern parts A, B, and C, as they now appear on the enlarged grill.

2. Place the calfskin leather upon a hard, smooth surfaced board or a hard-pressed composition board, with the smooth or right side of the leather facing upward.

3. Using a small sponge or cloth, soaked in water, moisten the underside of the leather. After this is done, place the cutout patterns on the leather, arranged so that only a small amount of leather will be wasted. Use paper clips to hold pattern securely to the leather during this tracing step.

4. With sharply pointed pencil or the pointed end of a leather modeling tool, trace over all exterior outlines and interior detail lines of each paper pattern. Use sufficient pressure to assure a clear impression of all lines in the surface of the leather. When finished, remove patterns and paste them in a design scrap book for future use. For a more detailed explanation of tracing patterns to leather, see Fig. 3, Illustration 34.

C. Tooling butterfly tracings on the leather

1. With leather still in position on the hardwood or composition board working foundation, with the top or traced surface of

the leather facing upward, use sponge or cloth to moisten leather again, just as prescribed for the pattern tracing step.

2. Using the pointed end of a leather modeling tool or a nut-pick, go over all the outlines and details of each traced pattern part, until deep, clean-cut impressions are produced in the surface of the leather. To obtain the proper result, it is necessary to use a strong, downward pressure to avoid scratching the leather with the point of the tool.

3. When the tooling work is completed, allow the leather to dry completely, before proceeding with the next step. For additional details concerning leather tooling, see text under project No. 82 and also Fig. 4, Illustration 34.

D. Cutting out leather parts

1. Place leather on work board with the tooled surface of the leather facing upwards.

2. Using a sharp, pointed knife, suitable for cutting leather, cut around the exterior outlines of each of the three butterfly parts, A, B, and C. This is best accomplished by holding the leather firmly over the working board, using the left hand, while the right hand is employed to operate the knife. Cut slowly and evenly, using a strong, downward pressure on the blade of the knife as each cut is made. Also, be sure to avoid slanting the knife to either side, as this will result in distorting the edges of the leather. For more complete directions for cutting leather, see directions under Project 82.

E. Preparation of wood and wire parts

As you will note by referring to Fig. 2, Illustration 36, the head and body parts of the butterfly are fashioned from a single, short length of 1/4 inch dowel stick. Also needed are a few short lengths of thin wire, to provide the butterfly's antennae, or feelers, and for fastening the body to the wings. These wood and wire parts are made as follows:

1. Using a coping-saw, back-saw, or pocket knife, cut a 1/4 inch dowel strip, or lollypop stick, into a 1-3/4 inch length.

2. Then, with a hand-drill, fitted with a 1/16 inch drill point, bore a hole about 1/4 inch down from the top part of the stick. Bore completely through, taking care not to split the stick at its forward side.

3. With a whittling knife, such as a sloyd or regular pocket knife, shape the top end of the dowel into the butterfly's round head, and taper the lower end into the shape of its tail, or lower section, just as seen in Fig. 3, D, Illustration 36. Next, cut three notches, about 1/16 inch deep, completely around the dowel, at points indicated by X, Y, and Z, in Fig. 3. These notches serve to simulate the sectional segments of the butterfly's body, and provide a convenient arrangement for using the wire connectors in attaching its body to the leather wings.

4. After the head and body parts are properly shaped with the knife, use a medium grade of sandpaper to smooth this wooden member of our project, until it is neatly and uniformly finished all around.

5. Using wire such as is furnished on the top of milk bottles, cut one length 3-1/2 inches, for the butterfly's antennae, and three 1-1/2 inch lengths, for connectors. These can easily be cut with snips, a file, or cutting pliers.

F. Coloring butterfly parts

1. For coloring both the wood and leather parts of this project, use small size brushes, of the pointed, water color type. No. 1 is best for coloring the very small areas, while Nos. 2 and 3 are suggested for the larger parts of the butterfly. As the coloring medium, use either water-proof inks, or aniline dyes, in assorted colors. To dilute the former medium, add necessary quantity of distilled water, while for the latter, add hot water in such solutions as desired.

2. Before applying any colors, it is a good idea first to determine which combination of colors will be most appropriate for this particular project. To do this properly, make a rough color sketch on a scrap piece of leather. Be sure that the colors used are in good taste and in effective contrast. Use small pans, such

as those provided with household food jars, as containers for preparing the necessary color mixtures. Do not mix too much of any single color, but only as much as is required for the job.

3. Apply selected colors to leather parts, using the lighter colors first and the darker ones last. Do not allow any of the colors to enter into the tooled design lines, but paint just along side of them. Do not "flood" the colors on. Instead, use just enough paint on the brush as is needed to cover the leather in a neat, uniform coating. Remember not to apply one color over another until the first color is thoroughly dry.

4. Following the coloring of the leather parts, paint the wooden body section, using a color which will allow the body to stand out in attractive contrast to the leather wing parts.

G. Assembling and finishing the butterfly lapel pin

1. Place part B over part A, in the manner shown in Fig. 1, Illustration 36, then draw a thin, pencil line around the upper edges of part B and the lower edges of part A. Next, using any good grade of rubber or household cement, and a small stiff-bristled pasting brush, coat the contact surfaces of these two wing parts, but do not as yet join the parts together.

2. Apply a second coat of cement to the same contact areas and join the two parts together. Place a heavy weight upon the jointed parts and allow the joint to set and dry for from five to ten minutes.

3. Following this first assembling step, cement part C in place over parts A and B, again referring to Fig. 1, Illustration 36, for exact position, and using same procedure as when joining the first two parts together.

4. Place wooden body part in its correct position over the three wing parts and then fasten it to the wings with three small strips of wire, as shown at N, O, and P, in Fig. 2. First twist the wires around the grooves in the body, then insert the points of the wires through the leather wings, and finally, twist the ends

of the wires together at the back of the butterfly, to assure a firm joint. The surplus parts of the wires may be cut off with snips or cutting pliers.

5. Insert a 3-1/2 inch wire through the hole drilled in the head of the butterfly, then loop its ends with round-nose pliers in the manner shown in Fig. 2, M. If the wire antennae seem loose, they may be made more secure by first twisting the wire around the butterfly's "neck," once or twice, before arranging them in their final position as antennae.

6. Using a needle and brown thread, sew a 1-1/4 inch safety pin to the back of the butterfly, as a clasp. A regular plastic pin-clasp may be used in place of the safety pin, and cemented or sewed on.

7. As a final finish, apply a little liquid wax on the wood and leather parts and polish with a soft cloth, until an attractive, lustrous finish is obtained.

Note:

If felt is used for the construction of this butterfly lapel ornament instead of leather, follow all directions as given above, with the following exceptions:

1. Cut out felt parts with a small, sharp pair of scissors instead of a knife.

2. Do not use any painting medium to produce the coloring effects. Instead, use already colored felt, in the particular colors desired, in cemented on, applique fashion.

3. Do not employ any wax finish. Instead, allow the felt to appear in its original brightly colored form, without any finish at all.

CHAPTER THIRTEEN

WORKING WITH OLD PIPE CLEANERS

A PIPE cleaner is simply a piece of soft, flexible wire, about 7 inches long, with white fuzzy cord wrapped around it. Because of the softness of the wire, a pipe cleaner will remain in whatever shape you bend it. This important characteristic, in addition to the fact that its white fuzzy cord wrapper can easily be painted or dyed makes discarded pipe cleaners a good craft material.

After pipe cleaners have been used to clean pipes, they must be thoroughly cleaned before they can be employed in handwork. To clean them properly, soak them for a while in a container full of soap suds and hot water. Later, while still soap-soaked, rub their cord wrappers with the bristles of an old tooth brush. When the pipe cleaners have dried, they will be ready for use in the construction of a wide variety of novelties, party favors, and gifts.

In using discarded pipe cleaners, first make a good collection of them, and clean them as you collect them. Then, you will be ready to construct the interesting and useful items described in the subsequent pages of this scrap craft unit.

As our key projects in the treatment of this form of scrap material, we are presenting two novel lapel pins. In these costume ornaments, pipe cleaners are used in combination with other scrap materials, although the pipe cleaners are the most essential and most novel factors in their construction.

Besides these key projects, several related pipe cleaner projects are described in this unit.

Working with pipe cleaners provides an especially fine handwork activity for children's craft groups in schools, clubs, camps, church classes, recreation centers, and so forth. This craft may also be applied to excellent advantage in connection with gift sales, charity bazaars, and similar occasions.

After you become familiar with the fine craft possibilities of discarded pipe cleaners, it is certain that an old pipe cleaner will mean more to you than just a device for cleaning pipes. You will find, too, that working with this unique form of scrap material is really lots of fun and that it puts into play one's imagination and creative powers. Furthermore, because of the ease with which this material can be manipulated, colored and so forth, you will be producing many original and ingenious little dolls, animals, lapel pins, party favors and other novel projects before you are aware of it.

Project No. 87, Cock-o'-the-Walk Lapel Pin

See Figure 1, Illustration 37

In this novel lapel ornament, just as in the case of the lapel pin shown at Fig. 5, Illustration 37, discarded pipe cleaners are the essential material of construction.

In this particular lapel pin model, in which a proud rooster is employed as the decorative motif, pipe cleaners are used for his gaily upturned tail feathers as well as for his legs and toes. In addition to pipe cleaners, other readily obtainable and easily manipulated scrap materials are employed, such as tin, felt, and plywood.

Because of its simplicity, this novelty pin is easy to make in quantity. It includes such handwork processes as the use of the coping saw, boring holes with a hand drill, cutting with scissors, gluing, forming pipe cleaners into various shapes with pliers, and coloring with tempera or enamel paints.

II. Materials

A. Three discarded pipe cleaners.

B. A scrap piece of deep red felt and a piece of white felt

C. A scrap piece of 1/4 inch thick plywood.

D. A scrap piece of tin-can tin.

E. Tempera paints in white, red, black, and yellow colors.

F. A small amount of white shellac.

G. A piece of medium grade sandpaper.

H. Liquid glue.

I. A small size thumbtack.

J. A regular small pin clasp or a small safety pin.

III. Tools

A. Coping saw equipment such as shown in Fig. 3, Illustration 10.

B. Metal cutting shears.

C. Hand drill fitted with a 3/32 inch drill point.

D. A gluing brush, a medium size, water color brush, and a 1/2 inch to 3/4 inch wide flat shellacking brush.

E. A pair of round-nose cutting pliers.

IV. Directions

A. Make a pattern grill of 1/4 inch squares on drawing paper, using same number and arrangement of squares as shown in the reduced form grill in Fig. 2, Illustration 37. Reproduce parts A, B, C, D, E.

B. Cut out paper pattern parts with small scissors, working carefully and exactly as outlined in pattern grill.

C. Trace pattern part A, body, to 1/4 inch three-ply wood, then cut out this part with a coping saw, using coping saw equipment shown in Fig. 3, Illustration 10. Later, sandpaper this part until clean and smooth.

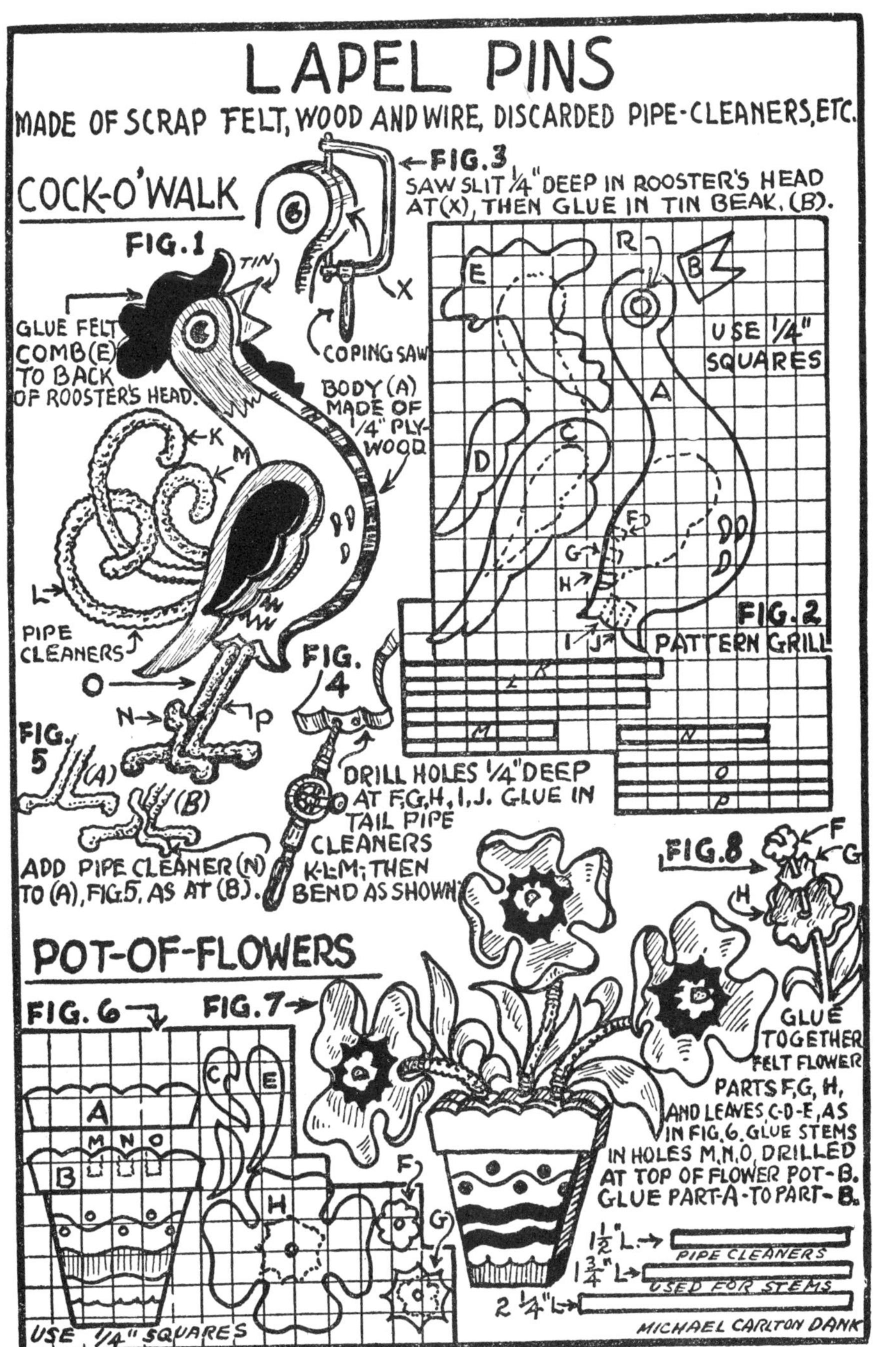
LAPEL PINS
MADE OF SCRAP FELT, WOOD AND WIRE, DISCARDED PIPE-CLEANERS, ETC.
COCK-O'WALK
FIG. 1
TIN
GLUE FELT COMB (E) TO BACK OF ROOSTER'S HEAD.
K
M
L
PIPE CLEANERS
O
N
P
FIG. 3
SAW SLIT 1/4" DEEP IN ROOSTER'S HEAD AT (X), THEN GLUE IN TIN BEAK, (B).
X
COPING SAW
BODY (A) MADE OF 1/4" PLY-WOOD
USE 1/4" SQUARES
FIG. 2
PATTERN GRILL
FIG. 4
FIG. 5
(A)
(B)
ADD PIPE CLEANER (N) TO (A), FIG. 5, AS AT (B).
DRILL HOLES 1/4" DEEP AT F, G, H, I, J. GLUE IN TAIL PIPE CLEANERS K-L-M; THEN BEND AS SHOWN.
POT-OF-FLOWERS
FIG. 6
FIG. 7
FIG. 8
GLUE TOGETHER FELT FLOWER PARTS F, G, H, AND LEAVES C-D-E, AS IN FIG. 6. GLUE STEMS IN HOLES M, N, O, DRILLED AT TOP OF FLOWER POT-B. GLUE PART-A-TO PART-B.
1 1/2" L.
1 3/4" L.
2 1/4" L.
PIPE CLEANERS USED FOR STEMS
USE 1/4" SQUARES
MICHAEL CARLTON DANK

Illustration 37

D. Cut a slit in front part of rooster's head, also using coping saw, as shown at X, Fig. 3.

E. Drill 3/32 inch diameter holes, 3/8 inch deep, at points F, G, H, I, J, shown in pattern grill in Fig. 2.

F. Insert a small thumbtack in front side of rooster's head. See R, Fig. 2.

G. Using tempera paint, color head yellow and body white. When dry, apply a coat of white shellac over all parts of body. If enamel paints are used instead of tempera colors, no shellac finish is required. For this coloring work, use a medium size pointed type water coloring brush, No. 5. To apply the shellac finish, use a 3/4 inch wide, flat, varnishing type brush.

H. Trace pattern part B, beak, on a small piece of tin, cut this part out with a pair of metal-cutting shears, then glue tin beak into slit previously cut in front section of head. See Fig. 1, showing beak glued into correct position.

I. Trace large wing pattern, C, to a red piece of felt and small wing part, D, to a white piece of felt, then cut out both felt wing parts with a small pair of scissors.

J. Glue wing part D to wing part C and then glue assembled wings to body Part A. For correct placement of these wing parts, see dotted lines showing these locations, in Fig. 2.

K. Trace pattern E, rooster's comb and wattles, to a red piece of felt, cut this part out with scissors, and then glue it into position at the back of the rooster's head. See correct position of comb and wattles as represented in Fig. 1, and as indicated by dotted lines in Fig. 2.

L. Using shears or cutting pliers, cut three lengths of discarded pipe cleaners for rooster's tail feathers, to measure 2-1/2 inches, 3 inches and 3-1/2 inches. You will find these tail feathers represented in the pattern grill, Fig. 2, as K, L, and M respectively. Later, glue these pipe-cleaner tail feathers into drilled holes, F, G, H, indicated in Fig. 2. After glue has dried, curl outer ends of the pipe cleaners with round nose pliers, into the graceful, upturned positions suggested by K, L, and M, in Fig. 1.

M. Using pipe cleaners again, cut three leg and toe parts. Make O and P leg parts 1-3/4 inches long and toe part N, 1 inch long.

N. Glue leg parts O and P into holes I and J (see Fig. 2) and then, using pliers, form two toes as at Fig. 5, A.

O. Glue pipe cleaner part N between the two already formed toes shown at A, Fig. 5, and then form part N into the third toe of the rooster in the manner shown at Fig. 5, B.

P. Using a small, pointed brush, color pipe cleaner legs yellow and toe tips brown or black, employing the same coloring medium as previously used for rooster's body. Also, color pipe cleaner tail feathers with spots of yellow, red and white. Do not use any shellac over colored pipe cleaner parts.

Q. Fasten a safety pin, or regular metal pin-clasp, to back of rooster's wooden body section, using the method shown in Fig. 2, Illustration 35.

Our proud Cock-O'-the-Walk lapel pin is now ready to wear. In addition to being used as a costume ornament, it may also be employed as a curtain tie back window shade pull, and as an ornament for a knick-knack shelf. When used for the last named purpose, this pipe cleaner novelty should be mounted on a small base or platform made of wood or heavy cardboard. In these additional applications, of course, no pin-clasp is required at the back of the project.

Project No. 88, Pot-of-Flowers Lapel Pin

See Figure 7, Illustration 37

I. Description

In this Pot-of-Flowers lapel ornament, pipe cleaners are used as stems to support the felt flowers and leaves, while the bottom ends of the pipe cleaners are firmly fixed into the top edge of a wooden "flower pot." Because of the flexibility of the pipe cleaner stems, the felt flowers which they support can easily be arranged in a fixed position, in any of several decorative forms, as represented in Fig. 7, Illustration 37.

As shown in Fig. 8, same illustration, each of the three flower units is built of three separate and differently colored felt parts, neatly glued together, just as seen in the sketch of our completed project, in Fig. 7. Each pipe cleaner stem is dressed up with two or three differently shaped leaves made of green felt. The "flower pot," made of two pieces of scrap wood of different thicknesses is neatly decorated in a harmonious combination of tempera colors, and is brightly finished with a coating of white shellac.

When completed, this charming Pot-of-Flowers lapel pin, shown in finished form in Fig. 7, looks most realistic.

II. Materials and Tools

The materials required for this Pot-of-Flowers lapel ornament are scrap pieces of felt for the flower and leaf parts, two pipe cleaners, small pieces of 1/8 inch and 1/4 inch three-ply wood (regular thin wood is also good), a piece of medium grade sandpaper, a little glue, a few appropriate colors of tempera paints, a little white shellac, and a small safety pin or clasp.

As for the tools, you will need a pair of round-nose pliers, equipped with cutting edges, a coping saw, a medium size pair of scissors, small and medium size water color brushes, and a 1/2 inch wide, flat-type shellacking brush.

III. Directions

The few, simple directions required for the construction of this novel lapel ornament are as follows:

A. On a sheet of drawing paper, make a pattern grill of 1/4 inch squares, consisting of the same number and arrangement of squares as shown in the reduced form grill in Fig. 6, Illustration 37.

B. On this grill of squares, reproduce wooden, flower pot parts A and B, felt leaf parts C, D, and E, flower parts F, G, and H, and then cut out these paper patterns with a small pair of scissors.

C. Trace pattern A to a scrap piece of 1/8 inch thick wood, either plain or three-ply, trace pattern B to a piece of 1/4 inch thick wood, and then cut out these two wood parts with a coping saw, using the equipment shown in Fig. 3, Illustration 10. Following cutting out of these wood parts, smooth all sawed edges with medium grade sandpaper.

D. Using a hand drill, fitted with a 3/32 inch drill, bore 1/4 inch deep holes at the top edge of wood part B, at points M, N, and O, as indicated in Fig. 6.

E. Glue wood part A over wood part B and then paint entire flower pot with a brick-red color of tempera paint. When dry, and using two or three other, though harmonious, colors of tempera paint, add some form of simple, ornamental design to lower, front section of part B, just as represented in Figs. 5 and 6. For the overall coloring of the flower pot, use a No. 5 and 6 water coloring brush. For painting on the decorative design, use a No. 2 or 3 water color brush.

F. Apply a coat of clear white shellac over the entire wooden flower pot and allow to dry.

G. Make three tracings of flower pattern part H to white felt and then cut out these parts with a small pair of scissors. Make three tracings of pattern part G to blue felt and cut them out. Make three tracings of pattern part F to orange felt and also cut these out.

H. Make three tracings each on deep-green felt of leaf pattern parts C, D, and E, and cut them out with small scissors, just as in the case of the felt flower parts.

1 Using side cutting pliers, cut three stems, J, K, and L, from pipe cleaner strips, to measure 1-1/2 inches, 1-3/4 inches and 2-1/4 inches respectively. Then, color stems with brown tempera paint.

J. On the upper tip of each pipe cleaner stem, glue a set of three felt flower parts F, G, and H, placing a drop of glue between each two parts, and using the formation shown in Fig. 8. Allow 1/8 inch of the top end of each pipe cleaner stem to extend above each assembled flower unit, just as seen in Figs. 7 and 8.

K. Glue a set of three felt leaves to each of the three pipe cleaner stems, using the general plan and arrangement for these leaves as suggested in the sketch of our completed project, in Fig. 7.

L. Glue lower ends of pipe cleaner stems into the previously drilled holes, M, N, and O, at upper end of flower pot.

M. Bend pipe cleaner stems to produce an attractive arrangement of the flowers as in Fig. 7.

N. Attach regular small metal clasp or safety pin to back of wooden flower pot section, using method suggested in Fig. 2, Illustration 35.

Our Pot-of-Flowers ornament is now complete.

Like the Cock-O'-the-Walk lapel pin model, shown in Fig. 1, this decorative unit, minus the pin-back clasp, may also be employed as a curtain tie back, window shade pull, wall decoration, and so forth.

Project No. 89, Pipe Cleaner Funny Figures

In addition to the pipe cleaner projects already described in this scrap craft unit, there are quite a few other interesting articles which can easily be made of this scrap material.

For instance, you can make a variety of little dolls, employing the pipe cleaners as foundations, and dressing them in colorful doll clothes made of felt or crepe paper. When completed, these dolls can be used as toys, ornaments, party favors, and so forth.

Much fun can also be had in making a wide variety of doll figures, such as puppies, snakes, monkeys, giraffes, fish, donkeys, rabbits, squirrels, and goats. Or two small boxers can be made in full action, fighting position. Another idea is to make the figures of little children at play: running, pulling a sled, climbing, and so forth.

Pipe cleaners may also be used effectively to form a name such as JOHN or JANE. They may also be employed in the construction of miniature furniture for doll houses. Youngsters can have lots of fun forming pipe cleaner numbers or alphabet letters.

If you wish, you may attach some of your pipe cleaner figures to wood or cardboard bases, so that they can stand up easily in whatever positions you place them. Also, you may add a few touches of color, to brighten the pipe cleaners with a regular pen and different colors of writing ink. By this simple means, you may color a nose red, eyes blue or black, hair brown, and so forth.

The only tool you will need for converting discarded pipe cleaners into these figures is a pair of round-nose, cutting pliers. However because of the extremely flexible nature of pipe cleaners, you will be able to produce a good number of these funny little creations without the use of pliers, working simply with the fingers.

This simple handwork skill offers teachers of children's crafts excellent possibilities in the development of creative expression. Little boys and girls like to manipulate and fashion things of these pipe cleaners, and often produce ingenious figures and devices with them.

CHAPTER FOURTEEN

WORKING WITH SCRAP PLASTICS

IN THIS final scrap craft unit, we are going to consider the handicraft possibilities of the most modern of our construction materials, plastics. This amazing new material is different from all other craft materials such as wood, metal, cork, leather and clay, and offers vast opportunities in fascinating handwork to home and school craftsmen everywhere.

Because of their usefulness in innumerable industrial processes, their adaptability, and the wealth of handicraft work which they make possible, plastics are recognized as the miracle construction material of all time. In fact, because of the rapid and tremendous development of industrial plastics, our times may become known as the Age of Plastics.

Since children and adult craftsmen everywhere will sooner or later find themselves working with this wonderful material, it will not be amiss to consider a few of the more important qualities, physical properties, practical advantages, and possibilities of plastics.

What are plastics? To answer this question properly, it must be stated at the outset that the term "plastics" is a commercially created name and not entirely based on the scientific properties of this material. Most technical dictionaries define plastics as those materials which can be formed, sculptured, or molded into various shapes by hand or machine processing. Generally speaking, therefore, clay, wax, plaster, rubber, glass, and a host of other widely used materials may also be called "plastics." However, the term "plastics," as it is popularly and universally used today, has come to mean those synthetic, organic chemical compounds or mixtures which can be cast, molded, formed, or pressed into various shapes by the application of heat and pressure, and which retain those shapes after cooling.

At the present time there are about two dozen basically different types of these plastics. Classified according to their chemical sources and properties, these plastics may be placed in four general groups as follows:

1. CELLULOSE PLASTICS, made from cotton or wood pulp. "Celluloid" is the oldest and best known example of this form of plastic.

2. SYNTHETIC RESIN PLASTICS, made from phenol, formaldehyde, petroleum, acetylene, and several other chemicals. Among the more extensively used plastics in this group are phenol formaldehyde, styrene, acrylic, and phenolic furfural plastics.

3. PROTEIN PLASTICS, essentially made from milk. Other protein plastics are made from soy beans, coffee beans, peanuts and various other agricultural products. The so-called "casein" plastics are the most popular and most widely used in this group.

4. NATURAL RESIN PLASTICS, among which are such commonly known materials as shellac, asphalt, rosin, amber, and pitch.

According to their physical properties, all plastics may be classified in two distinct groups: thermoplastic and thermosetting.

Thermoplastic plastics can be formed into any desired shape under heat and pressure and become solids upon cooling. If they are subjected to equal amounts of heat and pressure again, they can be made pliable as before and remolded into different shapes.

Popular and comparatively new products in thermoplastic plastics are represented by such trade names as "Lucite," "Plexiglas" and "Crystalite." These plastics are chiefly characterized by their crystal-clear transparency, their practically unbreakable quality, and by the important fact that they are tougher and lighter in weight than glass. These particular types of thermoplastic plastics are industrially known as "Acrylic" plastics, because of the acrylic resins which are chiefly employed in their production. They were originally designed for use in the construction of turrets and noses for commercial and military aircraft. They are also excellent for use in home and school workshops.

Acrylic, thermoplastic plastics such as Lucite, Plexiglas and Crystalite, become amazingly pliable when heated at temperatures from 220° F to 300° F, in any suitable type of oven. They can also be made pliable by immersion in hot water. In this pliable state, they can be molded and shaped over wood, metal, or plaster of Paris forms. Because these plastics may be bent and twisted into an endless variety of shapes and forms, and because they can easily be sawed, drilled, smoothed, polished, and jointed like wood or metal, craftsmen everywhere are enthusiastic about them. These transparent, thermoplastic plastics may be purchased in flat sheets of various thicknesses and sizes, as well as in tubes, rods and molding powders. In addition to a colorless crystal-clear form, they may also be obtained in beautiful tints of green, amber, and so forth. As in the case of other forms of plastics, considerable quantities of this material can be purchased in odd sizes and lots at low cost.

Thermosetting plastics differ essentially from thermoplastic ones in that they cannot be remolded once they are solidified by cooling. In this group, the cast phenolic resin plastics, earlier described under Synthetic Resin Plastics, are of special interest to us since, like the acrylic resin plastics, they provide us with an excellent handwork medium. These thermosetting, synthetic resin plastics are chiefly characterized by their deep opaque quality, their intense brilliance, their coral-like luster, and their range and beauty of color. Not only can synthetic resin plastics be obtained in almost any desired color or shade of color, but they can also be had in most combinations or mixtures of colors, including many beautiful marble-like effects. These opaque plastics may be obtained in sheets of various thicknesses and sizes, as well as in the form of tubes, rods, and novelty strips which are convenient for making costume jewelry.

These phenolic resin plastics, like the acrylic resin plastics, may be easily sawed, drilled, carved, filed, sanded, buffed, and polished with ordinary, inexpensive craft shop equipment.

Other questions which may be asked by the reader are "When did the plastic era begin and how did these miracle products of chemistry actually originate?"

After referring to most authoritative sources on this absorbing subject, the author found that the plastic industry really was born as early as 1870. It was then that John Wesley Hyatt, a young American printer, set out to find a new material which could be used as a substitute for ivory, in the production of billiard balls. As a result of his research and endeavors in this field, he produced a substance which he could mold into desired shapes through the application of proper amounts of heat and pressure. This new material, which soon won international recognition and prominence for its great industrial value, he called "celluloid." The essential ingredient used by Hyatt in the creation of this first new plastic material, was cellulose nitrate, formed by the action of nitric acid on cotton cellulose. The cellulose nitrate thus formed was later mixed with camphor and treated with proper proportions of heat and pressure.

In 1909, Dr. Leo Baekeland, also an American, succeeded in producing a new and different plastic which came to be popularly known as "Bakelite." This plastic, which chemically belongs to the synthetic resin group, was created by the mixture of phenol and formaldehyde.

Bakelite, like celluloid, was instrumental in inspiring the discovery of many new forms of plastics. Research in plastics today is not only seeking to discover new plastics, but also to improve those already known to us. According to present indications, the possibilities of this wonderful new material are still tremendous.

To craftsmen everywhere, plastics have created many new opportunities for absorbing handwork.

Arts and crafts enthusiasts who find it difficult to purchase plastic material in the regular sheet, rod, strip, or tubular form, as provided by the various handicraft supply houses, will find it a simple matter to obtain many satisfactory grades of plastics, entirely free of cost, in the form of scrap or discarded plastic articles. Thus, as later described in this scrap craft unit, an old tooth brush or hair brush can easily be transformed into an attractive novelty or piece of costume jewelry. Or, an old discarded plastic radio cabinet can be utilized in the production of various styles of brooches, pendants, novel lapel ornaments, buckles, cigarette boxes, book-ends, pen and ink stands, stationery racks, and a host of other equally fine projects. In this connection, the reader is referred to Chapter Two, Scrap List No. 2, where several common sources of supply are given for obtaining different forms of scrap plastic material of a workable grade at little or no cost.

In the scrap craft unit which follows, the author has endeavored to present some representative and popular types of handwork projects which are particularly suitable for simple construction work in plastics. After you have made these models, you will have little difficulty in producing many other plastic articles of your own design.

Project No. 90, Novelty Letter Openers

See Figure 9, Illustration 38

I. Description

Letter openers and paper knives of various attractive designs and styles provide an excellent project for beginners in work with plastics since any small piece of plastic of any color or grade can be employed and only simple operations such as sawing, filing, and polishing are involved.

Making letter openers and paper-cutting knives also provides an opportunity for the development of creative design. Not only can you use an endless assortment of abstract forms and design arrangements for the handles of these projects, but you can also apply such motifs as ships, animals, birds, flowers, or Mexican subjects. Furthermore, in the construction of plastic letter openers and paper knives you can introduce such decorative procedures as piercing or completely cutting out certain interior sections of the handle; inlaying, in which other, contrasting colors of plastics are imbedded in the handle in interesting designs; or by electric burning the design on the handle in various ways. Using a simple silhouette or contour design in the formation of the handle is still another effective ornamental treatment. The appearance of the handle can often be enhanced by the use of one or more appropriate colors of good grade enamel.

The cutting blades of these letter openers and paper knives also provide opportunities for creative designing. You may use symmetrical, tapering shapes, scimitar-like shapes, or regular knife shapes, depending, of course, upon the particular purpose of the article.

An interesting variation of this project is the construction of plastic cheese-cutting knives. These knives are made in practically the same manner as the letter openers except that the blades must be considerably thinner and that the cutting edges must be very sharp.

As you will note later in our discussion, fine little letter openers can be made from the plastic handles of old, discarded tooth brushes and hair brushes. As you know, these plastic handles come in a wide variety of attractive colors, all of which are appropriate for letter openers.

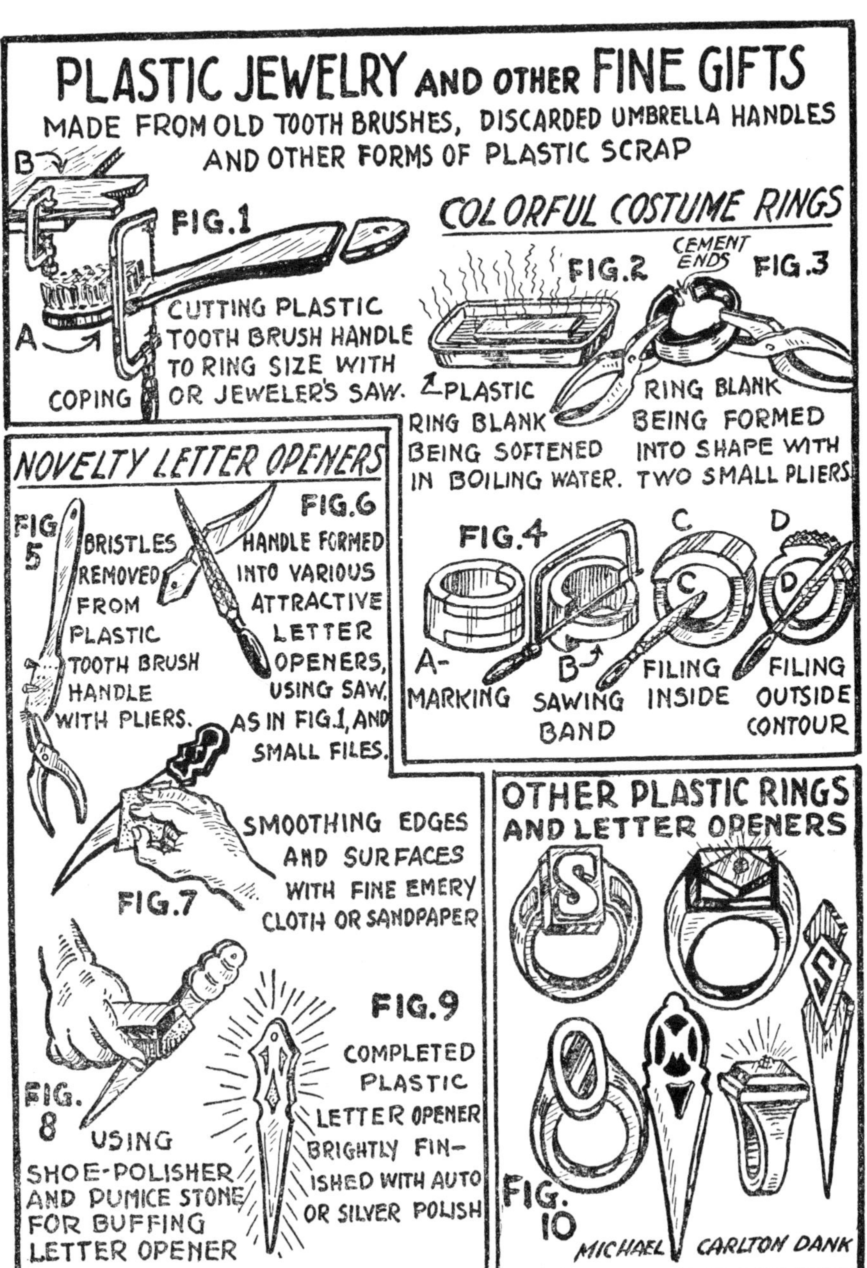

PLASTIC JEWELRY AND OTHER FINE GIFTS
MADE FROM OLD TOOTH BRUSHES, DISCARDED UMBRELLA HANDLES AND OTHER FORMS OF PLASTIC SCRAP
B
FIG.1
A
CUTTING PLASTIC TOOTH BRUSH HANDLE TO RING SIZE WITH COPING OR JEWELER'S SAW.
COLORFUL COSTUME RINGS
FIG.2
CEMENT ENDS
FIG.3
PLASTIC RING BLANK BEING SOFTENED IN BOILING WATER.
RING BLANK BEING FORMED INTO SHAPE WITH TWO SMALL PLIERS
NOVELTY LETTER OPENERS
FIG 5
BRISTLES REMOVED FROM PLASTIC TOOTH BRUSH HANDLE WITH PLIERS.
FIG.6
HANDLE FORMED INTO VARIOUS ATTRACTIVE LETTER OPENERS, USING SAW, AS IN FIG.1, AND SMALL FILES.
FIG.4
C
D
A- MARKING
B SAWING BAND
FILING INSIDE
FILING OUTSIDE CONTOUR
SMOOTHING EDGES AND SURFACES WITH FINE EMERY CLOTH OR SANDPAPER
FIG.7
OTHER PLASTIC RINGS AND LETTER OPENERS
S
FIG.9
COMPLETED PLASTIC LETTER OPENER BRIGHTLY FINISHED WITH AUTO OR SILVER POLISH
FIG. 8
USING SHOE-POLISHER AND PUMICE STONE FOR BUFFING LETTER OPENER
FIG. 10
MICHAEL CARLTON DANK

Illustration 38

Of course, if you wish to make large letter openers or paper knives, you will have to use larger plastic material than is provided by old tooth brush handles. Whether you employ an old tooth or hair brush handle or some other form of plastic scrap, the method of construction, as given below, is practically the same.

In addition to using colored or opaque scrap plastics for these projects, you may also employ such glass-like, crystal-clear plastics as lucite, plexiglas, or crystalite.

After you become familiar with the basic working procedures described below, you will find it a simple matter to make many other one-piece plastic articles such as pendants, earrings, brooches, watch-fobs, and so forth. You will find several such projects shown in Illustration 39.

II. Materials

A. An old plastic tooth brush or hair brush handle or any scrap piece of plastic at least 3/16 inch in thickness and from 3/4 inch to 1-1/2 inches in width and 6 inches to 8 inches in length.

B. Squared paper, having 3/16 inch to 1/4 inch squares.

C. Rubber cement and any good grade of plastic cement such as acetone, Duco Household Cement, and so forth.

D. Medium and fine grades of sandpaper or emery cloth.

E. Any good grade of buffing compound suitable for polishing plastics.

F. Any good grade wood or metal polish.

G. Scrap pieces of heavy felt as polishing rags.

III. Tools

A. A medium size jeweler's saw frame fitted with a No. 1 jeweler's saw blade. Any type of coping saw with a fine grade coping saw blade can also be employed satisfactorily for cutting plastics.

B. Saw board with a V-shape cut out of one end. A good size board for this purpose, is one which measures about 4 inches wide, by 10 inches long, by 5/8 inch thick. Any hardwood is satisfactory. See Fig. 1-B, Illustration 38.

C. A small, metal "C" clamp, used to clamp the sawboard tightly to bench or table.

D. Regular shoe polisher or a heavy piece of felt. See Fig. 8, Illustration 38.

E. Assorted shapes and sizes of medium and fine grade files.

IV. Directions

A. Preparation of design

1. Draw several full size shapes of letter openers or paper knives on a sheet of squared paper containing 3/16 inch to 1/4 inch squares. See Figs. 6, 7, 8, and 9 for a few suggested shapes. If you wish, you may also use for the handles such motifs as ships, animal forms, Mexican subjects, flower forms, etc. If an old tooth brush or hair brush handle is to be the construction material, first trace around the outlines of the tooth or hair brush handle on the squared paper, and then work out your letter opener design accordingly.

2. After completing the desired letter opener pattern on the squared paper, cut out the pattern with scissors and then cement it to a proper size piece of plastic material, using rubber cement. If an old tooth brush handle is used as the plastic material, first remove brush bristles with a pair of pliers in the manner shown in Fig. 5, Illustration 38. Then cement properly prepared paper pattern to the plastic handle, just as when using scrap sheet plastic.

B. Sawing out plastic letter opener

Sawing out irregular shaped plastic projects is very similar to cutting out irregularly formed wood or metal articles. Here, as in wood or metal sawing, a wooden saw board, having a "V" notch at one end, is attached to the work bench or work-table top by means of a small "C" clamp, in the manner shown by Fig. 1, B, Illustration 38. When fastening the saw board into position for working, have half of its length extend forward beyond the edge of the bench top. The saw board in this position acts as a rest or foundation which is very helpful and convenient for this sawing procedure.

With the saw board clamped to the table top in this manner, cut out the plastic letter opener as follows:

1. Place plastic material with the paper pattern cemented to its upper surface over the "V"-notched end of the saw board. Hold the piece of plastic firmly with the left hand while the right hand is used to operate the saw. In this connection refer to Fig. 3, Illustration 10, which shows this same sawing arrangement employed in the cutting of irregularly shaped wood parts.

2. Using a medium size jeweler's saw frame, fitted with a No. 1 jeweler's saw blade, or any type of coping saw which can accommodate a fine toothed coping saw blade, cut out the letter opener as represented by the paper pattern. Be sure to follow the outlines of the paper pattern carefully and to hold the saw in a perfectly vertical position at all times when cutting. Use fast short sawing strokes. Avoid pulling or forcing the saw as doing so will cause the saw blade to snap.

3. If you wish to use a pierced design for the decoration of the handle in which certain parts are completely sawed out, as in the model shown in Fig. 9, Illustration 38, proceed as follows: First, drill a small hole within the section to be cut out, detach one end of the saw blade from the frame, place this detached end through the drilled hole and attach loose end of blade to frame again. Now cut out the interior section of the handle in the same manner as when cutting the outside contours. When finished, detach one end of saw blade again, remove saw from project and then attach loose end of saw blade to the frame again. Repeat this same procedure for each separate interior section which requires cutting out.

C. Filing cut-out letter opener

1. File all sawed edges until they are uniform and true all around. Use flat, half-round, three-cornered taper, and rat-tail styles of files, as required by the particular contours of the project in

work. Use only medium and fine-toothed files of a small size, such as regularly used by jewelers, for the filing of all outside and inside edges and for all small carving effects. See Fig. 6, Illustration 38. To facilitate the filing you may use the "V" notched saw board or a bench vise as an aid.

2. File the flat surfaces of the cutting blade of the letter opener until the blade is much thinner than the handle and tapers to a very thin edge at its tip, making the tip sharp enough to cut through paper easily.

3. File both sides of each cutting edge of the opener, until the edges are sufficiently sharp for cutting paper and opening letters. The bevels thus formed at the cutting edges should be neat and uniform all around.

4. For filing pierced work or interior sawed sections, use very small files of appropriate shapes and styles.

D. Sandpapering filed edges and flat surfaces

1. Rub all filed edges and flat surfaces of the plastic letter openers with a medium grade sandpaper (No. 1/2). This will remove the heavy file marks and will cause the plastic material to take on a dull, grayish appearance. You may use a similar grade of emery cloth in place of the sandpaper.

2. Smooth all edges and surfaces of the opener with a piece of fine grade sandpaper (about No. 00). Here also, emery cloth of a similar grade may be employed in place of the sandpaper. Keep on smoothing the work in this manner until all edges and flat and round surfaces are perfectly smooth to the touch and free of all scratches. See Fig. 7, Illustration 38.

E. Polishing and finishing the letter opener

1. Apply some suitable plastic buffing compound to a regular shoe polisher and then briskly buff all edges and surfaces of the finely sandpapered letter opener until they appear brightly polished and finished. See Fig. 8, Illustration 38. If a regular shoe polisher is unavailable, you can apply the buffing compound to a heavy piece of felt and produce an equally satisfactory plastic polishing result.

2. After sufficient polishing, use a clean cloth with soap and warm water to wipe away all remaining particles of the buffing compound.

3. For added luster and a more protective finish, rub all surfaces of the buffed and wiped plastic letter opener with any good wood or metal polish, using a soft piece of cloth and a light, though brisk, polishing motion.

F. Additional decorative treatments

1. Electric pencil etching

Trace the design on the handle and then scratch or engrave it surface of the plastic material with an electric pencil. After a little experimenting with this decorative technique, you will soon be able to produce good results. The method is similar to that used for burning a design on wood and a variety of styles of burning points may be used.

? Scratching or engraving the design

Trace the design on the handle and then scratch or engrave it into the surface of the plastic, using for this purpose a regular scratch awl, an engraving tool, or any similar sharply pointed metal instrument. Small needle files or sc called carborundum pencils may also be used effectively for this purpose. After going over the design once repeat the same procedure once or twice again, until a sufficiently deep and clear engraving result has been produced. For added artistic effect, you may rub any desired contrasting color of paint filler or enamel paint into the engraved surfaces, wiping away any surplus filler with a piece of soft cloth.

3. Inlaying

Here a contrasting color of plastic may be partially or completely embedded or set into place to form an interesting design. First, saw out the exact shapes or sections of the handle which you wish to have inlaid. It is important first to prepare a careful pattern which must be traced to the handle and then scratched in with a sharply pointed metal instrument. Then, using a contrasting color of plastic of the same or even slightly greater thickness, saw out the same shapes as the pierced or cutout sections in the handle. After the inlay pieces are made to fit exactly by filing or sandpapering, cement them into their respective places on the handle with any good plastic cement. Duco cement, which is transparent, is fine for this purpose.

4. Overlaying or applique

This decorative treatment is simpler than inlaying since the cutout contrasting color of plastic which is to be used as the ornamental unit, is just cemented to the upper surface of the handle. First, make a paper pattern of the overlay design unit and then, with rubber cement, cement it to a contrasting color of plastic, preferably a little thinner than the thickness of the handle stock. After carefully smoothing and finishing all sawed edges of the overlay unit, cement it neatly in place, using Duco Household Cement, acetone, or any other good plastic cement. It is important that very little of the cement be allowed to ooze out around the edges of the overlay unit. Use clear nail polish remover to wipe away any of this surplus cement. Besides using one-piece overlay designs in a simple silhouette effect, you can also use overlay designs consisting of two or more pieces effectively.

Project No. 91, Plastic Rings

See Figures 1, 2, 3, and 4, Illustration 38

I. Description

Like letter openers, attractive costume rings can easily be made from such discarded articles as umbrella handles, tooth brush handles, and various other forms of plastic scrap. In plastic ring making, there is no limitation as to color, style, and design.

These colorful plastic costume rings are an excellent project for beginners in plastic work since they can be made of a small single piece of plastic material in comparatively little time.

An excellent source of material for making plastic rings is provided by an old plastic umbrella handle. In fact, from a single umbrella handle you can make several rings of various types. Using discarded umbrella handles as ring-making material is advisable as no cementing or bending is required. All you need to do is to cut the tubular handle into small sections, thus providing the fundamental ring shape as seen at A, Fig. 4, Illustration 38. Already-formed fundamental ring shapes, of various tubular diameters and styles and in a wide variety of plastic colors, may also be obtained at all handicraft supply houses at very little cost.

If fundamental ring shapes in the types suggested are unobtainable, you can use as your construction material for making the rings any scrap pieces of flat or sheet plastic, at least 1/8 inch in thickness. An old tooth brush can advantageously be employed as the material for these rings simply by cutting off a proper or measured size section of its handle, in the manner shown in Fig. 1, Illustration 38. Cut to required size, this strip can easily be formed and cemented into a circular shape, ready for carving and the other interesting steps involved, by the simple method demonstrated in Figs. 2 and 3 and described in the directions given below.

Attractive little plastic rings can also be made from odd Mah Jong dice, now commonly made of some form of plastic material, simply by first drilling the finger hole through the center with an ordinary brace, fitted with a proper size metal-working drill.

The remaining steps in plastic ring making include simple handwork procedures such as designing and preparing the pattern, sawing, filing, engraving, and polishing.

After you complete your first few simple plastic rings, you may then make rings of a somewhat more advanced form, incorporating other decorative treatments such as piercing, carving, electric pencil etching, inlaying, overlaying, stone setting, and so forth.

II. Materials

A. An old plastic umbrella handle, odd Mah Jong dice, an old tooth brush handle, or any scrap piece of sheet plastic in the desired color.

B. Remaining materials needed are the same as listed under "Materials," items B, C, D, E, F, and G, Project No. 90, Novelty Letter Openers.

III. Tools

A. Same as item Nos. A, B, C, D, and E, as listed under "Tools," Project No. 90 Novelty Letter Openers.

B. Two pairs of small size pliers of the type seen in use in Fig. 3, Illustration 38.

C. A metal pan suitable for boiling water, of the type seen in use in Fig. 2, Illustration 38.

III. DIRECTIONS

When using flat pieces of plastic material for ring making such as provided by old tooth brush handles, as in Fig. 1, Illustration 38, it is first necessary to form the flat strip of plastic into its fundamental circular shape, as represented at A, Fig. 4, Illustration 38. A simple method for forming these fundamental ring tubes or blanks is as follows:

Note: This same method may also be applied wherever any bending or curving operations are required, such as in the construction of bracelets (see Fig. 12 and 13, Illustration 39), and picture frames (see Fig. 8, same Illustration), spiral-formed flower holders, etc.

A. Method for bending plastics to form rings, bracelets, etc.

1. Using 3/16 inch to 1/4 inch squared paper, draw several varieties of ring designs, making the lengths of the patterns in accordance with the particular ring size of the finger for which the ring is intended. This can easily be determined by wrapping a 3/4 inch wide strip of paper around the finger and pencil-marking the length of strip required. In this ring designing step, you may use various treatments for the head or top section of the ring, and the band may vary by being straight or tapering in thickness toward the bottom.

2. After you have completed your paper pattern of the ring, cut a scrap piece of sheet plastic, about 3/4 inch wide and in the desired color, to the same length as the paper pattern. Do not cement the pattern to the plastic material, as the pattern in this instance, is only used as a guide or plan. If a plastic tooth brush handle is employed as the material for making the ring, cut a strip off the handle, in the required length, using a coping saw in the

manner shown in Fig. 1, A, Illustration No. 38. As an aid in this sawing step, use the "V"-notched saw board and "C" clamp, shown at Fig. 1, B, Illustration 38. Following the cutting of the tooth brush handle to required length, file the slanted edges of the strip until they are parallel with each other and a straight strip is produced such as seen in Figs. 2 and 3, Illustration 38.

3. Boil water in any suitable shallow pan, large enough to conveniently hold the plastic ring strips to be bent. After water reaches boiling point, remove pan from fire and allow water to cool for a minute before inserting the plastic strip.

4. Place plastic strip in the hot water and allow it to remain in the water about three minutes. If the plastic strip is more than 1/8 inch thick, allow it to remain in the water a little longer than three minutes. For instance, a 3/16 inch thick strip of material may remain in the water from four to five minutes, a 1/4 inch thick strip, about six minutes, etc. Never place the plastic in the pan while the water is over the fire and heating as this will cause the plastic material to disintegrate and spoil. See Fig. 2, Illustration 38.

5. Using a pair of cotton gloves as protection and two small pairs of pliers, remove the now pliable plastic strip from the hot water and then gradually bend and form the strip into a perfect circle, in the manner shown in Fig. 3, Illustration 38. In this bending procedure it is important to work fast and you must complete the bending of the strip into the desired ring form before the plastic cools. Be sure to press both ends of the plastic strip together tightly so they will remain pressed against each other after the plastic cools off.

In place of using pliers for bending the plastic, you may work as follows: Remove heated, plastic ring strip from the hot water with a pair of cotton gloves as a protection; bend the pliable plastic strip over a round stick or rod of proper diameter, such as an old mop handle or dowel rod; place a thin sheet of metal over the plastic strip; bind all three members together tightly with a strip of thin wire or string; after the plastic cools, remove the wire or string, slide the metal sheet and formed plastic material from the round wooden form and you will now find that the cooled plastic strip will remain in the form of a circular little tube or foundation ring shape, ready for further processing, just as produced by the "pliers method," shown in Fig. 3, Illustration 38.

6. Cement the ends of the now formed circular ring blank with any good grade of plastic cement such as transparent Duco cement, making certain that the seam holds very tightly. To produce a permanently secure seam, it is best first to apply a thin coat of cement to each end of the ring form and allow this first coat to dry without pressing or joining the ends together. Then, apply a second coat of cement to each end, clamp the ends together tightly by winding a thin strip of wire several times around the ring, and by twisting the ends of the wire securely together. The wire here acts as a clamp and if the work is left clamped in this manner for a few hours, or better still, overnight, a permanently secure seam will be produced.

The originally straight strip of plastic material has now been transformed into a fundamental ring blank shape, practically as good as the already molded tubular ring blanks which are sold at handicraft supply houses. Following this bending procedure, you may go ahead with the sawing, filing, decorating, and polishing steps. These additional working procedures are as follows:

B. Marking design on foundation ring tube

1. Using a sharp pencil and carefully following the ring pattern previously prepared on the squared paper, mark off the head and band sections of the ring.

2. Using any sharply pointed metal instrument, such as a scriber or pointed brad awl, carefully go over all pencilled outlines on the ring and scratch them deeply into the plastic surface.

3. Wipe away all remaining pencil marks with a soft cloth to allow only the scratched in design outlines to show around the ring. See Fig. 4, Illustration 38.

C. Sawing away surplus ring stock

1. Place scratched-in plastic ring tube in a bench vise in a convenient position for working, being careful not to use too much vise pressure.

2. Cut away the surplus material at each side of the ring band, using either a jeweler's saw or a coping saw equipped with a fine-cutting saw blade. This step is called "rough shaping the ring." See Fig. 4, B, Illustration 38.

3. Do not saw too close to the scratched in design lines, as a little stock must be left for the filing step which follows.

4. Hold saw in a perfectly vertical position with handle at bottom and saw blade teeth facing downward toward the handle just as seen in Fig. 1, A, Illustration 38.

D. Filing ring to desired shape

1. Do all filing operations with work either clamped in a bench vise or held tightly against the "V"-notched end of the saw board. The saw board, of course, must be firmly clamped to the bench top, just as in the sawing step.

2. Using either a small size, all-round file, commonly known as a rat-tail file, or a small half-round file, file the inside of the ring band until it exactly fits the finger for which the ring is intended. Keep filing round and round to make the inside curve perfectly uniform. See Fig. 4, C, Illustration 38.

3. Using a small-size, half-round file, smooth and round off the outside sections of the lower portion of the ring band until that part of the ring is shaped exactly as planned in the prepared pattern.

4. Using a small-size, three-cornered taper file, shape the head or top-face section of the ring until general desired shape is produced. A small-size, rat-tail file, which is completely round, is also very useful for filing this upper and more complicated section of the ring. See Fig. 4, D, Illustration 38.

5. For specially complicated design shapes on the head or top face of the ring, use assorted types of jeweler's needle files or a small size carborundum pencil. Since this top section is the most delicately formed part of the ring, it is important to work out this part very slowly and as carefully as possible in order to produce good workmanship.

6. After all sections of the ring band have been properly filed to the desired shape, look over your work carefully again to make certain that all parts have been formed accurately and uniformly.

E. Sandpapering, polishing and finishing the ring

After correctly forming the ring, it is necessary to remove all file marks and scratches, until the ring is perfectly smooth to the touch. For this smoothing step, use small pieces of medium and fine grade sandpaper or emery cloth, in the manner described under section D in the directions given for Project No. 90, Novelty Letter Openers. Be sure to smooth all inside and outside surfaces of the ring. Also neatly smooth and round off all edges.

Finish the ring by buffing it to a bright luster, using any good grade of plastic buffing compound, and either a regular shoe polisher or a piece of felt as the buffer. Of course, if you are fortunate enough to have the use of an electric polishing head, all you need to do is to apply some of the buffing compound to a cloth buffing wheel, press the ring against the revolving wheel (be sure the wheel turns in the direction toward you), and in a minute or two, your ring will have a beautiful, sparkling finish.

F. Additional decorative treatments in plastic ring making

Besides using little files of different types, in the preparation of the design for the head of the ring, you may also produce good decorative effects by applying any one of the following ornamental treatments:

1. Using a small size countersinking tool, drill a shallow hole in the center of the face of the ring. In the small conical-shaped hole thus formed, cement a small imitation diamond or any suitable inexpensive ring stone as an added bit of ornamentation. In this decorative scheme at least part of the head of the ring must be flat.

2. Using an engraving tool or a scratch awl, carve either one or two initials on the head of the ring. An electric pencil may also be used for this decorative treatment. In this initialing procedure, the entire head of the ring must be flat to allow for sufficient carving room.

3. Cut out a separate initial, using a contrasting color of plastic, and cement this initial to the face of the ring. Be sure the initial is properly located and that a suitably designed initial is prepared for this purpose. It is also best that the plastic used for the initial be of a fairly thin grade.

4. Use three separate pieces of plastic of different size, color, and shape to form the head of the ring. Cement these three separate parts together carefully in an overlay fashion, to form various abstract designs.

You will find the above decorative schemes and several other interesting ideas for decorating your plastic rings in Fig. 10, Illustration 38.

RELATED PROJECTS

Constructed of scrap pieces of plastic material requiring the same basic handworking methods and procedures used in our key projects in this scrap craft unit, No. 90, Novelty Letter Openers, and No. 91, Plastic Rings.

Project No. 92, Carved Plastic Pendants

See Figure 1, Illustration 39

Lovely pendants, in a wide variety of styles and decorative treatments, may easily be made from small scrap pieces of plastic material. The plastic used for this type of costume jewelry may be of the crystal-clear, transparent kind such as lucite or plexiglas, or the colored opaque resin plastics. Here are the simple directions:

After preparing the design and tracing the pattern to the plastic stock, saw out the outside contours or shape of the pendant. Then, by filing and sandpapering, round and smooth all sawed edges until they are neat and uniform all around. For these pattern-tracing, sawing and smoothing operations, see sections A, B, C, and D, in the directions for Project 90, Novelty Letter Openers.

The next consideration is the selection of an appropriate decorative treatment for the front or face of the pendant. One effective method is to carve the design so that the lower level extends downward to half the thickness of the plastic. Before proceeding

Illustration 39

to carve the design, however, boil some water in a flat pan, remove the pan from the fire, and then place the plastic piece into the water for about three minutes. This will soften the plastic and make it easy to carve. For carving tools, you may use a scratch awl, jeweler's needle files, engraving tool, or carborundum pencil.

After carving the background designs to their proper depths, you may simply smooth out these lower levels with small pieces of fine sandpaper or emery cloth and leave them clean and plain; or stipple them with any pointed tool, or paint them in an appropriate contrasting color of enamel. Another good idea is to fill the depressed areas right to the top level of the plastic with some kind of wood or cement filler which contrasts in color to the plastic. After levelling the depressed areas or cavities with the filler, smooth the entire top face of the pendant with fine steel wool or emery cloth wrapped around a small smoothing block. As a final finish, polish all parts of the pendant brightly, using any one of the plastic polishing methods described under E, Project No. 90, Plastic Letter Openers.

For a representative example of a carved plastic pendant, see Fig. 1, Illustration 39. Note the small hole drilled at the top for attaching pendant to a metal chain. Bore hole with a 1/16 inch metal drill. Use a small metal ring to link the completed plastic pendant to a suitable form of necklace chain.

Project No. 93, Pierced Plastic Pendants

See Figure 2, Illustration 39

In this piercing method of ornamenting plastic pendants the background areas of the design are completely sawed away, as shown by the black areas of pendant in Fig. 2, Illustration 39.

For complete details concerning this effective decorative technique which is also used a great deal in art metal work, see Section IV-B-3 under Project No. 90, Plastic Letter Openers.

When preparing the designs for pierced plastic pendants, it is important that they be arranged in a stencilled manner in which the background areas only (shown black in Fig. 2), are to be cut completely through and away. Also, that the design motif itself (shown white in Fig. 2), be left intact, in effective silhouette. The use of a bordered effect for the designs here employed, just as represented by our model in Fig. 2, is also both effective and expedient, in this piercing method of ornamenting plastic pendants. It is also important that all designs employed for this form of decorative treatment be especially simple and free of any unnecessary detail. Following the sawing out of the pierced areas, make certain that all cut edges are neatly smoothed and rounded off, using either small needle type files or small pieces of fine emery cloth or sandpaper.

To complete this type of plastic pendant, drill a small hole at the top for attaching it to necklace chain, and polish brightly, as directed for the pendant shown in Fig. 1, Illustration 39.

Project No. 94, Plastic Earrings Using "Overlay" Construction

See Figure 3, Illustration 39

The construction of earrings of various simple designs provides an excellent form of easy and inexpensive plastic work. Plastic earrings are always popular with girls and women because of their decorative appeal.

Plastic earrings in the overlay form of ornamentation, made of either opaque or transparent types of scrap plastic, as represented by the model in Fig. 3, Illustration 39, are especially effective. You will find this simple, decorative process fully described in Section IV-F-4, under Project No. 90, Plastic Letter Openers.

For these earrings, use a 3/16 inch thick piece of plastic for the base of the earring, and a somewhat thinner grade of plastic for the overlay unit. The overlay unit may be variously carved or embellished with small files, just as represented by the center of the flower motif in earring 3, Illustration 39. For the overlay unit use any appropriate contrasting color of plastic.

For the cementing, smoothing, and polishing operations, refer to instructions given in Section IV, Project No. 90. As clasps for the back of the earrings, you may use either the plastic or the metal types, employing Duco, or any other good grade of plastic cement as the adhesive. See Fig. 5, Illustration 39. When cementing the ear clasp to the back of the earring, be sure that the clasp is properly located so as to show the front of the earring to best advantage when worn.

Project No. 95, Plastic Earrings with Veined Designs

See Figures 4 and 5, Illustration 39

These "veined" earrings are easier to make than the overlay type since they are made of a single piece of plastic. Furthermore, the design which, in our model earrings seen in Fig. 4, represents the veins of a leaf, is simply scratched in or grooved just about 1/32 inch deep into the surface of the plastic. This shallow grooving or "veining" provides a dramatic contrast to the rest of the plastic earring.

As veining tools, you may use a scratch awl, an engraving tool, or a carborundum pencil. A good finish for the shallow, veined sections, is provided by the use of a contrasting color of enamel or metallic paint. Simply apply the paint to all the veined sections of the earring, allow it to dry a little, then wipe away all excess paint with a small piece of cloth so that the paint will show only in the veined, lower levels. After the painted, veined sections have thoroughly dried, the entire earring may be brightly polished and finished.

Fig. 5 shows the back section of this leaf earring, with either a plastic or metal clasp cemented on. For all other working operations here involved, such as sawing, filing, and proper methods of polishing, see directions as given for Project No. 90.

Project No. 96, Plastic Initialed Earrings

See Figure 6, Illustration 39

Initialed earrings are especially attractive because of their personal quality and their simplicity of design. You may either use the same initial for both earrings or a first initial on one earring and a second initial on the other. In addition to the initials you may employ a few simple design lines or carved effects such as those used in the decoration of earring 6, in Illustration 39. Both the initials and the added design treatments may be worked out in a shallow veining style, as in the ornamentation of the leaf earring, Fig. 4. Here, also as in the leaf earring, use a contrasting color of enamel or metallic paint as a filler for the veined or engraved areas.

Besides square or oblong shapes for these plastic initialed earrings, shown in Fig. 6, you may also use such interesting shapes as diamonds, circles, octagons, ovals, or stars. A good thickness for the scrap plastic material used in the construction of these initialed earrings is from 1/8 inch to 1/4 inch. Although you may use the colored, opaque form of plastic for these earrings, the crystal-clear, transparent variety such as lucite or plexiglas is more effective. The clasps used at the backs of these earrings may be of the plastic or metal grade and attached as at Fig. 5, Illustration 39.

Just as in the case of all the other styles of earrings, it is important to finish all edges carefully, and to vein the initials and all other ornamentation employed as neatly and attractively as possible. A bright polish is also essential for these appealing, initialed, plastic earrings.

Project No. 97, Plastic Cigarette Box

See Figure 7, Illustration 39

Although this novel cigarette box is built of twelve separate pieces of plastic, it is very easy to make and requires less plastic material than one might at first suppose.

The entire box is built of 3/16 inch or 1/4 inch plastic of either the opaque or the transparent type. The latter, however, is preferable since it permits the cigarettes to show even when the cover is in place.

As you will note from Fig. 7, A, no hinges are required for the cover of this unusually styled cigarette box. This is because the little triangular pieces at the corners of the top of the box are cemented solidly in place and hold the cover neatly in its proper position as shown in Fig. 7, B. To remove a cigarette from the box, simply lift the cover by its two little streamlined handles, which are cemented to the top of the box, and then replace the cover within the four fixed triangular corners.

The directions for constructing this useful, plastic cigarette box are as follows:

1. Make a bottom piece 3-1/2 inches wide by 4-1/2 inches long, making certain that its edges and ends are perfectly square and true all around. Use a try-square as the testing tool, just as

you would do in testing the edges and ends of a wood board. Finish this base piece by smoothing its edges and ends with fine emery cloth or sandpaper, wrapped around a small wood block.

2. Make two long side strips 1 inch wide by 4-1/2 inches long and cement these side strips to the top of the base piece, exactly flush with its 4-1/2 inch edge. See Fig. 7, C. Be sure these side strips are made perfectly straight and square at their edges, to assure a good fit when these strips are cemented to the base.

3. Make two short end strips, also 1 inch wide and long enough to fit tightly between the two long strips. Then cement these two end strips in place, applying the cement to the ends and the bottom edges of these strips to assure strong construction. See Fig. 7, D.

4. Make a piece for the top section of the box, in exactly the same measurements as the base part, namely 3-1/2 inches wide by 4-1/2 inches long. Then, using a scratch awl, mark off the four triangles, one at each corner, measuring 1-1/8 inches along the end and side parts of the cover, from each corner of the box. After marking off these 1-1/8 inch measurements, connect these points to form the corner triangles, just as in Fig. 7, E.

5. Using a jeweler's saw, equipped with a fine blade, carefully saw off each corner triangle, thus dividing the top piece into five separate parts. Be sure the cuts are made perfectly straight and square, since irregular sawing of these straight lines will detract considerably from the appearance of the completed cigarette box. After using the saw at these corners, finish each cut edge with fine emery cloth or sandpaper wrapped around a small sandblock, to produce a neat result at each corner.

6. Cement only the triangular pieces securely in place, making certain that their outer edges are exactly flush with the sides of the box. The large octagonal section of the top remains uncemented so that it can easily be removed or replaced as desired.

7. Cut two strips of plastic to measure 1/2 inch wide by 1-1/4 inch long for the cover handles. Round off the top edge of each

of these strips in a neat, streamlined fashion and then cement these two strips to the top of the octagonal cover section, placing one handle at each end. See Fig. 7, F.

8. Decorate the cover with some form of monogram or some simple, appropriate design motif such as a flower, a ship, an animal, or a geometric design. For applying the design, you may use any one of the decorative treatments described under Project No. 90, Plastic Letter Openers.

9. To finish the plastic cigarette box properly, round all edges neatly and polish all surfaces, following the directions for finishing and polishing plastic projects given under Project No. 90.

These attractive, plastic cigarette boxes can also be made smaller or larger than the size in our model in Fig. 7, Illustration 39. Different handle and cover arrangements can also be employed. This particular model, however, has proved very popular in the author's own handicraft classes.

Project No. 98, Plastic Picture Frame

See Figure 8, Illustration 39

The particular kind of picture frame here represented is only one of the many varieties and sizes of attractive picture frames which can easily be made from scrap pieces of plastic. Because of its curved construction, it is necessary to use only the thermoplastic type of plastic material which can be made pliable under heat. It is best to make this frame out of any transparent, crystal-clear plastic such as lucite, plexiglas, or crystalite.

The directions are as follows:

1. Make a straight piece of crystal-clear plastic to measure 1 inch wide by 12 inches long. The material used for this purpose may vary from 1/8 inch to 1/4 inch in thickness, although a thickness of 3/16 inch will be found to be most suitable and practical.

2. Using a jeweler's saw, cut a slit 3/16 inch wide and 1-3/4 inches long, in the exact center of the width at each end of this plastic strip. See Fig. 8, A.

3. After all sawing and filing work is completed, smooth all cut edges of the plastic strip with fine sandpaper or emery cloth until neatly finished. Also round off the sharp corners of the ends of the strip a little.

4. Bend the ends of the strip into the scroll arrangement seen at Fig. 8, B, using either a pair of round-nose pliers or some round shape form, such as provided by a broom handle, as working aids. Heat and bend only one end at a time. Later, bend the bottom or central section of the plastic strip a little to produce the arrangement seen at Fig. 8, C. For these plastic bending procedures, apply the immersion in hot water method, given under Directions, Section A, for Project No. 91, Plastic Rings. Be sure the scroll at the left and the one at the right are neat and uniform. Also make certain that the upward bend in the center of the frame is properly executed. Refrain from denting or otherwise marring the surfaces of the plastic material during these bending operations. Should the scrolls turn out to be uneven or not quite correct, simply place the uneven or incorrect part into the hot water again and rebend it properly.

5. As an added decorative feature, though not really necessary, cement two round foot rests to the undersurface of the base of the now formed frame, in the manner represented by D, Fig. 8. Make the strips just as long or a little longer than the width of the frame material. The foot rests may be made of any round strip plastic material from 1/4 inch to 1/2 inch in diameter.

6. The plastic frame may be attractively decorated with some simple design motif by using a scriber, an engraver, or an electric pencil, but all such embellishments must be applied before the plastic frame strip is bent or formed into position.

7. Polish all parts of the formed frame neatly, following the directions given for polishing plastic articles under Projects Nos. 90 and 91.

8. After the plastic frame is completed, insert two thin pieces of glass of an appropriate size, into slits, A, Fig. 8. Be sure the width of these glass pieces is exactly the same as the distance be-

tween the slits at the ends of the frame. The height of the glass pieces may vary as desired. Then, insert photograph between the glass sheets in the manner shown at E, Fig. 8.

If a larger or smaller size photograph is to be framed, use a correspondingly larger or smaller size strip of plastic for the frame and the frame scrolls. Attractive results can also be produced by bending the scrolls at the ends of the frame in an outward instead of an inward direction. Another good idea is to make one of the scrolls higher than the other.

Project No. 99, Ornamental Plastic Buttons

See Figures 9, 10, and 11, Illustration 39

Making attractive costume buttons of various colors and types of scrap plastics, offers home and school craftsmen another interesting project.

Insects, birds, fish, flowers, animals, ships, humorous figures, and geometric forms, are only a few of the possible designs which make attractive plastic buttons. The possibilities for original designs are endless. Decorative treatments include such handwork processes as electric burning, enamel coloring, veining, inlaying, piercing, and overlaying. You will find all of these decorative methods fully described in the directions given for Projects 90 and 91 above.

In the construction of these plastic costume buttons it is important that all edges and surfaces be neatly smoothed and that the buttons be polished to a bright luster. Either two or four holes may be bored at the centers of the buttons, using for this purpose a 1/16 inch drill point fitted in a hand-drill. See Figs. 9, 10, and 11 in Illustration 39. The buttons can be sewed on to the dress or coat simply as ornaments, or they can be sewed on to serve actually as regular buttons. When applied for the latter purpose, however, it is necessary to design the buttons in a smaller size so that they will function satisfactorily.

An especially effective idea in the construction of these costume buttons is to use a transparent or lightly tinted plastic material and fill in the veined or incised detail design lines with appropriate colors of enamel. Another good idea is to use two contrasting colors of opaque plastic in an overlay form of construction, as shown in Fig. 11, Illustration 39.

One of the author's students in a girls' handicraft class, made a series of pretty little plastic buttons in the form of butterflies, as shown in Fig. 9, Illustration 39, and in addition made a pair of matching earrings in the same motif.

Plastic buttons of the types shown in Figs. 9, 10, and 11, may also be sewed to a leather belt, thus producing a very attractive sport belt.

Project No. 100, Plastic Bracelets

See Figures 12 and 13, Illustration 39

Attractive bracelets in various colors and in a number of styles and designs can easily be fashioned from scrap pieces of transparent or opaque plastic material. These plastic bracelets may either be made in the all around form such as represented by the model shown in Fig. 13, Illustration No. 39, or in the open end form shown by model No. 12.

The method required for the construction of these plastic bracelets is very similar to that employed in making plastic rings, described above. The simple steps here involved are as follows:

1. Use a strip of paper to determine the required wrist size.

2. Draw a careful pattern, preferably on squared paper, and in the determined size, and indicate on this pattern the proposed design and form of ornamentation which you intend to apply.

3. Paste the paper pattern to a strip of plastic material slightly longer and wider than the pattern size, using rubber cement. Be sure to use only the thermoplastic type of plastic material, which can be made pliable and bent to required shape when immersed in hot water.

4. Using a coping or jeweler's saw, fitted with a fine toothed blade, cut out the plastic strip carefully and just as indicated by the pasted-on paper pattern. When finished sawing, remove the pattern, and clean off all traces of the rubber cement.

5. With the plastic bracelet blank still in its flat form and cut to its proper size and shape, neatly smooth and finish all its

edges and flat surfaces with fine emery cloth or sandpaper. If necessary, use a file before employing the emery cloth or sandpaper.

6. Transfer the prepared bracelet pattern to the plastic strip, this time tracing all design or ornamental details, such as the name "Mary" used in the bracelet model shown at Fig. 12, or the Mexican motif employed in the model at Fig. 13. To obtain an accurate tracing of your design, you may use carbon paper. Or you may first cover the entire top or outer surface of the bracelet blank with an even coating of paraffin wax and then place your pattern, with drawing side facing downward, upon the waxed surface of the plastic and produce a good tracing of the design simply by rubbing the entire plain side of the pattern sheet with the edge of a coin or any blunt instrument, such as a tongue depressor or a wooden handle. This rubbing procedure will cause the pencil marks of the paper pattern to be transferred to the waxed surface of the plastic bracelet blank. Be careful pattern is not permitted to move during this rubbing step.

7. Remove the paper design from the plastic strip and then, using a sharply pointed scratch awl or scriber, carefully scratch all traced design outlines deeply into the surface of the plastic. Following this scratching-in step, remove all carbon or wax marks with soap and warm (not hot) water.

8. Work out the design details in a veined effect or in low relief, using an electric pencil, an engraver, or a scratch awl, or, carve the design details with assorted styles of needle files. For these decorative treatments, see directions under Projects Nos. 90 and 91.

9. Applying the method for bending and forming plastic articles as outlined in Project No. 91, Plastic Rings, bend the plastic strip, now neatly decorated, into the curved form of a bracelet. See models 12 and 13, Illustration 39. If the bracelet is of the all around type such as represented by the model in Fig. 13, cement ends tightly together with a good grade of plastic cement, using a string or a thin strip of wire as a clamp, until the cement dries thoroughly.

10. Finish bracelet by smoothing and polishing all edges and surfaces, following the method and directions for finishing and polishing plastic articles given under Project Nos. 90 and 91.

After a little experience in making plastic bracelets, you will soon discover that you can apply several other decorative treatments. You will find, for example, that they can also be made attractively by piercing, inlaying, or overlaying the designs. The directions for these additional ornamental processes are also given above.

Project No. 101, Ornamental Plastic Buckles or Belt Slides

See Figures 14 and 15, Illustration 39

Individually designed buckles or belt slides can easily be made of scrap plastics at small cost.

These buckles or belt slides can be fashioned from opaque, variously colored plastics, or from crystal-clear, transparent plastics. There is no end to the styles or shapes which can be employed in these practical, attractive plastic buckles. For instance, they can be built in square, rectangular, round, oval, diamond, or hexagonal shapes. To these general, popular, geometric shapes, additional simple contour modifications can be worked in, just as represented by the design treatments of the contours in the models shown at Figs. 14 and 15, Illustration 39.

A most effective method for decorating these plastic buckles or belt slides is that of simple line veining, which is described in the directions for Project No. 95. For this decorative treatment you may use either a scratch awl, an engraving tool, or a carborundum pencil. Another good method for the simple embellishment of these novelty buckles is to use an electric pencil and burn the design markings into the plastic material in a uniform, shallow, etched effect.

Multicolored buckles or belt slides can be made by cementing one color of plastic over another, contrasting color of plastic in an overlay or applique form of construction. You will find this form of ornamental treatment fully treated under Project No. 94.

When making these buckles, it is important to have the inside, open sections of a suitable size, to accommodate the particular width of the leather, felt, or cloth belt on which the buckle or belt slide is to be used. Ample room should also be provided in the width of these inner openings to allow the belt to pass through easily. Still another important consideration, is to make the outer or frame sections at least 1/4 inch wide to avoid possible cracking of the plastic when the buckle is used.

The construction of these ornamental buckles or belt slides provides handicraft teachers and home craftsmen with an excellent opportunity for combining various types of plastic with some other form of craft material, such as plastic with leather, felt, cloth, elastic band, and so forth. Sport belts fashioned by the combination of plastic with any of these belt materials are smart.

As a final finish for plastic buckles or belt slides, round off all edges neatly and buff all surfaces to a bright polish.

Project No. 102, Novelty Candle Holders Made of Plastic

See Figures 16 and 17, Illustration 39

Candle holders made of opaque or transparent scrap plastics are both attractive and useful.

For the construction of these novelty candle holders in plastic, you can employ any interesting and appealing form of decorative motif or design subject. If you wish, you can use the same motif for both units of a set of two candle holders or you can use two different, though related, types of subjects. For instance, you might employ marine subjects such as the two different types of fish represented in the candle holder models shown in Figs. 16 and 17, in Illustration 39. Or, you can use two different forms of birds, two different types of ships, two card symbols such as a diamond and a heart, and so forth. Other interesting and appropriate motifs are provided by the use of two different animal figures, such as a cat and a dog, two different types of leaves, a boy and a girl, or two kinds of flowers.

To determine the proper size of the plastic figure or ornamental unit which is to form the base or support section of the candle holder, first draw a 4 inch to 4-1/2 inch diameter circle on a sheet of squared paper. Then, within this circle, draw your fish, bird, ship, or other form of design motif which you have selected for your candle holder base. Make the units very simple in contour and free of unnecessary detail, similar to the treatment used in the formation of the candle holder bases in models Nos. 16 and 17. After drawing the outside contours of the bases, add a few detail lines such as the eye and scales seen in model No. 16, A.

Having thus completed the paper patterns for the bases of the candle holders, trace the prepared designs to suitable size pieces of plastic. You may use either opaque plastics or the transparent kind, such as Lucite or Plexiglas. For the most practical results it is best to use plastic which is at least 1/4 inch in thickness.

For tracing the base patterns to the plastic material, use either a sheet of carbon paper, placed face down underneath the paper pattern, or use the paraffin wax method for tracing designs to plastic, described under Project No. 100, Plastic Bracelets. Still another good tracing method is to paste the pattern to the plastic, with the design side of the pattern facing upward, and then, with a sharply pointed metal instrument such as a scratch awl, prick through the outlines of the pattern, in close formation, making tiny dots or holes in the surface of the plastic.

After completing the tracing of the designs for the candle holder bases, cut out the bases with a fine toothed coping or jeweler's saw. Following this sawing step, file and smooth all cut edges of the bases and neatly round off all top sections of the edges to produce a round-beveled effect. Next, use a scratch awl, engraving tool, or an electric pencil, to carve or vein in all detail lines represented in the designs of the bases, such as the eye, scales, and fin grooves in our fish model, shown at Fig. 16. As a final step in the processing of these base sections of the candle holders, brightly polish all edges and their upper surfaces, employing the method for polishing plastic material detailed in Project No. 90, Novelty Letter Openers.

In order to provide a practical receptacle for the candle, make a small disc of 1/4 inch thick plastic, about 1-3/4 inches in diameter, and using a color of plastic which will show up in effective contrast against the novelty base unit over which the receptacle is to be mounted. Then, cut a hole from 3/4 inch to 7/8 inch in diameter in the center of each circular disc. After smoothing and polishing all edges and surfaces of the cutout discs, mount them to the central section of the upper surface of the base of the candle holder, just as represented by Fig. 16, B, and Fig. 17, B.

The plastic candle holders are now complete and ready for use. Insert a candle of a suitable size and color into the circular cutout section of the cemented-on receptacle piece of each holder. When not in use on the dining room table, you may place your set of candle holders on the mantle or buffet.

Project No. 103, Plastic Brooches

See Figures 18, 19, and 20, Illustration 39

Brooches or lapel ornaments made of opaque or transparent scrap plastic, fashioned in attractive designs, provide still another interesting project for enthusiastic craftsmen.

The number of possible decorative motifs or design schemes which can be employed in the construction of these plastic costume accessories is indeed limitless. When selecting or planning the brooch motif, however, be sure it is of a simple, appealing character. Also make certain that the design is of a proper size, since a brooch which is made either too small or too large will lose its effect even though it is well designed.

Excellent design motifs for these plastic brooches are provided by such popular subjects as a ship (see Fig. 18), a heart and arrow (see Fig. 20), a deer, a scottie, a butterfly, a Mexican figure, a palm tree, a flower, an oak leaf in combination with two or three acorns, a fish, an elephant, a woman's head, and so on.

To make the ship brooch shown in Fig. 18, proceed as follows:

1. Trace a prepared pattern of the ship, in full size, to the selected piece of scrap plastic material.

2. Saw around the outside contours of the ship, using either a coping or jeweler's saw frame, equipped with a fine-toothed blade.

3. Saw out the inside or interior sections of the brooch. For piercing or sawing out interior areas in plastic work, see directions given for Project No. 90, under Section B, 3.

4. Using a scratch awl, an engraver, a carborundum pencil, or an electric pencil, carve down the wave sections, shown in outline form just below the hull of the boat, to a depth of about 1/16 inch.

5. File, smooth, and polish to a bright luster all edges and surfaces of the cutout and carved plastic ship. Before polishing it, be sure to round all top sections of the outside and inside sawed edges, to produce a round-beveled effect all around the front or face side of the brooch.

6. Fasten either a plastic or metal form of plain clasp to the back of the ship brooch, using the type of clasp shown in Fig. 19. You will find it a practical idea to attach the clasp in a vertical position to the back of the large sail as shown by the dotted lines in Fig. 18. Locating the pin clasp in this manner will make it invisible when the pin is worn. If crystal clear plastic is used, before fastening on the clasp, it is a good idea to apply white enamel paint over the underside of the sails, orange enamel over the underside of the hull, and blue or blue green enamel over the underside of the water section. In addition to being very effective, this will also make the clasp invisible. In this particular case, it is best to attach the pin clasp to the back of the large sail with melted beeswax. Using either glue or plastic cement over enamel paint will produce a weak joint and is therefore impractical.

The combination heart and arrow brooch shown in Fig. 20, may either be made of a single piece or of two separate pieces of scrap plastic. If made of a single piece of plastic, simply trace the arrow and heart design to the plastic material and then saw it out neatly, using a coping or jeweler's saw, fitted with a fine-toothed saw blade. In this single-piece form of our heart and arrow brooch, it is a good idea to use the crystal-clear form of plastic in a thickness of about 1/4 inch. Following this sawing step, file all cut edges until perfectly uniform and true all around, and then smooth the edges with fine sandpaper or emery cloth. The next step is to file down the top surface of the front of the arrow (see Fig. 20, A), and the back of the arrow (see Fig. 20, B), to one half of its original thickness. After filing down these arrow parts, smooth and finish them neatly and then polish both the arrow and heart sections of the brooch to a bright luster. The top sections of the edges of the heart should particularly be well beveled and rounded off.

To complete this single-piece heart and arrow brooch, built of clear plastic, paint the under surface of the heart (see Fig. 20, C) with scarlet red enamel paint, leaving the extended ends of the arrow (see Fig. 20 A and B), in the original, crystal-clear color of the plastic. Then, simply fasten the pin clasp to the back of the heart section of the brooch, placing it, preferably, in a horizontal position. Use either a metal or plastic type of pin clasp of the kind shown at Fig. 19. Because of the enameled undersurface of the heart, the pin clasp will remain invisible. Here, as in the case of the ship brooch, Fig. 18, it is wise to fasten on the pin clasp with melted beeswax, rather than with glue or cement.

To make this charming heart and arrow brooch of two separate pieces of plastic, one for the heart and one for the arrow, proceed as follows:

1. Cut out the heart part, using 3/16 inch thick, bright red-colored plastic. If you so desire, you may use crystal-clear plastic and paint the undersurface of the heart with bright red enamel paint. Finish the edges and surfaces of the heart neatly and polish all parts of the heart unit to a bright luster.

2. Cut out a complete arrow part, using 3/16 inch clear plastic. To obtain a correct pattern of the arrow, use the dotted lines seen drawn through the heart in Fig. 20, as a guide. Finish the edges and top surfaces of the arrow neatly and polish all arrow parts to a bright luster.

3. Fasten the arrow to the back of the heart, following the arrangement in Fig. 20. Use plastic cement, if red-colored plastic material is used for the heart section, and use beeswax as a fastening device if the back of the heart is colored with red enamel.

4. Fasten pin clasp to the back of the arrow, placing the clasp in the same direction as the length of the arrow. The pin clasp may here be attached with plastic cement since it is being joined directly to a plastic surface.

Another good idea for constructing this heart and arrow brooch is to make the heart of clear plastic and suspend it from a separately cutout arrow, made of red-colored plastic (or enameled red on its underside), and which is arranged in a horizontal position. The heart may be suspended from the arrow by means of a thin, metal chain, by drilling a tiny hole at the top of the heart (see Fig. 2, Illustration 39), and one at each end section of the arrow. The pin clasp may then be fastened to the back of the arrow, according to the fastening methods outlined earlier in the discussion of this project.

Made in any one of the three different ways described above, this little heart and arrow plastic brooch is sure to be attractive.

Project No. 104. Artist's Palette Lapel Pin

See Figure 1, Illustration 40

For this palette pin, as well as the pin shown in Fig. 2, Illustration 40, plastic is combined with various other materials.

For the palette itself, you may use any scrap plastic material from 1/8 inch to 1/4 inch thick. Especially effective is either the amber or clear glass forms of transparent plastic. After sawing the outside palette shape, following the pattern in Fig. 5 A, Illustration 40, drill a small hole at N, Fig. 5 and then saw out that interior section. For method of cutting out interior parts, see directions given under Project No. 90, Plastic Letter Openers. Next, smooth and bevel all edges of the palette neatly and buff and polish it, as directed in Project No. 90.

For the palette "paints," you may use scrap pieces of plastic of different colors, cut to the shapes shown at B, Fig. 5. After you have cut out the small plastic discs, smooth and bevel the edges at their top surfaces only, and then cement them to the palette at the locations shown in Figs. 1 and 5. For plastic cementing directions, see Project 91, Section III, A, 6.

The "paints" can also be made of different colors of felt cemented to the plastic palette. Or different shades of oil paints can be employed.

The "brushes" may be made of a contrasting color of plastic material. Saw out two thin strips of plastic and neatly shape and finish them, as shown at C, Fig. 5. Note that the bristled end of each brush should be neatly flattened out and lined to imitate the brush hairs. After the plastic brushes are finished, cement them in place, in the arrangement shown in Figs. 1 and 5. If you wish, you may make the brushes of 1/16 inch to 3/32 inch diameter strips of wire, or even tooth picks or match sticks. Whether you use plastic, metal wire, or thin sticks of wood, it is important to shape them neatly.

To finish the palette, cement a plastic pin clasp to its back. Then, with a small piece of cloth and a little nail polish remover, carefully wipe away any excess cement.

Project No. 105, Storkie Lapel Pin

See Figure 2, Illustration 40

In making this novel lapel pin you are given wide latitude in the selection of materials to be combined with plastic.

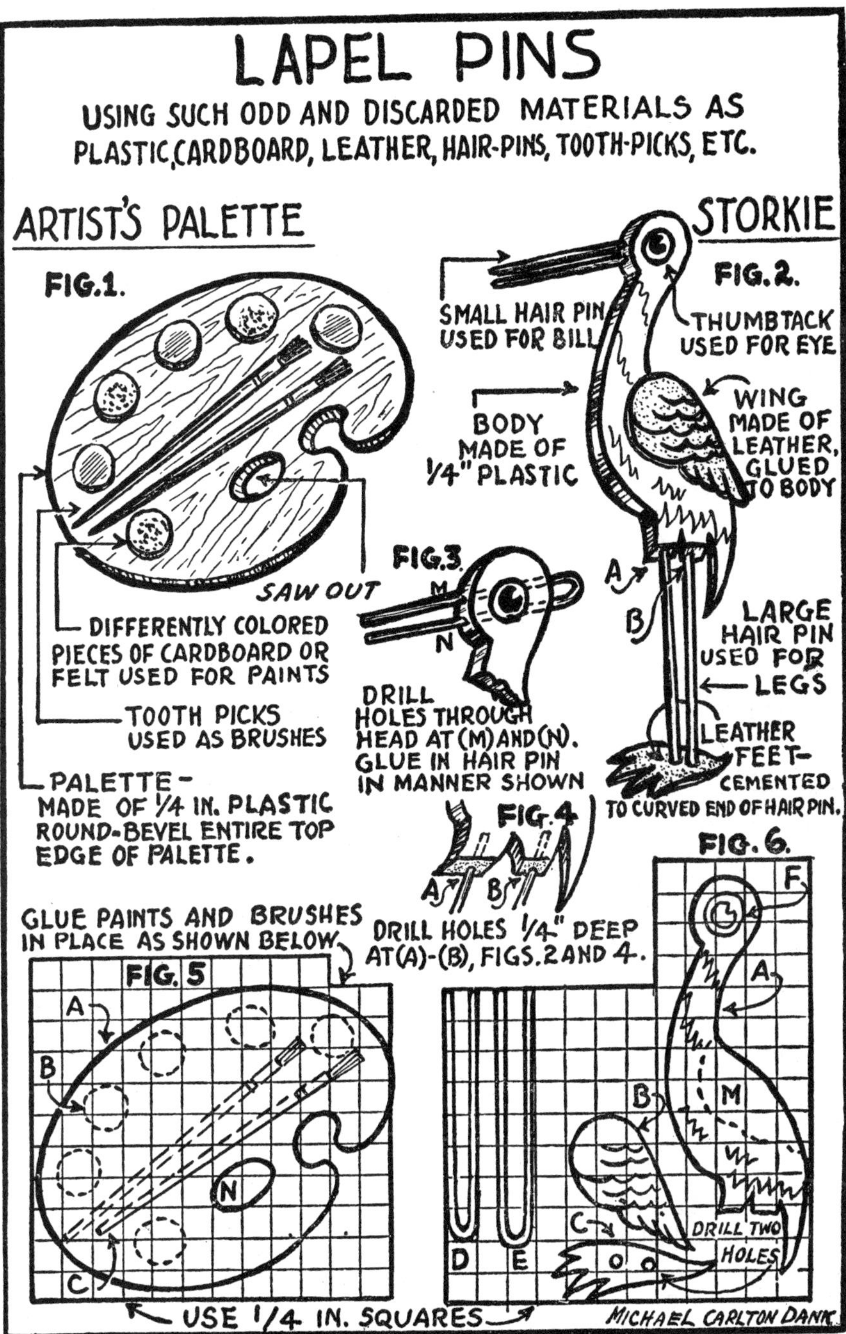

Illustration 40

As you will note in Fig. 2, Illustration 40, an odd thumb tack is used for Storkie's eye, a small hair pin for his bill, a large hair pin for his legs, scrap pieces of leather for his wings and feet, and a scrap piece of plastic for his body. You will find Storkie very easy to make and a lot of fun.

1. For the body, which is the first part to be made, use any suitable color or type of plastic which is at least 1/4 inch thick. Use either the opaque type of plastic or better still, the transparent type of plastic, in either the colorless or amber variety.

2. Using the pattern of the body part as shown in the pattern grill at Fig. 6, A, Illustration 40, cut it out according to the method of sawing out plastic work described under Project No. 90, Plastic Letter Openers.

3. After cutting out the body part, smooth and bevel the edges around its forward or top surface. Buff the plastic body part until a bright finish is produced.

4. Using a hand drill fitted with a small drill point a little larger than the diameter of the hair pin to be used for Storkie's bill, drill two holes through Storkie's head section at points M and N as shown in Fig. 3, Illustration 40.

5. Using the same drill, bore two holes about 1/2 inch deep at the base section of Storkie's body at points A and B in Figs. 2 and 4, Illustration 40.

6. Using either a contrasting color of thin plastic material or scraps of leather or felt in appropriate colors, make the wing part B, and the feet part C, following the patterns of these parts given in the pattern grill in Fig. 6. It is best to use the same type of material for the wing and feet.

7. Cement wing to Storkie's body.

8. Pass ends of small hair pin through the little holes previously drilled in Storkie's head, and then cement this hair pin in place to form the bill. See M and N, Fig. 3, also sketch of completed pin in Fig. 2.

9. Pass the ends of the larger hair pin through the two holes drilled in the feet part (See Fig. 6 C), and cement the feet to the round end of the hair pin. Then cement the two pointed ends of the hair pin into the holes previously drilled in the lower section of the body. (See Fig. 4 A and B.)

10. Drill a hole in the center of the head section and cement a thumb tack to the forward side of the head as shown in Fig. 2 and Fig. 6 F.

11. Apply all necessary colors with enamel paints. The hair pins may be left in their original black color or enameled in orange or brown.

12. If Storkie's wing is made of leather, the feather lines in the wing may be tooled. If made of felt, the feather lines can be cut out of a contrasting color of felt and cemented to the wing. If wing is made of plastic, they can be made with an engraving tool or an electric burning needle.

13. Cement a plastic or metal pin clasp to the back of the plastic body section, using a pin at least 1-1/4 inches long and fastening it in a vertical position.

INDEX

A CATALOGUE OF SELECTED DOVER BOOKS IN ALL FIELDS OF INTEREST

A CATALOGUE OF SELECTED DOVER BOOKS IN ALL FIELDS OF INTEREST

TWO LITTLE SAVAGES; BEING THE ADVENTURES OF TWO BOYS WHO LIVED AS INDIANS AND WHAT THEY LEARNED, Ernest Thompson Seton. Great classic of nature and boyhood provides a vast range of woodlore in most palatable form, a genuinely entertaining story. Two farm boys build a teepee in woods and live in it for a month, working out Indian solutions to living problems, star lore, birds and animals, plants, etc. 293 illustrations. vii + 286pp.
20985-7 Paperbound $2.50

PETER PIPER'S PRACTICAL PRINCIPLES OF PLAIN & PERFECT PRONUNCIATION. Alliterative jingles and tongue-twisters of surprising charm, that made their first appearance in America about 1830. Republished in full with the spirited woodcut illustrations from this earliest American edition. 32pp. 4½ x 6⅜.
22560-7 Paperbound $1.00

SCIENCE EXPERIMENTS AND AMUSEMENTS FOR CHILDREN, Charles Vivian. 73 easy experiments, requiring only materials found at home or easily available, such as candles, coins, steel wool, etc.; illustrate basic phenomena like vacuum, simple chemical reaction, etc. All safe. Modern, well-planned. Formerly *Science Games for Children.* 102 photos, numerous drawings. 96pp. 6⅛ x 9¼.
21856-2 Paperbound $1.25

AN INTRODUCTION TO CHESS MOVES AND TACTICS SIMPLY EXPLAINED, Leonard Barden. Informal intermediate introduction, quite strong in explaining reasons for moves. Covers basic material, tactics, important openings, traps, positional play in middle game, end game. Attempts to isolate patterns and recurrent configurations. Formerly *Chess.* 58 figures. 102pp. (USO) 21210-6 Paperbound $1.25

LASKER'S MANUAL OF CHESS, Dr. Emanuel Lasker. Lasker was not only one of the five great World Champions, he was also one of the ablest expositors, theorists, and analysts. In many ways, his Manual, permeated with his philosophy of battle, filled with keen insights, is one of the greatest works ever written on chess. Filled with analyzed games by the great players. A single-volume library that will profit almost any chess player, beginner or master. 308 diagrams. xli x 349pp.
20640-8 Paperbound $2.75

THE MASTER BOOK OF MATHEMATICAL RECREATIONS, Fred Schuh. In opinion of many the finest work ever prepared on mathematical puzzles, stunts, recreations; exhaustively thorough explanations of mathematics involved, analysis of effects, citation of puzzles and games. Mathematics involved is elementary. Translated by F. Göbel. 194 figures. xxiv + 430pp. 22134-2 Paperbound $3.00

MATHEMATICS, MAGIC AND MYSTERY, Martin Gardner. Puzzle editor for Scientific American explains mathematics behind various mystifying tricks: card tricks, stage "mind reading," coin and match tricks, counting out games, geometric dissections, etc. Probability sets, theory of numbers clearly explained. Also provides more than 400 tricks, guaranteed to work, that you can do. 135 illustrations. xii + 176pp.
20338-2 Paperbound $1.50

LAST AND FIRST MEN AND STAR MAKER, TWO SCIENCE FICTION NOVELS, Olaf Stapledon. Greatest future histories in science fiction. In the first, human intelligence is the "hero," through strange paths of evolution, interplanetary invasions, incredible technologies, near extinctions and reemergences. Star Maker describes the quest of a band of star rovers for intelligence itself, through time and space: weird inhuman civilizations, crustacean minds, symbiotic worlds, etc. Complete, unabridged. v + 438pp. 21962-3 Paperbound $2.50

THREE PROPHETIC NOVELS, H. G. WELLS. Stages of a consistently planned future for mankind. *When the Sleeper Wakes,* and *A Story of the Days to Come,* anticipate *Brave New World* and *1984,* in the 21st Century; *The Time Machine,* only complete version in print, shows farther future and the end of mankind. All show Wells's greatest gifts as storyteller and novelist. Edited by E. F. Bleiler. x + 335pp. (USO) 20605-X Paperbound $2.25

THE DEVIL'S DICTIONARY, Ambrose Bierce. America's own Oscar Wilde—Ambrose Bierce—offers his barbed iconoclastic wisdom in over 1,000 definitions hailed by H. L. Mencken as "some of the most gorgeous witticisms in the English language." 145pp. 20487-1 Paperbound $1.25

MAX AND MORITZ, Wilhelm Busch. Great children's classic, father of comic strip, of two bad boys, Max and Moritz. Also Ker and Plunk (Plisch und Plumm), Cat and Mouse, Deceitful Henry, Ice-Peter, The Boy and the Pipe, and five other pieces. Original German, with English translation. Edited by H. Arthur Klein; translations by various hands and H. Arthur Klein. vi + 216pp. 20181-3 Paperbound $2.00

PIGS IS PIGS AND OTHER FAVORITES, Ellis Parker Butler. The title story is one of the best humor short stories, as Mike Flannery obfuscates biology and English. Also included, That Pup of Murchison's, The Great American Pie Company, and Perkins of Portland. 14 illustrations. v + 109pp. 21532-6 Paperbound $1.00

THE PETERKIN PAPERS, Lucretia P. Hale. It takes genius to be as stupidly mad as the Peterkins, as they decide to become wise, celebrate the "Fourth," keep a cow, and otherwise strain the resources of the Lady from Philadelphia. Basic book of American humor. 153 illustrations. 219pp. 20794-3 Paperbound $1.50

PERRAULT'S FAIRY TALES, translated by A. E. Johnson and S. R. Littlewood, with 34 full-page illustrations by Gustave Doré. All the original Perrault stories—Cinderella, Sleeping Beauty, Bluebeard, Little Red Riding Hood, Puss in Boots, Tom Thumb, etc.—with their witty verse morals and the magnificent illustrations of Doré. One of the five or six great books of European fairy tales. viii + 117pp. 8⅛ x 11. 22311-6 Paperbound $2.00

OLD HUNGARIAN FAIRY TALES, Baroness Orczy. Favorites translated and adapted by author of the *Scarlet Pimpernel.* Eight fairy tales include "The Suitors of Princess Fire-Fly," "The Twin Hunchbacks," "Mr. Cuttlefish's Love Story," and "The Enchanted Cat." This little volume of magic and adventure will captivate children as it has for generations. 90 drawings by Montagu Barstow. 96pp. (USO) 22293-4 Paperbound $1.95